**Matthew Boulton College of Further
& Higher Education**

Learning Resource Centre

THE HARDWARE MAN'S DAUGHTER

My Dear Papa

I am quite unhappy at not having heard from Soho since I saw you last but I hope you will ease my mind by writing a few lines as soon as you conveniently can Matty drank tea here yesterday she was perfectly well and in very good spirits she desired me to ask you to send him 3 of Sʳ Gᵗ Rodneys medals which he said he should be very much obliged to you for I hope my Dear Mama yourself and all my Friends at Soho are well Mʳˢ & Miss Wilkes present their Compliments to you and Mama and I remain Dear Papa your Dutiful & Affectionate
                                        Daughter
                                  Anne Boulton

Richmond May 18ᵗʰ
                1781

The earliest surviving letter from Anne Boulton to her father, written from school in Richmond in May 1781. (Birmingham City Archives)

THE HARDWARE MAN'S DAUGHTER

Matthew Boulton and his 'Dear Girl'

Shena Mason

Phillimore

2005

Published by
PHILLIMORE & CO. LTD
Shopwyke Manor Barn, Chichester, West Sussex, England
www.phillimore.co.uk

ISBN 1 86077 374 5

Printed and bound in Great Britain by
CAMBRIDGE PRINTING

Published with the assistance of:

Contents

List of Illustrations

Black and white figures

Colour plates

between pages

Acknowledgements

This book traces, for the first time, the story of Anne Boulton's life as the daughter of an extraordinary father, the industrialist Matthew Boulton.

Most of the research has been carried out in the Matthew Boulton Papers and the James Watt Papers in Birmingham City Archives, and I am immensely grateful for the help of all the staff there, especially Fiona Tait. Thanks are also due to: Soho House Museum, Birmingham; the County Record Office, Stafford; Lichfield Record Office; Erasmus Darwin House, Lichfield; the Museum of Costume, Bath; the Herbert Museum & Art Gallery, Coventry, and to private owners who have allowed me access to paintings. Special thanks to Alistair Thompson, Consultant Orthopaedic Surgeon at the Royal Orthopaedic Hospital, Birmingham, for his interest and the attention he has given to studying some of the documents for me. For suggestions, encouragement and help of various kinds I thank Val Loggie; Dr Jenny Uglow; Rita McLean and Chris Rice of Birmingham Museums & Art Gallery; Professor Maxine Berg of the University of Warwick; Professor Jennifer Tann of the University of Birmingham; and the Barber Institute of Fine Arts.

This publication has been made possible with the generous support and co-operation of the George Cadbury Fund; Birmingham Museums & Art Gallery; Birmingham Museums & Art Gallery Development Trust Fund; Birmingham Reference Library; Birmingham Assay Office; the Birmingham Common Good Trust; and the Firs Trust. I thank them all.

Picture credits

Picture sources are included in the captions. The Matthew Boulton Papers reproduced as illustrations are the copyright of Birmingham Assay Office Charitable Trust and Birmingham City Archives, where they are housed. The photographs of the Tilly Kettle portraits of Matthew Boulton and Mrs Ann Boulton are the copyright of Sir Nicholas Goodison. The photograph of the Tilly Kettle portrait of Miss Anne Boulton is by David Rowan.

S.M., 2005

Introduction

I wanted to write about Anne Boulton (1768-1829) because in all the books about her father, Matthew Boulton (1728-1809), she gets little more than a passing mention, yet she was a hugely important presence in his life, his 'fair Maid of the Mill', the 'greatest blessing and comfort' of his old age. She was stoic in the face of adversity and not lacking in courage. In situations where some women might have become bitter, she seems to have remained philosophical and pragmatic and not to have borne grudges.

Anne Boulton was in a real sense a daughter of the revolution: her father was one of the leading protagonists in that process now generally known by the label of the Industrial Revolution. With his partner, James Watt, Boulton had powered Britain onto the world industrial stage at a time when the 'mechanick arts' were as astonishing and unstoppable as CADCAM is today. The business had had unremarkable enough beginnings, just one among many of the Birmingham 'toy' manufacturers who earned the town Burke's epithet of 'The Toyshop of Europe'. 'Toys' (small personal accessories, such as buttons, buckles and snuff boxes) and other decorative metalwares ('hardware' in 18th-century parlance) were its stock-in-trade, before the arrival of James Watt and the building of steam engines turned it into a heavy engineering powerhouse. Boulton described himself in later life as 'an old button-maker', and it is tempting to think of the Boulton story as the rags-to-riches rise of a humble button-maker, but (setting aside the fact that 'humble' is not an adjective which would ever have suited Matthew Boulton) a glance at the family background reveals that the Boultons were well-connected and not without means (*see* Appendix). They straddled the increasingly blurred boundary between landed and mercantile fortunes, and were bent on gentrification. The family lived in some style, albeit on a modest scale, and welcomed an astonishing range of guests to their home. Piecing together Anne's life has allowed me to explore the social and domestic world which hummed away quietly (and sometimes not so quietly) behind all the science, technology and industry.

I have tried to focus primarily on Miss Boulton throughout this book and it has not been easy – for she is very quiet and her father is very talkative! Early in her school career Anne promised her parents that they should never go longer than a fortnight without a letter from her and, though she may have slipped a little from this routine, it is clear from her father's letters to her that she wrote to him often (her mother seems never to have written). Anne kept a great many of her father's letters, so that today we see her to some extent through his eyes. He kept few of her letters to him – or if he did, later members of the family did some 'weeding' of the papers for their own reasons. In consequence we do not hear Anne's own voice very often and the research is inevitably skewed.

Nevertheless, the letters which do survive between Anne and her father give us insights into their relationship and the personal and family preoccupations of a man whom we are inclined to think of somewhat two-dimensionally as one half of Boulton & Watt. More importantly for us here, they provide tantalising glimpses of Anne's life. Beyond the letters between father and daughter, much of the detail in this book has had to be gleaned from postscripts to letters between Matthew Boulton and his many other correspondents, and from household bills and other records.

The information which emerges from all the sources gives us a picture of a woman who from infancy had mobility problems. Anne's health and medical treatments are a recurring theme throughout the book. The documents give us information on her education, too. At a time when even middle-class girls had at best a perfunctory education, she was sent away to boarding school – though it has to be said that her schooling suffered frequent interruptions, and her younger brother received a far more thorough grounding, intended to equip him as a future captain of industry. I have compared Anne's life with that of her brother and some of the other young people who were part of their circle, and tried to set it in the context of the times.

When Anne was about seventeen her father forecast that she would have 'great choice of husbands', but she never married – though not from choice, and the sad story of the marriage which never happened is related. Instead, she seems to have resigned herself pragmatically to life as her brother's housekeeper, until his marriage. Miss Boulton and her new sister-in-law could not agree and it became impossible for her to stay on under the same roof. So, at the age of 50, she left the house where she had been born and set up her own home.

Anne Boulton had just under eleven years as mistress of her own house, during which time she kept careful accounts of all her spending, on the house and on food, journeys, clothes, stable expenses, and so on. As a result, we can get a good idea of the furnishings, garden planting, the household's diet, the style and running costs of the carriage – and of Miss Boulton's penchant for rather splendid headgear.

It has been a particular joy, shortly before publication of this book, to come face-to-face for the first time with the portrait of Anne as a young girl. As I write, there is no known image of her as an adult, though a miniature is mentioned in a family will in the 1920s. Almost certainly, more information remains to come to light.

Amanda Vickery has written in *The Gentleman's Daughter*, 'To be mistress of oneself was paramount – genteel ladies aimed to be self-possessed in social encounters, self-controlled in the face of minor provocations, self-sufficient in the midst of ingratitude, and, above all, brave and enduring in the grip of tragedy and misfortune.' This description seems to sum up perfectly the character of Miss Anne Boulton. She never travelled abroad (she would have liked to visit France); she did not take the literary world by storm by writing novels, describing herself as 'no authoress, only a mere scribe'. She did not, as far as we know, ever take part in a chemistry experiment (though she may well have watched them). Hers were the quieter preoccupations of the dutiful daughter – botany, reading, drawing, embroidery, music, and being ever ready to please her dear Papa. For all his enlightened views on the universe and his regular dealings with strong, independent and intellectual women, to whom he was clearly attracted, Matthew Boulton seems to have had conservative views on the kind of life his daughter should live. She was, like most women of her class and period, under the permanent necessity of being amiable, and this is the word most often used to describe her by her contemporaries. She seems to have accepted this as her lot, and never to have kicked over the traces. How I wish she had, for her sake as much as for the biographer's!

A note on spellings and dates

This is a book constructed from, and about, letters – letters which have given me great pleasure in the reading of them. In the hope that they will give others equal pleasure, I make no apology for quoting at length from Boulton family correspondence. In doing so I have retained the original spelling and contractions, because they provide part of the character of the original documents. I have, however, added a little punctuation here and there and broken some of the text into paragraphs, to make them easier to follow.

With regard to the spellings of names, these vary a good deal in the 17th and 18th centuries, in particular, the spelling of 'Ann' or 'Anne' when referring to Matthew Boulton's second wife and his daughter. As Mrs Boulton generally appears as 'Ann', I have kept to that spelling for her. Miss Boulton's name appears in both forms in various documents, so I have kept to 'Anne' for her in order to distinguish her from her mother. With dates, where there is documentary evidence of actual dates of births and deaths I have used it, but in some cases only baptism or burial dates are available. This is indicated in the text.

Friday's Child

Lichfield Races. Crowds milling, ribbons and flags fluttering, bookies shouting odds. Smell of horses, smell of people. Starters line up, urged by excited onlookers.

One of those watching is a young woman. Her gown and bonnet are fashionably elegant. As she makes her way through the jostling crowd with two friends, eager to see all that is going on, she walks with a noticeable up-and-down gait which is nothing to do with the uneven ground. From beneath her skirts there is the occasional glimpse of her feet, the right foot shod in a dainty brocade shoe, the left matching it in colour but with a thick, built-up sole two or three inches high. Her name is Anne Boulton, and she is 24 years old. It is September 1792.

Miss Boulton is staying with her friends the Turners at Shenstone, near Lichfield. After the races her hosts will go to one of the race-week balls but Anne finds dancing awkward, and prefers to return to the house and write letters. Her father, Matthew Boulton of Soho, near Birmingham, is far away in Cornwall, busy about his steam engines. When he reads her letter he will approve of her going to the races (which she has done more than once), not because he has any great interest in racing himself, but because he believes in the value of varied experience (and fresh air). On Sunday Anne sits down in her room at the Turners to write to him in Truro. 'We are to be very Godly to day, to say our prayers at Shenstone Church this morning & at the Cathedral in the Afternoon,' she tells him. 'I am going to Church in a quarter of an hour when I shall most fervently pray (as I do every day of my life) for the health & happiness of the best of Fathers, who, I hope, will always believe me his Dutiful & affect. Daughter A. Boulton.'[1]

*

Anne was the first surviving child of Matthew Boulton and his second wife. She had grown up used to the fact that Papa was always busy and frequently absent, but as a result she enjoyed all the advantages he could give her: a comfortable and stylish home, an education which was better than most girls of her time could expect, the best medical treatment that his money could buy, fashionable clothes, visits to London. As one of the rising class of industrial-scale manufacturer-merchants, Boulton was what Samuel Johnson called 'a new species of gentleman'.[2] By extension, his daughter was a new species of lady, living in genteel style from an income based on manufacturing and trade. The early years of her parents' marriage built the foundation of that lifestyle, and reveal Boulton energetically pursuing his ambitions, in business and in love.

Anne's parents had risked opprobrium to marry, and the story of their courtship and almost clandestine marriage reveals a driving impetuosity, at least on Boulton's side. Mrs Boulton was Ann *née* Robinson of Lichfield. She was the daughter of a prosperous mercer, Luke Robinson, and she was the second of his daughters to marry Matthew Boulton. Not long before Luke died in 1749 his first daughter, Mary, had married the young Birmingham button-maker. Luke Robinson's settlement on his elder daughter had included £3,000 and land at Curborough, near Lichfield. Matthew and Mary Boulton had three daughters, none of whom survived long, and in the summer of 1759 Mary herself died (*see* Appendix). With Luke and Mary gone, there were now just three Robinsons left in the family house in Bore Street, Lichfield: Luke's widow Dorothy, and her two surviving children, Ann and her elder brother, Luke Robinson junior. The Robinsons and the Boultons were distantly related, for Mary and Ann's grandfather and Matthew Boulton's great-grandmother were brother and sister, John and Mary Babington (*see* Appendix).

A month after his wife's death, Matthew Boulton lost his father too. At the age of 31, he now took control of the family button and buckle business in Birmingham. He went over to Lichfield to visit his in-laws as often as he could, hiring a chaise to take him there from Birmingham, at 16s. a time.[3] Ann Robinson probably looked forward to his visits. In spite of losing his wife and his father in quick succession, he was charming and flirtatious. There was a strong attraction between the young widower and his 26-year-old sister-in-law. Before long the flirtatious banter and Boulton's letters to her took on a more serious note:

> Think not my dearest Creature that it is in the Power of Enemys or Friends, or Abscence, Sickness, or any other Circumstance to abate one Spark of that Fire thou hast kindled in my Breast. No I will sooner be torne to pieces by Savage Wolves than I will ever abate one jot of that Resolution I have so often repeated to thee. Therefore my Dear as thou hopest for mercy thy selfe, shew Mercy unto me; & not torter me by keeping me in doubts, wither I am to be happy & live in thy blisfull bosom, or wither I may dye some ignominious death ... & now in all the Seriousness of my Soul I again most Solemnly declare to thee, that I will never live to see thee in the Arms of another; for if I do my brain will be overturn'd with madness, & I should do some desperate deed: but if I was once assured my dear that thou wert mine, & that it was out of the Power of all my Conspiring Enemys to delude thee from me (for they are now busy) then should I be Chearfull & happy ... Adieu God bless & preserve you & keep your heart & mind in Sincere & Constant Love towards me who am
> Dear Creature, Your unchangable Lover & most affectionate Friend
> I wish I could say Husband, MB:[4]

From a man who only some two months before had been writing a poetic eulogy to his dead wife (*see* Appendix), this letter to her sister is disconcerting to find. It marks the beginning of a barrage of ardent love-letters from Boulton to Ann Robinson. Generally he addresses her as 'Nanny' or 'Nancy' – when he is not beginning letters with 'My dear lovely creature', 'My dear Charmer', or 'My dear Precious Life'. Often, in London on business, he would drop into a coffee house to read the paper, collect his thoughts, listen to the buzz of gossip – or write to Ann, though the coffee house did not provide the ideal setting for composing love-letters: 'My dear Creature, I am now in the midst of a crowded Coffee House & therefore cannot write to thee all I wish to say … everything I see thats pretty I have a mind to buy for thee but then I consider thou art in mourning & cannot ware it at present & by the time thou art out of it I hope to bring thee to choose for thy selfe …'[5] He did, however, send her 'a pretty Toy made from the very Golden Guinea I won & received from my Lovely, Dearest, Sweetest Charmer'.[6] One letter he addressed on the outside simply to 'An Angel at Mrs Robinsons in Boar Street, Lichfield'.

Many of Matthew Boulton's early letters to his 'angel' speak of 'enemies' trying to drive them apart. Just who these enemies were is not revealed, but one of them was possibly Ann's brother, Luke Robinson junior, for Boulton wrote to Ann:

> The behaviour I perceived in your Brother yesterday, his non acceptance of the trifles I brought him, & the information you & your Mamma gave me of his insinuations & conduct, added to what I have otherways heard makes me so very uneasy that at present I am incapable of either eating, drinking, sleeping or minding any business & indeed I am quite ill with uneasiness … I find it is told thy Brother that you & I are laying our Heads together to perswade thy Mamma to give all she has from him unto us which is a most villainous, Enveyous, & Malicious insinuation yet it is such a one that I need take but little pains to convince either thee or She of the Falsety of.[7]

Luke may have been angered by Boulton's pursuit of his second sister so soon after Mary's death; or he may have been concerned about the financial implications of the affair, as Boulton seemed to think; or he may have feared (perhaps not without reason) that his sister was risking her reputation.

There was undoubtedly Talk, behind the fluttering fans at card tables. Early in December 1759 Ann went to Boulton's Birmingham home on a visit, and although they were no doubt chaperoned by his mother and his sisters Mary and Catherine ('Kitty'), when he wrote to her afterwards promising to send a skirt over to Lichfield by the wagon he added: 'I am quite overjoyed to hear that your mama was not in the least angry at your staying here & I hope to God the length of Your Visits here will be increased instead of being shortend untill you reside wholy here.' He had joked to a Mr Barker about getting some printing done on a Sunday, to which Barker had retorted sharply that he hoped, 'I did not hazard my Soul more on Saterday night … & hopes I sat up late on some good & Virtuous action which was the cause of my not riseing before Eleven o'Clock on Sunday morning, which you know is faulse for as I remember I rose about Nine & if I had layn Till Twelve what was it to any body.' He concluded the letter with a sentimental flourish, 'God bless my dear angel & preserve her in peace & happiness till I again Clasp her to a heart that Bleeds & pants for her & if she would do a good, kind & Charitable act she must favour with a Line her Most affectionate Loving & ever dutyfull Friend & Husband Matthew Boulton at the George Inn in Aldersgate Street London.'[8] Though he signs himself 'Husband' the letter is addressed to Miss Ann Robinson at Lichfield.

Shortly after writing it he set off for London with his brother John and did not return to Birmingham until Christmas Day, when he sat down to write to his mother-in-law. Dorothy's attitude to the increasingly passionate relationship between her second daughter and her son-in-law is unclear, but judging from the tone of his exuberant (and possibly slightly tipsy) letter they seem to have been on cordial terms. Boulton wrote:

Behold I send you glad tydings, glad tydings of great Joy! which shall be unto you & unto my People, Tydings of great Joy: for unto them this day hath the Lord restored me ... He hath upheld & preserved me, He at length hath restored me to mine own tribe, & set my Feet in mine own Habbitation ... Hallaluja Hallaluja.

I wished to have left the Great City sooner but could not accomplish all my Business, before the very end of the Week & on Sunday morning I stayed to behold the Wickedest part of it near Covent Garding [sic] smote to the Ground by a dreadfull Fire. Even Thirty six Houses in less than two Hours were laid in Ashes. – Oh: dreadfull Scene – for these causes I was under a Necessity of Travelling on this day yet I faild not to Visit the Church at Dunchurch this Morning & though I have traveld 47 Miles to day yet my goodly health enableth me to write this Epistle. I shall tomorrow begin to set in order the things that are wanting & shall do my dilegence to come shortly unto thee. for my Soul Loveth thee, & my Song shall be always of thy Loveing Kindness ... I will not now write more with Ink (I having no more room on this Paper) but I trust to come unto you shortly & speak Face to Face that our Joy may be full. Peace be with you all amen

written at Birmingham about 8 o'clock in the Evening of Xmas Day.[9]

Squeezed in sideways along the left-hand margin of the letter is an apology: 'excuse my manner of writing for know that I must write always in that Style which Floats uppermost.'

Dorothy Robinson died in the spring of 1760 after a long illness. She had undergone some kind of surgery the previous autumn – a surgeon, William Bailye, sent in a bill to her executors for eight guineas for surgery, visits and dressings, with a note saying 'n.b. the above Surgery in such a case was worth £10.10s.0d.'.[10] Dorothy was buried at St Giles' Church at Whittington, near Lichfield, on 25 May.[11] William Wyatt charged a guinea for 'making steps and turning an Arch in ye Wall for Mrs Robinson's Vault at Whittington',[12] though there is no trace to be found there today of any Robinson vault, graves or memorials. Dorothy went to her grave with due ceremony, in a shroud of white swanskin.[*] John Barker's funeral bill of £59 19s.7¼d. includes, apart from the shroud, two coffins at £4 10s. od. for the pair, £3 10s. for hire of a hearse and a coach, and the usual range of mourning cloaks, black hatbands (36, of silk or crape), men's and women's gloves, scarves, black handkerchiefs, and yards of 'Norwich crape' (some of it for the maids) and 'superfine raven grey broadcloth'.[13]

In her will Dorothy left the furniture and other household goods in her best parlour, hall, common parlour, kitchen, closet and three upstairs chambers (presumably in Bore Street), as well as some silverware and a gold watch, to her son, Luke (who had already inherited most of his father's estates). The rest of her estate went to her surviving daughter, Ann, who with Matthew Boulton is named as an executor. Dorothy included an acknowledgment of Ann's 'dutiful and affectionate behaviour and constant attendance on me during my long and tedious Illness'.[14] Ann was already receiving the interest on £3,000 which her father had left her at the age of twenty-one.[15]

Matthew Boulton and Ann Robinson were married at Rotherhithe, London, on 25 June 1760, witnessed by Boulton's sister, Mary.[16] They must have left Lichfield

---

[*] Swanskin: a type of finely woven flannel cloth.

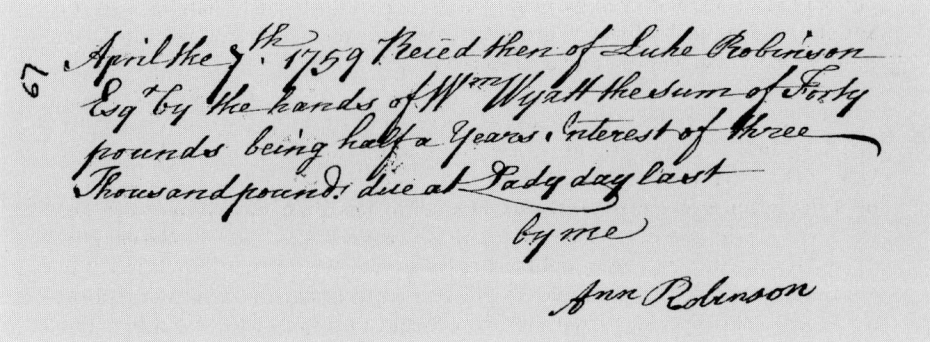

FIG. 1   *Receipt written by Ann Robinson for one year's interest on her father's legacy.*
(Birmingham City Archives)

and headed for London immediately after Dorothy's funeral, for they would have had to be in residence there for a month before the marriage could take place and the 32 days from 25 May to 25 June were barely time to accomplish the journey and this requirement. Marriage to a dead wife's sister was not illegal at the time, but it was certainly frowned upon by the Church, their objections being based on a passage in Leviticus,[17] and in a defensive gesture before the marriage (and a month before Dorothy's death) Boulton had ordered and distributed to friends and acquaintances, and probably to anyone else who would listen, 180 copies of a booklet which he referred to as *Fry on Marriage*, in which marriage to a dead wife's sister was judged to be 'opposed neither to law nor morals'. With binding charges they cost him altogether £10 11s. od. (though that was a discounted price for his bulk order), so he must have felt under some pressure of necessity to prove the point.[18] Nevertheless, the reason for the marriage taking place so far from home must be contained in a letter Boulton wrote many years later to Richard Lovell Edgeworth, who was likewise contemplating marrying his late wife's sister. Boulton recommended the Fry book to his friend and went on:

> I advise that you say nothing to any body of your intentions, but go quickly & snugly to Scotland, or to some obscure corner in London where you are not likely to be known (suppose Wapping) & there take Lodgings to make yourself a parishioner. You need not sleep there every night but may amuse yourself by excursions where you please; & when the month is expired & the law fulfilled, Live & be happy, & defy the Devil. The Dignitaries of the Church will then say, it ought not to have been done, but being done ought not to be undone. It will not be even one days wonder in the Capital nor 7 days wonder in a country Town, nor more than 9 days in a Cathedral Cardplaying Town ... therefore I recommend Silence, Secrecy & Scotland ... [19]

The new Mrs Boulton and her sister-in-law took the opportunity to do some shopping while they were in London. On the day after the wedding they were to be found in the establishment of one Henry Paulin, Haberdasher and Habit-Maker to Her Royal Highness the Princess of Wales, whose shop was at the Princess's Arms and the Statue of Queen Elizabeth in Tavistock Street. Here Mrs Boulton bought 'A Rich white Sattin Quilted Coat double diamond & Boarder' for £3 os. od.[20] She

FIG. 2   *Billhead from Henry Paulin of Tavistock Street.*
(Birmingham City Archives)

also ordered from Elizabeth and Hannah Concher various items including a white silk flowered negligée with body lining and Persian sleeve linings, trimmed with sleeve knots of 'love ribband'[21] (the 18th-century negligée was an informal, loose-fitting gown in which a lady could receive morning visitors). The ladies liked their ribbons – the bill includes a total of 203 yards of various kinds of ribbon. The clothes (some of which were perhaps for Mary) were made up and despatched in a box to Birmingham on 17 July, along with the bill for £8 4s. 10d.[22] Another supplier, Thomas Welch, sent 19 yards of 'laylock [lilac] and green lustring'* at £5 14s. 0d., with a note saying it was 'the last of the pattern and cannot be equalled by the whole trade'.[23]

Apart from going shopping, before returning home all three called at the office of Thomas Hurst, a solicitor with whom Boulton was friendly. Hurst was out but Boulton probably left a copy of the Fry book at his office, for Hurst wrote to Boulton a few days later that he was sorry to have missed them,

as from the Description of the Ladys that came with you, I with pleasure conclude that one of them is Mrs Boulton, whom I am very ardently Desirous to Congratulate on her Nuptials with One that is so well deserving of her; Her Choice sufficiently Evinces her prudence, and nothing will be more pleasing to me, than to hear that the reciprocal affection that subsists between you, may be permanent & productive of the truest uninterrupted Conjugal happiness. I have perused the Book you left, which very evidently proves the validity of the subject it treats upon, as well as the insolent injustice of those that (thro' lucrative motives) Endeavour to oppose it.[24]

A day or two after this Hurst wrote to Boulton again, hoping that he and the ladies had all arrived home safely, adding

I shall be glad to hear that no Sinister Accident during your journey happen'd to give either you or them the least uneasiness – I am so well acquainted with the Soft timidity of them both, as well as the *nice* Circumstance one of them is in, that I am a little anxious on their Accounts … You have very often given me some friendly hints (for such I esteem them) of my too passionate fondness of musick, but I believe it is now unnecessary for me to take the Liberty of

---

* 'Lustring' or lutestring, a type of light, glossy silk worn in the summer.

reminding you that you was formerly immoderately & inconsistently fond of
Electricity – But the pursuit of so dear a prize as you are in poss[n] of (I need
not tell you that I mean dear Mrs Boulton) was sufficient to take [the] place of
& Suppress every other ...[25]

This sounds suspiciously as though Hurst believed one of the women was, or
might be, pregnant, an interesting possibility to contemplate but there is no other
evidence for it.

Many commentators have suggested that Boulton's successive marriages to the
Robinson sisters were contracted on purely financial grounds, and it is easy to
understand why. Ann's brother Luke Robinson himself probably thought so. But
whether or not the marriages had a mainly mercenary foundation, the opposition to
them almost certainly did, as Thomas Hurst had hinted. It is true that both marriages
ultimately brought a substantial amount of capital within Boulton's control, especially
as Luke was to die unmarried at the age of 33 in 1764.[26] However, Boulton would
have had no expectation of this at the time of his marriage to Ann, when her own
capital was relatively modest and her brother would still have been expected to
marry and have a family. Boulton put Ann's financial 'value' at the time of their
marriage at £6,000, in a letter to his banker twenty years later, but added that two
years after the establishment in 1762 of his business partnership with John Fothergill
(therefore in 1764, after Luke's death), her fortune had risen to £28,000.[27]

In the pragmatic way that the 18th century viewed these things, the marriage
had obviously brought him great advantages, but the gaining of the prize was not,
as so often happened, the end of the courtship. Throughout their 23 years of
marriage Boulton continued to write to his wife whenever they were apart, if not
with the same degree of youthful passion, certainly with the warmest affection.
But not a single letter survives from Ann to her husband – who frequently and
plaintively begs her to write him a line or two of news from home, or chides her
for her reluctance to do so.

If Luke was put out by the marriage, he and his sister must have been reconciled
afterwards, for Ann sometimes stayed with him at Lichfield. In 1763 Boulton wrote
to her there from Birmingham that he had engaged maids for her and that 'we
now only want a Servant man', adding 'I have got an excellent Cookmaid'. He was
having to chase 'the Upholsterer, the Painter & the Cabinit Maker' to finish their
work.[28] Written three years after the marriage, this sounds as though Boulton was
having work done at the Boulton family home in Snow Hill in the town centre,
perhaps to bring it up to the smart standard his wife demanded. The eight-day clock
was chiming again in the hall, for he had had the Birmingham clockmaker George
Donisthorpe repair it, and also Mrs Boulton's 'larg Gold Watch', a repair which cost
9s. 6d. Donisthorpe also made him 'a new Electrical Orrery' for £1 8s. od., so he
was still, in Thomas Hurst's teasing phrase, 'immoderately fond of Electricity'.[29]

Mrs Boulton was to want for nothing. The only known portrait of her, painted by
Tilly Kettle at about this time, shows a rather solemn woman, looking older than her
30 years. There are pearls in her hair and at her throat and ears. She wears a dark
red velvet shawl or loose jacket edged with fur, over a deep décolletage trimmed
with lace (Plate 2). Her expression seems to belie the taste for lavish be-ribboning

already hinted at. By contrast, Tilly Kettle's portrait of Matthew Boulton himself, done as a companion piece to the portrait of his wife, shows a youngish, slightly preoccupied-looking man in a plain dark red coat, with modest lace cuffs and cravat (Plate 1). There are more bills for Mrs Boulton which include a cloak and bonnet trimmed with lace, linings for hats, various muslins, ribbons, silk mitts, and kid gloves. Elizabeth Sabet's dressmaking bill of 1763-6 (paid in 1768) lists two gowns and four negligées, including 'a striped silk gown made & pinking the silk' (five shillings), a 'Bombazine Neglegee & Petticoat made up' (ten shillings), body linings, 'a silk gown & petticoat made' (seven shillings and sixpence), and other things.[30] These making-up bills would be in addition to the fabric costs. Ann's dress sense and fashion contacts must have been admired among her acquaintance, for her husband's friend Erasmus Darwin's wife, Mary, wrote to her asking her to get a black silk negligée painted for a friend.[31]

With Ann's moderate capital available to him following their marriage in 1760, Boulton was able to contemplate the expansion of the family business. Though they were already established exporters at the time of Boulton senior's death, the business was not on a particularly large scale. When Boulton junior took over the running of it, it soon became clear that the cramped Snow Hill premises would be unable to contain his ambition. In 1761, the year after his second marriage, he took a lease on 13 acres of high, open heathland in Handsworth, some two miles north-west of Birmingham town centre, and then just over the Staffordshire border. Here he set about having built what was to become the world-famous Soho Manufactory, a great industrial complex fronted by an impressive 'principal building' (Plate 4). The building project took several years, but eventually John Fothergill, who had joined him in the business in 1762, was able to write to him, 'The buildings now begin to look so very sumptuous as to engage the attention of all ranks of people.'[32] The area was already known as Soho – the name is said to have been taken from a local inn sign showing a huntsman blowing a horn, from the bell of which issued the word 'Soho!'. The building cost Boulton some £10,000 – which was £8,000 more than the architects' estimates. He probably sold the Curborough Estate, which had once belonged to his Babington ancestors (*see* Appendix) and had come down to him as part of Mary Robinson's marriage settlement, to Luke Robinson around this time to help finance the project.

With the new Manufactory in production, the range of steel buckles, buttons and jewellery formerly produced at Snow Hill began to be augmented (Plates 5 & 6) by decorative sword hilts, Sheffield plate, ormolu ware, sterling silver tableware, and, later, coins and medals. Boulton & Fothergill embarked on a vigorous export sales drive. They appointed agents in London who handled much of the Continental business; Fothergill, who was a good linguist, travelled widely in Europe on sales trips (Plate 13).

The business required Boulton's frequent presence in London. By and large he enjoyed the buzz of the capital, but sometimes complained of the fogs and the coughing population and longed for the 'pure air' of Soho. If all was not well at home he found it trying to be so far away. He was in London early in 1764 when 'Cousin Kitty' (his sister Catherine) wrote to tell him that Mrs Boulton was ill. Kitty's letter made him anxious to get home as soon as possible, and he wrote to Ann begging that 'nothing may be delayd that is necessary for thy safety & restoration'.[33] Whatever the problem was, it did not last long; Boulton was relieved to get reassuring letters from both John Fothergill, and his own brother, John. Then one of his own letters to Ann, dated 9 February 1764, was returned to him with a note on the back from Kitty, dated 13 February. Addressing her brother rather formally as 'Sir', and in an uncertain hand and employing an archaic use of 'cousin', she wrote:

> Cousin Boulton [Ann] is obligd for your Kind Concern but now I have good news which will make you rejoice for she is got very well again we yesterday had the pleasure of seeing Cousin Luke who is here now & hope your Business will be transacted as soon as possible, that we may have the pleasure of seeing you here Cousin Boulton hopes youll remember the Tea & other things she mentiond before you went to London, she joynes with me in Love to you wishing you a good Journey ...[34]

Delighted with Kitty's news, Boulton wrote to Ann again on 15 February, a newsy letter describing various events he had witnessed including two weeping prisoners being taken in a cart to the gallows, and a serious fire at the Star Alehouse in Eagle Street, Haymarket. Flames were 'bellowing at every window in the House, nor could any Water be had untill the House was burnt but at length a water pipe was oppend & then the Engeons soon stoped its progress.' There was no need for Cousin Kitty's reminders about the tea, he added – 'I shall forget nothing that relates to my *Love* nor should I know how extatically I Love her was it not for these abscences. I beg you will make my kind Compliments to your Scribe...'[35] For his own part, he was sick and tired of London and missing home comforts: 'nor shall I have any repose until I am got into my old green Bed. Miss Russell being upon a Visit to Mrs Jeffrys I have been obliged to pig into a Cold dirty Garrett at ye George wch has given me a little Cold ...'.[36] 'Mrs Jeffrys' may have been the wife of Nathaniel Jefferys in the Strand, for in an earlier letter Boulton mentioned that he was lodging 'at his Majestys Cuttler'.[37] Boulton perhaps liked to keep in with Mrs Jefferys – he had paid £3 1s. 3d. for a rather splendid hat for her in 1760, a black velvet turban with a gold tassel, cord and button and one-and-three-quarter yards of fine long lawn.[38]

Boulton had taken Kitty's comment about Luke Robinson's presence at the family home in Birmingham as a sign that his brother-in-law's health was improving, but he was mistaken. During the summer Luke was unwell, and by September 1764 he was dangerously ill at his Lichfield home and deteriorating rapidly. The nature of his illness is not recorded. His cousin, Charles Blackham, visited him often and noted the frequent presence at the house of the solicitor, Charles Simpson (who in 1764 became Lichfield Town Clerk and Coroner). Simpson was pestering the invalid to make a will. Blackham thought him incapable of it. The solicitor insisted that the will was already drawn up; Luke needed only to sign it to execute it. Blackham was so concerned about the solicitor's behaviour that some time later he and other witnesses made long statements about it, which were written down in a foolscap notebook.

On the morning of Friday 14 September, Luke was rambling and delirious. Anxious and fearful, Blackham

> wrote a letter to Mr Boulton Mr Robinson's brother in law to inform him that Mr Robinson was much worse and desired either him or Mrs Boulton to come over to Mr Robinsons with all expedition, but did not chuse to make the worst of Mr Robinson's condition for fear of frightening his Sister who was far gone with child, and sent a messenger on purpose on horseback between the hours of ten and eleven on Friday morning the 14th of September.[39]

Just after the messenger had gone, Simpson the solicitor arrived. He was asked not to disturb Luke but 'ran up the stairs immediately'. When Blackham went up, 'Mr Robinson had been got out of bed and was sitting on the side of a bed in another room very weak and poorly and much ado to sit up & was obliged frequently to lie down.'

Simpson urged Luke to sign the will immediately, and neighbours were sent for to witness it. The solicitor read the will aloud – Charles Blackham said Luke plainly did not understand a word of it. He was asked if he wanted to change anything and said he didn't know. William Kennedy, one of the witnesses, said Luke ought to leave more to John Wootten, who had been his faithful servant for many years after giving up his job: 'You have taken the poor fellow from his trade, he perhaps may never be able to work at it again.' The solicitor agreed, and according to Blackham he altered the will to increase Wootten's legacy from £5 to £50. The name John Wootten does not appear in the probate copy of Luke Robinson's will, though there is a £50 bequest to a servant John Oughton, whose name also appears on other documents. The alteration having been made, poor Luke Robinson was then badgered into executing the will by repeating the words after the solicitor and making his mark.

After this the witnesses went downstairs and began grumbling among themselves at how they had fared in the will. Blackham said,

> I think Mr Robinson ought to have considered my Mother who is as near a relation as any he has except his Sister, you know very well my Mother attended Mrs Robinson in a long illness for a month together and did everything she could to please him [Luke] and that he has told several persons that he was greatly obliged to his Cousin Blackham for her kind attendance, that she was the best nurse he had, and that there was always a good understanding between his Mother & her, for that she visited him & her more than any relation he had – surely she is entitled upon that account to some reversionary interest upon the death of Mr & Mrs Boulton without issue...

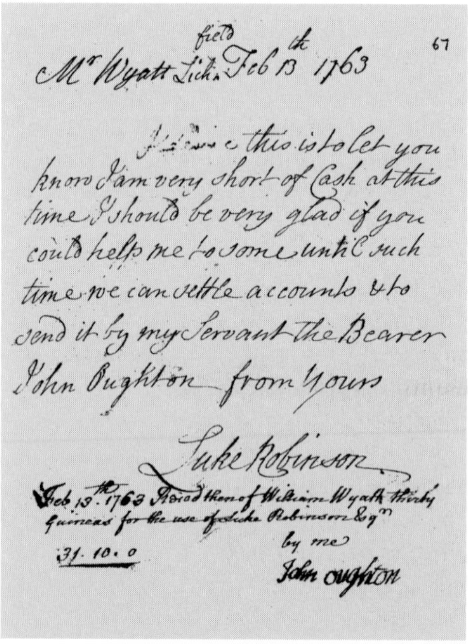
Mr Wyatt Lichfield Feb 13th 1763 67

Sir this is to let you know I am very short of Cash at this time I should be very glad if you could help me to some until such time we can settle accounts & to send it by my Servant the Bearer John Oughton from Yours

Luke Robinson

Feb 13th 1763 Recd then of William Wyatt thirty Guineas for the use of Luke Robinson Esqr
31. 10. 0 by me
John Oughton

FIG. 3 *Letter from Luke Robinson junior to William Wyatt, receipted by his servant, John Oughton. (Birmingham City Archives)*

Others pointed out that as Mr and Mrs Boulton were still young there was no guarantee of legacies which were dependent on them dying without surviving children. Simpson the solicitor said he had suggested to Luke that he leave his Yoxall estate, after Mr and Mrs Boulton's death without issue, to Charles Blackham, but Luke had said no, because 'I know if my Sister Nanny had it in her power to leave any thing she wou'd have left me all she cou'd. Therefore I wou'd leave her what I have in her own power.'[40] Luke had also told Simpson that the Farm at Curborough was 'a settlement upon his [Boulton's] first wife & tho he has sold it he wou'd like to have it again.'

Some time shortly after 14 September, Luke Robinson died. His servant, John Wootten [or Oughton?], said that Charles Simpson had been endeavouring to get his master to make a Will 'all this last summer' and Luke could not understand why he was so keen, unless he just wanted the business. The solicitor had visited him every day during his illness. Martha Silvester the housekeeper said that Charles Simpson had 'tais'd' [teased] Mr Robinson to make his Will, always leaving him very disturbed:

> The evening Simpson attak him upon ye subject [of the Will] he was so agitated & affected wth what Simpson had said to him that when his physician [Dr Darwin] came to see him he found Mr Rs pulse, Body & Mind so agitated that he [Darwin] was almost in a Passion with his serv^{ts} for suffering him to be disturbed & asked them what [they] had been doing to him & who had flurryd him thus. They answered that nobody had been wth him but Mr Simpson.

Another witness reported that 'About 6 weeks before Mr R's death he requested his Blacksmith to kill him, telling him he would forgive him for that he was tired of his Life.'[41]

On one of the blank pages at the end of this extraordinary document is the following satirical 'advertisement':

> Soon will be published
> The Modern Art of Will-making
> By Charles Smiler Gent
> With Notes Critical & Explanatory
> To which will be added
> An Essay on Bribery & Corruption
> And its Utility
> In Borough Elections
> As practised by ye Author
> In the City of Litchfield
> Subscriptions are receiv'd
> At the late Mr Luke Robinsons in Bow Street
> And at ye Bowling Green Litchfield[42]

(Charles Simpson was known in the town by the nickname of 'Young Smiler', his father, Stephen, being 'Old Smiler'.)[43]

After some bequests to cousins, servants and charitable causes in Lichfield, Luke left Ann and Matthew Boulton the estate at nearby Curborough which Boulton had received from Luke Robinson senior as part of the marriage settlement when he married Mary Robinson, but had subsequently sold back to Luke junior. Income from Luke's leasehold property at Lichfield, Bowling Green House and the Bowling Green, was to be distributed annually to the poor of St Mary's Parish, Lichfield, Charles Simpson being named as one of the trustees. Simpson and his heirs were left 'the House I live in' for a term of 21 years from Luke's death, for which they were to pay Matthew Boulton an annual rent of £14. The rent income from Luke's other lands was to be paid to Ann Boulton for her personal use. A codicil to the will gives the Yoxall estate in trust for the Blackhams in the event of Ann dying without issue. Matthew Boulton is named as the sole executor of this will, which was not proved until June 1767.[44]

The strange and disturbing affair of Luke Robinson's will tells us one thing of particular note here: that Mrs Ann Boulton was 'far gone with child' at the time of her brother's death. This must account for the concern expressed by John Fothergill's wife and sister, who sent a message on the day of the funeral, 24 September, begging Boulton to 'prevail if possible on Mrs Boulton to be absent from this day's scene as it may be too much for her spirits'.[45]

If Mrs Boulton was indeed heavily pregnant in September 1764, it may throw some light on her illness earlier in the year. If her indisposition in February was due to the early stages of pregnancy, she would have been about eight months pregnant by September – 'far gone with child' – but no evidence of a resulting birth or baptismal record has been found around that time.

On the other hand, in the early spring of 1765 the Boultons *did* suffer a major disappointment. At the end of a letter dated 9 March 1765, to an agent, John Lewis Baumgartner, Boulton added a postscript condolence for a bereavement Baumgartner had suffered, and then added, 'thus are our Lives Chequer'd. I myself lost a Son but yesterday'.[46] A customer, John Cantrel, having also received the news, wrote to him at Snow Hill on 18 March,

> I cannot omit letting you know that I am quite inconsoleable for your sake; but, at the same time, do most fervently wish that your next efforts may be blessed with greater success. This loss of yours is, what you cannot think I can so sensibly feel as yourself; yet I can draw some outlines of your disappointment together ... My best compliments to Mrs Boulton; and with your leave, I hope to take her by the cheek next Monday ...[47]

Was this son, lost on 8 March 1765, the five-month-old child of Mrs Boulton's pregnancy the previous year? Or was he the miscarried or very premature result of a new pregnancy (which could not have lasted much more than five months, if it followed immediately after an unsuccessful pregnancy which ended in September 1764)? Or might Ann have been only about three months pregnant at the time of her brother's death, and been delivered in early March 1765 of a stillborn son or one which did not survive long enough to be baptised? No record has been found of a Boulton burial that March, but burials of stillborn children are often entered anonymously in parish registers, if at all. Perhaps the first of these suggestions is the most likely, though if so it is strange that the correspondence contains no mention of the baby.

Although it was to be three years before Luke Robinson's will was proved, as a result of his death Mrs Boulton's fortune – and thereby her husband's – was expected to increase substantially, and when Benjamin Franklin wrote to Boulton in the spring of 1765 to introduce a new friend, Dr William Small, he congratulated Boulton candidly on the 'considerable Addition to your Fortune', which their mutual friend John Baskerville had told him about.[48] Small ('an ingenious Philosopher, & a most worthy honest Man') was a Scottish-trained doctor, who had been Thomas Jefferson's tutor in natural philosophy at Williamsburg, Virginia, before returning to Britain. After he arrived in Birmingham bearing Franklin's letter, he became Boulton's physician and a close friendship based on their shared scientific interests soon developed between the two men.

In the autumn of 1765, just as Boulton was planning another trip to London, Ann was taken ill again, an illness said to be 'dangerous'.[49] After a day or two she rallied, and her husband set off for London reassured. On 3 November Fothergill wrote to him about an order, adding that Mrs Boulton was now perfectly recovered except for her speech, which was 'owing to the heat of her disorder yet unintelligible'.[50] She must have regained it promptly, for by 5 November Boulton was getting messages that his wife wanted a new cap, and a ring engraved, and even had thoughts of joining him. Meanwhile, family and colleagues endeavoured to keep her amused at home. One of the Soho managers, John Scale, reported at the end of a letter about an order for chains that he, Mrs Boulton and Mr and Mrs Walker (Boulton's sister Mary and her husband Zacheus Walker, who was the senior clerk at Soho) had had 'one very merry Game at Whist & beleive we are going to have another tonight'.[51]

While Ann contemplated going to London to see her husband, Boulton had plans of his own which he had not shared with her. In November 1765, shortly after sending a barrel of oysters off to Birmingham, he left London for what was probably his first trip abroad, to France. Perhaps it was because of her recent illness that he did not want Ann to know about the trip until he was well on the way, for John Fothergill wrote to their London factor John Motteux: 'the Secret of Mr Boultons departure was this morning at his request communicated to his Lady who beares his abscences very feelingly.'[52] As soon as he reached Calais, Boulton wrote to his wife, explaining that on Motteux's advice he had gone to France to try to recover some Boulton & Fothergill goods which had been supplied to a Paris importer whose business had failed. His letter, written on Sunday 18 November, provides a graphic description of the journey. He and an associate, Daniel Bureau, had set out from London for Dover the previous Wednesday but, in spite of travelling all night, they had arrived in Dover too late to catch the Thursday 'packett' (ferry). Anxious to get to Paris as soon as possible, they had chartered a vessel to take them across the Channel, but the wind ('blowing a hurrican') had kept them in port at Dover until Saturday, when his patience would brook no more delay and he had ordered the captain to set sail, come what may. Their troubles had barely begun:

> On Board we went, twixt 10 & 11 yesterday morng, accompanied by 4 or 5 shabby French Gentlemen who could not raise Mony to pay their passage in ye Cabin; an old Duch Womn, her Son, her niece & her nieces little Girl abt 4

yrs old, with Mr Bureau & Self were all ye Cabin Guests. In about half an Hour
after we were got out to Sea we all began to be very sick. I opened ye Ball wth
throwing up my Breakfast & all ye rest soon followed my example, I continued
upon deck till I was so ill that I was obliged to go to bed in ye Cabin, my Friend
Bureau soon followd, & presently after the old Womn wth her Friends all packed
to Bed (for there are Ten Beds in ye same Cabin) the Captn finding me so very
ill (having almost strained my Stomach up) offerd to return to Dover but I was
resolvd to weather it through although both Wind & Tyde were against us ...
Dureing all this time we continued employing one of the sailours to wait upon
us, the Old Womns Fountain below playing very often ye young one cascading
above, the Child Crying, the Sailours tramping over our heads cursing Swearing
& manageing their Sails, added to my own extream sickness, produced a species
of pleasure I wish you never to partake of. After fasting & pukeing near 24 hours
we arrived at Calais betwixt 7 & 8 this morng. I have got my pattns [patterns,
or samples] safe on shore by the help of wide Breeches & Pocketts & I have
just hired a Chaise ... by wch means I hope to get my Self & pattrns to Paris on
Tuesday morng. I have found here a very usefull Friend that hath furnished us
wth Mony & good advice, his Name is Monsr Le Sage. I have had Two Breakfasts
& am got shaved washed & Shifted so that I am now not a tittle ye worse for
my Voyage. I expect to stay abt 8 days at Paris & then shall return & finish my
business in London. 53

Concluding with greetings to his brother John, sisters Molly (Mary) and Kitty,
'and little Niece I'll not forgett' (probably Kitty's daughter, Anne 'Nancy' Mynd,
who would have been about two years old), he adds a PS: 'every thing appears
very droll & strange to me here. There are many parties a-playing at Shuttle-cock
in ye Streets, the Womn are all dressd wth Square old fashioned pinners, Great
Hoods, & little Slippers &c.' He did not like French food, complaining a couple
of days later: 'I have not eat one meal since I left England half so good as our
Birmingham Bread, Chees & Small Beer. I have quite lost my belly having had
little in it for this week past ...'54

The following Sunday, 25 November, Boulton wrote to his wife again, from Paris.
He had planned to write her a long letter, he said, 'with my reflections & observations
by wch I intended to give my Love some Idea of this grand & paltry Country, a
Country that abounds wth pompous poverty & is in most particulars quite in the
papier mache style: except their palaces, churches, Sculpture, Carving, Painting;
& in general their Designs are beyond all things I have ever seen' – however he
had been too busy, so would have to 'reserve 'em for those sweet winter evenings
I hope to soon pass wth my Dear Wife.'55 He was feeling the cold, since he had
been unable to wear a greatcoat or hat, these not being *de rigeur* in Paris. Instead
he was obliged to dress in black, with a bag wig and sword, and carry his hat under
his arm instead of on his head where he would have preferred it. The formal bag
wigs were curled at the front, with the longer hair at the back encased in a black
silk bag. The French fashion of carrying the hat under the arm (the '*chapeau
bras*') arose from the impossibility of wearing a hat on top of the higher wigs of
the earlier 18th century, and continued for formal occasions even after wigs had
assumed more modest proportions.

It being Sunday, Boulton had been on an outing to Versailles where, he told
Ann, 'I saw I suppose ye largest palace in Europe'. He had admired the paintings,

marble sculptures, 'water works' and 'curious workmanship without end or number'. Back in Paris in the evening, they were too late for the opera, and the playhouses were full, but they had seen a harlequin performance on a candlelit stage in the street. He concluded the letter with love to all in Warwickshire and Staffordshire, and signed himself 'your most affectionately & sincerely Fidell, alias MB'.

Boulton managed to get back some of his goods and hoped that with the tenpence in the pound being paid to creditors, Boulton & Fothergill would lose no more than £40, but the visit lasted longer than he had expected, for which he made excuses to Ann, writing virtuously to her:

> … my affection for my dear Nanny encreases wth my abscence: for all ye Variety I have seen will only teach me to enjoy home & value my good Wife more & more if possible, as all my observations rather induce me to think there is scarcely such a thing in this Country, if paint, patches, powder, Silks, Diamonds & flirting airs render ye Sex agreeable the Garden of ye Tulleries abound; but for that Gem call'd Virtue whose brightness puts ye Diamd out of countenance, I have scarcely seen a glimps of it in any Face here.[56]

By 8 December he was at last looking forward to setting out for home. As a peace offering he was bringing her some silk which she could get made up 'a la mode de Londre for as its a good silk I could wish to have it well made'.[57]

If Ann had been sulking about her husband's absence abroad, her temper had improved by this time for on 9 December John Baskerville wrote a letter to await him at John Motteux's near the Mansion House. He had been to see Ann at home that morning, evidently to placate her on Boulton's behalf, and to suggest that she take the opportunity to accompany Boulton's friend and physician Dr William Small to London to meet up with her husband. Baskerville had found Ann

> quite reconciled to your Journey to Paris & [I] urg'd the Necessity of your stay there to establish the Trade that Oppenheim used to have thro' his Hands. I told her that your sudden Departure left most of your London Business unfinished; that a Journey thither to meet you would agreeably accomplish the whole, that you would range 'till Dinner & attend her [in] the Evening, that Dr Small would advise this, & observed that it would be as good as a Journey to Bath, & the Consequence no doubt a Son & Heir, at which she laughed heartily, & said, then she would not go.[58]

But she did go. Fothergill wrote to her, hoping that she had arrived safely. He dwelt a little suggestively on their reunion: 'It gives me great pleasure to reflect what mutual happiness will attend your Approaching meeting in London, sure that lucky minute is now in agitation.'[59] To Boulton he wrote rather more racily a day or two later, 'Your mentioning that travelling excites in you such youthful vigour will be the best means to prevail wth my Wife for a little Widowhood, *Je suppose qu'a l'heure presente votre courage est un peu diminué, com[m]e la foire dure long temp[s] il faut être discret,* your taste for going abroad pleases me much as I doubt not in time we must practice it pretty often…'[60]

When Mrs Boulton did not join her husband on visits to London, left to his own devices in the capital he could not resist shopping, both for her and for himself, in between business calls. Shopping was the new amusement of those with money to indulge in it, and shopkeepers were becoming increasingly assertive in their efforts to attract trade, with elaborate, finely-engraved letterheads proclaiming the superiority of both their wares and their customers. It was usual for small discounts to be given for ready money 'paid same time', but where (more often) goods were bought on credit, retailers frequently had to wait months (sometimes years) for payment, torn between the need to hang on to high-profile customers and the need for working capital to keep afloat. Boulton seems to have enjoyed buying fabrics and clothes for his wife; there are many comments in letters about items purchased, and there are shopping lists in his notebooks – one such list, in 1765, is headed 'a handsom silk for my wife' and also includes earrings and 'a blew & green hoop ring'.[61] He sends home small gifts such as cotton stockings and lace caps. Jewellery is altered or engraved, cloaks are dyed. [62]

In October 1766 he was in London and spent the enormous sum of 65 guineas on 'a suit of Lace' for Ann, which he had asked the lace merchant's wife Mrs Grossett ('a Lady of tast') to send to a good milliner to get made up. 'If I have failed in my test you must take the will for the deed but I hope it will please & then I shall be happy...'[63] Good lace was inordinately expensive and the 'suit of lace' probably included one or more pairs of sleeve ruffles, a skirt flounce, a neck ruffle and possibly lace for a bonnet too, for at this period milliners worked on gowns as well as head-dresses.[64] A day or two later he wrote that the lace was made up, he was setting out for home and wanted his wife to meet him at Hall Green on the outskirts of Birmingham to keep him company for the last few miles of the journey (something he often asked her to do when he was returning home alone from London). He began to cut a dash about town himself, in a scarlet flannel waistcoat and a dark brown Ranelagh frock suit of 'superfine cloth', with rich gold embroidered buttonholes with pearls and spangles, among many stylish items in a 1767-8 tailor's bill of £49 14s.2d.[65]

The year 1766, when Ann received that expensive gift of lace, was also the year in which the Boultons moved from Snow Hill in Birmingham town centre to Soho House at Handsworth. Matthew Boulton had acquired the house in January 1761, when it came with the land he leased to build the Soho Manufactory. The house, on the windy, barren hilltop just above the Manufactory, had been built c.1757. It accounted for £300 of the £1,000 he paid for the lease, but when Boulton acquired it the interior was unfinished, and in any case the house was not the chief attraction of the site. He was far more interested in the potential for industrial development offered by an old mill and millpool. Nevertheless he had the house decorated and in March 1761 his mother and one of his sisters moved in. But some time in the summer of 1762, his new business partner John Fothergill needed somewhere to live, so Boulton 'turnd his mother & sister out of his house at Soho & Fothergill entered upon it'.[66] Mrs Boulton senior and her daughter may have gone back to the house at Snow Hill, where Boulton and his wife were probably living.[67] By 1766, however, Boulton felt he needed to live nearer the Manufactory himself, and set about evicting Fothergill, who understandably put up vigorous objections, Boulton countering them with a long list of complaints of his own, including Fothergill's neglect of the garden which had not 'received the assistance of one Load of Muck since Fothergills residence'. Further, he demanded petulantly, 'As Fothergill is not of the least use in the Manufactory if he will not live near a warehouse in Town Qr of what use will he be?'[68] Then for good measure he added a pinch of pathos:

> B. now approaches that time of life when it would be madness in him to risque his health by a daily going backward and forward in all seasons and weather, and, without he doth attend at Soho every day and almost all day long, F. will share but small profit. But, waveing all consideration of health, is it reasonable that B. should sacrifice his domestick happiness, and likewise the happiness of his wife, by such a continual absence from home that the manufactory at Soho will require? For as F. talkes of going abroad for 12 or 14 months, then surely B. must attend it. According to the common course of things B. has but about 10 years good for business to come, as he is now enter'd into his 38th year ...[69]

Eventually, of course, Boulton got his own way; Fothergill went protestingly to a house in town, and Boulton and his wife moved into Soho House. In October 1766 John Motteux observed, 'I am glad to hear that you are at last settled at Soho'.[70]

Soho House at this date was a modest brick house, smaller and different in appearance from how it came to look later. Boulton had some work done on the house before moving in, the first of many alterations over the next forty years, and we shall return to this subject later (Plate 3). Still muttering about Fothergill's neglect of the garden, he instituted a lengthy programme of soil improvement, carting loads of manure out from the numerous stables in Birmingham, and planting 'above 2,000 firs' to form a windbreak.[71]

Ensconced in his new house, the sociable Boulton enjoyed playing the host; in an early letter to James Watt he reminded him that there would always be a bed and a friendly reception for him at '*l'hôtel d'amitié sur Handsworth Heath*'.[72] The two men had begun corresponding on steam engine matters in 1766, but not until 1768, in one of those pivotal moments in history, did they meet, when Watt called at Soho on his way home to Glasgow from London.

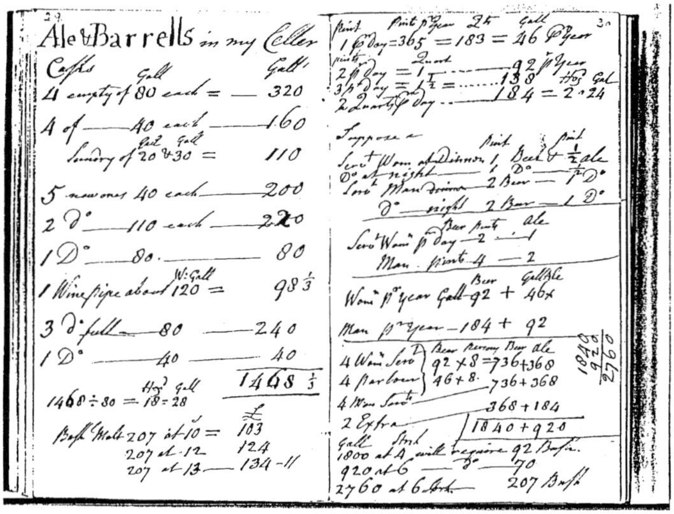

FIG. 4 *'Ale & Barrells in my Celler', from Matthew Boulton's notebooks. (Birmingham City Archives)*

Many other guests were welcomed at '*l'hôtel d'amitié*' from 1766 onwards. While the cook busied herself over the venison, in anticipation of their visits Boulton must have made many a trip down the worn steps, candle in hand, to inspect the state of his wine cellar, for he made a number of lists of its contents. And after dinner Mrs Boulton would entertain their guests on her new forte piano by Johann Zumpe.[73]

The most regular among the visitors were the members of the Lunar Society.[74] Boulton, who had been interested in natural philosophy (what is now called natural science) since boyhood, was a founder member of this small but influential group; members met at one another's homes on or near the night of the full moon, so that they might have better light to travel home by afterwards – not an unusual idea in itself, for in the 18th century many societies chose the full moon period for their meetings, for the same reason. Over a good dinner, washed down with Boulton's best wines, the Lunar Society members – 'Lunaticks' to the folk in town – discussed their latest scientific hobby horses and probably teased each other about their pet theories, before adjourning to the study for a few experiments or to peer at 'animalcules' through Boulton's good Dollond microscope.

In the early summer of 1767 Boulton had more than animalcules on his mind. Mrs Boulton was pregnant again. It was now seven years since their marriage, and they had had at least one disappointment. As the end of the year and the time for his wife's delivery approached, Boulton became the stereotypical anxious expectant father (understandably, in view of previous experience). In a letter to Francis Garbett at the New Year he wrote, 'as I am hourly expecting the delivery of my Wife I cannot think of leaving home on any account until her anxiety is at an end'.[75] On 15 January he wrote to John Motteux, excusing himself from coming to London because 'my Wifes pregnancy being now *expired*, in ye Counting Way, I can not reconcile myself to leave home untill she is safely deliverd which I am in hourly expectation of ...'[76]

The child, a daughter, was born on Friday, 29 January 1768. This raises the possibility that, even allowing for mis-counting the pregnancy, she may have been two weeks or more overdue. They named the baby Anne, and before long Boulton was writing to Richard Levett, one of his wife's cousins, thanking him for his congratulations and declaring 'my Wife & little one are in as perfect health as can be possably expected'.[77] On the same day he wrote to his German business agent, J.H. Ebbinghaus, 'I have the pleasure to inform you that my wife was deliver'd the 29th January of a very fine girl, and both are likely to do very well.'[78] He could not tear himself away from them. On 2 March he wrote to another business contact that he had put off a journey to London due to the bad weather, his rheumatism, and the fact that 'my Wife at this time lyes in of a Daughter'.[79] If he had hoped for a son, there is no hint of it. From the beginning, there is no question of Boulton's love for his daughter, which makes subsequent revelations all the more puzzling.

2

Doctors

At the time of Anne's birth, Matthew Boulton was 39 and his wife about thirty-five. In a period when the average age at marriage was generally rising, and the mortality rate, especially among women, was high, second and even third marriages were common and it was not unusual for marriages and births to take place well into the thirties and even forties.

With her pregnancy over, Mrs Boulton ran up a lengthy bill for dressmaking and alterations from one Mary Greaves. The bill included alterations to 'a blue Sattin' and a cotton gown, making several 'stumachers', making gowns in green silk, 'gray stuff' and gingham, making 'a Chince gown and petty coat trimmd with Lace' (5s.), 'turning' various silk gowns, 'altring a white silk neglege' (10s.) and 'a gaye neglege made into a gown' (2s. 6d.).[1] There is little evidence of what was spent on the new baby, apart from a bill for a cradle and a child's chair, which cost 17s. 6d.[2]

Like many new parents, Mr and Mrs Boulton probably regarded the infant with a mixture of love and fear. What to do with so small a creature? Boulton had already lost the three children of his first marriage and knew all too well how fragile they were. For guidance and reassurance they may have turned to their Lichfield friend Dr Erasmus Darwin. Darwin (Plates 8 & 9) was a larger-than-life character: big, ungainly, genial, poetical, inventive and scientific. He already had three sons of his own, by his first wife Mary Howard, and another son and a daughter had died, so he was fully sensible of the pain of parental anxiety. An early, undated note from him in the Boulton papers contains pointers on babycare. Whether it was sent as advice on caring for Anne there is no indication, but it includes recommendations that infants should sleep in a cool room, wear light clothing, and 'a child should not be fed as it lie on its back because then it is obliged to swallow till it bursts'.[3] As in so many other areas of knowledge, Darwin the physician was well ahead of his time in his ideas on childcare. The cool, airy room and light clothing which he recommends are in distinct and enlightened contrast to many of the accepted practices of the day, including the exclusion of fresh air at all costs and the habitual tight swaddling of infants.

But there was a cloud on the horizon. By the time Anne was 18 months old they could see she was not going to walk properly. Boulton discussed their worries with Darwin, and with the family doctor, Dr William Small (Plate 7). In June 1769 Darwin wrote Boulton a long letter, complete with diagrams showing deformities of the spine and hip joints, and considering various possible causes. Beginning in a reassuringly light tone, he wrote:

> WOMAN, says Aristotle, is a two-leg'd animal *without Feathers* – He certainly meant very young Women! – after being given a Definition of the Subject of my Letter, the next thing necessary is a drawing, here it is, *abc* is the said animal, *a* the Head, *b* the Body, *cc* the Legs. When this animal stands erect, & careless, the Line *xy* should be horizontal, if it be inclined a few degrees from the perpendicular, by whatever means this is occasion'd, the whole Figure [will] undergo the changes express'd in the 2nd f[ig].[4]

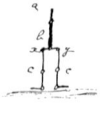

Darwin went on to outline various possible causes and effects, and described how the calf muscles could become so contracted by spasm that they would no longer function properly, so that the patient developed a tendency to walk on tip-toe, which in its turn produced some turning of the foot. He had evidently discussed a possible way of treating the problem with Dr Small, but did not repeat his recommendations in this letter. He advised Boulton how to see the problem for himself:

> If you see the Child play sprawling on the Bed, quite naked & on its Feet for some time, repeatedly, you will see the Defect … pray all of you come over to Lichfield that we may have a general Consultation, Ladies & Gentlemen, for if it be remediable, it must be NOW. And for this Purpose the defect must be absolutely ascertain'd – Delay is damnable …[5]

There is no record of whether this 'general consultation' did take place, or if Anne received any treatment. By the end of the year her mother was pregnant again, and in the meantime Boulton's hectic round of business activities continued unabated, perhaps pushing the problem into the background. In the early part of 1770, leaving his wife and little daughter at home, he set off for London, where he was about to achieve a long-cherished ambition: an audience with the King and Queen. George III had come to the throne in the autumn of 1760, not long after the Boultons' marriage, and attendance at Court was something which went a long way to establish one's credentials – Lady Northumberland had once recommended it to young James Boswell, telling him: 'I'm sure that's a cheap diversion; it costs you nothing, and you see all the best company, and chat away. It is the best coffee-house in town.'[6]

Boulton wrote triumphantly to his wife about his reception at the Palace, 'which I cant help saying was passing agreeable to me, I saw 4 of the young princes who are very fine Boys but not prettier than my little darling.' The Queen (the German Charlotte von Mecklenburg-Strelitz) was, he added,

> much improvd in her person & she now speaks English like an English Lady, she draws very fine, she is a great Musician & works with her needle better than Mrs Betty*, however without joke she is extreamly sensible, very affable & is a patroness of English Manufactorys.[7]

In the course of the royal audience, which lasted over three hours, the Queen invited Boulton to her bedchamber, where she showed him the chimney piece and told him she wished to replace all the china ornaments on it with his ormolu vases and candelabra. He asked his wife to get the works manager, John Scale, to send

---

* 'Mrs Betty' – Mrs Elizabeth Marklew, the housekeeper at Soho House.

him immediately '7 or 8 good Vases for ye Queen lower part of her Chymney piece, all sorts, Blew John ... as I was made to promise they should be delivered in less than a fortnight ...' He also wanted to know how many blue john vases could be finished within a month. Soho was certainly not short of blue john – the previous year over fourteen tons of the blue-and-yellow-banded Derbyshire fluorspar, which took its name from the French *bleu-jaune*, had been delivered, at a cost of £81 1s. 6d.[8] (Plate 10)

Boulton was clearly expecting further orders to flow as a result of the royal patronage.[9] It certainly helped the first of three sales at Christie's auction room in Pall Mall the following month, Boulton writing to his wife: 'I made so great a bussle amongst the Nobility even to such a degree as to stop up Pallmall with Coaches.'[10] Going to auctions was a fashionable amusement – Fanny Burney describes a similar scene in Pall Mall in *Evelina*. In spite of all this excitement, Boulton promised, 'I will not forget my little Maids Bu bonne [perhaps a representation of Anne's childish pronunciation of 'blue bonnet'?] God bless her as well as her Mamma whom I wish good night & am her truly affectionate Matthew Boulton'.[11] At a shop on the corner of Shoe Lane and Fleet Street, he spent £5 19s. 0d. on 'a fine blond Dress & Cap' at £1 12s. 0d., and other items,[12] but there is no indication of whether these garments were wife- or daughter-sized (children's clothes were virtually miniature versions of those for adults).

On Wednesday 8 August 1770, when Anne was just over two-and-a-half, her brother, Matthew Robinson Boulton, was born. He was known in the family as Matt. Elizabeth Montagu visited Soho in 1771 and saw the baby, writing to Boulton afterwards: 'I hope the little Gentleman whose Beauty eclipsed all your gold on Cupids is in perfect health'.[13]

Boulton proved an affectionate and concerned father, writing regularly to his wife when away from home with worries and advice about the children's health. In one letter he told her that to avoid 'a putrid soar throat' during a heatwave, 'I have heard that it's a good thing in such hot weather to wash the out side of the neck & throat of Children with a decoction of Bark'.[14] This would probably be quinine bark, which was widely used in the treatment of fevers or, as here, as a preventative.

With the new baby safely settled down, the Boultons' attention turned again to Anne's leg. If Erasmus Darwin's proposed discussion had taken place in Lichfield in 1769, it cannot have produced the desired result, for early in April 1771 they took her to London for a consultation with the top surgeon, John Hunter. Fothergill wrote to Boulton expressing the hope that 'Miss' would receive 'the desir'd benefit of being in London with her Mother'.[15] After the consultation Hunter wrote to Dr Small about his examination of the child, adding diagrams. He had measured her legs from the tops of the thighs to the soles of the feet and found them to be nearly the same length, but drew the pelvis raised on one side, with some twisting in the spine. The three-year-old tended to walk with the left foot on tip-toe, though whether this was cause or effect is not clear. Hunter thought rickets was the likely explanation. He said (presumably drawing on what Boulton had told him) that from birth the child had been put to a wet-nurse who had insufficient milk and took inadequate care of her during the first three months, 'so that she was nearly cut off from weakness'. Having next been put with a better nurse she had recovered, but since that time her left leg had appeared shorter than the right, something her parents had tried to compensate for when she began to toddle by having the sole of the left shoe built up. The child did not seem to be in pain, but walked awkwardly. Hunter thought the built-up shoe was doing more harm than good and recommended, with a sketch, a shoe longer than the foot, which would tend to make the child put her heel down. He also recommended sea bathing, cold baths all the year round, and 'strengthening medicine'.[16] The belief in the efficacy of cold water in treating all manner of ailments and for general character-building was widespread.

Setting aside for a moment the problems with Anne's leg, Hunter's letter raises questions about the child's care in early infancy. For a start, why had her mother not nursed her? Putting babies out to a wet nurse was common enough in the 18th century in aristocratic families, but the Boultons were hardly aristocratic, though they were certainly aspirational. In any case, as the century wore on breast-feeding became widely promoted (even fashionable) and the use of wet nurses declined. Perhaps for some reason Anne's mother was unable to feed her. But given that situation, it seems curious, and even rather careless, that she was put with a plainly unsatisfactory nurse. At a time when babies' lives were so precarious, both Boulton and his wife would have been well aware of her vulnerability.

While Anne was coaxed to take her strengthening medicine, Boulton's Lunar Society friend John Whitehurst happened to meet another 'Eminant Surgeon', James Bent of Newcastle (the man who in 1768 had amputated Josiah Wedgwood's leg), and took the opportunity to speak to him about Anne: 'I told him the defect did not arise from disproportion of the Limbs, but from a weakness in the Hip or Back.' Bent had put forward some suggestions including 'suspension' (probably a form of traction).[17]

Based on the evidence of the letters and diagrams, with the help of Mr Alistair Thompson, a consultant orthopaedic surgeon at the Royal Orthopaedic Hospital, Birmingham, an attempt has been made at a modern diagnosis of the little girl's problem. Possibilities which have been considered include John Hunter's diagnosis of rickets, and also tuberculosis (a 'TB hip', or 'consumption'), polio myelitis, cerebral palsy, and *talipes equinovarus*, or club-foot deformity. Darwin's drawing of a bent thigh-bone might suggest rickets if there were any indication that other bones were bent, but this does not appear to be the case. A 'consumption' which started so young would have been likely to prove fatal long before Miss Boulton's age at death of 61 and there is no other archive evidence to support a diagnosis of tuberculosis. Polio myelitis was common in Europe in the 18th century, but there is no evidence in the correspondence of the acute febrile illness which generally accompanies polio. In a child both cerebral palsy and *talipes equinovarus* may be accompanied by the contracture of the calf muscles which Darwin described, and both of these conditions remain possibilities, but, on balance of probability from the diagrams and descriptions in the correspondence, a diagnosis of *talipes equinovarus*, or club-foot deformity, is suggested.[18]

Whatever the actual nature and cause of Anne's problems, it seems likely that they had a bearing on her for the rest of her life. Ten years later Hunter would examine Anne again and report that the left leg still gave the appearance of being shorter than the right, though in other respects the child appeared healthy and 'free from her compt' – a contraction here taken to mean 'complaint'.[19] Miss Boulton has sometimes been described as an invalid or a cripple. She certainly did have some mobility problems, and later in her life the congenital problem was compounded by the after-effects of an accident, but in the main, though her problems hindered her dancing, they did not prevent her travelling or even riding, though her father always regarded her as delicate, perhaps being over-protective as a result of his anxiety (maybe tinged with guilt) during her early infancy.

In the spring of 1772 the third of Boulton's ormolu sales took place in London, but this time several major pieces failed to sell including his two great golden 'philosophical' clocks, the geographical clock and the sidereal clock (the 'star' clock[20]), on which he had put a price of £250. He wrote to his wife about the sale, grumbling, 'If I had made the Clocks play Jiggs upon bells & a dancing bear keeping time, or if I had made a horse race upon the faces, I believe they would have had better bidders'. He brought the clocks back to Soho. Later, the sidereal clock would travel all the way to St Petersburg and languish there for years, equally unappreciated (and unpaid-for) at the Imperial Court because it did not play tunes. In the end, it was brought back to Birmingham and a place of honour in the Boultons' drawing room, where it stands today – a technological triumph but a financial failure. There was some compensation for the disappointment of the 1772 sale, though, for Boulton went to the Palace again and the King bought a pair of cassolettes, a 'Titus' clock and a 'Venus' clock. Ever the businessman at heart, Boulton wrote to his wife:

> I was with them, ye Queen & all the Children between 2 & 3 hours, there was likewise many others of the Nobility present. Never no man was so much complimented as I have been but I find Compliments don't fill the pocket nor make me fat. The Queen shewd me her last Child which is a beauty but none of 'em are equal to the General of Soho nor to the fair Maid of the Mill.[21]

A day or two later he wrote to say he would be home soon 'to sup wth own dear Wench'. In the meantime Mrs Boulton was to remind John Scale to ensure that some earrings were got ready in time to send to London before the botanist Joseph Banks departed in Captain Cook's ship for his proposed round-the-world voyage. The earrings (long, in green, white and other colours) were to go on board as bartering goods for tribal peoples. He added a greeting to the children: 'God bless my sweet soft little Nanney & my jolly little General, kiss 'em both for me good night my love, goodnight, MB.'[22]

Although their father was away from home so much, the garden at Soho in which Anne and Matt played and were taken for walks was often on his mind. He had planted a thick belt of conifers to provide a windbreak when he first took over the property, and subsequently added some more ornamental varieties, including arbutus, 'Neapolitan evergreen cytisus', Swedish and English junipers, variegated hollies, '20 Scotch Firs' at ten shillings, '3 shining leav'd laurestinum' and various others, costing altogether £2 16s. 9d. The nurseryman, Roger Eykyns, added a note to the bill wishing him success with them.[23]

In July 1772 Boulton paid what was clearly an inspirational visit to Charles Hamilton's garden at Painshill Park in Surrey. He made five pages of notes there, interspersed with rough sketches of its sculptures, porticos and other features. In among them is a page headed firmly 'Improve Soho'. It lists walks, pools, and planting. The following year these ideas began to take shape. On the slope below the house a small pool was made, which after the addition of an ornamental stone shell feature in 1778 was known as the 'Shell Pool'. A Temple of Flora, smaller but similar in style to Hamilton's Temple of Bacchus at Painshill, stood above the Shell Pool. A cascade was constructed from the little pool down to the lake, which was in reality the old mill pool, greatly extended when the Manufactory was built to provide it with the water needed to power the machines. Later, Matt would have a little sailing boat on the lake. Near the bottom of the cascade a little gothic tower

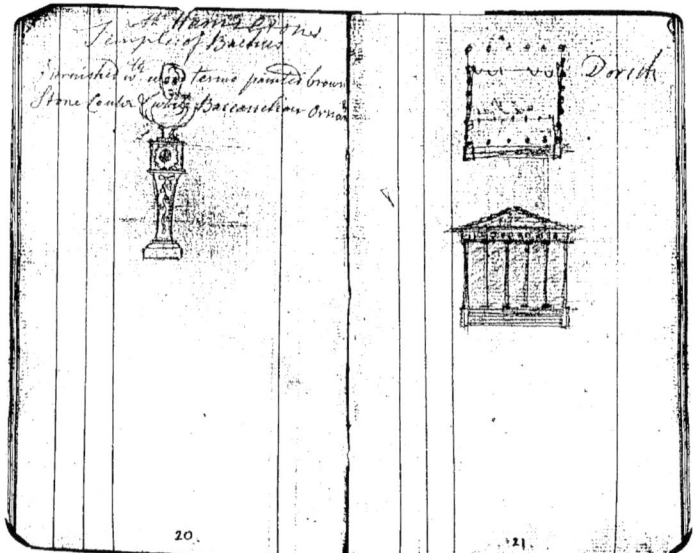

FIG. 5   *Matthew Boulton's Painshill Park notes, from his 1772 notebook. (Birmingham City Archives)*

FIG. 6   *The Temple of Flora (See also plate 34), Soho House gardens, by John Phillp, c.1795. (Birmingham Museum & Art Gallery)*

FIG. 7   *The Cascade Library Building, Soho House gardens, by John Phillp,* c.1795. *(Birmingham Museum & Art Gallery)*

was built (again perhaps inspired by Painshill), described as 'the Cascade Library Room'. Nothing of this garden survives today.

Household bills at this period reveal a taste for oysters and a high consumption of sugar in the Boulton household. A 'large round tin sugar box' was supplied, costing 3s. 6d., in which to store it. Christopher Greatrex in Birmingham regularly supplied quantities of lump or loaf sugar, ranging from 20 pounds' weight to over 40 pounds' weight (it would have needed a very big box!). In October 1769, just a month after supplying '20½lb. fine lump sugar' at 14s. 6d., Greatrex supplied a further 38lb.1oz. at £1 2s. 6d. Some of the sugar was probably used in brewing ale. At least the Boulton children had fresh fruit as well – other Boulton housekeeping bills from this period include one from a Mr Hector, who supplied 3s. 6d.-worth of oranges and lemons. The same bill includes 'a tub of butter' at £1 2s. 6d., while in London in November Boulton bought five pounds (weight) each of Bohea and green tea, eight ounces each of cinnamon, mace, cloves, and white pepper, two pounds of black pepper, and pimentos and 'long pepper', costing altogether £4 9s. 8d.[24] From William Fenter the following year came 'half a pound of tae' at 6s., eggs, 'apels', '1 copel of fouls' (2s. 4d.), rice, brimstone, a lemon, 'oisters' (1s. 0d.), yet more 'sugger', and the single most expensive item, 'a cod fish 10 pound' (4s. 2d.).

Apart from food bills, William Richardson supplied '2 watering pots' at 7s. and '1 small ditto with a long pipe' at 2s. 3d., and there was a costly bill of £14 10s. 10½d. for coach overhaul from the appropriately-named Samuel Wheeley, which included 'guilding all the frame work to the Body & varnishing with Mr Baskerfields [Baskerville's] varnish £2. 10s.'[25]

Anne and Matt were too young to realise it, but their Papa had a finger in many pies. Between 1771-1773 he was in London even more than usual, busily engaged in an energetic campaign for Birmingham and Sheffield to be allowed to establish their own Assay Offices for the testing and hallmarking of sterling silver articles (Plate 11). In spite of his enthusiasm for the project, there were times when the trip to London tested his patience; one cold January day he wrote to his wife about a journey 'that a fretfull person would have thought disagreeable'. For a start, the company in the coach had not been particularly congenial, consisting of:

> ... a young Welch singing Lawyer, a long-grace-saying Schoolmaster, an antiquated mumbling House Keeper & a silent country born Londoner. We arrived at Warwick about one oClock, [and] was put into a dirty room with dirty linen dirty knives dirty plates & stinking Butter to a stinking fowl ...'

The next night, at Towcester, was no better:

> The London down passengers arrived 2 hours before us & eat all the supper except some pork griskins of Doctor Hunters pigs, we went to bed before we had done belching up the foul air produced by the fermintation of the pork. We were calld up again at half past three but did not set out before half past four, went 16 Miles to breakfast, now the roads became better but the Inns we eat at were all of the shabby class, however I amused my self with the conversation of my fellow travilers & thanked my Stars that I was not an out side passenger (for it has raind great part of ye day) & arrived in good health about six oClock. Mr Matthews is gone to the play, the Old Woman was glad to see me & says she made some broth for me 3 days ago in full expectation of my coming which shall be nicely warmd up again for my supper with a woodcock & some apple pye.[26]

'Mr Matthews' was William Matthews, Boulton's banker in London since about 1767; he and his wife, Charlotte, became close friends of the Boultons and on occasion almost surrogate parents to Anne and Matt. With the Matthews providing a comfortable refuge once he reached town, all the effort, discomfort and stinking chicken en route paid off: the Bill was passed and Boulton returned home to triumphantly pealing church bells. Birmingham Assay Office opened for business on 31 August 1773.

During one of his many London visits that year Boulton had perhaps seen the work of the Swiss artist Jean-Etienne Liotard, for Liotard was in England in 1773 and staged an exhibition at his London studio. Among the works on show were some of Liotard's exquisite pastel portraits of children, and these may have impressed Boulton enough to invite the artist to Soho, for some time that year, on what was probably his only English visit outside London, Liotard painted a pastel portrait of three-year-old Matt Boulton, signing it 'À Soho par Liotard 1773'. (Plate 12) If Liotard charged for doing the portrait, the bill has not been preserved. Strangely, there seems to be no evidence that Liotard painted Anne, who was almost exactly the same age as his own daughter, of whom he had painted a delightful portrait earlier the same year.[27]

Mrs Boulton liked to keep up-to-date with fashion, a predilection in which she was seconded by her husband (who wanted a fashionable wife). When in London he sent her regular reports of what was and was not being worn: 'I saw a fashionable

Muff & Terissa[28] making for ye Dutchess of Grafton & therefore I bought one for my Nanny,' he wrote, but 'I have enquired about Ear Rings & find that they are left off amongst people of fashion except when they are in full dress & then nothing but pearls or diamants is worn.'[29] Mrs Boulton probably did have some diamond earrings – in 1770 the London jewellers John Duval & Sons supplied four alternative designs and quoted for making up earrings, an aigrette and four pins, using rose diamonds which she already had, perhaps in an older piece of jewellery from her mother. The fashion (the making-up) would cost about £10. Alternatively, they could take the rose diamonds in part exchange for some brilliants and make a pair of single drop earrings for about £8.[30]

Occasionally Mrs Boulton left the children at Soho and went to London with her husband. They were both in London in March 1773 when John Scale wrote to reassure her that 'the King & Queen' (two-and-a-half-year-old Matt and five-year-old Anne) were well, adding 'the little Queen wants to be pack'd up in a Box and sent to London to see her papa'.[31] Who generally looked after the children, especially when both their parents were away, is not clear; there appears to be no record of anyone specifically charged with the function of nursemaid or nanny, and how much hands-on childcare was carried out by Mrs Boulton herself, or whether it was incorporated into some servant's job, or whether aunts may have helped, is not known. More often than not when Boulton travelled, Mrs Boulton stayed behind at Soho House with Anne and Matt. It's clear from his letters home that he missed them all; on one occasion he wrote to his wife: 'Your picture I kiss every night, its very like you'[32] (presumably a miniature, whereabouts now unknown), and on another, 'My desire for incircleing my dear Nanny in my arms will induce me to leave much of my business undone … I have not bought ye little books yet but shall not forget my little folks.'[33]

The range of books written specifically for children at this period was quite small, but growing. Fairy tales, 'improving' moral tales, rhymes and books of instruction were being produced for younger children, while abler readers had the likes of *Gulliver's Travels*, *Robinson Crusoe*, *Aesop's Fables* or *Pilgrim's Progress* available to them. As for toys, among many others with which children (or at least the children of the well-to-do) played at this period were whole families of dolls, dolls' houses and furniture, Noah's Arks and animals, puppets and peep-shows, hobby-horses and rocking horses, skipping ropes, toy soldiers, drums and trumpets. No bills have been found for toys, but Boulton probably came home from London often with some small plaything in his pocket for Anne and Matt. More than once he reproached his wife for not writing more often with news of the children:

> … it is not kind of you not to let me know more particularly how you & my little dears go on: tell me that you are free from Colds, that you & they Eat heartily & that you all grow fat, tell me of some pretty thing that Nanney says, or that Matty does …[34]

Apart from shopping, food also features often in Boulton's letters home. In one he wrote to his wife: 'The most fateaguing part of my Journey is Feasting'[35] and in another, written in weather 'so amazeing hot that I have scarcely been able to exist in Solid form either night or day',[36] he regaled her with an account of a dinner, attended by ten people including William and Charlotte Matthews:

> We had nothing but a fine Turtle, Ducks, Chickins, Lamb Souls, a larg haunch
> of Venison, puddins, Tarts, Ice Creams, pine Apple, Melons, fruit of various sorts
> & such like things with Wines of various kinds, after wch we had Coffe & Tea
> & concluded with drams of Danzig Water ... You may easily suppose that I shall
> go supperless to bed.[37]

In 1774 something happened that would have a profound influence on Anne's later life. Her father invited James Watt (Plate 18) to move down from Scotland and join him in the business at Soho. Watt had worked on scientific instruments and as a canal surveyor in Scotland, but it was his development work on the steam engine which attracted Boulton, who could see its potential. Watt's patron, Dr John Roebuck, was in financial difficulties and without a new backer Watt would have been unable to continue the work. The introvert Scot and the extrovert Midlander were a good foil for each other.

Watt arrived in Birmingham a widower, his first wife, Peggy, having died in 1773; when he came south he left his two children, Margaret (also known as Peggy), and James junior (b.1769) with relatives in Glasgow. In 1776 he went back to Glasgow for a visit and returned to Birmingham with the two children and a new wife, Ann McGregor (Plate 19). Annie and James Watt would go on to have a son, Gregory (1777-1804) and a daughter, Janet ('Jessie') (1779-94). The Watts initially took up residence at Harpers Hill, about halfway between Birmingham town centre and Soho, and Anne and Matt Boulton were introduced to their new playmates.

3

Lessons

The Boulton children probably had their earliest lessons at home, but by the time Anne was seven years old Boulton was looking around for a school for his daughter (by now gracing the house in a little gown of pink silk, solemnly invoiced to 'Miss Ann Boulton', which cost her father £1 13s. 6d.[1]). In doing so he was rather going against the conventional wisdom that held that a girl had little need of schooling beyond what her mother could teach her. For girls, even middle-class girls and the daughters of upwardly mobile manufacturers bent on gentrification, education was somewhat perfunctory and frequently limited to what were perceived as the desirable feminine accomplishments of music, drawing and embroidery, with additional and careful attention paid to deportment, how to enter and alight from a carriage and curtsey properly, and the graceful handing of tea-cups.

Boulton's own formal schooling had finished at the age of about fourteen, but he had a clear belief in the intrinsic as well as the practical value of learning. He was, moreover, possessed of that boundless curiosity about the world around him which is the greatest spur to self-teaching. He had a wide-ranging and open-minded approach to education, as something to be derived as much from a variety of experience as from the classroom. He told Lord Dartmouth that one of the reasons he thought Birmingham should have a new and better theatre was because it would tend to improve public taste, adding

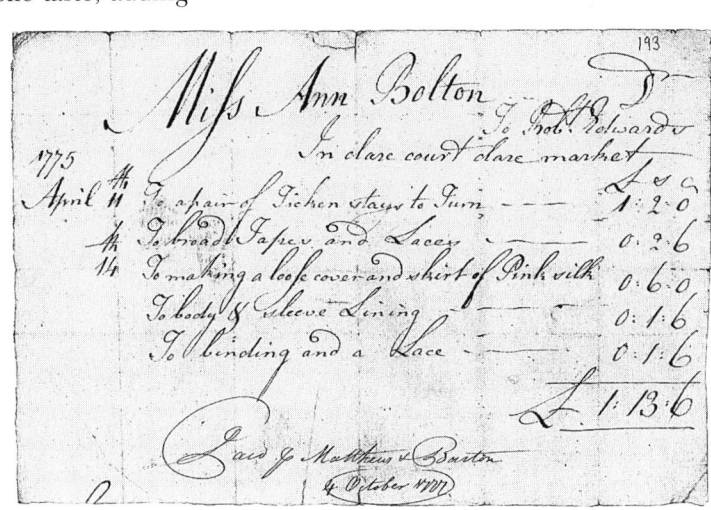

FIG. 8 *Dress bill for seven-year-old Anne Boulton, 1775. (Birmingham City Archives)*

I have frequently given my designers, painters & modellers Tickets to the play, in order to improve them in those Arts, by which they are to live & gain reputation … it is impossible for a person to paint or moddell an attitude or a passion which he never saw well express'd … Of late Years Birmingham hath been visited much in the summer season by persons of fashion, & it is some inducement to prolong their stay when their evenings can be spent at a Comodious airy Theatre. This is a fact I mention from experience & it is certainly our interest to bring company to Birmgm as it contributes much to the publick good not only from the mony they leave behind them but from their explaining their wants to the manufacturers themselves, & from their correcting the Tast & giving hints for various improvements which nothing promotes so much as an intercourse with persons from different parts of the World.[2]

He read widely and made copious notes on subjects as diverse as biology, astronomy and chemistry. In one notebook he allowed himself to day-dream of:

A round building for my Study, Library, Museum or Hobby Horsery to hold 6 handsome Book Cases with drawers in the lower parts to hold things which relate to subjects of the books wch are in upper parts, e:g: a Book Case containing Chymical Books should have drawers under wch contain Metals Minerals & Fossells – between each Book Case should be a Sophie [sofa] & under the Space between ye upper parts of ye Cases should be fixed such instruments as, Baromotor, Thermomotor, Pyromotor, Quadrants, all sorts of Optical, Mathematical, Mechanical, Pnumatical & Philosophical instruments also Clocks of Sundry kinds both Geographical & Syderial, Lunar & Solar System & one good regulator of time. A table in ye middle of ye room & a skylight in ye middle of the domical roof wch roof may be covered either with Sail Cloth or brown paper. Out of this round room should open a private door into a passage in which passage should open doors into sundry conven[ien]t rooms such as Cold & Warm Bath, a Labritory [laboratory], a dressing & powdering room & an observatory for a transit instrumt, &c.[3]

Though this 'hobby horsery' was never built in quite the way he visualised, he did have a small observatory built in the grounds, in which a telescope was installed. His 1772 notebook contains a list of equipment for it and the plaintive query, 'What are all the things done by astronomers?'[4] But he was away from home so much that he had little opportunity to make himself an astronomer, though on 25 June 1778 he noted in his diary that he had 'showed Watt's dau. ye eclipse' – this must have been Peggy, Watt's daughter by his first wife, who would have been about eleven years old. Later that year Boulton sold his telescope to the astronomer Alexander Aubert for £20, but much later he would have a replacement installed on the roof at Soho House.

He also set about collecting books, instruments and specimens and – an inveterate list-maker – made lists of them. He enjoyed Sterne's *Tristram Shandy* (where he perhaps found the expression 'hobby horsery') and furnished his embryo library with an eclectic selection of volumes ranging from the classics to Hogarth's *Analysis of Beauty*, English and Roman history, agriculture, *Halfpenny Architecture*, and books on the new art of landscape gardening including Sir William Chambers' *A Dissertation on Oriental Gardening*, Thomas Whateley's *Observations on Modern Gardening*, and William Mason's *The English Garden, a Poem*, as well as works of practical use such as law, accounting and chemistry. Attached to the booklist is a rough sketch of a

FIG. 9 *Matthew Boulton's sketch of a bookcase, attached to a list of books (undated). (Birmingham City Archives)*

bookcase to hold them, which may have been made[5]. Samuel Aris in Birmingham supplied him with copies of Spenser's *Faerie Queen* in three volumes (£2 7s. od.), *Robinson Crusoe* (18s.), Bird's *Method of Dividing Astronomical Instruments* (1s.), Hill on Fruit Trees, *Elements of Criticism*, and other volumes, totalling 18 guineas, for which he was finally billed by Aris's executors in 1775.[6]

One of the items on the list was Dr John Gregory's new book, *A Father's Legacy to his Daughters*, published in 1774. If Anne was to be brought up according to Gregory's precepts, she would be urged, among other things, to 'Be even cautious in displaying your good sense. It will be thought you assume a superiority over the rest of the company. But if you happen to have any learning, keep it a profound secret, especially from the men, who generally look with a jealous and malignant eye on a woman of great parts, and a cultivated understanding.'[7] Gregory also approved of blushing as 'the companion of innocence' (and very fetching, to boot), but cautioned women never to boast of having good health but to 'enjoy it in grateful silence'. Feminine 'fragility' was looked upon by some as woman's greatest asset, kindling in the male breast the desire to protect her; therefore, warned Dr Gregory, 'when a woman speaks of her great strength, her extraordinary appetite, her ability to bear excessive fatigue, we [men] recoil at the description in a way she is little aware of'.

Gregory was not the only writer to hold such limited opinions of women's capabilities. Rousseau's view was that, 'What is most wanted in a woman is gentleness. Formed to obey a creature so imperfect as man, a creature often vicious and always faulty, she should early learn to submit to injustice and to suffer the wrongs inflicted on her by her husband without complaint.'[8] Like Gregory he abhorred the intellectual female and thought that a girl should be encouraged to dress dolls because 'In due time she will be her own doll.'[9] 18th-century polite society was generally repelled by the thought of the learned female, who was considered to be unmarriageable; the 'blue-stocking' intellectual ladies were regarded by many as an aberration of nature and it was not only Dr Gregory and Rousseau who advised women of intellectual ability to keep it carefully hidden from their husbands (or

FIG. 10 *The Hermitage, Soho House gardens, by John Phillp, c.1795. (Birmingham Museum & Art Gallery)*

better still, never to allow it to develop in the first place). Swift would have girls put away their books because 'a humour of reading books, excepting those of devotion or housewifery, is apt to turn a woman's brain ... All affectation of knowledge, beyond what is merely domestic, renders them vain, conceited and pretending.'[10] Through the promulgation of such views a sort of tacit conspiracy arose whereby both women and men adopted the pretence that women (middle-class women, at any rate) were incapable of much exertion, either physical or mental. Some of them even believed it.

If Boulton was at all influenced by reading his copy of Gregory, a conversation or two with Erasmus Darwin would have put him straight, for Dr Darwin, though he approved of 'mild' female characters, had little patience with a male culture which required girls to be vacuous, vain and vulnerable. Darwin's own *Plan for the Conduct of Female Education in Boarding Schools* was published in 1794, for the use of his two illegitimate daughters, Susannah and Mary Parker, when they set up their own school in Ashbourne, so it was long after Boulton was making decisions about Anne's education, but Darwin's ideas on the subject were probably well-formed by then. He believed girls should have educational visits to factories, and spend less time on music and dancing and more on exercise in the fresh air, including ice-skating and swimming. Bedrooms should be well-ventilated, stays done away with. They should learn modern languages and science including chemistry (virtually unheard-of for them at the time, though in 1801 Boulton's and Darwin's friend and fellow Lunar Society member James Keir would write a substantial chemistry book for girls, *Dialogues on Chemistry between a Father and His Daughter*. This his 21-year-old daughter Amelia took down at dictation, but it was never published.[11]).

With conflicting views ringing in his ears, Boulton tried to decide what kind of education would be best for Anne. Typically, he enlisted the help of another Lunar Society friend, John Whitehurst (Plate 15), asking him in October 1775 to investigate a girls' school in Chelsea, Blacklands. He may have been led to the idea of this particular establishment by Josiah Wedgwood, whose eldest daughter Susan ('Sukey') was a pupil at Blacklands from 1775-78.[12] Wherever the suggestion came from, it indicates that Boulton felt confident enough of Anne's health to contemplate sending her away from home. He could no longer consult his great friend and physician Dr William Small on the matter – Small had died in February 1775, just after Anne's seventh birthday, a loss which Boulton felt so keenly that he had a monument to Small erected in his garden, near to a little thatched woodland hermitage which he described as 'a building adapted for contemplation'.[13]

Whitehurst, who by this time was establishing himself in London as Keeper of Stamps and Weights at the Royal Mint, went to look round Blacklands School for his friend and reported back as requested, but urged a re-think. The school was satisfactory as schools went, he thought, but the education of girls was a sensitive matter: 'The education of girls appears to me of more real importance than that of boys.' He thought Anne would be much better off being educated at home,

> Where you might daily judge the propriety of her Tutoress's conduct. Was I in your Situation I should certainly persue such a plan, as circumstances at present occur to me. Mr Day is not yet return'd, so nothing more is done in the Plan we named to you. Only, it manifestly appears from calculations that £25 per annum will include every species of Education and every other expense whatever, clothes excepted. I mean to include all the branches of Education wch in a general way cost £70 per annum.[14]

Whitehurst's and Day's plans for Anne Boulton's education have not been found. Thomas Day (Plate 16) was another Lunar Society member, and his head was full of Rousseau. The story of Day's failed experiment in which he 'adopted' two orphan girls and, applying Rousseau's principles, attempted to mould them into the pattern of his ideal 'simple' wife, with the intention of marrying whichever proved most amenable to this 'training' (neither did), is well known. Day's chief claim to fame, however, was as the author of an 'improving' children's book, *The History of Sandford and Merton*.

While Boulton dithered over Anne's education a decision about young Matt's was made much more promptly, and some time in 1776-7 he started at his first school, a small establishment run by the Rev. Henry Pickering at Winson Green, about a mile from Soho House, where one of his school-fellows was James Watt junior. The Rev. Pickering's school was just one of hundreds of small private day- and boarding schools for boys around the country, many of them run by clergymen, some of them taking only a handful of pupils to supplement a poor stipend. Matt was perhaps ahead of his age-group, for Pickering wrote rather altruistically to his father 'as to my good Friend Matthew I think 3£ per Ann. (which is the Sum I have with day-scholars) will be too much for him this Year, as his Improvements have been acquired with very little trouble on my part, so that any trifle you think proper to give me on his acct. I shall be satisfied with.'[15]

With Matt settled at school, Boulton continued to ponder what to do about his daughter's education. Although by the 1770s girls' boarding schools were increasing in number, they were very variable in the quality of both education and board which they provided. The Birmingham businessman William Hutton, whom Boulton knew well, had flatly refused to consider boarding school for his daughter Catherine (11 years older than Anne Boulton), dismissing them all as 'hives of contamination', and only reluctantly, after much pestering on her part, allowed her to attend a Birmingham day school.[16] But the idea of boarding school for girls was already accepted in the Boulton household, for Matthew Boulton was paying boarding school fees for his niece, 'Nancy' Mynd (Ann Mynd, the daughter of Boulton's sister Kitty and her husband Thomas Mynd). Nancy was about five years older than Anne Boulton and around 1776 she had started at Cambden House School, London (where one of Erasmus Darwin's step-daughters later became a pupil). The establishment was run by a Mrs Elizabeth Terry. In 1777 her assistant, Mrs Gandry, wrote to Boulton:

> We have eight young Ladies left, & three Teachers to take care of them, they read French & English constantly … if Miss Mynde returns during the Holidays I will take care she shall be employ'd for I much fear too much Time or Money has already been threwn away.[17]

Nancy pouted. Nancy flounced. Nancy threw tantrums. Mrs Gandry wrote, 'I found … that they had made too much a Woman of her at the first setting out, and since that, they found it difficult to manage her … [I was told that] Miss had always had a Parlour & Fire to Herself, and that she *would* have it.'[18]

The girl was troubled with a recurrent large swelling in her neck. John Hunter was consulted, and the fact that he advised drinking sea-water and also sea bathing suggests she may have had a goitre, or enlarged thyroid gland, a condition which can result from an iodine deficiency. Sea-water contains iodine (sea-weed contains it in greater concentration). Acting on Hunter's advice, in May 1777 Boulton took Nancy to Margate, telling James Watt 'there is a necessity for her bathing in the sea or she will never get a husband'.[19] He left her there in the care of her schoolmistress, Mrs Terry, but after a month Mrs Terry wrote anxiously to Boulton that as the doctor had said Miss Mynd was not ready to return to school, she had been obliged to leave the girl to her own devices in Margate. She had, however, removed her from Mrs Hawes' lodgings, chosen for her by Boulton, because

... I thought that Miss began to value herself upon being fit Company for the Gentlemen & Ladies there, which I am sure would spoil her for a School Girl, & make her very troublesome to her friends here at her return, & so thought Mrs Hawes, who was seemingly rejoiced at my removing her. I certainly had no reason to dislike the people but in short that mode of situation for a Girl is a dangerous one & I could not prevale on myself to leave her in it ... I have placed Miss Mynd with Miss Wild, who seems a discreet good kind of woman ... I have left her with strict orders to go no where & not even to bathe, without Miss Wild ... I have desired her to be imployd in needlework & her accounts; & making exercises in French & English for her Masters here. I have agreed for a guinea per week for which the Washing as well as Tea is to be included. I should be very glad if you would write to her & to enforce all I have said by your Orders, for Miss cryed so ... that Mrs Hawes was so kind to desire her Company some times, to which I absolutely refused by wch I fear I offended her, but if you would be so good to write to yr Niece signifying yr approbation of what I have done I imagine it will in some measure remove any prejudice against poor me, who certainly did undertake a disagreeable office to serve a young creature that cannot act for herself ...[20]

By December, when Nancy finally set out from Margate to travel back to Soho for Christmas, calling at Cambden House *en route*, she seems to have been under the impression that fashionable Margate was her true *milieu*, and on Boxing Day 1777 poor Mrs Terry wrote exasperatedly to Boulton:

I understand they have had trouble enough with Miss; who chose to do just as she pleased, wch I believe was not always right. Miss Mynde call'd here, but I was not return'd so did not see her, she was full of her journey to you; & I believe thinks she has done with School. I wish she was capable of doing without it, for her sake, but I am sure that is not the case, I suppose I shall see her soon when I shall endeavour to set her right again & hope to succeed ...[21]

Back 'Miss' went after Christmas, to be 'set right' again by the long-suffering Mrs Terry. A typical half-year's bill for Miss Mynd's education gives an indication of the somewhat limited curriculum; totalling £22 4s. 8d., it includes board and lodging, masters' fees, some books, and personal expenses, as follows:

Boarding	£9	9s	od
English	£2	2s	od
Drawing	£2	12s	od
A year's English omitted in a former Bill	£4	4s	od
Minister		5s	3d
Grammar 2/6, Lambert 3/6, Letters &c 5d		6s	5d
Mending Stays; ye Pumps 16/6	£1	3s	6d
Coat Makers Bill	£1	6s	od
Apothecary's Bill		9s	6d
Mantua Makers Bill		7s	6d[22]

While his niece tested Mrs Terry's patience, Boulton made a decision about his daughter, and certainly by the beginning of 1778 Anne was attending a day-school in Birmingham, for shortly after her tenth birthday John Fothergill mentioned in a letter to Boulton that 'Mrs Boulton was gone to take Miss Boulton to Moseley Schoole'.[23] Nancy Mynd had earlier received instruction in writing from a D. Williams at Moseley, so it is possible that Miss Boulton was sent to the same teacher.[24] The 1770 Birmingham Directory contains an entry for a David Williams, a teacher of writing and Latin, though his address then was in the town centre.

In the end, Anne's spell at the Birmingham day-school turned out to be just a preparation for going away to school. After the summer holidays in 1778 Boulton and his wife set out again for London. In the coach with them this time was ten-year-old Anne, off to join her cousin at Cambden House. Boulton's notebook records bleakly: 'I put Nanney to School on Monday ye 7th Sept.'[25] What is (at present) the only known portrait of her was possibly painted shortly before she went away to school. Attributed to Tilly Kettle, it shows Anne in a creamy coloured gown of silk or satin, with a pink underskirt. She wears a flower-sprigged muslin cap over her dark curls and is adding summer flowers to a flower stand, from a collection she holds in her apron. Her face is alert but composed and there is a hint of determination about the mouth (Plate 17).

At about the same time that Anne left home, eight-year-old Matt also went away, to a school run by a Mr Stretch in Twickenham. Soho House was quiet.

The Boultons' decision to send both children away to school when they did may have been prompted by the fact that Matthew Boulton intended to spend the three months up to Christmas 1778 in Cornwall, and wanted his wife there with him. Boulton & Watt supplied and erected a number of steam engines for the Cornish mining industry, and the business required frequent and lengthy attendance on site by either Boulton or James Watt or both of them. Watt and his wife had already spent part of the previous year in Cornwall and had expected (vainly) that Boulton and his wife would join them then, for the Cornish business had great potential. While awaiting their arrival, Annie Watt had written from Chacewater, west of Truro, to give Mrs Boulton the low-down on Cornwall and the Cornish. She had put off writing for a long time, she told Mrs Boulton, because she 'evry day wishd to find something pleasing to write' – which she seems to have found difficult:

> Mr Watt & I on our arrival found there was no such thing as a House or Lodging to be had for any money within some miles of this place where the Engine was to be erected, which obliged us to except [accept] of Mr & Mrs Wilsons very kind invitation to stay at their house where we are treated in the kindest manner & evry thing in their power is done to make us comfortable and happy, it gives me pain to think I must give trouble to such good people, for I am very certain our being here must be inconvenient to them as their family is large and their House very little & to add to all the Cornishe Servants are a set of Laziest Wretches that now Breathes on the Earth to say nothing of their Nastiness. Mrs Wilson is a Yorkshire woman & is teased to death with them I am sure few people wou'd bear the plague she has with them half so well as she does. I don't know what to say to you of the Country, the spot we are at is the most disagreeable part of the whole County. The face of the Earth is broke up in ten thousand heaps of rubbish & scarce a tree to be seen … Don't think that all Cornwall is like Chacewater, the place we are now at. I have been at some places that are very pleasant nay Beautifull, the Sea Coast to me is charming but not easy to be got at in some places, my poor Husband has been obliged to mount me behind him

to go to some of the places we have been at … I wish to see you here, one thing
I must tell you of is to take care Mr Boltons principals [principles] are well fixt
before you trust him here, poor Mr Watt is turned Ana Baptist & duely attends
their meetings, he is indeed and goes to Chapel most devoutly.[26]

If Mrs Watt's letter had put Mrs Boulton off the idea of accompanying her
husband to Cornwall in 1777, he did manage to persuade her to go with him in
1778, and after leaving the children at school they travelled down to join the Watts.
In their absence, matters at the Soho Manufactory were to be managed by James
Keir. A gifted chemist and metallurgist, Keir was also an astute businessman. He had
agreed to help out at Soho in return for a quarter share of Boulton & Fothergill's
profits, but his close examination of the state of B&F's books soon persuaded him
that entering into a full partnership might not be a wise move.

The Boultons were back home again in time for Christmas, when Anne and Matt
also came home from school. Boulton perhaps presided at the Christmas dinner
table resplendent in the new warm waistcoat of figured green and white velvet,
costing £3 9s. 9½d., which he had had made that December by the London tailor
who earlier in the year had made him a 'Parrott Green mixt cloth French Frock
& Breeches & a green and Gold Tissue* Waistcoat', at £9 19s.[27]

The short Christmas holiday over, Boulton took Anne and Matt back to school
and stayed on in London on business (probably one reason why London schools
were chosen, as he was so often there). 1779 did not get off to a good start. One
dark January evening he was crossing Ludgate Hill into St Paul's Churchyard when
he was knocked down by a coach. This accident could easily have cost him his life.
Bruised, battered and bespattered he was taken to the Matthews' house in a state
of shock and dosed with brandy, but with books in his breast pocket protecting his
ribs, it seemed there were no bones broken, though breathing was painful.[28] By
March, now fully recovered, he planned to return home. He wrote to his wife:

> … to make my self the more welcome I shall bring my two little friends &
> favourites with me. I forgott to tell you that Matt hath had 3 teeth drawn at his
> own request, as he had the tooth ache very bad … He has acquired the Character
> of a Bold Fellow on Horse back. Miss Nanny hath been forbid by the Writing
> Master to write Letters untill her hand is well formed under his eye in writing
> a good large round hand. She hath got her Clothes made & is well. There are
> 2 Bottles of Tea sent down by Mr Matthews, the one is for you & the other for
> Mr Fothergill. It was sent us from Moscow to which place it was brought from
> Pekin in China by land.[29]

The children returned to school promptly after this short visit home, and the
following month the young ladies at Cambden House put on a dancing display.
Anne, being awkward on her feet, was not picked to take part and instead sat
inconspicuously at the back watching the other girls, not noticing that Papa had
crept into the room. He had arrived to find the road up to the school

> filld with Gentlemens Coaches but I soon found it was a publick day, however
> I ventured in & saw such a sight of Tulips & Rosebuds as I never before saw. I

---

* Tissue: a woven fabric incorporating gold, silver or silk threads.

stayd in the Room near an Hour & saw all the best dancers dance but my poor Nanny sat modestly behind & never saw me untill all was over. I then had her to myself in a room for near an hour, she liked her Buckles. I requested Miss Gandry to get the Stays made, a Silk Slip & a muslin frock & they are to be done by next Wednesday which is another publick day. I think Miss Mynd dont look so well as usual but she has no swelling. Brother Matt came to see Sister Nanny in his road to school. He is very well but I have not yet had time to go see him ...[30]

Boulton wrote this letter later the same evening after visiting Anne. He asked his wife to have his new wig packed up and sent to him, as he wished to get it altered. He said nothing about the fact that at midnight he was setting out for the port of Harwich. The coach arrived in Colchester in time for breakfast and by three in the afternoon of 24 April he was eating his dinner in Harwich, before embarking for Holland, on what proved to be a successful mission to get a two-year extension on a loan of £2,000 from 'a very rigid person'. Back home in Birmingham, Mrs Boulton would know nothing about this trip until he was back in England. He did, however, keep a detailed account of it in his notebook. The 15-hour crossing was stormy and the captain of the packet boat was worried about the danger from French privateers which prowled the channel and north-sea coasts like predatory wolves. Boulton was, as usual, seasick, but recorded with a certain amount of satisfaction that so too were a Mr and Mrs Cummins who 'became very sick & puked although they declard they had crossed the Atlantick 4 Times & had been accustomed to ye Sea 19 yrs without ever being sick before, for great Ships have not so much Motion as ye Packett Boats have'. The Cummins had 'a good Estate & plantations upon ye River Demerara near Surinam in ye West Indias'.[31]

Boulton was clearly fascinated by the differences between England and Holland and described what he saw in some detail. At Rotterdam:

the weather had been so warm that they had left off fires & their Chymneys were stoped up & clean painted & therefore we were obliged for the sake of preserving neatness & cleanness to sit without Fire. We supped & went to Bed. Their Beds are boarded round so that you lye in a Box. There was 3 very long Pillows each, the whole Breadth of the Bed by which you almost sit up in bed but every thing is remarkable Clean ... I was much delighted to see in every thing extream Cleanness, the Ships in their Canals are minutely Clean, every pulley is scraped & every thing that can be painted in oyl is painted & afterwards is constantly washed.

Through most of ye streets are larg Canals filld with Shiping, on each side is a row of green Trees mostly limes & then a very neat pavement either of Bricks or Stone, for Coaches or hand 2 wheeled Carts, & next ye houses is a foot path. Every House seems new painted, the Windows Clean, & as many live upon ye 2nd floor they fix on each side of the Windows without side a looking glass abt 1 foot Squr upon a joynt, so that it may be placed at any angle, by wch they may within see who & what passes either one way or ye other in ye Street. The tast of ye Houses in respect to architect. ornam[ts] are rather French but the cleanness is only Dutch. At the front of many houses for a Yard broad they are layd with squares of black & white marble, many of the passages in the House are coverd with white Dutch tyles, some of the upper floors are layd with marble & many best rooms are wainscoted dado high with Marble.

Their Houses & their streets are as Clean as if it was the sole employment of ye people to paint & clean them & that there was nobody to dirty them. The most remarkable irrational looking thing is the walls of the Houses lean forward, some of them so much that they are obliged to be kept up with Iron screws within but now the magistrates have made an order that they shall lean forward no more than 1 inch in every 12 feet high. There is not that Crowd of people in ye Streets that one sees in London & there are very few Coaches. All the people have an air of Seriousness & both Merchts & peasants Cloath much in Black. Prudence, Industry, Oeconomy & Seriousness are Characteristicks of the Dutch ...

Leyden he thought 'a most beautyfull Town' and its University 'well regulated', and thinking ahead with Matt in mind added

I think it is a better place to bring up young men than at Oxford as they have not so many temptations, bad examples nor Gayeties to take off their attention but study & application is the prevailing fashion among ye young men & tis disgracefull to do otherwise. There is another advantage of ye Dutch & German Schools which is that ye young men are learning two liveing useful languages besides the dead ones & these they acquire with little trouble. But as I think the Dutch Language more vulgar than the German I should prefer a German School where French is learnt very well.[32]

Not until he got back to London did Boulton write to tell his wife about the trip, explaining the purpose of it and adding that he had not told her beforehand as he did not want to worry her. He liked Holland, but the crossing had been very bad and he doubted she could have stood it: 'Indeed tis horrable to lye (for to sleep is impossable) in a Cabin with ten or a doz people all groaning & pukeing ...' In spite of this he thought it would be good for Matt to go to school abroad, preferably Germany, at some stage.[33] He could not give her any news about the children, he added, as he had not yet had time to visit them but planned to shortly. Two days later he wrote again, asking for detailed instructions about some silk his wife wanted, and also to say he had been to Twickenham to see Matt at school, but was a little uneasy about him:

I think he grows so fast as to prevent him from being so strong as I could wish; he seemed rather shy & not in such good spirits as he used to be. He says he is well & so doth his Master but I am not satisfyd. I hope to recruit him a little at Soho & perhaps may bring one of his school fellows with him. I hear Nanny is well but I have not yet seen her.[34]

As Mrs Boulton did not seem inclined to write letters, Boulton had to rely on reports from other people who had seen her, and on 13 May wrote to say that he had learned that she wanted a new cap. Therefore he had been to fashionable Tavistock Street, where he had ordered 'a genteel Cap &c for a Young Lady about 40' (gallantly overlooking the fact that she was now approaching forty-six). The London social round, an essential part of his business networking, was proving irksome: 'I have not been very well for 2 days past & yet I was obliged last night to go to Ranelagh contrary to my inclinations, where I had as much pleasure as if I had drawn so many Hours in a Horse Mill.' At least he was looking forward to seeing Anne:

I shall on Saturday visit a Young Lady near London who is a great favourite of mine as she makes no scruple of saying she loves me & I am vain enough to believe her. I shall make her a proposal to take her to Soho & I don't believe she will refuse & I make no doubt but you will be very civil to her even more so than Wifes generally are to their Husbands favourite Ladys. However never mind my Dear I continue to Love you most ardently & affectionately.[35]

Mrs Terry perhaps took the opportunity, when he called at Cambden House, to hand over her bill for Miss Boulton, covering the half year to 1 May 1779. The bill gives us some idea of both the scope and the limitations of the establishment:

	£	s	d
To Half a Years Boarding Miss Boulton	14	14	0
Dancing	2	2	0
English	2	2	0
Writing	1	19	0
Drawing	1	1	0
Minister	0	10	6
Hair Cutting 4s.; ? 1/6	0	5	6
Allowance	0	13	6
Tea & Sugar	1	1	0
Mercer	2	9	0
Milliner	1	4	0
Coat maker	2	6	1½
Entrance to drawings [perhaps an exhibition?] 1 1.0., & Ball Tickets 1 1.0.	2	2	0
?Gram 1/6, Advice 6s, Letters & parcels 1/6	0	9	0
Muslin for a Frock	2	2	0
Gloves 14s, Pins 2s, Laces 1s, Lock & Key 1/6	0	18	6
Materials for a Purse & making up	0	11	9
Cariage of ye Box 2s, Extra Washing 2/6	0	4	6
Spelling dictionary	0	1	0
Teachers & Servants	3	3	0
	£39	18	10½
Omitted, Drawing materials	0	9	0
	£40	7	10

It's clear from this that Anne was not receiving tuition in much beyond English, drawing, sewing and learning to write a good hand, all useful attributes to be sure, but hardly an education. The two guineas for the dancing master tell us that Anne was still trying to learn to dance (of all feminine accomplishments perhaps the most desirable), but her disability may have made this difficult for her. Setting aside the paucity of the curriculum, the fact that tea and sugar are charged extra is an indication that these were still expensive commodities, notwithstanding the large amounts of sugar which, as we have already seen, were bought by the Boulton household – and may have had more than a little to do with the many instances of toothache which crop up in the letters. Added to Miss Boulton's bill is the further sum of £17 0s. 3d. for Nancy Mynd over the same period, a much shorter account which includes 'powder & Root for Teeth' (3s. 6d.), making a total of £57 8s. 1d.[36]

A day or two after visiting Anne at school, Boulton headed home. In the coach with him were five children, 'our own 3 and the 2 young Motteux's'. Their 'own 3' were Matt, Anne, and Nancy Mynd.[37] Matt liked the two Motteux boys who, Boulton thought, would keep him 'out of improper Company'. Matt had a slight cough and seemed dull and listless; Boulton suggested his wife might speak to Dr Withering (Dr Small's successor and another Lunar Society member) about it if she happened to see him. The children stayed at home for some time, because early in July Boulton (who was now back in London for trials of the Chelsea Engine) wrote to his wife to ask how they were, and whether she thought Matt was well enough to return to school yet. 'The health of my Children is the first consideration with me & next to that the improvement of their minds,' he wrote. 'I fear they are looseing all they learnt at School & thereby they will have the more painfull task of learning all over again & seeing their School fellows get before them.' If Mrs Boulton and Dr Withering thought the children ready to return to school, she was to bring them or send them to London either by the two-day diligence or by post-chaise, and he would meet them. He could not spare the time to come back to Birmingham to fetch them himself. He had been to see Matt's schoolmaster, Mr Stretch, and had learned that on his return Matt was to go up into a higher class, and that 'The Boys now go a-batheing once or twice a week according to the desire of their parents'. He added, 'I beg my little Nanney will bring with her some handsome thing for a present to her teacher Mrs Steward, suppose some pretty filigree thing or a fine pair of Steel Ladys Buckles or any thing worth 2 or 3 Guineas.'[38]

The children returned to London, but were no sooner back than Boulton took them out of school again, having decided London was an unhealthy place in the summer. Instead he took them to Southampton for the bathing. He asked John Fothergill's sister, Mary, if she would accompany him to look after the children, to which she readily agreed, though with some puzzlement: 'Pray what is become of Mrs Boulton as you make no mention of her, surely you are not in the present fashion. I think you judge very right in not sending the Children to School this hot weather, its enough to give them fevers as they come of so airy a place as Soho.'[39] Boulton and the children duly set out from London, calling at Epsom to pick up Miss Fothergill. After a few days at Southampton, Boulton wrote to his wife that Matt was bathing every day with two schoolmates, and 'jumped in as bold as a Lyon & swam across'. Anne had been unwilling to bathe until he gave her the option of going into the cold water or returning to Cambden House, whereupon she 'stripd & went in overhead, the woman rubd her hip & she behaved upon the whole pretty well ...'.[40] The children were 'pert and & lively, yet they were exceedingly thin & weak,' he thought, and feared, if he had just left them at their schools, 'their constitutions would have been ruined & its probable they might not have got through the winter.' However, he had heard from Mr Stretch who was evidently instituting a healthier regime at Matt's school: 'Mr Stretch hath now got a bathing place for 'em at Twickenham, & gives them Sallits [salads] & Vegitables every day.'

He thought the children should stay at Southampton for the whole of August, and asked Mrs Boulton to arrange to send the small sofa from the front room at Soho House by the Oxford wagon for their lodgings, as 'Nanney wants to repose her self often in the day time and cant, for the Chairs are small and the beds two storeys high'.[41] If at some stage Mrs Boulton wanted to come to Southampton to see the children, '& will permit me to attend you, I am at your service', he added, but his wife did not take up the invitation. His next letter to her, a fortnight later, was from London; the children were still in Southampton with Miss Fothergill. Anne had evidently written to him for he told Mrs Boulton he was 'made very happy by my little Nanneys Letter'.

Some time during that summer of 1779 Boulton decided not to send Anne back to Cambden House, probably to the child's intense relief. Instead, he went to see a school recommended for his daughter by Mrs Montagu.[42]

Elizabeth Montagu (Plate 28), the London society hostess known as 'the Queen of the Bluestockings', was a customer for Boulton's silverware and ormolu, and a frequent correspondent. The school she had recommended was run by a Mrs Elizabeth Wilkes who took in '6 young ladies' at Richmond, Surrey. Having seen Mrs Wilkes's establishment and approved it, Boulton must have passed this news on to Mrs Montagu, who wrote to him the following month: '... I flatter myself you will have good reason to be pleased with Mrs Wilkes' attentions to Miss Boulton & if she inherits any share of her fathers genius the greatest attentions will find a subject worthy of them. When I go to London I will go to Mrs Wilkes & get acquainted with yr fair Daughter.'[43]

In October 1779 Mrs Terry wrote to Boulton, expressing concern that Anne's health had been so precarious, and regretting that he had withdrawn the child from Cambden House in favour of another establishment. The letter is tinged with a note of offended pride.[44] Two years later Mrs Terry was still chasing him for the outstanding school fees.

Mrs Montagu had expected that Anne would start at Mrs Wilkes's school immediately, but Anne and Matt were still in Southampton with Miss Fothergill and did not return home until the beginning of November, when Boulton and his wife went together to collect them. Mrs Boulton seems often curiously reluctant to involve herself much with the children, and it would be interesting to know whether her tendency to leave all the decisions, much of the contact and even some of the care to her busy husband was due to lack of interest on her part, or to an overbearing determination to be in charge on his. But on this occasion, when she did venture to Southampton with him to fetch the children, Annie Watt was scornful. Writing to her husband, who was back in Cornwall on his own, Annie declared tartly, 'Mr Henderson says Madam B & Husband are gone for Southampton in the Pheaton [sic] I pray she may be drenchd to the skin for her folly in going there, spending both money & time to her Husband when the Children was just going to return home & had so carefull a person with them as Miss Fothergill to take care of them on the road.'[45] A day or two before this, Boulton had written to Watt himself, mentioning that the children had caught 'the itch' (possibly scabies) while at Southampton. 'How Madam will fume', observed Annie Watt, not without satisfaction.[46]

4

'Holding the Ballance of Love even'

By the time 'Madam Boulton' arrived back in Birmingham with her scratching children, Annie Watt had taken little Gregory and Jessie up to Scotland to visit relatives during her husband's long stay in Cornwall, writing to him, 'O Jimmy you have robb'd me of my better half by taking your self a way'.[1] She nursed the hope that he would join them later. Annie and the children travelled north via Newcastle, where they met a family friend, George Anderson, who advised her to be sure to 'nocolet [inoculate] the children, it was the best thing [in] the world his daughter had nocoleted four why all did very well two of them was just such pretty babies as mine'.[2] Jessie was teething, and at her husband's insistence Annie had weaned her, 'contrary to the opinion of every body here, nine month you remember is the shortest they are suckled in this place of the world'.[3] Jessie was doing well, however – as was Gregory, who was growing fat. 'I am sorry to tell you I do the same,' wrote his mother. 'I am mortified to find every gown I put on that has not been worn for some time confines me as much as if I was bound in ropes, I am vext at it as I am afraid you will not like me so well as if I was thinner tho here they say I am the better for the fatt I have got.'[4]

Annie had a grumble at Watt's refusal to leave off the business in Cornwall for a while and join her and the children in Scotland: 'I think it very hard if you can not spare as much time in three or four years on your friends as Mr B spends every year on his wife & children', she wrote, adding, 'you are a miser in good news my Jamie & deals it out with a very sparing hand.'[5]

Having spent some days in Glasgow, Annie and the children went off to Clover, near Edinburgh, to visit more friends and relations. Just as they were planning to return to Glasgow word came that smallpox had broken out in the town and the question of inoculation arose once more. Annie was reluctant and fearful, but James had written and instructed her to have it done, so the doctor came to the house at Clover to carry out the procedure:

> I was sure the infection had took place as their arms were much inflamed. Jessy was very sick for three days & had a good number of fine Large pox, Gregory has never been sick worth the mention he had three Large pox on the three wounds which was very much inflamd, he had two or three small pimples on his face but one could not tell if they were pox or not. I woud have been very well pleased if he had been favoured with as many as Jessy had. Mr Wallace & Dr Irvine say he will never have any others without [unless] he shoud catch the infection from his own arm but they think it woud have taken place before

now, it is the 17 day since he was inoculated. They are both very well they have been out & come in as cold as frogs, I cant tell how happy & gratefull I am my Dearest James that they have got so well over so fatal a disorder.[6]

Annie had complained about Boulton not being with Watt in Cornwall to share the workload (by implication due to the capricious demands of his wife), but in mid-November, having got the children back from Southampton, he was finally able to set off to the south-west and remained there until the following February. This time he left Mrs Boulton at home at Soho – she had probably refused point-blank to go. Mrs Montagu, not knowing about 'the itch', was puzzled by the non-appearance of Anne at Mrs Wilkes's school. She wrote to Boulton in November: 'Mrs Wilkes daughter was at Sandleford with me for some weeks, she is a most amiable & well behaved & well inform'd young Person, & I imagine will make an agreeable part of the Society at Richmond when Miss Boulton is placed there. I heard a little while ago she was not yet arrived, I hope it is not want of health that has delay'd her.'[7]

The children were improving – Keir told Boulton they were 'pretty well, but not quite recovered of the scratching disease',[8] but no school would want them back with 'the itch', so Anne would stay at home until her father returned from Cornwall in the New Year, as would nine-year-old Matt, for whom Boulton had also been considering a change of school. By Christmas 1779 Matt was well enough to be at school and went back to his old school, Mr Pickering's in Winson Green, as a day boy. His father was not at all happy with this arrangement: 'I am realy at a loss where to place Matt. I only know that home is the most improper of all places. If I send him again to Twickenham I shall be apprehensive of bad health', he wrote to his wife, adding that 'On Saturday I shall drink a bumper to my two Nanneys, wishing they may both live to be as good, & as old as any of their great great great Grandmothers. I hope to find Matt improved in arethmatick, I dare say he is in skiteing [skating], my love to him, to my Mother & to Nanney Mynd. God bless & preserve your body & soul.'[9]

With Matt back at Winson Green as a day scholar, Henry Pickering felt it was an opportune moment to propose to his father that the boy should remain with him as a boarder. He wrote to Boulton in Cornwall on the subject, underlining his friendly relationship with his pupil by referring to the boy as 'Matty':

> Finding that you are undetermined where & in what manner to fix Matty so as to be most to his advantage & your conveniency ... I mean that you sh[d] place him with us as a Parlour Boarder, for then I should have frequent opportunities of introducing him into good company, which I think would be of considerable service to him. I have no mercenary end to answer by this proposal, for I am willing to take him as a P[arlou][r] Boarder on the same terms as a Common one, because I consider myself under great obligations to you, you have been a Friend to me several years, & this to me would be an agreeable opportunity of manifesting my gratitude to you.[10]

It would also, undoubtedly, have been a feather in his cap to be able to say to other prospective parents that Mr Boulton's son was one of his boarders. As a 'parlour boarder' Matt would take meals with Mr Pickering and his family, and probably have a bed to himself (beds were commonly shared in boarding schools unless parents were prepared to pay extra). Pickering offered to take Matt at 20 guineas a year, adding 'I am sure the advantages arising from Boys being constantly in the Family & always under the Eye of a Master are much greater than they are generally supposed to be ... I do not mean to say that we are calculated to finish his Education on the liberal & genteel Plan that you I know wish & intend to adopt, but I think at his age we can do as well for him as Schools in general at a greater distance.'[11] Another advantage of becoming a boarder would be that Matt would be less likely to fall into bad company (presumably on his way to and from school and after hours). Mr Pickering told Boulton:

> The present plan of attendance Matty is upon, I for several Reasons disapprove of. He is necessarily exposed at times to such Company as will have a great tendency to viciate his Taste & perhaps his Morals too ... so situated he must necessarily acquire a vicious pronunciation & vulgar dialect & may possibly after some time sink into vicious Habits, tho' [he added hastily] I never discovered in him the least propensity that way in my life – but it is certainly best to keep Youth as far as possible out of the way of Temptation.[12]

One of the bad influences Pickering may have had in mind was Matt's cousin George Mynd, Nancy Mynd's brother (1764-1813). Boulton had paid for George's education at Mr Pickering's, and had then taken him into the business, where he was a thorough nuisance. In exasperation he dismissed him in 1781, berating him roundly:

> Your idleness and negligence in business, the bad example you set in my Manufactory, your lying out of nights, breaking the peace of my family, shooting the birds in my garden, robing my orchard of apples, my walls of their fruit, and my kitchen garden of its produce; your conduct in general is so bad and so wicked that some of my friends have forbid their sons from comeing to my house on your account. And as your behaveour is so highly disgracefull to your self and me, I am therefore now resolved to return you to your father, and never suffer you again to disturb my peace, nor the peace of my family and friends ... You must therefore return to your father, who is obliged by law to provide for you. I am not.[13]

Some idea of the school at Winson Green can be gleaned from a few later bills for John Scale's sons, who also attended. School in Birmingham was evidently much cheaper than in London. The half-year bill for George Scale at Christmas 1782 came to a total of £8 1s. 10d., of which £7 was for board, with small sums for servants, washing, a seat in Church, a knife, fork and spoon, 2s. for fire, and 13s. 4d. for stationery. There are printed headings on the bill for mathematics, French, drawing, dancing, and for the apothecary, draper, tailor, shoemaker, barber, hatter and glover, but none of these have been filled in (the last seven presumably because the boy's parents lived nearby and would provide for him themselves).[14] English and Latin are not included on this bill, but the boys must surely have had lessons in both. Mr Pickering liked to give his pupils the opportunity to show what they could do, and their pre-Christmas production in 1779, in which Matt Boulton perhaps took part, was reported in *Aris's Gazette*:

> On Wednesday evening last, previous to their breaking up for the Holidays, the Young Gentlemen educated under Mr Pickering, at Winson Green, near this

Town, delivered several select Orations, from various Authors, with a Propriety and Ease, which reflected great Credit on the Master's Care and Attention, and afforded the utmost Satisfaction to a genteel Audience, assembled on the Occasion.[15]

Whether Mrs Boulton formed part of that genteel Audience is not recorded, but it does not seem that she and her husband accepted Pickering's recommendations for Matt's education. Their decision may have been influenced by a comment from James Keir. He had arranged for Matt and James Watt junior to spend a couple of hours every day during their Christmas holiday working in the Soho Manufactory Counting House, learning 'to reckon & to draw' under the supervision of Mr Playfair, the Counting House manager. Keir told Boulton he did not think Matt had yet lost too much ground by his absence from school the previous summer and autumn, but in order to acquire studious habits and a manly character, 'he must be removed more than a hundred miles from Soho'.[16] In a letter to Watt at about the same time he reported that Jimmy had been 'a very good boy'.[17]

Boulton spent a gloomy Christmas in Cornwall, writing home from Truro on Christmas Day full of cares about problems with the Cornish mines, the unreliable supplier of the copper pipes for the engines, and Watt's constant moping. The one thing that had cheered him up was a letter from Anne:

> I received my dear little Girls letter dated the 14th instant which I have kissed without fear of the Scotch Piddle. As it is one of the greatest pleasures I enjoy I beg she will write me often & I should also be glad to receive a letter once a week from Marcus, Cato's Son [ie Matt] – Oh ye immortal powers that guard the just, watch round your Couch & soften your repose, banish all sorrow & becalm your Soul with easy Dreams, remember me & let my darlings be your care ...[18]

'Marcus, Cato's Son' may have been a reference to a production at the Theatre in New Street, Birmingham, earlier that year, of *The Celebrated Tragedy of Cato*. This clearly ambitious school production, which the Boultons may have seen, was performed by 'Young ladies and gentlemen under the tuition of Mr Dunning'. The programme began with Dunning himself delivering a Eulogy of Shakespeare, together with 'An Exordium to Elocution and an Address on Behalf of his young Performers'. Between each act the schoolmaster delivered a comic oration, and the evening concluded with a 'Humorous Epilogue by a CHILD not above EIGHT Years of Age'. The playbill concluded: 'Mr DUNNING takes the liberty of assuring the Ladies and gentlemen of Birmingham, that he has spared no pains for many months past, to render his pupils worthy of public attention; and flatters himself with having so far succeeded in his endeavours, as to have every reason to expect the whole will prove an agreeable and rational evening's entertainment.'[19]

By mid-January Boulton thought the Cornish business was near to being settled and promised to bring home 'a very handsome dish of Parchments which will serve us to live upon all the remainder of our lives'.[20] In spite of this, he and Watt were about to walk part of the way to Marazion to save money and would hire a chaise just for the last part of the journey. From Cornwall he would have to go up to York for some other business, and invited his wife to join him on the trip and see the sights of that ancient city – an invitation which she accepted. And as soon as they returned from York, he said, Anne must be ready to go to her new school.

In February Mrs Wilkes herself wrote to Boulton to enquire if he still wanted the school place, or whether she could let it go to someone else – though she would 'prefer Miss Boulton to any other young lady'.[21] Following this Anne started at Mrs Wilkes's probably in March 1780, much to Elizabeth Montagu's satisfaction: 'I hope Miss Boulton will be pleased with her society at Mrs Wilkes, the young ladies there live very agreably and friendly with each other, Mrs Wilkes' good sense, good humour & pleasing manners reign through the whole house ...'[22] At the same time, in the absence of any better idea, Boulton sent Matt back to school at Twickenham.

For most of May and June 1780 Boulton was alone in London, where he took lodgings for eight weeks at £25 13s. plus 2s. 6d. for washing sheets.[23] This was probably cheaper than staying in a hotel. He took his meals at an eating house run by a Thomas Hoyland, whose statement for meals taken in the week ending 1 June happily gives us the menus. On 24 May Boulton enjoyed a dinner of bread and butter (6d.), mock turtle soup (2s. 6d.), pigeon pie (4s. 6d.), currant pudding (2s.), and cream cheese and radishes (6d.). Mr Hoyland's currant pudding seems to have been something of a favourite – it appears on the menu four times in the week. Other courses taken on different days include neck of veal, 'sallad egg and oyl', ribs of lamb with mint sauce, beef steaks, poultry, asparagus, and salmon with lobster sauce. The dinners bill for the week is £15 6s. 9d.[24] On another occasion he noted the expenses of staying at a hotel in the Adelphi for three weeks: lodgings £12 13s., servants £1 1s., maid 2s. 6d., stockings 9s. 6d., barber 15s., and the coach back to Birmingham £1 11s. 6d. Before leaving he bought 'a Hatt for Matt' costing 10s. 6d.[25]

While Boulton was tucking into his currant pudding, Matt fell sick at school. Mr Stretch wrote, 'Mr Gilchrist the apothecary apprehends your Sons disorder will turn out to be the Meastles ... We can put him in an apartment distinct from the other young Gentlemen, where he shall have faithful and unremitted attention paid him by night and day.'[26] Measles was potentially life-threatening, so when Anne went down with it too at Richmond, her father was beside himself with anxiety. He took his daughter out of school and, fearing that she was too ill to stand the journey home to Birmingham, took her to stay with William and Charlotte Matthews who, childless themselves, were fond of Anne. Clearly frantic, he wrote to his wife on 5 July:

> This morning I receiv'd my Dear Daughter ... with a red face & a feverish pulse which proved to be the Measles ... since dinner the Eruption is come out extreamly thick and she is just as Matt was, very feverish. I went this morning to consult Dr Sir Richard Jebb respecting the general state of her health which is by far too delicate but Sir Richard was not at home & this I did before I had seen her or knew she had the Measles. After I saw her I went to J. Hunters but he was out of Town. I then went again to Sir Richard Jebb & saw him but he could not see her to night. He hath told me all that is proper to be done & hath recommended a sensible apothecary & will see her tomorrow. She is now at Mr Matthews's & cant be moved at present. I have paid for my place in tomorrow nights Coach but I will lose my Fare for I cant leave her till she is recoverd & I will write to you every day. God preserve you. I am your uneasy but affectionate Husband, MB.[27]

The next day he wrote to Mrs Boulton again, a more reassuring letter, at the end of which he noted, 'I will excuse your droping a tear upon the receipt of my letter of yesterday because I found myself very womanish, but as all seems likely to go well let us thank God and be satisfied.'[28]

For the next week Anne's mother received daily letters from her husband, who on 7 July announced:

> It affords me unspeakable satisfaction to tell you that our dear Child is going on very well & nothing more need be done than to let the disorder take its course, she requires no physick as nature doth her own business, except she takes a white powder with a white emultion every 3 Hours. She conforms to everything she is desired to do & her mildness is as conspicuous in sickness as in health.[29]

Mrs Wilkes wrote offering Anne expert care from 'the woman of the house', a 'professed nurse', and every attention during her convalescence (at no extra charge), as soon as Sir Richard Jebb said the child was no longer infectious and could return to school.[30] Meanwhile, Mrs Montagu wrote from Bath with good wishes: 'I am greatly rejoyced the amiable Miss Boulton is recovering her health so well after the measles; it is a very good symptom for her general constitution, for the measles are apt to make great impression where there is any weakness or defect.'[31]

As soon as Anne was better Boulton made plans to return to Cornwall, taking along young Erasmus Darwin junior for company: 'He hath softened the rigour of my bleak and lonely existence in this steril peninsula.'[32] While Boulton went about his business Erasmus junior travelled along and amused himself collecting mineral specimens for his father. The boy had lost his elder brother, Charles, a couple of years earlier when, shortly before his 20th birthday, the gifted medical student had died of septicaemia, arising from a finger cut while dissecting the brain of a dead child at medical school in Edinburgh.

For news from home Boulton had to rely almost entirely on John Scale, who wrote to him in late August, 'Mast[r] Matthew has been much plagued with the tooth Ach & last night he determind to have it out this morning.'[33] Mrs Boulton had told the dentist that the boy had two bad teeth together and did not know which one was hurting, so both were taken out without forewarning him. 'He met the operator with all the firmness & resolution you cou'd wish … almost with an oh!,' said Scale.

Far away in Cornwall, on his 52nd birthday (14 September new style) Boulton wrote to his wife from Plengwarry Green, addressing her as 'My dearest Joan' and beginning:

> So sure as there are 1728 Inches in a Cubic foot so sure was I born in that Year & so sure as there are 52 Weeks in the Year, or what you will better remember, so sure as there are 52 Cards in a Pack, so sure am I 52 Years old this very day, and yet I fear you think so little of me that you will neither have a plumb pudding for your dinner nor drink my good health. I shall not forget the same day in Novr next for I find a great deal of Old Darby about me, at least that part of his Character that I am ever uneasy asunder from my Joan. Well, the older we grow the better friends I hope we shall be, & though Time has a spite against Cupids Wings yet Friendship never comes to Maturity unless it hath been long nursed & cherished by Old Time.[34]

There was little news that she would find interesting, he added; the business was going slowly, though he would be content if only she would join him. He asked for news of the children. A fortnight later he wrote again, from Redruth, that he had concluded a deal to erect six large engines for the Wheal Virgin adventurers by Michaelmas the following year. This enormous amount of work would necessitate both of them living in Cornwall for the whole of next summer, he said firmly, holding out the promise to his wife of her own servant and carriage, and better weather to make the prospect more agreeable than last time. The business promised to be

> the greatest & most profitable that will ever fall to our lott as it will at least be an addition to our income about 4 Thousand a year which is the best grease that can be put to the Wheels of a Coach. I have rode on horseback so hard that I have wore out my bottom & by not allowing it time to heal it is become so bad a sore that I am obliged to borrow friend Phillips's Chaise which waits now at the door to take me to Marazion.[35]

He had heard via the Soho grapevine that his wife had mobility problems of her own. John Scale had mentioned in a letter that Mrs Boulton had spent the day with Mrs Baskerville; playing blind man's buff after dinner she had fallen and sprained her ankle, but was hoping it would be better enough to allow her to attend a performance of *Messiah* the following day.[36] Boulton wrote reproachfully to his wife, 'I hope your ankle is got well, 'tis well it is no worse for Blind mans buff is a dangerous play as I have heard of many young Women coming off with a Broken Leg from playing at that game.'[37] More than once Scale took it on himself to act as informant (once writing of Mrs Boulton '… the bottoms of her Dancing pumps sufferd considerably as you may easily suppose for she kept it up till 3 oClock in the morning'[38]), and sometimes he was go-between. During the autumn of 1780, after writing a letter to his wife, Boulton subsequently received one from Scale which clearly upset him a good deal, though neither has been preserved. In some distress he wrote post-haste to Mrs Boulton, anxious to clear the air:

> I thought my self slighted because you promised to write to me & you have not. I repeatedly urged you in my letters to send me one line, one scrap of your pen, I talked, in my letters, of our meeting upon the road & was happy in amuseing myself with such like ideas, yet no reply no letter no scrap of your dear writing nor indeed any news whatsoever of you for this month past until this hour … If I could have borne your slights (or what I took to be slights) with indifference, you might then have concluded I had little regard for you and although I am exceedingly concerned to find that you are made uneasy by my letter, yet I must own it affords me more satisfaction than if you had laughd at it …
>
> I wish you had come to Cornwall with me, all would have been well, but now the Winter is too far advanced, & my business approaching I hope to a conclusion, so that I may soon return & be happy … I shall be obliged to return back to Cornwall in April & then I hope you will come with me & bring one Man & two Maids with our own Horses that you may not be imprisond as you was the last time. It is impossible my residence here can be agreeable to me without you …
>
> I referd you to your serious midnight thoughts because they extend further than those of smileing noon and I am at a great distance from you. You will not be surprised at my uneasiness when you consider my regard for you & when you

reflect that you have not sent me one mark of your Love since I have been here
... Give me your Love & Confidence, I ask no more. Dear Nanny I am & I hope
I ever shall be your faithfull & most affectionate Husband, Matthew Boulton.[39]

Though Boulton and Watt were prepared to rough it to some extent themselves,
the lodgings they had been able to get in Cornwall had never been really satisfactory when their wives accompanied them. Now, possessed of the idea that if he
could find some way of providing an agreeable second home in Cornwall, the two
wives would be more amenable to going with them, Boulton wrote to Annie Watt
explaining one idea:

> One might build of Timber a comfortable & portable dwelling house one story
> high consequently no staircase. I would have a good dining room & a good
> drawing room I mean a room to draw & write in with 2 Bedchambers for 2 pair
> of married folks, with 4 dormitories fitted up in the stile of a Ships Cabin one
> for Female & one for Male friends, one for male & another for female servants,
> they are the cheapest sort of beds & take up little room. The house we may place
> in the most agreeable & convenient situation that can be found ... it may at any
> time be changd for another. Mr Henderson says such houses are sold ready to
> put together in ye American markets ... After all I dare say you & I shall agree
> upon one point, which is, that tis a very disagreeable thing for Husbands &
> Wives who love each other, to be so far & so long separated as hath falln to the
> lot of a couple of Engineers of your acquaintance. For Charity sake go see my
> Wife as often as you can, & tell her she shall never serve me so again, for I will
> force her along with me when ever I come back to Cornwall.[40]

How the Boultons' and Watts' friends would have reacted to having to sleep in
male and female dormitories is questionable, and the plan for the flat-pack house
was evidently abandoned as soon as thought of, for shortly afterwards he wrote to
Watt that he had found a suitable house, Cosgarne (Plate 20). Near Truro, it was
convenient for 14 of the mines where Boulton & Watt had steam engine business,
and the roads in the district were being improved. The landlord had wanted 150
guineas a year; Boulton had agreed 'upon condition that o was struck off from
the rent and accordingly we did agree upon these terms and there remains to be
paid so long as we keep it 15 Guineas pr year'.[41] Having struck this extraordinary
deal, Boulton added that if Watt disagreed, he would in any case keep the place
to use himself. Watt agreed.

Cosgarne House now provided the partners with a comfortable base during their
extended visits to Cornwall. Boulton had taken it part-furnished, and the inventory
shows the house to have been well-equipped, with china, glass, linen, blankets,
kitchenware and furniture for its occupants and for entertaining visitors. Twelve
people could sit down to a table spread with linen tablecloths and set with blue
and white china, and drink tea from two brown teapots. There were a coffee pot,
a dozen cut crystal wine glasses, two crystal decanters, and 17 jelly glasses. Beds
were made up comfortably with feather beds, linen sheets and pillowcases, flannel
blankets, 'Manchester counterpanes', and check bed-hangings. The cold Cornish
floors were softened with a large blue and white carpet and a stair carpet. In the
bedrooms there were three chests of drawers, four looking glasses, mahogany tables
and wash-stands, and six bedsteads. In the kitchen, the maids clattered about among

milk pails and pans, a copper stew pan and cover, saucepans, a fish kettle, '2 tin pans for baken bread', coffee and pepper mills, and an egg slice; they worked at two deal tables and took their breaks on 'common chairs'.[42]

But in spite of the home comforts of Cosgarne, Cornwall was a dreary place in the winter and Boulton was still low-spirited from his wife's coolness. No sooner had he settled on the house than he wrote to Watt announcing his intention of giving up either the business at Soho or the business in Cornwall, as 'my days are now short, and my health & faculties declineing, [and] I am desirous of bringing all my worldly affairs into some distinct order before I am quite superannuated'.[43] At the same time he wrote to the Rev. Tremain at Helligan, apologising for not having had time to call on him and promising to do so next time he was in Cornwall, so he was clearly in a somewhat distracted and indecisive state. He was looking forward to seeing his wife and repairing hurt feelings, and to the tonic of a family Christmas at Soho House.

However, he was worried about whether Anne was strong enough to undertake the journey home from Richmond and, if she couldn't travel, then he wondered whether he ought to leave ten-year-old Matt at his school in Twickenham for the holidays too, as he explained to both head teachers in letters which suggest a rather modern approach to child psychology. On 5 December 1780 he wrote to Mrs Wilkes:

> Now my Dear Madam I must beg the favour of your advise respecting a certain weakness I am possessed of: it is of a species which young Ladies are sometimes liable to at School when they want to see Papa & Mamma and as I am perswaded that you have the agreeable art of dispeling that disorder from your own Mansion I must beg you will also from mine, either by letting me have the specific calld Miss Boulton to spend the Xmas holodays at Soho, or give me such a portion of reason as will palliate the infirmity. If you do not put a negative upon my plan I shall prevail upon some friend to accompany my Children to Oxford, where I will meet them & convey them home. But if you think my Dear Child's health not sufficiently strong to encounter with this rugged season, & that I ought to suppress my Desires, I will endeavour to do it. In which case I must hold the Ballance of Love even, & not seem to let it preponderate in favour of my Son & therefore wave fetching him home ...'[44]

To Matt's headmaster, Mr Stretch at Twickenham, he wrote on the same day:

> Dear Sir,
> I have now been exil'd from my Family & friends into this barren peninsula about 4 months; where, from illness & overmuch business, I have been prevented from holding much correspondence with my Children or Friends but as I have now brought all my business to a conclusion, I propose setting out homeward in 2 or 3 days. I cannot help owning that I should be glad to see both my Children at home during the holydays & yet grim Winter seems to forbid it. I am not so much afraid of Matt encountering with ye journey, as I am of his Sister, whose present state of health I am not sufficiently inform'd of, to judge of the propriety of fetching her home. I have therefore, by this post, wrote to Mrs Wilks, desireing her opinion upon the matter, and if she disapproves the undertaking I must hold the Ballance of Love even, & not let either of them think it preponderates in favr of the other by fetching either, in which case I must contrive to give them a little change of scene amongst some of my Friends about Town ...[45]

Mrs Wilkes wrote back promptly, her letter giving Boulton the news he wanted, and us an insight into her approach to education:

> I should at any time, dear Sir, be unwilling to withhold from you a cordial which is I imagine at all times necessary to your comfort; but as it is more especially so at the present, I am happy that your dear child's health will permit her to administer it with perfect safety to herself. She is, I bless God! charmingly well & has been so ever since she took the Asses milk. She has eat, drank, slept & looked well & is grown we think rather plumper; of which I hope you will be a witness – but she has (since her Journey has been arranged) caught a cold which *may* possibly make some little alteration in her looks; although I rather flatter myself, that with the help of good wrapping & care, the Journey & change of air may prove beneficial & remove the little cough so recently contracted. I am just now informed by a letter from Mrs Matthews that she will fetch Miss Boulton & her brother to morrow, as she has found a proper person to take care of them to Birmingham. Had there arisen any difficulty in this matter, I would with pleasure have conveyed them safely to Oxford, or even to Soho if you had wished it: but Mr Stretch telling me he would accompany them & had offered to do so, prevented my offering myself.
>
> I hope Sir, you will think your dear child already something improved; although I generally appropriate some time at first to the purpose of gaining the affection & confidence of those intrusted to my care & laying the groundwork of improvement; rather than venture the disgusting them of those things I wish to inculcate by too much hastening their acquirement. Miss Boulton's health being so very delicate & her spirits in consequence weak, makes this treatment particularly necessary with regard to her & I make no doubt it will succeed to my wish – I beg you to believe that no attention on my part shall be wanting & from her good sense, great memory & sweet disposition I dare hope that sometime hence, her progress in her learning will be very apparent. [46]

Boulton had paid Mrs Wilkes a preliminary fee of £31 10s. 0d., and had asked her to send him an up-to-date account, which she did, with compliments and good wishes to Mrs Boulton and thanks for 'the many obliging presents received'. The accounts with this letter total £72 3s. 6d, less the £31 10s. already received. They include a bill of £1 9s. 3d. for a daily supply of two gills (half a pint) of asses' milk throughout August (asses' milk was generally prescribed as a restorative food – Sir Richard Jebb advised Fanny Burney to cease taking it as 'too nourishing' in 1781[47]). There is a bill of six guineas for the dancing master, J. Gallini, for March to September 1780. The drawing master's bill for the half-year came to £4 8s. 3d. and included tuition (four guineas) and 4s. 3d. for black and red chalk, poster crayons and drawing paper. Half a year's board, June–December, was charged at £52 10s. 'Cloaths' come to £5 8s. 7d. and include 'making 2 new frocks', 9s.; 'new bodying one', 2s.; four pairs of shoes, 19s. 6d.; '8 yds edging for a cap', 4s.; a pair of gloves at 1s. 6d., an ivory comb at 1s. 8d., a black cloak with edging, £2 2s., and a matching bonnet, 8s. There were also a few sundries, including postage, pins, 'going to the Play' 4s. and the coach fare for this outing, 1s. The balance of £40 13s. 6d. was paid in full and receipted on 17 April 1781.[48]

Matthew Boulton finally set out from Cornwall for home on 12 December 1780. As a peace gesture, Mrs Boulton travelled as far as Worcester to meet him, where they spent a couple of days together before returning to Soho House. With the children back at home for the holidays, there was a joyful family Christmas reunion – a letter from Boulton to Mr Capper (probably Peter Capper, of Redland, near Bristol, with whom he had business dealings) refers to them all being together at Soho for Christmas 'in good health & good humour'.[49]

Though Anne and Matt did not get home to Soho to see their mother very often, their father took the opportunity to visit them whenever he was in London, and they and he were sometimes able to spend time together, thanks to the kindness of business friends. At Easter 1781 John Motteux sent his chaise to collect Matt from school in Twickenham and bring him to the Motteux's home in Banstead, where Boulton spent Sunday with his son; Matt stayed at Banstead until later in the week, when he went on to stay with the Matthews. Then Boulton picked up his daughter from school in Richmond and took her with him to visit the Veres at Sunbury overnight. The Veres were business friends of the Boultons, the Fothergills and the Matthews. Charles Vere was a banker and also a tea and china dealer in London, and they had houses at Sunbury near London, where they generally lived, and at Astley between Fillongley and Nuneaton in Warwickshire.

When Boulton delivered Anne back to school after the visit he paid Mrs Wilkes £66 and chatted with her about the child's progress. 'I am most heartily sick of London,' he wrote to his wife, '& wish not only for my own health but for the sake of my dear lonely Dove to be at Soho. I have a torrent of Vexations but I will not trouble you about them ...'[50]

A week later he went to see Anne again, this time accompanied by John Whitehurst, writing home to her mother:

> I think [she is] much better than ever I saw her before, & she appears to more advantage as she holds up her head. Although she has not improved so much as we expected during the last year yet I have no doubt but she will make much more proficiency in the present year as I hope she will not be pulled back by illness & Mrs Wilkes intends to push her forward now as her health will better bear it. I mentiond all that was necessary respecting her Cloaths & she has promised me to write once a fortnight to you.[51]

He was also busy with commissions from his wife, and conscious of the type of fabric she would need for the season, the light, glossy silk known as 'lutestring' rather than a heavy winter satin:

> Pray send me word directly how many yards of Silk you must have for the Gowns you want – I suppose they must be Lutestrings as Satins will not be made up till next Winter. I think you would have them made up & trimed smarter here than at Birmingham. I have seen many plain Silks trimd with white – Burgundy Couler is much wore.[52]

Soon Boulton was heading back home with two silks, one for his wife and one for Miss Fothergill. Mrs Boulton was to have first choice: 'One is a plain Quaker-like Couler calld the Bou de Pari: which I am doubtful if you will like although it is fashionable. But if you do not like one you may perhaps like the other ...'[53] The fabrics came from Barton & Nelthorpe of Covent Garden, grandly entitled on their billhead 'Mercers to His Majesty's Great Wardrobe'. Twenty yards of 'stript lustring' cost £7 and 20 yards of 'Bou de Paris plain' £5 15s. The shop allowed a discount of 12s. 9d. for ready money.[54] Boulton may also have bought his wife a gown already made up, for on a separate slip of paper he wrote a gift-note: 'May this easy cheerfull sprightly Dress be emblematical of the heart, health & spirits of the wearer. Mrs Boulton is requested to be that wearer for the sake & pleasure of him whose choice it is.'[55] The upset of the previous autumn seemed to be behind them.

By mid-May 1781 Anne, at school in Richmond, was feeling homesick, and wrote a plaintive little letter to her father: 'My Dear Papa, I am quite unhappy at not having heard from Soho since I saw you last but I hope you will ease my mind by writing a few lines as soon as you conveniently can. Matty drank tea here yesterday, he was perfectly well and in very good spirits … I hope my Dear Mama, yourself and all my Friends at Soho are well …' In a wistful PS she adds, 'I hope I shall hear from you by the return of post'.[56] Evidently Mrs Boulton was no more inclined to write to her children than she was to her husband. This is the earliest of Anne's letters to be preserved in the Archive.

Anne does not mention being unwell in this letter, but soon after writing it she had some kind of health problem, for in June Mrs Wilkes wrote to tell Boulton that his daughter was nearly recovered (she does not say from what), and passed on the advice of John Hunter, who had been to the school to examine her. This is the examination about which Hunter also wrote to Boulton, which was referred to in Chapter 2. According to Mrs Wilkes, Hunter's recommendations were:

> … riding was not necessary unless she could not take sufficient exercise otherwise; & that she would be better without Wine or Porter; eating little butter & much vegetables & plain Meat or Fowl – Mr Robertson [the apothecary] had desired she should for a day or two (at the first of her Illness) eat no animal food but very soon allowed her chicken or boiled Mutton which she has had almost every day, except once or twice the Muttn at her own desire & great plenty of oranges, rusks & bunns which agreed extremely well with her – she does not like Sago, Panada*, or such kind of things & therefore she has been allowed as much latitude in other things, as possible & it is a great comfort to me since she dislikes that sort of light diet that Mr Hunter says solids are best for her – Mr Robertson too, having nearly observed the turns of her constitution, tho for only one week is of the same opinion & had given me directions accordingly – the dear Child eats with appetite, has no remaining sickness & sleeps charmingly, which I hope will contribute to make you & her dear Mama easy …[57]

By this time the Watts had gone to Cornwall again, from where Annie Watt wrote to Boulton to tell him how Mr Henderson had been 'struck all of a heap' by their arrival and her request to hire a maid, because he had not been expecting a lady. Watt had been much put out by their reception and had reacted with one of his headaches, but it had abated enough to allow him to finish some drawings.[58]

In February 1782, after a Christmas holiday at home, Anne and Matt and their father set out for London in the coach, giving a lift to Mr Garbett. When Matt got back to school Mr Stretch had to chase Boulton for his fees, writing to him that as Matt had 'mentioned *very slightly* that you had not sent [payment] I was a

---

* Panada: a preparation of bread, boiled to a pulp and flavoured.

little afraid he might have dropt it by the way'. By way of a sweetener he added, 'Your son went yesterday to see his sister who as well as himself is perfectly well.'[59] Mr Stretch's half-year account had amounted to £23 16s. 11d. This included two guineas for the drawing master, 7s. 10d. for Mrs Stretch ('sewing and laundry'), £1 3s. 5d. for 'new shoes, pumps @ 5s. 9d., and shoe repairs', and 6s. 5d. for mending – including a pair of breeches which had to be mended several times. Board and tuition came to £13 2s. 6d. Books included *The Art of Speaking* at 5s. and a Latin Grammar at 1s. 6d. There was an additional charge of 14s. 6d. for a 'party of pleasure to the play *Military Master*'.[60] Stretch's next account, at midsummer 1782, included a copy of Telemachus at 3s. 6d., two guineas for the dancing master, and sums for the tailor (4s. 3d.), barber (1s.), shoemaker (£1 8s. 7d.) and apothecary (8s.). Ushers and servants cost 10s. 6d. and the use of a study 10s. 6d. Fires were charged at 2s. 6d.[61] A later bill includes 4s. for mending a window, and three guineas for the fencing master.[62]

The midsummer of 1782 brought them all a great shock. Boulton's partner in the silverware and jewellery business, John Fothergill, died suddenly. They had been locked in disagreement over some aspects of their partnership but Boulton wrote to William Matthews, 'This great and sudden shock distresses me almost beyond the power of supporting myself, for let the conduct of any part of that family have been what it will, their present distresses turn every passion into pity.'[63] The company of Boulton & Fothergill was formally dissolved on 22 June, and a new company, Matthew Boulton & Co., registered on 24 June.

The following month Boulton took his son on a tour to Derbyshire. They called to see their old friend Dr Erasmus Darwin, who had moved from Lichfield to Radburn, near Derby, with his second wife, and at Matlock they met Richard Arkwright and toured mills where they saw velvet-dressing and other processes. On 1 August they stayed at Castleton, where next morning they rose before six and went into Peak's Hole and heard the singers. The expenses for the 244-mile round trip came to £32 1s. 0d. which included £1 4s. for 'fossills'.[64]

Some time during that summer of 1782 Anne Boulton changed schools again. The new establishment was run by a Mrs M. Moore and was in central London – in Portman Square, in fact, so she was almost a neighbour of Elizabeth Montagu. Mrs Montagu had had a grand new house built in the Square, as a suitable setting for her famous *salons*. The construction went on for so long, and aroused so much interest, that the site foreman was eventually forced to the expedient of selling tickets to view in order to manage visitor numbers, but Mrs Montagu had finally been able to move in some time in 1781. Boulton had supplied specimens of Soho's 'mechanical paintings' (a process developed by Francis Eginton) to decorate the ceilings, and seems also to have been landed with the task of sourcing plate glass for the windows. This commission gave him so much aggravation that he kept a special notebook in which to detail his searches for glass of a suitable clarity and size, and his negotiations with glass manufacturers. Mrs Montagu had definite ideas about what she wanted:

> My eating room & that Venetian window of my Great Room which looks to Hampstead &c & also one of the Bow windows of ye Great Room which looks

FIG. 11 *Interior of Mrs Montagu's house, Portman Square, for which Matthew Boulton supplied 'mechanical paintings' for the ceilings. (Country Life Picture Library)*

to ye Country must be of Plate glass the other 2 windows of the Bow only look upon houses & streets. What I have said on this subject gives testimony to that great truth that the clearer the medium through which we see the works & images of the great Creator the more beauty appears, but the works & occupations of Man appear better thro' a little mist ... I have very little hope of assistance from my architect Mr Stuart [James 'Athenian' Stuart] who is idle & inattentive & his assistant seems ... Tho' an ingenious draughtsman not very alert in business, I believe Mr Stuart made choice of him as men do of their Wives for their passive qualities rather than serviceable talents.[65]

In a later letter the Queen of the Blues added tetchily:

I am quite ashamed to be so often and so very troublesome, but you will pardon me on account of the importance of ye object. A Philosopher wd laugh at my reckoning a House an important Object, I am not a Philosopher & whoever is not, is apt to consider things according to their bulk, & I am sure in that view my House is not a trifling bagatelle.[66]

Apart from mechanical paintings from Soho, the adornments of the house included feather hangings about which Cowper was moved to write, 'The birds put off their every hue/to dress a room for Montagu'. Horace Walpole thought the house 'a noble simple edifice, magnificent, yet no gilding'. In Portman Square Mrs Montagu's *salons* assumed an even grander air. In the *Observer* Richard Cumberland wrote:

Vanessa in the centre of her own circle sits like the statue of the Athenian Minerva, incensed with the breath of philosophers, poets, painters, orators, and every art, science or fine speaking. It is in her academy young novitiates try their wit and practise panegyric; no one like Vanessa can break in a young lady to the poetics ... she can make a mathematician quote Pindar, a master in chancery write novels, or a Birmingham hardware man stamp rhymes as fast as buttons.[67]

Was Matthew Boulton Richard Cumberland's 'Birmingham hardware man'? It seems entirely possible, and it would be interesting to know what Anne Boulton thought of Mrs Montagu's house, which she would surely have visited with her father when he was in town, but she remains silent on the subject, being much more interested in when she can come home from Mrs Moore's: 'I think by the account you gave me of Cosgarne, it must be a very delightful place; but I own I am glad to hear that I shall see Soho at Christmas, as the vacation commences on the 18th of next month and not any of the young ladies stay after that day ...'[68] Garbett also wrote to Boulton, 'This day at noon I saw Miss Boulton. She is very well and looks delightfully. She desires duty to you and Mrs Boulton, and love to Miss Mynde. You will not wonder that she is anxious to hear that she is to be happy with you at Christmas. I observed Miss Moore said none of the ladies staid with her at Christmas.'[69]

Boulton had been at Cosgarne with his wife, their niece Nancy Mynd and some of their servants since September – so Mrs Boulton had finally succumbed to his entreaties and joined him again. While they were away, at Boulton's invitation Fothergill's widow Elizabeth, his sister Mary, and his daughters Elizabeth and Mary came to stay at Soho House – John Fothergill's death had left his family in financial difficulties and they had been obliged to move out of their home. Arrangements were being made for the youngest Fothergill daughter, Patty, to leave her boarding school and attend a day-school at Sunbury, which would be cheaper for her mother.[70] This was at the instigation of their old friend Mrs Vere, who lived at Sunbury. Mrs Fothergill later went to live at the Veres' Warwickshire house at Astley.

With Anne and Matt at school, and leaving the Fothergills in temporary residence at Soho House, Boulton's diary for September 1782 lists the expenses of the eight-day journey to Cosgarne with his wife, niece, two maids and a manservant.[71] The route took them via Bromsgrove, Worcester, Upton-on-Severn, Gloucester, Newport, Bristol, Bridgwater, Cullompton, Taunton, Exeter, Moretonhampstead, Tavistock, Liskeard, Lostwithiel and St Austell to Truro. In Bristol they bought cheese and five hams, and the chaise needed repairs at Exeter. Including overnight stops, the journey to Cosgarne cost £58 16s. 6d. Mrs Boulton was travel-sick more than once and may have regretted agreeing to go. She must have felt she had barely recovered from the journey down to Cosgarne when it was time to return to Soho for Christmas.

When Anne arrived home for the holiday she brought with her Mrs Moore's bill for the half year to December 1782, which gives us some indication of the subjects in her curriculum:

	£	s	d
Pens		1	6
A copy book		1	0
Chambaud's French grammar		3	0
A book for exercises			8
A wash ball			8
Two books for translations & French exercises		1	4
Chambaud's fables		1	6
Entrance to the music master	1	1	0
Chambaud's exercises		2	0
Ash's grammar		1	0
Chambaud's vocabulary		2	6
The history of England		1	6
The children's geography		1	6
A spelling book		1	0
A book for English exercises			8
A treatise on arts & sciences		2	6
A music book		3	6
Ribbon		1	10
Paid for the carriage of a parcel			6
A French prayer book		2	6
A large caravan box		5	6
A Hymn book		2	0
A letter			4
Powder, pomatum & pins		2	6
Gloves		1	3
Paper		1	6

A pr. of worsted stockings		1	6
A swing glass		6	6
A pr. of shoes		6	0
A black bonnet		16	0
A copy book		1	0
Pens		1	6
Persian for a work box		2	3
Ribbon for D°		5	6
Paste board for the box			3
A cap		8	0
A letter			4
Beads for a work box		1	6
A copy book		1	0
Six months board & education	26	5	0
Six months writing	2	2	0
Six months dancing	3	3	0
Six months music	3	3	0
Six months drawing	3	3	0
A seat at Chapel for six months		10	6
Tuning the harpsichord for six months		10	6
Six months subscription for books		6	0
D° for maps		4	0
Paid Mr Hill for shoes	2	10	0
Materials for drawing		10	0
Extra washing		10	6
A back collar	1	11	6
	£50	5	1[72]

This seems to reveal a rather broader curriculum than Anne had had at previous schools, though French, drawing, sewing, music and dancing still appear to be the chief ingredients in the school day. Her father could undoubtedly have taught her more about 'arts and sciences' than the school could, but he was certainly now spending more on his daughter's education than he had been doing previously. Mr Hill's bill for shoes, which Mrs Moore enclosed with her account, is for six pairs of shoes over the half year; each pair has one shoe with a cork sole, which indicates that although John Hunter had advised against it years ago, Anne was still wearing a shoe with a thick built-up sole on her left foot. Cork was the material of choice for the thick soles of such shoes, because it was lightweight, easily shaped, and resilient and comfortable to walk on, though only the well-to-do would have been able to afford such special orthopaedic shoes.[73]

Strolling unsteadily in the Soho House grounds in the holiday, Anne would have noticed a few changes. The tea house which her father had first had built in the 1770s, and where visitors to the Manufactory were entertained, was either extended or adapted to include at one end a laboratory and at the other a fossilry, equipped with specimen trays supplied by Wedgwood.[74] So Boulton had at least got some way towards his 'hobby horsery'.

Mrs Boulton was unwell during the early part of 1783. Mary Fothergill, on a visit, thought her 'very indifferent' and was concerned. Fothergill's widow Elizabeth suggested a change of air might do her good and invited her to Astley.[75] But she stayed put at Soho House. Nobody was too worried. She had been unwell before, and spring was on the way and would surely put her back on her feet. Boulton launched into a scheme to fill the gardens at Soho with colour for her. In April 1783, over 300 herbaceous plants and 18 varieties of pinks and carnations were delivered, costing £3 1s. 3d.

That hot summer, notwithstanding weird weather precipitated by the giant volcanic explosion in Iceland, the beds and borders at Soho House burst forth in a riot of colour with iris, thalictrum, doronicum, phlox, polygonum, aconitum, spiraea, valerian, ranunculus, betany, anthemis, peony, verbascum, artemisia, veronica, solidago, lychnis, 'delphinium Americanum', aquilegia, anchusa, oenothera, hellebore, potentilla, sedum, trollius, epilobium, centaurea, viola, saponaria, achillea, rudbeckia, coreopsis, pulmonaria, geum, aster, saxifrage, *gentiana acaulis*, hemerocallis, salvia, primula, physalis, stachys, allysum, caltha, campanula, fritillary, hyacinth, crocus, scilla, euphorbia and scabious.[76]

Planting them all must have kept the gardeners busy for ages.

5

'An amiable female character'

In the midst of all this summer glory, Mrs Boulton was found face-down in the water in a little pool in the grounds at Soho House. She was dead.

The day it happened Boulton had been to Coventry for the day, and when he returned home in the evening a distraught Anne and Matt rushed across the garden and flung themselves on him sobbing.

Because of the circumstances in which 50-year-old Mrs Boulton had been found, there was gossip in the neighbourhood that she had committed suicide, but one of the Boulton family's oldest friends, Samuel Garbett, moved quickly to dispel the rumour. He attended the inquest and wrote on 13 July to another old friend, Mrs Barker of Lichfield, describing symptoms which are consistent with Mrs Boulton having had some kind of stroke, as a result of which she probably fell into the water.[1] In his letter to Mrs Barker Samuel Garbett wrote:

> As there hath been different stories propagated about Mrs Boulton's Death I know it will be agreeable to you to be assured by me that there is the utmost Reason to believe her Death was accidental. The Coroner's Inquest have upon minute Examination been unanimous of that opinion.
>
> It appears she was preparing with great satisfaction for a journey with her Husband & Children to Buxton, that she had often complained of a Giddiness in her head, was very liable to fall in Consequence of that & weak Ankles & high Heel shoes. She had Fits sometimes, & for a year last paralytic symptoms that were alarming, & so apprehensive was she of water that she could not think of bathing at Buxton.
>
> The Morning of her Death (Friday) she was walking by the Water side, when a woman passed by for Beer for Haymakers. The woman apologized for coming that way, & Mrs Boulton answered it was very well, it was the nearest. In about ten minutes the Woman returned & found her upon her Face on the Water in a shallow Part of it. She was immediately got out & when Trials were made for her Recovery there was such Appearances as plainly proved that water was not the occasion of her Death ... [Mr Boulton] is extremely affected indeed, but it is some comfort to him that there is not the smallest Circumstances to shew that Mrs Boulton had any Intention of destroying herself. I attended when the Inquisition was taken, I know many of the Particulars here related to be true, & I believe every one to be strictly so ...[2]

James Watt gave a similar account to the chocolate maker Joseph Fry, explaining that Mrs Boulton had, it was supposed, been seized with an apoplectic fit as she was walking by herself in the Garden near the edge of the pond into which she fell, at a place where it was not much above knee deep, and in about 10 minutes after she had been seen there by a servant, was found dead. Every means that could be devised was used for her recovery, but in vain, from which and some previous symptoms the doctors supposed an apoplexy, not drowning, to have caused her death.[3]

A dark shadow fell over Boulton and the two children, Anne now fifteen, and Matt, thirteen. Mrs Fothergill, who had been hoping for a visit from Mrs Boulton, wrote to Boulton as soon as she heard of the 'melancholy event that hath deprived you of a Fond and Affectionate Wife and [your children] of a tender Indulgent Mother. She poore woman I make no doubt is Happy & freed from the Distresses of this Troublesome World'.[4] Boulton replied to Mrs Fothergill on 2 August 1783, giving his own account of the events of that day:

> I set out early on the Fatal Fryday morn … to Councillor Whealers beyond Coventry, who gave me a very satisfactory opinion, I thought & talked of you & wished much to have come to Astley but my heart was at home when I arived early in the evening & was met in the garden by my distressed Children with the fatal news.
> I cannot say more on that subject. The scene is not discribable by pen or tongue neither do I wish to revive such poignant sensations which you have too recently felt & which none can conceive but such as like me have lost a most sincere & affectionate wife after liveing together upward of 23 years and I can say with truth & with satisfaction that our Mutual Love affection & friendship increased with our years the which she took more pains & opportunities latterly to express than even in the Meridian of our youth …[5]

Joining her mother Dorothy, sister Mary and brother Luke Robinson, Mrs Boulton was buried at St Giles' Church, Whittington, near Lichfield, on 9 June.[6] Unlike the earlier funerals, the bill for this funeral does not seem to have been saved. If many of the Boultons' friends wrote letters of condolence following Mrs Boulton's death, their letters have not been preserved, either, nor are there any surviving letters between Boulton and his daughter for almost a year, and only one or two between him and young Matt, who was still at school in Twickenham. Boulton threw himself into work, and not long after his wife's death he went to Ireland, which James Watt thought would help to lift him out of his melancholy as well as dealing with some necessary Irish business.[7] Kindly as ever, William and Charlotte Matthews stepped into the breach, taking charge of Anne and Matt while he was away. Charlotte wrote to him,

> This will be accompanied by two others, which almost makes it unnecessary for me to acquaint you that we arriv'd safe about twelve to-day, both Miss Boulton and Matt were as chearfull or more so than we cou'd expect, and be assur'd nothing on our part shall be wanting with regard to them. I therefore hope you will make yourself perfectly easy on that head, and that you will regain your good spirits – the quantity of business you will be engag'd in will, I trust, effect it …
> I trust you will let us hear from you upon your arrival at Dublin[8]

Boulton's Irish trip is recorded in a notebook. Samuel Garbett's son went with him for company. For a man deep in mourning, Boulton's account of the Snowdonia landscape and the costume of the women at a fair on Anglesey is surprisingly observant and engaged. At the inn in Holyhead he even jotted down a multi-lingual verse he found there which took his fancy:

> *In questa Casa troverete*
> *Tout ce que l'on peut souhaiter*
> *Vinum Panem Pisces Carnes*
> *Coaches Horses Chaises Harness*[9]

Once across the Irish Sea, he wrote with admiration of the beauties of the Irish countryside and of the many fine houses and gardens he saw or visited, during what was essentially a sales trip. From Ireland he went on to Scotland before returning home, and the earliest of Matt's letters to survive reached him in Falkirk, where he was visiting the Carron company. Matt wrote from school:

> My Dear Papa ... Mr Vere call'd on me Saturday and took me to [...] but I returnd on Sunday morning. He said that my sister had been at Mrs Matthews, that she had just returned to Mrs Moores [and] that she was very well. Miss Stretch was married on Monday ... when we all had a holiday. Tomorrow I intend writing to my sister ... I remain My Dear Papa your dutiful Son, Matthew R. Boulton.[10]

In odd juxtaposition with such newsy personal letters are studiously formal ones, probably taken at dictation or copied from a blackboard by the class, written in careful copperplate, for example in October 1783:

> Hon'd Sir,
> As usual, at the beginning of the Month, I present you with a Specimen of my writing and embrace the opportunity of informing you that I am in perfect Health and I hope making such improvements in my learning as will meet your approbation and do credit to the Care and attention of my Masters.
> Mr and the Miss Stretches present their respectful Compliments.
> I am
> Hon'd Sir
> Your dutiful Son
> Matthew Boulton.[11]

Boulton returned to Soho at the beginning of December 1783, noting that he had covered a total of 1,054 miles. He did not settle for long. By 18 December he was on his way to London again and stopped in Oxford, where he noted that 'a balloon was turned up ... in the park. The ladies wore balloon hats and the ballad singers sing balloons about the streets'.[12]

Before returning to Birmingham he probably collected Anne from school. She brought home with her Mrs Moore's bill for the half-year, amounting to £46 0s. 9d. Among the usual lengths of ribbon, sewing silk, a length of 'Boue de Paris sattin', drawing materials, exercise books, wash-balls and so on were packs of 'historical cards' at 2s. and 'cards of mythology', a further 2s. Arnold's *First Book of Instructions* cost 10s. 6d. Anne had had a tooth out (10s. 6d.) and was still having tuition in writing, dancing, drawing and music. In addition to music lessons there was a charge of 10s. 6d. for 'tuning the harpsichord for six months', and a copy of an overture at 6d.[13]

With the New Year of 1784 Boulton's spirits began to pick up (perhaps fortified by the 'two gallons of fine cogniac Brandy' supplied on 6 January by Richard Conquest, which cost him £1 10s. 0d.[14]). He also paid a tailor's bill of £46 13s. 10¾d. from Davenport & Farrant in Tavistock Street, his conscience perhaps stung by the note on it which read, 'To you as a Merchant there wants no apology for sending the enclos'd, some part of it is standing since 1781, our Creditors give us no such Indulgence.'[15]

By the summer, exactly a year after her mother's death, Anne was looking forward eagerly to travelling to Cornwall with her father in the approaching holiday when she went down with the 'Chincough' (whooping cough) at school in Portman Square. She was seen there by Sir Richard Jebb. Sir Richard must have thought she would be better off at home, although William and Charlotte Matthews were keeping a friendly eye on her. The fact that there was to be a resident physician at Soho House for the summer probably influenced the decision to return Anne to Birmingham immediately.

The physician was Dr William Withering (Plate 14), one of Boulton's Lunar Society friends. Boulton had offered Dr Withering and his wife Helena and their children the use of Soho House while their own house, Edgbaston Hall, was being re-painted. They should have had Soho House to themselves, for the original plan had been for Anne, Matt, and Nancy Mynd to spend at least part of the summer holidays in Cornwall, but Anne's illness threw the plans into disarray. Dr Withering was willing to keep a careful watch over the patient at Soho as she recovered, so Boulton set off glumly alone for Cornwall. When he got there he found he could not face Cosgarne, where he had last stayed with his wife. Instead he took himself off to stay with Boulton & Watt's Cornish agent Thomas Wilson and his wife at Chacewater, between Redruth and Truro. It was not exactly peaceful there. On 28 June he was woken at 3a.m. by the sounds of Mrs Wilson giving birth to their sixth son.[16]

He had a look round Cosgarne and made a note of one or two jobs which needed to be done. More than once he wrote to Anne, reminding her that in the matter of her journey to Cornwall, 'reason should preside over inclination'[17] and adding 'I know by my self that inclination & judgment often point to opposite poles'.[18] Inclination was stronger. Determined that she should not be prevented from going to Cornwall at the earliest possible moment, Anne wrote to him that she was much better. Samuel Garbett seconded her wish, writing to Boulton that all three young people were keen to come.[19] Matt, he said, was only being held back by the fact that his trunk had not yet arrived from Twickenham and so he had only two shirts; as soon as four new ones were finished on Friday the boy was absolutely determined to set out alone for Bath.

Under this pressure from his children and friends, Boulton sent Anne suggestions of friends they could call on *en route* to break the journey (once the doctor approved), adding, 'I must apprise you that it is very difficult to pack up good Clothes to travil such a long Journey without their being wore through & you must bring some genteel Clothes here & not some to disgrace me.'[20] Withering meanwhile wrote to reassure Boulton that Anne was well on the mend; to prove it, he added that she appeared to have an aptitude for botany, in which he had been instructing her. Boulton hoped Anne would 'prosecute the study or rather amusement when ever opportunity permits',[21] and encouraged her to qualify herself to teach him botany on his return, '& then we will have a Botanical Garden'.[22]

Dr and Mrs Withering got on well with their two young charges. The Doctor described Anne as 'an amiable female character. I have not often met with one so perfectly feminine, there is so much shyness mixed in her disposition that it is not easy to know her, but I perceive a great deal of good sense enlivened by a vein of humour, and all the good nature natural to her age and sex.'[23] Anne, he said, was now well enough for the journey. Matt he found 'perfectly unaffected; he has an excellent disposition; strong solid sense, and does not want industry.'[24] Boulton was overjoyed, writing to his friend, 'Esculapeus himself could not have wrote a prescription more cheering to my spirits than yours of ye 25th Ultmo. Your account of my daughters health is a balmy cordial to me; and your too partial description of my Son is most palitable.'[25]

A day or two later, Anne received precise instructions for the journey. Papa had mapped it out to the last detail:

I am sure our Chaise is too much unwheeld for such a Journey and as there are 4 of you [Anne, Matt, Nancy Mynd and a maid], you may take the light Coach from the Castle Inn, drink Tea at Bromsgrove, go to bed early at Worcester, order the Maid not to call you before 6 oClock & to have a dish of tea ready pourd out with much Milk & this is to prevent you from being Sick as you will travil 3 or 4 hours before breakfast.

When you get to Bath go to bed early & next Morng dress yourself clean & neat & go & spend the day with Miss Capper who is much improved in Singing & Playing. You may spend the whole of that day in seeing Bath & our friend Mr Green, you may take the whole Coach either for the 2nd or 3rd Day to go to Exeter but as that Coach sets out between 3 & 4 oClock in the morning I wish you to go as far as Wells the preceding evening & see the Cathederal. Your self, Brother & Miss Mynd may go in a Chaise & the maid may come in ye Coach in the Morng & then all 4 proceed in the Coach to Exeter where I or somebody perhaps will meet you if I know time enough.

Any smart thing you may want you can buy at Bath or Exeter ... As there will be 3 of you & one Maid you may give each Coach Man 3 shillings & each Chambermaid 2/- & to the Man that asks you for something for putting on Luggage 6 pence. You must order what you like for Supper & one pint of Wine, you must take a purse & put 30£ or Guineas into it & let Matt or Miss Mynd keep an exact acct of all you pay & see each night that your acct ballances right. I have one Cornish Maid a Horse & a Cow besides which I have a groom, a footman, a Secretary, a Cook, a Gardiner, a Valet de Chamber & a Book Keeper all comprised in little Benjamin who is a quiet good Servant ... Whether you come or not come I insist upon Matt coming & I leave you, not to your own inclinations, but to your own judgment.

My love to Matt & Miss Mynd & my prayers for all travillers by Land & by Water.[26]

Impatiently, Anne began to sort out what to take, on what would be the longest journey she had yet made. But before they could set out, she caught a cold. It brought a return of the violent cough. To her dismay Dr Withering said she was not well enough to travel. Matt, who refused to wait for his sister any longer, went to Cornwall on his own. Boulton wrote to Anne, 'He rides out with me to the Mines & I expect he will become a Miner & Fossilist before he returns, he hath already picked up a little collection of Cornish productions.'[27] Anne wept with frustration. Reason was no substitute for inclination, nor botany lessons for a trip to Cornwall. As soon as she had recovered from her relapse she would brook no more restraint. She and Nancy Mynd and the maid set out for Cornwall, and were there by the end of the month.

Though Boulton evidently regarded botany as no more than an amusement (for young ladies, at least), Dr Withering was a serious, if cautious, botanist. While he and his wife stayed at Soho House he worked on his book *An Account of the Foxglove and some of its Medical Uses*, which was published in 1785 and established digitalis as an effective treatment for dropsy. He was also engaged in a long-term project of British plant classification. Withering's system differed significantly from the one devised earlier by Carl Linnaeus, in that Withering drew a decorous veil over plant sexuality. This made his approach to botany eminently more 'suitable' for the ladies, for whom Linnaean botany was held to be not strictly proper. (Erasmus Darwin, whose poems celebrated plant sexuality, was withering about Withering.)

Dr Withering liked teaching ladies; it probably flattered his ego to do so, though he reacted with puzzlement when he came across one who did not fit the conventional mould. The Quaker philosopher Mary Knowles, who may have met him when she once visited Soho, wrote to him:

> Scholars will more & more discover to the confusion of their pride, that *genius* is shower'd down on *heads*, as seemeth Heaven good, whether drest in caps of gauze or velvet – in large grey wigs or small silk bonnets. Here I blush to observe that my Antithesis has accidentally brought forward too picturesquely, the poor small head thus sedulously pleading, not for itself but for its injur'd Sisterhood.[28]

This was in response to what Withering had thought were some complimentary remarks about Mrs Knowles which he had made in a letter to a mutual friend; she took them to be patronising, and with a nice line in sarcasm, which may well have been entirely lost on the Doctor, she wrote that, pleased as she was to be esteemed by Dr Withering,

> to be *praised* by him, is *too* great a tryal for my humility. Yet what meaneth he by his ingeniously supposed feminine characteristic? To wit, 'There is however a vivacity & a *distinctness* in the operations of her imagination that mark her for a female.' Describe this distinctness, give me an illustration, that I may try to trace the symptom of its true cause, for much do I ween that it is deduceable to the circumstances of situation, early habits & all the etceteras that are pendant on our universal oppression ...[29]

Later in 1784, after the Witherings had left Soho and moved back to their own house, Dr Withering embarked on another female education project, effectively a three-year correspondence course for Catherine Wright, wife of Sir James Wright, the former British Minister in Venice. Sir James had bought a box of second-hand books at an auction, for the sake of one particular book. He gave Catherine the rest to dispose of, and to her great delight she found herself reading chemistry, classics, and philosophy. Eager to understand it all better, she wrote asking for

Withering's help, to which he consented. 'That the Generalty of Men have Agreed that Women ought to be kept in perpetual Ignorance & the most profound Darkness, respecting every part of Literature beyond a Book of Cookery, is to be accounted for, & not greatly to be wonderd at,' she wrote to him, thanking him for agreeing 'to Enlighten the Mind of a Female'.[30] Catherine was to send essays and notes which he would mark and return. Apologising profusely for her 'presumption' in having interests not appropriate to her sex, Catherine wailed, 'a married woman cannot always act just as she pleases ... just now I wish to sit alone & thus converse with you but am obliged ... to attend on a set of unentertaining beings who will do me the Honor of a Visit.'[31] As her understanding of chemistry grew, so did her confidence and she began to spread her wings into such arcane subjects as animal magnetism (a fashionable new fad), and to tease Withering gently. She had met 'a philosopher of some note', she told him, who had assured her there was no such thing as either matter or spirit. Besides feeling tempted to stick a pin in the man to test the theory, she added wickedly, 'If I was to tell you the effects I have produced or *fancy* I have produced (for possibly I do not exist) you would say, God help her poor weak mind...'[32] Withering solemnly annotated this letter, 'curious comments'. He was much more comfortable with the amiable young Miss Boulton; he knew where he was with Anne and botany.

With Anne, Matt and their father away in Cornwall it must have been strangely quiet at Soho. James Watt was also away, in London, but he was not out of touch. Annie, who before her marriage had been accustomed to helping her father in his bleaching business, acting as a sort of laboratory assistant in his chemical experiments, kept her husband abreast of business affairs at home. She dealt with some of the incoming post, passing on any necessary information, and recorded and passed on to the bankers payments received, such as the regular sums of £10 3s. 6d. coming in from sales of copying machines.[33] It is probably fair to say that she generally took a closer interest in the business than Mrs Boulton had done. It is hard to imagine Mrs Watt playing blind man's buff. In his letters to his wife Watt often included a certain amount of technical detail and diagrams, so he plainly shared his ideas with her. She complained frequently that Boulton was getting more than his fair share of the proceeds of Watt's genius, urging in one letter, 'I give you joy of Mr Goodison's Engine I hope the Rotative ones will turn out to good account. I think in justice you ought to have at least half the profits that arise from them, they certainly were no part of your original agreement with Mr B.'[34]

After the summer in Cornwall, Anne and Matt went back to Soho House and were at home for Christmas 1784, when they watched their father launch and detonate a large home-made balloon before a cheering crowd (an experiment intended – unsuccessfully – to determine whether the rumble of thunder was produced by one large explosion and its echoes, or a succession of smaller explosions, and described by James Watt in a letter to Dr James Lind headed 'The history of Mr Boulton's explosive balloon'[35]). After the holiday Matt, now aged 15, said goodbye to his sister and his father and set off from Soho House for Suffolk and a new school. He was to be one of the 'young gentlemen' instructed by the Revd. Samuel Parlby, curator of Stoke-by-Nayland, a pretty riverside village near Colchester.

Matt wrote his first letter home from Stoke-by-Nayland on 15 February. Having missed the coach connection to Colchester, he had stopped over in London,

FIG. 12 *Frontispiece from* Descriptions des expériences de la Machine Aérostatique de MM. de Montgolfier, *by Faujas de St Fond, who visited Soho in 1784. This is Matthew Boulton's own copy. (Birmingham Museum & Art Gallery)*

where John Rennie had shown him over the Albion Mill.[36] Built near Blackfriars Bridge in 1784, its two Boulton & Watt steam engines drove 20 pairs of mill-stones, making it the largest flour mill in the world until it was burned down in 1791. Boulton was proud of the Albion Mill, writing to Anne when it opened, 'if the Miller's daughter hath half the admirers which the Mill hath she will have great choice of husbands'.[37] By March Matt had settled in at Rev. Parlby's fairly new and spacious house facing the green near Stoke-by-Nayland parish church (Plate 21), where the boys construed Latin every day except Friday, 'which is the day appointed for Arithmiteck & Geography'.[38]

The same year that Matt Boulton went to Stoke-by-Nayland, James Watt junior, who was a year older, was sent to Bersham, near Wrexham in North Wales, to learn machine drawing and other subjects suitable to a future engineer with the Wilkinson family of iron found-ers. But James had barely settled in at Bersham when his father decided to take advantage of a contact offered by Aimé Argand to place the boy in Switzerland (Argand was the Swiss inventor of the Argand lamp, a new and more efficient type of oil lamp which was being produced at Soho). Watt sent James to Geneva, where he lodged with the de Lucs, who were friends of the Boultons and Watts. He stayed there for some months, studying under de Luc, Pictet and de Saussure, and taking fencing lessons with Joseph Priestley junior, the son of another Lunar Society member, Dr Joseph Priestley, who had arrived in Birmingham in 1780 to take up the post of Minister at the New Meeting chapel. After a spell in Geneva, James went on to Eisenach in Germany, and later to Freiburg, where he stayed until 1788. Matt had also been expecting to be sent abroad and was probably envious of James, for he wrote to him in Geneva that he would have liked to have gone to Switzerland with him, but his father appeared to have given up the idea, and he was to learn Latin in Suffolk for a year or two.[39]

James and his father kept up a regular correspondence while he was abroad, but Watt senior's letters make depressing reading now, as they must have done for his son. He criticised the boy constantly: his expenditure, his supposed lack of moral fibre, his use of English, his use of French, his handwriting, even his extravagant use of stationery by writing in too large a hand. It seems hardly surprising that James wrote his letters in large writing; he must have despaired of finding enough to say that would please his father to fill a sheet. Annie Watt may have fuelled some of her husband's critical comments, for she wrote to him,

> I am glad you have wrote James a trim[m]ing letter he deserves indeed to be severly reprimanded, you must either be his Master or he will be yours. The Arrogance Conceit and Insolence of his disposition I am much better acquainted with than you are from many Instances that never came within your knowledge, while he is under controul nobody does behave better but the moment the reins are let go his good conduct is forgot.[40]

Astonishingly, Annie concluded this diatribe against her 16-year-old stepson with a plea to her husband to ensure that Gregory and Jessie were left well provided for in his will and independent of their stepbrother after their parents' death. Almost as an afterthought she added that Mr Argand did not think James's expenses in Geneva were unduly high, as he was learning mathematics which was an expensive branch of education there. And Miss de Luc had told her that young Priestley's accommodation in Geneva was cheaper than Jimmy's because Priestley did not have a room to himself, and the room in which he slept, in a concealed bed, was used as a sitting room during the day, so he had to be very tidy. For once Annie overstepped the mark, for her next letter contained an apology to her husband, who had evidently been angered by her comments about Jimmy – but the stream of criticism continued unabated, nevertheless.

Anne Boulton did not return to Mrs Moore's school in Portman Square after the summer of 1784, but whereas her brother and James Watt junior found their horizons broadening and the world beckoning, Anne's own were becoming more circumscribed. She was certainly at home in Birmingham in early 1785, when she was about seventeen years old, and perhaps bored and tired of being bossed about by Nancy Mynd and treated insolently by some of the servants, for that March James Watt wrote to William Matthews that he had arrived at Soho House (Boulton being in London) to find the house in a ferment because Miss Boulton had just left for the capital in the company of Mr Argand. Miss Boulton had given the household no reason for her sudden departure and speculation was rife. In a spirit of *Honi soit qui mal y pense* Watt wrote, 'As they did not know the real cause of her being called away, they are in a sad panic supposing no doubt that somebody had informed him of their conduct, and in order to leave them under that impression I have not gone near them ...'[41] To Boulton, Watt wrote,

> I sent immediately on my coming home for Argand, but was informed that he was just set out with Miss B. and as ... the family at Soho were in great consternation at Miss B's sudden departure, and you had given me no message to any of them, I thought it best to leave them to the suggestions of their own minds as the proper punishment for their impudence. I have been asked if I knew the cause why she was called to London, but answered in the negative, only said that I saw no reason for the question as it was natural you should wish her to be with you ...[42]

William Matthews reported back that Miss Boulton was in high spirits, in London with her father.[43]

In May 1785 Grandmama Boulton died, at the age of ninety-five. Christiana, Boulton's mother, had outlived her husband, Matthew Boulton senior, by 24 years.

Ever since her son had moved her out of Soho House to make way for John Fothergill in 1762, she had been living either in the old family home at Snow Hill, or elsewhere in Birmingham town centre. Now, she was laid to rest at St Philip's Church[44] in the town, miles from her husband who slumbered on in St Chad's churchyard at Stowe, Lichfield. Christiana does not appear in the records often – Boulton sometimes asked his wife to visit her when he was away from home, or commented that he had called in to see her, but when, later, Sir Joseph Banks was obliged to postpone a visit to Soho House owing to the death of his own 85-year-old mother from a stroke, Boulton wrote consolingly to him:

> I know what your feelings would be (by my own on a similar occasion) upon the loss of an Excellent Mother: But when one reflects upon the Measure of her Days being full, & that she departed without Pain, one should be resigned: & you are a much more exalted Philosopher than myself.[45]

With her father away so much, and Matt at school in Stoke-by-Nayland, Anne was thrown largely onto her own resources and passed much of her time at Soho House playing the harpsichord. In June 1785 her father was rather sorry he had not thought of taking her to London with him for the annual commemoration of Handel, a performance of *Messiah* at Westminster Abbey. 'I scarcely know which was the grandest the Sounds or the Scene', he wrote. 'In the grand Hallaluja my Soul almost ascended from my Body.'[46]

An enjoyment of music was something Anne and her father shared. She had had music lessons from childhood, and bills for music, lessons and instruments indicate that this became a lifelong interest. There is no evidence that Boulton had ever learned to play any instrument himself, but he certainly had a keen appreciation of music and no shortage of opportunity to indulge it, for Birmingham was a musically active town, with an Oratorio Society and a Musical and Amicable Society, founded in 1762.[47] He had subscribed to the publication of sets of songs by John Pixell,[48] and was also a subscriber to and a member of the original Birmingham General Hospital committee which organised major music festivals as fund-raisers for the new hospital project, the earliest of them under the direction of the composer and Coventry Cathedral choirmaster, Capel Bond.[49]

In fact, music formed the one underlying consistent theme in Anne Boulton's education; her schooling had been anything but consistent. She had spent about a year at Mrs Terry's at Cambden House, about eighteen months at Mrs Wilkes's at Richmond, and a further two years with Mrs Moore in Portman Square. All of these periods had been interrupted by illness of various kinds, and by 1785 her education, apart from in music, was apparently regarded as finished. But then in July 1785, just before Matt came home from Stoke-by-Nayland for the holidays, Anne went off to Leicester for some months, to Mrs Linwood's school. Hannah Linwood and her daughter Mary ran the establishment, which specialised in teaching embroidery. This was one of the most desirable of feminine accomplishments – or, as Dr Gregory would have it, 'The intention of your being taught needle-work, knitting, and such like, is not on account of the intrinsic value of all you can do with your hands, which is trifling, but … to enable you to fill up, in a tolerably agreeable way, some of the many solitary hours you must necessarily pass at home …'.[50]

FIG. 13 *'View of the Orchestra and Performers in Westminster Abbey, during the Commemoration of Handel',* *by J. Collyer after E.F. Burney, 1785. Matthew Boulton attended this performance and wrote to Anne about it.* *(Private collection, courtesy of Handel House Trust)*

Mary Linwood (Plate 29), who came from a Birmingham silversmithing family, was famed for her embroidered pictures or 'needle paintings', said to be almost indistinguishable from oil paintings, from which they were often copied. The pictures were worked on fine linen in long and short stitches in specially dyed wools. By the time Anne Boulton went to her to learn embroidery techniques, Miss Linwood was well-established in Leicester. She had already exhibited embroidered pictures in London at the Society of Artists. Mary's pictures included a full size (six feet high) copy of Gainsborough's *A Woodman in a Storm*, and a copy of John Russell's *A Goldfinch Starved to Death in a Cage.*[51] Another needle-artist was Mary Knowles, the woman who had rebuked William Withering for his condescension towards women. Invited by Queen Charlotte to copy Zoffany's portrait of George III in needlework, she accepted the challenge, delivered the picture and followed it up with an embroidered self-portrait showing herself at work on the Royal portrait.

Boulton approved of Anne going to Leicester; he also rather fancied Miss Linwood. He wrote to Anne from Cornwall:

> I am happy to learn that you have accompanied Miss Linwood to Leicester, which I hope will prove so agreeable to you & all parties, as to prevent you from returning so soon as you talk of. I hope you will stay till you have caught a little

of that Lady's fire, even if it is but a little of those sparks which dart from her finger ends. A fire that revivifies dead Game, and makes e'en Lear live again. I beg you will present my kind Compliments & best wishes to Mrs & Miss Linwood & say everything for me that you think I should say to either if present, and that I feel the truth of the old proverb *Love me love my puppies & kittens.* I hope I shall see at my return a flower, a silkworm or even a humble strawberry growing from the point of your needle or pencil. You know what will please me, & I know you do not want disposition to do it, but you some times want Courage ...[52]

He went on to tell Anne about a great gathering of Quakers near Truro, a 'fete a la tremblant' as he put it, 'or rather what the junior Quakers consider it, Le Fete d'Amour as there is much Brotherly love going forward at these meetings & many matches are made'.[53] On 17 August, he wrote to her again. Acknowledging a letter in which she had told him she was 'going to paint a pretty border', he declared, 'I am more delighted to see your person decorated with ornaments of your own fabrication & fancy than I should be in seeing you loaded with all the diamonds & pearls of the Indias.'[54] He was still keen that she should derive the maximum benefit from her stay at Leicester: 'I hope you keep a post Chaise in your Pocket & that you use it as often as you are inclined to breath ye Country air. Pray is there any relics of Richard the 3rd at Leicester or have you been in Bosworth Field? Read the story of that Battle & then go and contemplate it upon the Spot.' When she was ready to return to Birmingham, he continued, she was to ask Mrs Scale or Miss Mynd to fetch her, 'for I do not like for you to go in the Stage Coach unless some very particular friend happened to be going in it, for there is often Company in these Coaches that is very improper for you ... I think there is less danger in going out whilst Sol is the illuminating power, than when Luna prevails, for the nights are now become cold'. He added a characteristically complimentary note for Miss Linwood's benefit:

> I hinted to you in my last that I wish you not to be in a hurry in leaving Leicester unless it be to return to it again speedily, for it is impossable that you can keep company with Miss Linwood without improving your tast, & your hand ... Pray present my Compliments to that Lady & tell her I hope she will give me leave to admire her at the humble distance of 300 Miles.[55]

Anne had evidently met one of the Dyotts at Leicester for her father added, 'You mention Mr Dyotts living at Leicester. I know not if you know that he is a relation of ours, but I must turn your Eyes further back than you can see to shew you the degree of Affinity. My Grandmother was a Dyott (viz my Fathers Mother) & was born at Litchfield.' (*See* Appendix)

Since his last letter a melancholy event had befallen the Quakers at Truro, which he related in appropriate style:

> Thou mayst remember I told thee in my last that there was to be a great meeting of Quakers at Truro, and a great meeting it was ... I did not go to the meeting till third Day, when I heard our friend Catherine Phillips preach with great energy & good sence for one hour & a half ...[56]

When the meeting was over, the assembly had repaired to an inn for dinner, and as prudence & oecconomy are distinguishing Characteristicks of their Society they had previously agreed to pay 1s/6d for their dinners & small beer, with 1d each for the waiter. My worthy cheerfull good & sensible friend Phillips (whom you know was always a great favourite of mine) asked me if I wishd to dine with the Quakers & he would introduce me. I accepted his invitation & dined at a Table containing upwards of 70 & I the only person who was not of that Society. I considered my self particularly favourd & obliged. We had a good dinner & I must say I never dined with more pleasure or satisfaction in my life. I sat next to my old friend, we joined our 7d apiece for a pint of wine & being affected with the spirit of Temperance we had not only enough for our selves but we spared a Glass for friend Catherine & for 2 or 3 other holy Sisters. We then paid our 18d for our dinner & gave 1d to the Waiter & then departed in peace.[57]

Two days later, Friend Phillips, Catherine's husband, was dead. It fell to Boulton to break the news to their son, 'which I did in the course of a little lonely walk … The particulars I cannot discribe without giveing my self & you too much pain. Light sorrows speak, great griefs are dumb,' he wrote. The funeral took place in the Friends' Meeting House at Come-to-Good, near Truro. 'It is at the Bottom of Mr Daggs Garden, you once saw it as we rode from Trelissick,' he reminded Anne.[58] (Plate 22)

When Matt left Soho for Stoke-by-Nayland at the end of August, he took with him an Argand lamp as a gift for the Parlbys, who, he reported, were very pleased with it. Rev. Parlby wrote to thank Boulton for it: 'We have lighted it several Evenings & found it succeed most admirably and indeed think ourselves much indebted to you for this very ornamental addition to our table furniture.'[59] Matt, however, told his father that, though the Parlbys' visitors admired the lamp, most of them thought it was too bright, adding, 'I cannot convince them that by putting on the shade that will be remedied'.[60] At 15 he was growing fast, and wrote to Nancy Mynd, who was now to all intents and purposes in charge at Soho House, to ask 'if any [new] cloaths were made for me at home as the Cloaths which I have here are worn out & she sent me some of my old Cloaths as she thought I had better not have another suit of mourning but I thought I better ask you whether you approved of that before I got them made …'[61]

As far as Matt himself was concerned, Rev. Parlby found him 'very obliging & his attention to business as great as you can wish. I shall hope to qualify him so far in the Latin Tongue by Xstmas that he may be enabled to read a Latin poet or Historian with tolerable fluency …' Parlby was concentrating on Matt's languages because, as he said, it would be absurd for him to attempt to teach the boy any philosophical subjects, 'as the advantages he may reap in that way from his Friends at home both in Theory & Practice are so infinitely superior to any I could pretend to hold out to him.'[62]

By October 1785 Boulton, still in Cornwall, was looking forward to coming home for Christmas. He had given up the house at Cosgarne and taken a house next to the Wilsons, which was more convenient, and thought he might extend it next summer – 'but what are Cornish paradices without my Children? I cannot live alone'. He was pleased, if a little cautious, to learn that Anne was well: 'I hear from Birmingham that Rosey health blooms in your Countenance & that you are grown quite handsome, nay some say beautyfull but that is going a step too far.' Anne had evidently written to him of attending a music meeting and some horse-races; he commented that he had never bet on or kept 'running horses', but was happy that she should have the experience of going to a race meeting. But the 'music meeting' was probably more to his taste:

> Persons who have musical feelings are never satiated with the pleasures that result from fine Harmony & beautyfull Melody but as I have lately heard in Westminster Abby a Musical performance that transcends even the imagination of a Handel I am therefore content untill next year when I hope to have the additional pleasure of accompanying my dear Daughter to the commemoration of that great Man.[63]

Annie Watt was sceptical about Boulton's long absence from home; indeed, she grew so irritated that she even dreamt about him. She told her husband, 'I wonder what Mr B is doing drawlling in Cornwall all this time, I dreamt last night that you and I went to search for him and found him very gaily drest standing with his back against the wall of a very fine apartment flourishing and talking a way to a parcel of white wiged [wigged] heroes somewhat like our Salt market Elders were formerly. I was so provoked at him for triffling of his time that I awoke.'[64] She thought he was not to be trusted with money: 'If he had millions he would find ways to spend it.'

Before Anne left Leicester her father issued a playful instruction to her to invite Mrs and Miss Linwood to spend Christmas with them at Soho:

> I desire you will contrive to render Soho as chearfull as possable at Christmas by bedecking it with the ever sweet flowering Linwoodbines … You say Miss L sends her double Love, tell her that I will accept it single, & pray present my single, singular, love to that Lady singly, hopeing she & Mamma will accept of your invitation to spend their Xmas at Soho, but if they insist upon one from me I will write them one upon as many Sheets of Paper as they please.'[65]

Mary Linwood herself responded to the invitation, writing to Boulton that she and her mother had tried unsuccessfully to persuade his 'amiable daughter' to stay with them longer, but 'if I had any fascinating spell, I am sorry to confess – "my charm dissolves apace" – for next week is absolutely fix'd for her return … I hope you will soon be at Soho, for I am certain you will have great pleasure in meeting with the charming spirits and blooming health she leaves us with…' She thanked him for the invitation, adding 'tis at present uncertain where I spend my X'tmas, but I shall whenever I've opportunity be happy in waiting upon Miss B.'[66]

Boulton occupied part of the Linwoodless Christmas holiday writing a critical letter to Rev. Parlby about Matt's progress, and giving notice of his intention to send the boy abroad later in the year. Matt took the letter with him when he went back to school, and on St Valentine's Day 1786 the Reverend sat down to compose a lengthy reply, in defence both of Matt and of his teaching methods. Boulton seems to have been trying to tell the schoolmaster how to do his job, advising him to follow the precepts of education laid down by Locke. Politely but firmly, and 'with the utmost deference to the judgment of so wonderful a man', the teacher addressed Boulton's complaints and countered what was evidently his one-size-fits-all recipe for boys' education.

For a start, there was the matter of Matt's pronunciation, not just in Latin but in English. Bad habits acquired early were hard to remedy, but 'I seldom fail to correct him whenever he omits the aspirate, his most inveterate provinciality in conversation'.[67] Then, Boulton seemed to have a poor opinion of Matt's application, but Parlby thought he was perhaps not being quite fair in judging the boy by his own exceptional character. Parlby had watched Matt tackling, with patience and attention, boringly repetitive Latin exercises which would try any boy of his age. He feared that by criticising him too much and pushing him too hard it would be all too easy to dampen Matt's spirits and extinguish his educational progress for good. He thought Matt's grasp of Latin, which was the foundation he lacked for his better use of English, was not yet firm enough for him to embark upon Greek, though some knowledge of the latter language would undoubtedly be useful to anyone likely to delve much into natural philosophy. Parlby took the opportunity to add his account for the period March-December 1785 to the foot of the letter:

	£	s	d
Turner's Exercises		1	6
3 bl^k books at 1/3		3	9
Pens		2	6
Writing paper		2	0
Play at Colchester		3	0
Gradus		2	0
Chisnall (Shoemakers) bills	2	1	2
Willson (Taylors) bills	1	17	3
P^d for wash^g Linnen	1	19	11
Andrews bill (horse hire)		2	0
P^d for part of post chaise hire		16	0
Cash to Mr Boulton		10	6
d^o	4	18	0
Educat^n &c 3 Q^{rs} of a y^r at £50 to Xtmas	37	10	0
	£55	8	4

When paying the account, Boulton may have insisted on the Greek, for the following month when Matt wrote to his father he announced that he was starting Greek lessons. He also had a request – he wanted some arrows.[68] Boulton was easily appeased; Matt wrote a few weeks later to thank him for some oranges, and the arrows 'which have afforded me much entertainment'. He had also been on 'a pleasant jaunt to Ipswich [with] Mr Parlby where I saw the College built by Cardinal Wolsey & the other curiosities of that town.'[69]

Meanwhile back at home, Soho House resounded with the sound of the harpsichord. Anne was putting a lot of effort into her music. A new instrument by Kirkman was delivered to Soho House in June 1786, a 'single keyed instrument with two unisons, octave and harp stops, with pedals for piano and swell'. With its leather cover and packing case, the new harpsichord cost £46 6s. 0d., and when he paid the bill Boulton added a note to Kirkman that his daughter was 'much pleased wth its excellencies'.[70] Anne was receiving tuition on the instrument from Joseph or Josiah Harris, who may have been the organist of Birmingham Parish Church, St Martin's in the Bull Ring. Thirty lessons at Soho House during 1786 cost £7 17s. 6d., and six more in Birmingham – perhaps at the teacher's house or in the church – cost 15s. 9d. Tuning the harpsichord cost 5s., and quilling the instrument cost 7s. 6d. (harpsichord strings were plucked by plectra made of raven or crow quills, which soon wore out and had to be replaced regularly). Anne bought sheet music including several arias from her father's favourite oratorio, *Messiah*, at 1s. each, and some Italian songs.[71] Learning the Italian songs perhaps inspired in her the desire to master Italian, either then or later, for she filled an undated exercise book with carefully written out Italian language exercises, with vocabulary, verb conjugations, declensions of nouns and practice phrases, such as '*I miei libri sono nella mia camera*' and '*La lingua italiana è più dolce e più graziosa dell'Inglese ma la Lingua Inglese è più energica e più maestosa dell'Italiana*'.[72]

Matt finally said goodbye to the Parlbys and his schoolmates at the end of the summer term of 1786. He may have spent some time at home, but by September was in Cornwall with his father, who wrote to Anne that they had been to a concert at Truro, 'where we had a great show of Ladies well dressd & six songs by Mrs Hasker who is a good plain English professional Singer'.[73] Matt had not wanted to stay on for the ball which followed, so they had gone to supper with the Daniels family instead. The Wilsons' house was 'full of measled children'. He was looking for a house in Truro, where a new ballroom, theatre and coffee room were under construction in the city centre.

Father and son came home in mid-October, and then there was a great bustle of stitching and washing, starching and ironing, folding and filling of trunks and boxes. Matt was going to Versailles.

6

Fly, fly from Calypso!

On a cold November morning, Anne Boulton and Nancy Mynd stood in the porch at Soho House waving goodbye as Matt set off in the carriage for Dover, with his father and James Watt. Boulton and Watt were combining delivering the boy to Versailles with a business trip. Crossing the Channel and sharing a coach into Paris with them were Josiah Wedgwood's eldest son, John, and Wedgwood's business partner and nephew, Tom Byerley, who were going over to appoint French agents for the Wedgwood business. It was only Boulton's second visit to France (he had last been there 21 years before) and his letters to Anne, like those he had written to her mother long ago, are full of excitement and the novelty of it all, as well as a healthy British scepticism with frenchified manners. After his customarily graphic description of sea-sickness, he wrote, 'I actually did not know Matt this morning when I first met him after his Hair was dressed a la Francois – youl be astonished at ye alteration…'[1]

At home in Birmingham, Anne received regular accounts of their busy schedule of business, official and social visits, interspersed with injunctions to her to learn to speak French well, and to persuade Mrs Watt to join her in the enterprise, for above all, said her father, he wanted her to come and see France, 'which is the Country for Magnificence & Jolity'. Boulton had a higher opinion of Annie Watt than she perhaps had of him, telling Anne that from her she would learn 'many good things such as the dutys of a good Wife & a good Mother &c &c'.[2]

After arriving at Versailles, Matt, his father and Watt went exploring. They visited the Palace and walked 'dressd with our Bags & Swords & our little silk Chapeau Bras, over the Gardins enriched with Fountaines & hundreds of fine Marble Statues'.[3] They spent Christmas together (Boulton bemoaning not being able to eat his pudding at home or enjoy the rejuvenating company of Miss Linwood at Soho House), and then the partners left Matt behind at the home of his new French tutor, M. Bourdon, and returned to Paris, where they attended a meeting of the *Académie Royale des Sciences* and afterwards took tea with Madame Lavoisier, whose husband, the chemist Antoine Lavoisier, would go to the guillotine in 1794.

Then they had another look round the shops. Boulton was entranced with the shops in the Palais Royal and found the French capital 'illuminated and thronged as much as Cheapside on a Lord Mayors Day'. Many of the shops sold both English and French goods, and were already selling some of the products of Soho. The Paris Vauxhall, he noted, like its London and Birmingham counterparts, was 'another Nonsense Shop for Musick and Dancers', and he wrote to Anne, 'These sights &

this way of keeping this good Sunday would shock all the sober & thinking part of English men but the French seem never to think of any thing but nonsense & gayity'.[4] Boulton and Watt also took an excursion to the south, travelling to 'within sight of Mount Blanc', a journey which 'would have been a very agreeable one had it been earlier in the Year', but they had endured 'nasty' inns and beds with 'not damp but *wet* sheets & withal very high charged'.[5]

Although the stay in Versailles was intended to make a man of young Matt, his father was anxious about the cold, writing to the boy from Paris:

> I have sent you a Flannel Wastcoat & if you find it agreeable this cold weather you may get another of them made & this wch I have sent should be made to fit you. I fear you will find fireing scarce at Versailles as the French accustome themselves to bear Cold more than the English. If therefore you find your self distressed for fire you may buy ... wood provided you can have a place to put it in under Lock & Key.[6]

Before Matthew Boulton and James Watt left France, Matt joined them in Paris for a day or two. They had been invited to a ball by their French bankers, the de Lasserts. This was exactly the kind of sophisticated social occasion from which Boulton hoped his son would benefit, and he instructed him to bring with him from Versailles 'the new Clothes that were made for you last summer wth ye new Silk wastcoat, white silk Stockings, pumps &c.'.[7] But to his father's chagrin Matt declined the invitation because he thought he could not dance well enough, something which needed to be remedied, and in the spring Anne wrote a big-sisterly letter to her brother telling him he should learn to dance a minuet properly.[8] She hoped to have the chance of visiting France while he was there, though could not see any immediate prospect of it as their father was planning another prolonged stay in Cornwall.

In the same letter Anne suddenly reveals herself capable of comment which could have come straight from the mouth of Jane Austen's Emma Woodhouse in her more acerbic moments. Telling Matt about a visitor expected at Soho, Miss Landell of Newcastle, the sister of the engineer David Landell, Anne reported,

> she is neither young, or handsome, has what some people call a *pleasing cast with one eye*, talks a great deal, & would be *glad* to be thought young, notwithstanding wrinkles and grey hair begin to appear, but with all these perfections and imperfections she is I am told a sensible and entertaining woman.[9]

Poor Miss Landell – on a later visit Anne reported she was

> as gay and as young as ever, and if I had not recollected four years had elapsed since she graced our Birmingham assembly in pink and lilac ribbons (which she wore yesterday in great abundance) I shou'd have supposed she had not been one day older than when I first saw her, but perhaps she is arrived at that happy period when a few years makes little alteration in a fair Lady's complexion.'[10]

If the generally amiable Miss Boulton grew a little sharp from time to time it was perhaps not to be wondered at. Life in Birmingham must have seemed tame after reading about Versailles and Mont Blanc, even in bad weather. While her father and brother explored France, Anne had to content herself with paying visits to some of the family's elderly Birmingham friends, gamely enduring the claustrophobia of the tea-table and the card-table, to the approval of her father who wrote, 'It is the duty of young folks to contribute all in their power to the smoothing of the furrows of age.'[11] Anne found it stifling. She told Matt, 'I remember reading in the history of England, & I think in the reign of Richard the 2, that cards were first invented for the entertainment of the King of France. I should much sooner have believed it to have been for an old woman of eighty who was incapable of amusing herself by any other means. Do tell me in your next letter if cards are still much played in France.'[12]

Once he was back from France, Boulton promised to write to his son often,

> & endeavour to keep you Company as much as I can. I wish you to go to Mr De Lasserts as often as they invite because you will there be always in good Company but there are other persons that may want you to go with them into improper Company & in all such cases I hope that you & Mr Bourdon will put a negative upon all such propositions, perhaps it may be proper that he should do it in order that you may avoid giveing offence. I desire that you will alternately write to me in English & French & endeavour to make all ye progress you can in the Language.[13]

Matt was not a very satisfactory correspondent and Boulton fretted at not hearing from him more frequently. In March 1787 he sent him instructions on how to organise his finances and his correspondence properly:

> I recommend it to you to keep such a pocket Book as I do wch is on one side ruled into 7 horozontal divisions for the 7 days of the week & on the other side into one set of Columns of L S D for Money received & another for money spent or paid. I will send you an example by young Toney who sets out in a day or two to France.
>
> I note down in every day anything remarkable that hath occurd or where I have visited & I recommend that you note down on the space of such day of the month as you write any letter the address of such letter, Exampl (Feb 25 wrote to my Father) & then when you write your next letter, begin it always by saying – My last was of ... (such a date) since which I have received Yours (or my sisters &c) of such a date—
>
> I will do the same & then our letters will always hang together in such manner that we cannot be lost without there being a Chasm in the Correspondence & the loss pointed out in our next letter.
>
> I beg you will seal your letters with one Waffer & also with Sealing Wax & never trust to any body to put them into the post office but do it always your self as you may be deceivd ... Mr Green & Mr Dean say that Mr Parlby & all your school fellows speak of you with great regard & say they shall ever retain an affection for you, one of the Young Deans desires you will never pass through Oxford without calling upon him at Christ Church College ...
>
> I beg in your next you will tell me ... how you spend your time from 6 in the m[orning to] eleven at night.[14]

Obediently, Matt set about following these instructions; he could not remember the date of his last letter, but promised to do better in future. However, he did set out his timetable for Boulton, from which it appears that it was largely under his own control:

> I have indeavoured to dispose the days of the different masters in such a manner as to have employment for every day, Monday, I rise at 7 oClock, when the hair dresser pay[s] his visit, after that till Breakfast at 9 oClock I generally spend in reading at ten I learn my dialouges [*sic*] & translate some English piece into french till twelve the Hour of the fencing Master who rests an Hour, I draw till two, when I prepare for Dinner a quarter past, we rest at Table an Hour, after dinner we walk or take other amusements as the weather will permit at five Mr Bourdon corrects my translation &c & I read to him to get the pronunciation as you wished
>
> At seven I return into my chamber, for the evening I prepare the sums & questions which the mathematical master gives me who I attend every tuesday Thursday & saturday, from half past eight to ten; the same day the dansinc [*sic*] master comes at six & [I] rest an Hour; Thursday Friday Saturday the drawing master, who will suit your taste, large heads in Crayons, I have the fencing master the rest. Any Alterations that you may point out I will with pleasure adopt …[15]

Like any 16-year-old, Matt was constantly preoccupied with his appearance: 'As the season in which I can wear my dressed suit finishes at the end of this month I wish to know if I may have some others made & of what kind you may judge proper.'[16] His father advised choosing to wear summer clothes according to the thermometer rather than the conventions of the French court, and recommended Matt to get a frock suit made for everyday wear, and to look after it: 'I must recommend you to be carefull in keeping them clean as a necessary & reputable piece of oeconomy.' He named a tailor in Paris but told Matt not to go there until he had paid the man's last bill.[17] The following month he wrote again, telling him the tailor had been paid and had been asked to make a new suit for Matt. He thought 'a Frock Suit is sufficiently handsome to dine out in whilst it is fresh & new.' He added in a PS that he was having a gift made for one of their Paris friends: 'I have got a fine Girdle making at Soho for Miss De Lassert with Camios & Steel tassells.'[18] Miss De Lassert was pleased with this – Matt wrote to his father:

> Last Saturday I dined at Mr De Lasserts where I met Mr [Charles] Startin when he delivered me the Swords &c &c for which I return you my sincerest thanks & I feel how unable I shall ever be to repay you the numerous obligations which you have had the bounty to confer on your Son. Miss Delassert had on the Girdle you sent … which I think extremely elegant & I assure you she entertains the highest opinion of your favours.[19]

Instead of a frock suit, Matt changed the tailor's order to a dress coat and breeches, 'on account of the numerous ceremonies which I cannot see without being dressed'. His father was none too pleased about this, and perhaps began to doubt the wisdom of sending Matt to France. Seizing a few minutes while at the Albion Mill ('wch is going merrily') he cautioned the boy:

> There is some danger in a young Englishmans head becoming giddy by the pagentry of Courts & the Folly of Fashion for in proportion to the predominence of those things good sense & good tast dwindle although there is as much difference between the one & ye other as there is between Water Gilding & Solid Gold. It seems to be agreed on all hands that Germany is the place to make a Man & Paris the place to make a Man of Fashion (i.e. a Gambler & a Rake). I

PLATE 1 *Matthew Boulton, by Tilly Kettle, c.1762-4.*
(Private collection)

PLATE 2 *Mrs Ann Boulton, by Tilly Kettle, c.1762-4.*
(Private collection)

PLATE 3 *Soho House, late 19th-century watercolour. (Handsworth Historical Society)*

PLATE 4   *The Soho Manufactory, from Bissett's* Magnificent Directory *(1800).*

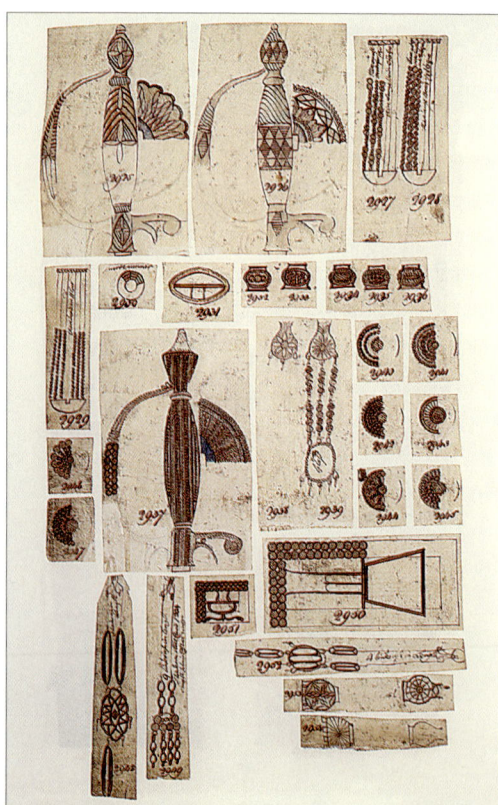

PLATE 5   *A page from the Boulton & Fothergill pattern books, showing sword hilts, steel jewellery and buckles and buttons. (Birmingham Assay Office Charitable Trust/Birmingham City Archives)*

PLATE 6   *Gilt chatelaine, the belt clasp stamped with the figure of Venus and the other panels with Venus and Cupid. Boulton & Fothergill* c.*1765. (Birmingham Museums & Art Gallery)*

PLATE 7   *Dr William Small. (Birmingham Assay Office)*

PLATE 8   *Dr Erasmus Darwin, by Joseph Wright of Derby, c.1792-3. (Derby Museum & Art Gallery)*

PLATE 9   *Erasmus Darwin's house at Lichfield. (Erasmus Darwin House)*

PLATE 10   *Pair of ormolu and blue john ewers,*
Boulton & Fothergill C.1772, *now displayed at*
Soho House Museum. (Birmingham Museums &
Art Gallery)

PLATE 11   *Silver and silver-gilt sugar bowl,*
Matthew Boulton, 1789. (Birmingham Museums
& Art Gallery)

PLATE 12   *Matthew Robinson Boulton, aged three, by Jean Etienne Liotard, 1773.*
(Birmingham Museums & Art Gallery)

PLATE 13   *John Fothergill, c.1770, artist unknown. (Private collection)*

PLATE 14   *Dr William Withering, after C.F. Von Breda, 1792. (Birmingham University Medical School)*

PLATE 15   *John Whitehurst, by Joseph Wright of Derby, c.1782. (Private collection)*

PLATE 16   *Thomas Day, by Joseph Wright of Derby. (National Portrait Gallery, London)*

PLATE 17   *Miss Anne Boulton, by Tilly Kettle, c.1778. (Private collection)*

PLATE 18 *James Watt, mezzotint. (Birmingham Museum & Art Gallery)*

PLATE 19 *Mrs Ann Watt, attributed to John Graham Gilbert, c.1820. (Private collection)*

PLATE 20 *Cosgarne House, the Cornish base for Matthew Boulton and James Watt. (Note: this is a private house.)*

wish, & beg you will constantly be employd & that you as speedily as possable get possession of the Language & that you read such History, such anecdotes & such sentiments as tend to teach & to inspire sentiments of Honour & benevolence for it is the possession of such like principles that constitute the real Gentleman. Fashion & Foppery has nothing to do with it. But at the same time I mean to be understood that you should dress your self in ye Character of a Modest young Gentn & never suffer your self to be laught out of a becoming decent Modesty by puppys, Blockheads, Rakes, or Impertinents.[20]

The two swords Boulton had sent to Matt via Charles Startin had not actually been intended for Matt at all, but as gifts for other people; however Boulton acknowledged that as he had forgotten 'that School Boys wear Swords at Paris & Versaills, upon further recollection I believe you must wear one of them your self ...' In the meantime, he recommended to Matt a new book which he had been reading, and which Anne had now sent on to Miss De Lassert: '2 Vols entitled *Evalina* which I beg youl borrow & read as I think them the prettyest Novel I have read & were wrote by Miss Burney, Daughter of the Musician who wrote Musical Travils.'[21]

By the autumn of 1787 Matt was tired of Versailles and thought he would improve faster in Paris. His father was inclined to agree, but confided in Anne that he did not dare trust her brother in Paris without a reliable mentor at his side – although (of course) he had 'a high opineon of Matts discretion, honour and virtue'.[22] For help, Boulton turned to the De Lasserts, and later that month Miss De Lassert wrote to recommend a certain Mr Manuel as the ideal person, a recommendation which Boulton promptly accepted. Miss De Lassert assured Boulton that they would make a point of seeing Matt often, adding that he was accepted in their home

> comme un enfant de la maison, et autre que la bonheur qu'il a d'etre votre fils, lui donne mille droits à nos attention, et à notre meilleurs accueil, il est d'ailleurs un excellent garçon, fort doux, fort bon, et parlant fort bien française à present.[23]

Mlle De Lassert added her thanks for the copy of *Evelina*, which she had much enjoyed, and hoped Boulton would keep his promise to return to Paris with Anne before long.

Having found a mentor for Matt, Boulton wrote to him, 'As it is impossible that you can know or even suspect the dangers of Paris, I must request of you not to go any where without the knowledge or consent of Mr Manuel.'[24] The said Mr Manuel was also to help Matt improve his written French (and to give the boy his due, as instructed he wrote to his father often in French), and to accompany him to

> lectures of chymistry, mineralogy, or natural philosophy ... and I must request you to make short notes of such lectures to assist your memory, and at leasure times you and he may converse upon and explain the same. At the same time, I advise you to allow a little time each day for the preservation of your health by takeing air and exercise, or you may go to some rideing school, as learning to ride is a usefull accomplishment. I beg that you and Mr Manuel will consider that I do not wish you to go to Paris to take what is commonly call'd pleasure, by going to balls, operas, or publick places of dissipation, or to contract habits of indolence; but, on the contrary, I am desireous you should be incessantly

employ'd in gaining knowledge or strength of body or of mind, and must beg
you will not indulge one idle moment in the course of the day. But above all I
must insist upon it that you do not form any improper acquaintance, or keep
any improper company; particularly I desire you will avoid the company of young
English puppys, fops, bucks, rakes, &c. Madam and Mademoisell de Lassert are
exceedingly kind in inviteing you to come often to their house, which I beg
you will never decline, as the company you will generaly find there will tend to
refine your manners and exalt your sentiments, and consequently tend to make
you a happy and virtuous man.

  I don't love to find fault with you, because I think upon the whole you do
not merit it; but you must excuse me if I express my wishes to see you write a
more regular hand, and state accounts with neatness and regularity.[25]

It was settled that Matt should spend the winter in Paris, pay a short visit home,
and then in 1788 go to Germany, where James Watt junior's former tutor, the Rev.
M. Reinhard at Staedtfeld, was willing to take him on the same terms as Jimmy
Watt, namely £40 a year for his board and instruction in German, geography,
arithmetic and music. James was not long returned from there, and Boulton was
impressed by the progress he had made and the 'manly turn of mind' Reinhard
had inculcated. Boulton was prevented by Cornish 'commotions' from sending
Matt to Germany as early as he had planned, and wrote to Mr Reinhard offering
to pay to secure his son's place from January 1788, even if he was not able to
send him until later in the spring. After a longer stay at home than had been
intended, due to Boulton's wish to 'gratify his paternal affection', Matt set off for
Germany in August 1788, accompanied by a former Soho apprentice. The two
young men spent a few days at the Frankfurt fair before heading for Staedtfeld.
In a letter informing Reinhard that they were on their way, Boulton said he
thought it 'but justice to your self that you should take from me a larger sum
in proportion for my talle Boy of 18 than you take for little Boys of 12 Yrs of
Age & which I shall pay you with great pleasure'.[26] Two other young Birmingham
men well known to Matt, Charles Startin and the son of a Mr Marindin, were
also at Staedtfeld so he would have some familiar companions. Reinhard took
to Matt immediately.

As when he was in France, Matt was supposed to write home regularly; in return,
his father, who was busy with plans for a new contract to produce the English
copper coinage, promised a regular supply of letters carefully set out to be of the
greatest benefit to the boy:

> My letters to you will in general consist of three parts:
> *1st,* a narration of all events and news that may be interesting to you on this
> side the water, and
> *2nd,* observations respecting what may occur on your side, with answers to the
> contents of your letter, and
> *3rd,* such advice and directions for your conduct, both moral and political, as my
> experience may enable me to give, and your youth and inexperience may stand
> in need of receiving; and in so doing I shall avail my self of such sentiments
> of wise, learned, and sensible philosophers as accord with my own, for, alass, I
> am too much absorb'd by business and by constant new inventions to think of
> – and for – my son so much as I wish to do.[27]

One of the first items of 'events and news' Matt learned was that 'Jim Watt is gone to Manchester and is to be an apprentice to a respectable house who are manufacturers of cotton, printers of calicos, and dyers in general, which will suit James's chymical turn of mind for one half the day, and for the other half he will find use for his German and French in the counting house. I have no doubt but he will be happier there than at home.'[28]

Relations between Watt and his elder son had been strained for a long time, and Annie Watt was also very critical of her stepson, so that when the time came for Jimmy to return from Germany, his father wrote to him, in a letter describing the young man as 'dogmatic, contemptuous of others, self opinionated and impatient' and told him that it was no longer possible for them to work together.[29] Accordingly, James had been apprenticed to learn the mercantile trade with a Manchester textile firm, Taylor & Maxwell. In the Watt household, James and Annie Watt's daughter Jessie and son Gregory were growing up, and the two children of James Watt's first marriage seem almost outsiders to this family unit.

In his letter to Matt, Boulton added some advice which he would have viewed as coming under item three of his correspondence agenda, but part of which Matt might justifiably have viewed as contradicting some of the instructions he had received in Paris:

> I beg you will write letters to your Paris friends, that they may not conclude you are ungratefull, or that you have forgot them: rules of politeness require it, as well as principles of gratitude, for you know not whose friendship or good offices you may stand in need of. A private individual can hurt but few, but he may please many, and therefore he should endeavour to be loved, for he cannot be fear'd in general. Popularity is his only rational and sure foundation ... I advise you to endeavour to secure a general refuge in the good will of the multitude, which is a great strength to any man, for mankind in general chuse and prefer popular and fashionable characters. A man who solicits a minister backed by the general good will and good wishes of mankind, solicits with weight and great probability of success, and women are biassed in favour of men whom they see are in fashion and hears every body speak well of.[30]

Boulton returned to this theme in his following letter, telling Matt he should

> associate with the few *gentlemen* of the village and cultivate their esteem and friendship. In great commercial and manufactureing countries the distinctions between one class of men and another are not so great as in remote inland villages, where agriculture is the principal employ. In such situations the distinction between the landed barons and the peasant is something similar to king and subject, and consequently the higher class is accustomed to be treated with ceremony and respect; and I think a benevolent good hearted baron is a blessing to his neighbourhood. Yet nevertheless I must own I am partial to trade, inasmuch as it extends a man's powers of doing good; and I had rather be distinguished as the greatest manufacturer in Europe than as a Count of the Holy Empire, because I suppose I pay weekly more money for ingenious labour than the first lord in England doth for common labour; and, after all, I am only a greater slave than my servants.[31]

As usual, he was concerned about the severe winter and wished he could instantly send Matt

> some of our soft fine Welch flannel to wear under your shirt, for 'tis immensly cold; however, I beg you'l get some such good non conducter of heat to keep you warm and to keep you from takeing cold, there being nothing worse for your constitution than sudden obstructed perspiration. Last night, Ferhenite's thermometer sunk to 15 degrees, which is 17 degrees below the freezing point (which is 32), but as it's probable the German's may use Raumeur's [Reaumur's] thermometer I must beg you to remember that 2¼ degrees of Farhenite's is equal to one degree of Raumeur's.[32]

If only Matt were not so far away, lamented his father, he would send him 'flannel, thermometers, and news papers', as he wished him to read the Parliamentary debates between Pitt and Fox concerning the Regency:

> The King continues yet deranged, and incapable of performing the functions of the kingly office; and therefore Mr Pitt proposes for Parliament to petition the Prince of Wales to solely take upon himself the Regency, and that he shall choose his own ministers and not be fetter'd with any perminent Council … As Mr Pitt hath acted so liberaly and manly towards the Prince, I shall hope that when he is invested with the regal powers he will not be so bad a politician as to change the ministry, particularly as the whole nation are satisfy'd with Mr Pitt, who found the nation in distress and who hath now restored it to its highest pitch of prosperity.[33]

George III's bout of insanity, now thought to be due to the effects of porphyria, had struck close to home where Boulton was concerned, for it had interrupted the plans for the new coinage. He had spent some £4,000 on buildings and machinery on the strength of the order he had received from the Privy Council the previous year, but having seen Pitt and Lord Hawksbury he was much disquieted to find he had 'nothing to expect from the intended ministers', and to receive no more than their 'concern for the disapointment'.[34] But to the surprise of everyone – not least the Prince of Wales and his supporters – the King recovered. Boulton heard the news from Fanny de Luc, daughter of his old Geneva friend the geologist Jean André de Luc, who was now Reader to the Queen at Windsor. Fanny wrote from Windsor of the

> general joy at the restoration of our *beloved* King to his faithful and affectionate subjects, indeed the pleasure we felt last Tuesday at seeing him again at Windsor in *good health* is not to be described, I could scarcely believe my senses, but feared it was almost a Vision which only delighted for a moment, but shouts, acclamations and general joy of the people convinced me of the charming reality; our good and amiable Queen too, with the Princesses, how delightful, how transporting the whole Scene! At night illuminations were general, and to-morrow the day on which our beloved Monarch visits us, we are to be most splendid.[35]

In spite of Boulton's worries about the cold and Matt's progress, the news he and Anne received from Germany was highly satisfactory. Reinhard was impressed with Matt's ready grasp of things mechanical and his quickness at picking up the language, telling Boulton, 'In nine months he has learnt more than young Watt has in a whole year'.[36]

It was all going so well.

And then Matt fell in love.

Reinhard wrote to Boulton: 'For some days my young friend was very sad, and he owned that he was in love with the young Baroness de Wangenheim, who returned it. He told me yesterday that they were engaged.'[37] Reinhard went on to extol the young Baroness's attractions (chiefly a considerable fortune), and at Matt's request allowed him to read the letter before sending it. But on the same day he wrote an additional letter to Boulton, which he did not show to Matt. This painted a rather different picture:

> The poor young man is a stranger to the wiles of a not too innocent girl. He isn't the first young man she has had a fancy to. Mr Watt knows that in his time she was sent away because of an affair with a servant. At the beginning I told your son of this and my mind was at rest. I cannot speak frankly at present or I should lose his confidence. I must be wary to save him, and for your tranquillity. I like the girl, and if I tell him she is not worthy of his love he will resent it and be drawn closer to her ... I think he believes himself bound more in honour than by passion.[38]

Matt had certainly been smitten, though his 'Amie Julie' had written to him, assuring him she was in no great hurry:

> *Écrivez votre Père, parlez lui ouvertement, ditez lui que vous aimez une Fille qui est trop honnête pour former une liaison secrete avec vous, ditez lui que son plan qu'il a formé envers vous ne sera point du deranger; Dieu nous preserve de vouloir demander que vous me préniez pour Femme tout de suite, non mon Ami, si vous croyez être heureux avec moi, voyagez encore une couple d'années tant que votre père le demand, je vous restera Fidèle ...*[39]

Boulton was full of sympathy for his lovelorn 19-year-old but warned: 'Fly instantly; fly without a pause from Calypso and all her enchantments ... you see not your own danger.'[40] It would be better to wait until he was older and more worldly wise, he added – which after all was pretty much what Fräulein Julie had said.

A day or two later Reinhard wrote to Boulton that it was all over, Matt had acknowledged his mistake and had a good cry, and he and Reinhard were off to Freiburg and Leipzig together, out of temptation's way. By the time they returned, Fraülein Julie had resumed her affair with the footman, a matter of some relief to both Reinhard and Boulton, who hoped Matt would find a nice, well-to-do English wife – if only he would learn to dance the minuet. He wrote to Matt:

> If you have any time for amusements, for Godsake don't employ it at cards or any paltry game, but I think it an agreeable amusement and an elegant accomplishment to dance with ease and grace, particularly minuets, as I have some times known elegant dancing introduce a young man to fifty or a hundred thousand pounds and a good wife, for though I would not have you sacrifice your happines for money, yet, nevertheless, there are as many good wives to be found with good fortunes as without them – at least, a good fortune cannot be consider'd as an alloy to a good wife, nor an objection; but when ever you marry, I advise that you marry an English lady, that your manners, customs, language, and religeon may accord. However, it's time enough to talk of these things a few years hence.[41]

7

Live Transplants

While Matt navigated himself uncertainly through the mysteries of continental manners and the treacherous narrows of teenage love, Anne remained firmly tethered in what Boulton called 'Miss Linwood's soft silken fetters' – the seemingly tranquil female world of embroidery and music lessons. In 1787 Mary Linwood, seeking to promote her embroidered pictures, applied to Boulton for help in getting an introduction at court. Ever ready to do a lady a favour, Boulton turned to his friend Jean André de Luc, telling him, 'If I was not persuaded that Miss Ls work exceeded all other of the kind that her Majesty had ever seen I would not have presumed to have requested your assistance but as I know you have great pleasure in promoting the fine arts & much satisfaction in being instrumental in rewarding real merit & promoting the happiness of the Fair, I will not trouble you with any further appologies but will assure you what ever favr you do Miss Lin I shall consider as to me.'[1] De Luc agreed to see Miss Linwood, who wrote to Boulton in high expectations of the outcome:

> … you are more than good in your attention to me, and if ever I am admitted to the Royal presence, 'tis to you and you alone I shall be indebted for the Honour, whoever is my conductor. I have not the least acquaintance with Miss Burney and tho' she may, and I believe has great merit, yet I know the Ladies of the Court so well, that those dependant upon the Queen, are jealous even of a smile, therefore I'm not very anxious for a female Pilot, but be assur'd whoever Mr D Luc shd think proper, will be agreeable to me … [2]

A month later Miss Linwood sent a detailed account of her audience with the Queen. She had met Mr De Luc at the Queen's House (Buckingham House at the end of the Mall, which the King had bought in the 1760s from Sir Charles Sheffield, the illegitimate son of the Duke of Buckingham for whom it had been built). De Luc had helped her to set up the pictures in the drawing room. There were twice-weekly *levées* and 'drawing-rooms' at the Queen's House; the *levées* were all-male affairs, while the drawing-rooms were presided over by the Queen and open to both sexes. Whether Miss Linwood made her appearance at one of these or was granted a private audience is not clear, but it was certainly a great success. The Queen spent an hour looking at the pictures and sent for the Princesses Augusta and Elizabeth to come and see them. Her Majesty had also sent for her Keeper of the Wardrobe, the acid-tongued Mrs Schwellenberg, who was ill, to come and see, telling her it was worth walking as far as the drawing room for. The Queen had further suggested some public rooms which would be suitable for Miss Linwood's projected sales exhibition, and had said she would commend the exhibition to the nobility. Finally, the Queen had asked for the pictures to be left so that the King could see them later. The Queen was 'graciously condescending … and as flattering in her encomiums as a Monsieur Boulton.'[3] It was all most exciting. Miss Linwood hoped to see Anne and her father in London again soon.

Anne was back in London that summer of 1787, but not feeling much like viewing Miss Linwood's exhibition. She was plagued with severe toothache in a front tooth, and because, as her father observed, 'the pulling out of foreteeth is a matter of great consequence to a young woman',[4] she was packed off to consult Charles Dumergue (Plate 23), a London society dentist who looked after the Royal teeth. Dumergue had attended to Anne's teeth before, and the two families were already good friends. In their letters to each other the two heads of family are referred to as 'Daddy Dumergue' and 'Pappa Boulton' respectively, and their correspondence is full of affectionate banter.

Charles Dumergue was a Frenchman full of gallic charm. He lived at No.15 Piccadilly with his daughter Sophia (Plate 24), nephew Charles (also a dentist), ward Charlotte Charpentier or Carpenter (who became the wife of Sir Walter Scott), and Mrs Sarah ('Sally') Nicholson. Mrs Nicholson seems to have overseen the Dumergues' household affairs and had perhaps looked after Sophia from childhood, for Sophia in her will in 1831 described her as 'my more than mother'. Certainly from the tone of her letters she was on more intimate terms with the family than a servant, and the letters she writes to Boulton to cheer him up when he is ill are positively saucy, written on the understanding that he would keep his promise to burn them (which he clearly didn't). Mrs Nicholson generally refers to herself in letters as 'Old Nick', while Boulton refers to her as 'Nursey Nickey'. The Dumergues had friends in London society including the likes of Mrs Siddons (Plate 25) and the singer Elizabeth Billington, and letters from both Charles Dumergue and Mrs Nicholson playfully pass on to 'Pappa Boulton' the good wishes and numerous kisses of these ladies, Charles Dumergue regretting in one letter that Boulton's 'rencrontres' have not been of the 'amoureux' kind[5] and 'begging he might be god-pappa if a little accident should happen'.[6]

Having examined Anne, Dumergue decided on the drastic but then accepted solution of a tooth transplant. The transplanting of live teeth was practised until the end of the 18th century, poor people being paid a few shillings to have a healthy tooth extracted and inserted immediately into the gums of the rich, who had undergone the more or less simultaneous extraction of a rotten tooth (Plate 27). The extractions were done without anaesthetic, of course, though possibly with a certain amount of alcohol or laudanum to dull the pain. At least Mr Dumergue seems to have taken the trouble to clean the replacement tooth before inserting it into Anne's gum – very often the operation caused serious infection, sometimes even fatal septicaemia.

Boulton stayed in London to be with Anne, writing to Matt in Versailles on 29 June:

> your Sister hath had a tooth drawn & at the same time another was drawn out
> of a young Girls head about 14 & after cleaning it & washing it in Spirits of

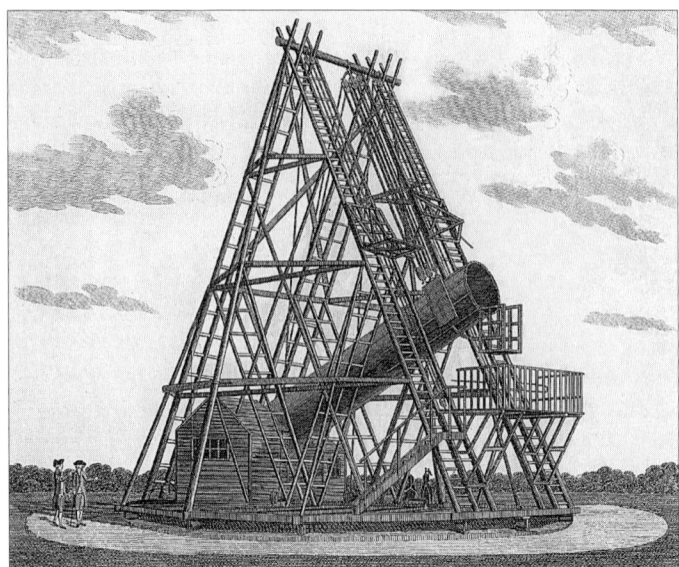

FIG. 14   *William Herschel's forty-foot telescope at Slough. (Herschel House Museum, Bath, 1879)*

Wine & Campher it was planted in your Sisters jaw where it seems to fix firm & I have no doubt but it will prove a good tooth & usefull.[7]

When Anne was sufficiently recovered from this ordeal to return home, she and her father set out from London for Birmingham via Windsor and Slough. Visiting was probably the last thing she felt like doing, but at Slough they called on the astronomer William Herschel (Plate 26). Boulton had been eager to see his astronomical friend ever since receiving a letter from Sir Joseph Banks earlier in the year in which Banks told him: 'Herschel has discovered two Satellites revolving round his Georgian Planet but has not yet completed his 40 Feet Telescope, what great discoveries may not we expect from that?'[8] Boulton could not wait to see the instrument, and to tell Matt about it:

> [we] saw his great telliscopes. The largest of which are fixed in the open air & weigh several Tons. It is governd by Wheels by pullys & Ropes, in such a way as to point it to any of the Planets or any of the Stars near the Ecliptick the great speculum is full 4 feet diameter, the Tube of it is 5 feet diameter & 40 feet long & Mr Herschel gets into it by a door on one side & runs up & down it as easy as up & down his own stairs. He hath discovered lately 2 burning mountains or vulcanos in the Moon & when the largest Teliscope is quite compleat he expects to make many other important discoveries & extend our ideas of the immensity of the Creation.[9]

After this they resumed their journey back to Soho House, Anne cradling her tender jaw against the jolting of the carriage while her father pondered the immensity of the Creation.

Fortunately, shortly after they returned home there was a sympathetic and understanding visitor in the person of Charlotte Matthews, wife of the banker William Matthews. Charlotte, who came to stay in August 1787, took a close and affectionate interest in the life of the Boulton household. She even took it upon herself at times to keep Boulton on the straight and narrow, sartorially speaking, writing to him on one occasion:

> Dear Sir, I understand your coat to be the inclosd Cloth & that *you* had fixd upon the silk pattern with *pink* in it. Now as I wear only black, I can not permit you to wear *pink*, but a still stronger matter is that I think the other silk pattern which I enclose is neat & handsom & at your age a similarity rather than a diversity of colors ought to be preferr'd.[10]

Charlotte was especially fond of Anne Boulton. Watching Nancy Mynd bossing her about, she did not like what she saw and thought Anne's cousin was inclined to overstep her authority. Charlotte did not feel able to talk to Boulton about it, and he was in any case so busy that it was impossible to get five minutes alone with him, so instead she sat down in his small library and wrote him a letter. She did not want to interfere, she said, but she felt bound to speak up for Miss Boulton (who had made no complaint herself). As for Anne,

> Her good sense is the more conspicuous to those who know her well from her great diffidence in displaying it ... Miss B's conduct I am thoroughly satisfied will command the respect and esteem of every well disposed person that knows her, but she ought also to be treated with respect by every one who resides under your roof, and if her own good nature prevents her from exacting it she is the most entitled to it, and your *authority* shou'd command it for her. My opinion of Miss M (who with not one hundredth part of Miss B's good sense or prudence pretends to be superior to her in both) has been long formed; but I wish her no greater harm than a husband to take her off your hands; and even that wou'd be a matter of total indifference to me but from the great esteem I have for Miss B which will not suffer me to see (with patience) her consider'd in a great measure as a non-entity in your house by Miss M, who from what I can see of her conduct seems to consider *herself* as mistress.[11]

Although Anne had not complained about Nancy Mynd, she did perhaps hanker for more independence, for in October she had her eye on a horse and wrote to her father asking if she might buy it, and whether £25 would be a reasonable price. Boulton was not against it in principle. He believed the fresh air and exercise would be good for her. As to the price, without seeing the animal he couldn't say – it might be dear at £5 or cheap at £25, the main thing was that it should be safe, and she should test-ride it for a few miles before coming to a decision.[12]

He was too far away to look at horses for Anne himself – he was once more in Cornwall, where he was unwell, perhaps a presage of things to come. He had been caught in a hailstorm near Truro and got very cold and wet ('the severity of the Storm hath left a pain in my teeth'), but this soaking was perhaps unrelated to the problems he experienced shortly after. He had been taken violently ill during a performance at the Truro Playhouse. The excruciating pains on the left side in the small of his back and in his abdomen, accompanied by vomiting, were the same he had felt during the jolting coach journey to Cornwall from London, but much worse. His Cornish host, Mr Wilson, had slept in the same room to keep an eye on him, and eventually sent for a doctor, who pronounced the problem to be in the left kidney. By the time he wrote to Anne about the horse he was feeling much better, though 'a little tender' and looking forward to returning home the following month. In the meantime he had been pleased to learn that she was visiting some Birmingham friends, the Salt family. 'I am particularly happy to find that you are at Mrs Salts for I assure you I have felt very unpleasant ever since I set out, at the idea of leaving you to the wide world, but consol my Self by my reflections on your Discression & good sense – I beg you will present my best respects to Mr & Mrs & Miss Salt with Thousands of Thanks for takeing in & nourishing a deserted Orphan.'[13]

Although she may only have gone to Cornwall with her father once, Anne seems often to have accompanied him to London. Nevertheless, much of their contact was by letter, even on special occasions. On her birthday, 29 January 1789, she was alone at home when he sat down in London to write to her, underlining the date many times:

> I cannot let slip this happy day without congratulating my dear daughter & congratulating my Self upon the return of that day which gave Birth to the greatest blessing & comfort of my old age. May you live to enjoy at my time of Life those pleasures & Satisfactions I now feel in the contemplation of my daughter being now 20 years of Age & possessed of Fillial affection & duty with an unspoted Character & every Virtue that can endear her to a Father a Friend or a Husband – may she live long & be happy is my fervent prayer.[14]

The odd thing is, he was mistaken. In January 1789 Anne was 21, not twenty.

That summer of her 21st year Anne faced another tooth transplant in Piccadilly. Mrs Nicholson wrote to Boulton that Dumergue proposed to remove the remains of an old tooth including the root, and would then 'place a live one in the Socket & he hopes from his care she will not suffer so much as you or Miss Boulton may fear ...'[15] She added reassuringly, 'I hope when she has spent some time with my lasses [Sophia and Charlotte] she will not consider it so unpleasant a visit.' In a subsequent letter Dumergue himself explained that he would place tin foil round the pivot of the new tooth to 'keep it fast', adding 'one must be very attentif in not putting too much of tin foil'. The ladies were expecting Anne '& will be very much disappointed if [they] don't Injoye her Dear Sweet Compagny'.[16]

It is hard to imagine Anne 'injoyeing' this visit to London, being fully aware this time of what lay in store. Her father told Matt that she had borne 'much pain by an operation upon her teeth' and still needed further treatment.[17] The amiable stoic endured what must be endured and the following month the Dumergues brought her back to Soho. After a few days' rest all of them headed north. Having dealt with some business in Manchester and attended a music meeting there together, Boulton and Anne joined the Dumergues in Buxton, where, he told Matt (now at Leipzig), he had intended 'to give my self a little holoday and to wash away all my rhumatick pains, but on the fourth day I was sent for by express to attend the Privy Council in London, where I was detain'd near a fortnight ...'.[18] Before leaving the others in Buxton he made arrangements for them to visit James Watt junior in Manchester, where he asked James to show them some of the sights. By the time he returned to Soho he found 'your sister return'd from Buxton with her dentist Mr Dumergue, his daughters, and three other ladies, who stay'd a fortnight at Soho, singing and dancing with all the vivacity of Frenchmen ...'.[19]

For James the pleasure of showing Anne and the Dumergues round Manchester must have come as welcome relief, for the steady succession of critical and parsimonious letters from home continued unabated, and it is noteworthy that he found Matthew Boulton easier to approach than his own father. Watt kept him terribly short of money and in late 1789 in desperation he turned to Boulton for help. On Boxing Day Boulton sent James £50, promising not to tell anyone and especially not Watt senior: '... you may tranquilize your self in respect to your Father as I promise you that he shall not know anything of the Transaction.' Boulton was kindly and sympathetic, trying to see both points of view:

> It is possible your Fathers Ideas may be too limited in regard to the quantum necessary for your expences but I think it equaly probable that yours may be too defuse [diffuse] I therefore can't help wishing it in my power to expand the one & contract the other. I know, & I speak from experience, that the principal articles of Expenditure in the generality of young men who live in large Towns, are such as produce the least additions to their happiness or reputation, for which [reason], as well as for some others I know of, I cannot help urging you to *cut your Coat according to your Cloth*, as the sure means of preserving the good opinions of your Father & the most likely of inducing him to open his hand more liberal to you ... If he speaks to me upon the subject I will do the best I can for you.[20]

Boulton ended this 'lifesaver' letter: 'I am writing within the sound of sundry musical Instruments which so confound me that I must stop.' Anne was 'obliging the company' on the harpsichord.

Although Anne was now 21 (or 20, by her father's reckoning), there was as yet no husband on the horizon. Boulton had earlier predicted she would 'have great choice of husbands',[21] and plainly expected that a suitor would come along sooner rather than later. There had been talk in the neighbourhood linking Anne's name with that of another local resident, for in June 1791 John Scale wrote to Boulton in London, adding in a PS: 'I think it but friendly to tell you that it is very generally reported that Miss Boulton & Mr Whately either *are* or *are to be* married before you return – how far this may be agreeable or otherwise I cannot say, if it is so I most sincerely wish her happy.'[22] John Whately and his brother Henry Piddock Whately were friends and business contacts of the Boultons – which one's name was being linked with Miss Boulton, or if it was another Whately altogether, is not clear, but there is no further mention of this 'marriage' in the correspondence so it seems to have been no more than rumour.

The simple pleasures of such drawing-room gossip were rudely shattered in the summer of 1791 by an event in Birmingham which had its origins in the shockwaves spreading from far away across the Channel, in revolutionary France. In the aftermath of the Revolution of 1789 there was much political unease in Britain and any groups perceived as radical were viewed with suspicion. This applied particularly to the nonconformists, or 'dissenters', notwithstanding the fact that in Birmingham a number of them were benefactors to the town and involved in public life in one way or another. One of the chief figures among the Birmingham dissenters was the Unitarian minister Dr Joseph Priestley. Priestley had arrived in the town in 1780 after leaving the service of Lord Shelburne, and was appointed minister to the New Meeting. In addition to his theological preoccupations, Priestley was one of the foremost 'natural philosophers', or scientists, of his day, having written books on colour, light, optics, electricity, gases and airs, and chemistry. These interests made him a natural addition to the Lunar Society, and he and his wife, Mary (the daughter of the 'ironmaster' Isaac Wilkinson of Wrexham) and their children became a regular part of the Soho House visiting circle.

But Priestley's nonconformism made him a target for the anti-radical portion of the community, especially when word got round that, on the evening of 14 July 1791, a dinner would be held at *Dadley's Hotel* in Temple Row, to mark the second anniversary of the storming of the Bastille and to celebrate what the diners saw as the liberation of the French people. Whipped into a state of high excitement by rumour-mongers, a hostile mob gathered outside the hotel chanting 'Church and King for ever!' Above all they were on the lookout for Dr Priestley, the 'political priest'. But Priestley did not attend the dinner. Disappointed of their quarry, the mob smashed the hotel windows and then headed down to the New Meeting chapel, which they destroyed. After that they made their riotous and drunken way to Priestley's house, which they ransacked and burned. Priestley had had a short advance warning and he and his family managed to escape, first to the home of their Moseley friends the Russells, and from there to the home of their married daughter in Dudley, but he lost his house along with his library and all his scientific papers and equipment. He was only the first: in five violent days the homes of a number of prominent townspeople, including William Hutton and the Russells, were destroyed.

By keeping his head down, Boulton managed to escape the attentions of the mob, and by supreme diplomacy (in the shape of a feast) to persuade his workforce to maintain production and not go off and join in the mayhem. Soho was in any case some way out of town and Boulton was not a nonconformist – in fact, he declared, in a letter to Charles Dumergue, 'I am happy in living alone in the Country & am almost silent upon this dissonant Subject. By minding my own business I live peaceably & securely amidst the Flames, Rapine, Plunder anarchy & confusion of these Unitarians, Trinitarians, Predestinarians & tarians of all sorts.'[23]

He added an invitation to Dumergue, Sophia, Charlotte and Mrs Nicholson to visit Soho, assuring them they would be perfectly safe:

> I now beg you will make my Love acceptable to your amiable Trinity & assure them they may Sleep in peace at Soho & I think it would do you no harm if you can come ... I will give you the keys of my Citydel & as much liberty as my Rabits. The ladies may trust my Son for I dont think he is so liable to that disorder calld Love as his Father. My daughtr & I are agreed upon another Love subject & begs to join with me in every thing that is kind & Lovely to you & your Lovely Three. Come, come, come away to Soho.[24]

Matt was back at home, having returned from Germany in 1790 and joined the business. James Watt junior was still working in Manchester; much to his father's disapproval he took some time off in the summer of 1791 to go to Scotland for the marriage of his sister Margaret (Peggy) to James Miller. When he returned he announced that he had received an offer from Thomas and Richard Walker, Manchester textile merchants, to travel for them in France, Italy and Germany, and had accepted it. His employer Charles Taylor agreed to release him from his indentures, and in March 1792 Jimmy set off for two years of travelling on the Continent for his new masters. He was no sooner in Paris than he was declaring his support of the French Patriots. 'We are now a nation of rebels,' he wrote to his father, aligning himself firmly with the Party of the People. 'I have the friendship of most of the Patriots here, so that I am infinitely more safe than any Englishman in Paris, but had the other party prevailed, I probably should have been in the list of the proscribed.'[25] Paris was in violent mood:

> I am filled with involuntary horror at the scenes which pass before me and wish they could have been avoided, but at the same time I allow the absolute necessity of them. In some instances the vengeance of the people has been savage & inhuman. They have dragged the dead naked body of the Princess de Lamballe through the streets & treated it with all sorts of indignities. Her head stuck upon a Pike was carried through Paris and shown to the King & Queen, who are in hourly expectation of the same fate.[26]

While James lived on the edge in Paris, Anne had to give her father some bad news. For some time he had been worried about the health of his banker, William Matthews. William and Charlotte were on a visit to the Watts at Heathfield (the house, not far from Soho House, designed for them by Samuel Wyatt in 1789-90), but Boulton suggested to Anne that she try to persuade them to stay at Soho instead, which he thought would be more cheerful. However on 1 April Anne wrote to tell him that Mr Matthews had died at Heathfield that morning.[27] Only the previous day, she said, she had drunk tea with Mrs Watt and Charlotte Matthews, and Charlotte had maintained brightly that her husband was much better but, said Anne, it was evident to them all that 'she thought as she wished'. Boulton was dismayed at the loss of a man who was not only important to his business but had become a trusted friend. Much dispirited, he wrote to Anne, 'I am thankfull that I keep my health & that my spirits tho low do not fail me'.[28]

In his will, William Matthews left £500 each to Anne, Matt and their father, and similar sums to Zacheus Walker and John Scale; there was £1,000 to James Watt. Scale and James Watt were two of the four executors.[29] Anne's legacy was used to open an account in her name at Boulton & Watt's London agency. Charlotte, who had always taken an active role in her husband's business, now took it over, continuing as Boulton's banker for a time until, in her 70s, she reluctantly handed over to John Mosley and retired to her country house, Croydon Lodge.

Boulton had addressed Anne in his last letter as 'my dear helpless Daughter'. In reality she was not in the least helpless, but her childhood legacy did continue to affect her, for in her letter about William Matthews she also mentioned her father's plan to get some shoe lasts made for the family in London, and commented, 'If you thought of having a pair of Shoes made to mine it will be necessary for me to send directions respecting the height of the heel, thickness of the cork &c &c but I think I could get them made in Birmingham by a man who has just finished me a pair which are tolerably easy.'[30] At the age of 24 she was still having one shoe built up to compensate for her limp.

The summer following her husband's death Charlotte Matthews, with Mrs Vere, and the younger Fothergill daughters Mary ('Polly') and Martha ('Patty') invited Anne to join them on a trip to Sussex; they were taking two post-chaises, there was a spare seat, and they would enjoy her company. Boulton thought this an excellent idea: 'I own I think the next best thing to Sea Batheing is to live a little while upon the Coast. I am sure it will do you good.'[31] He himself was back in Cornwall where at least the roads were getting better:

> The Town of Truro is vastly improved, the main Street is open & spacious since the Middle row has been pulld down, all the Streets are new paved & layd with flags, on each side as in London, all their Houses are repaired & new painted within & without & every thing carrys the appearance of Riches & prosperity, every mine being in full work, all which may be fairly said to be owing to Boulton & Watt for if our Engines had not been introduced not any of the present Mines could have worked & the Country would have been a heap of Barren Ruins, depopulated, as Miserable ... as it is now void of honour & gratitude.[32]

He had found Cornwall full of French refugees and commented:

> When we see the horrid Massacres in France, when we see the highest ranks of Men & the most oppulant either Savagely Butchered or obliged to escape to a foreign land, without other attendants than empty pockets, deprived of their Estates & every means of Subsistance as well as every ray of Comfort in this World – separated from a Murderd Husband or Wife or Child or Friend or torterd with anxiety for the safety of some tender life they have left behind – I say when one considers & reflects upon these, & greater misery which I can foresee: Let our hearts expand with Gratitude to the Divine being for the Blessings we enjoy & let us stretch out our hand to the relief of the afflicted & unfortunate as we our selves hope to be comforted in the day of affliction which no one is exempt from.[33]

He passed on to Anne the regards of the Tremains at Helligan and various other Cornish acquaintances, and asked her to remember him to Mr Von Breda. The Swedish artist, Carl Frederik Von Breda, was currently in Birmingham, where he was finishing portraits of Boulton and Watt, and hoping for further commissions. Anne said everyone who had seen Von Breda's portrait of her father had greatly admired it, saying it did all but speak. Von Breda had now begun a portrait of Dr Withering: 'the Doctor is drawn in Black, sitting in an arm chair with a flower in his Hand which Matt says is intended for a Foxglove.'[34] The artist must have been trying to get as far forward as possible with this portrait as quickly as he could, for Withering was due to leave for Lisbon that month, where he was going to spend the winter for the benefit of his health, taking his daughter Charlotte along for company. Anne meanwhile was staying with friends at Shenstone. They were planning an outing to Lichfield Races, and there was to be a ball, 'but as I don't dance & should perhaps not know a person in the Room ... I have beg'd to be excused'.[35]

8

'Sublime' Matlock

The New Year of 1793 opened on a sombre note, with Boulton relaying to Anne the contents of a letter which Lord Landsdowne had read out to him in London, from a friend who had witnessed the execution of Louis XVI in Paris. The French king had gone to his death with composure, protesting his innocence and forgiving his executioners, his words to the assembled crowd drowned out by drums and trumpets. Boulton found this account very moving. 'I cant wt [write] more', he wrote to Anne.[1] It was a long hard winter and in March James Watt had difficulty travelling the short distance to Soho House for the Lunar Society meeting and even greater difficulty getting home again, due to six-foot snowdrifts which had obliterated the road across the common and forced Boulton's coachman, who was taking him home, to dismount and lead the horses on foot, 'so covered with snow that he was like a walking mummy'. The snowfall was followed by a violent thunderstorm and heavy rain for four hours, so that the fishponds at Heathfield overflowed and some of the Soho gravel walks were washed away.[2]

The gardens were put to rights and blooming again by the time their old friends the Fothergills arrived in the summer: John Fothergill's widow Elizabeth, her sisters-in-law Mary and Ann Fothergill, and her daughters Mary ('Polly') and Martha ('Patty'). The five ladies arrived at Soho on 6 August at about seven p.m. According to Patty (Plate 31) they had been accompanied by 'a very droll Postilion, he was quite in an half dress, and put me very much in mind of Humphrey Clinker'.[3] Each afternoon or evening they took an airing, strolling in the gardens with Anne Boulton, but Patty, who liked dancing and gaiety above all things, found this a bit tame. On 8 August it was Matt's 23rd birthday and she was looking forward at the very least to 'a dance or something very gay', but was disappointed to find the event being marked only by a small dinner party. Bored by the dinner table, after the meal Patty, her sister Mary and Nancy Mynd decided to go for a walk in the grounds; seeing Matt's small boat (Plate 32) moored at the lakeside, the three flibbertigibbets hit on the idea of going for a sail:

> ... we sent a messenger with our compts to Mr Holbrook a gentleman who was staying in the House [probably Thomas Holbrook, whom Nancy Mynd married the following year], and begg'd he would come to the water side to us which he very good naturedly did and took us in the Boat, but unfortunately Mary was in such a terrible fright when we put up the Sails we were oblig'd to make to the shore as fast as possible, and as we cou'd not get quite close Mr H. carry'd Mary out of the Boat in his arms. Miss Mynd and myself staid till a very heavy shower

of rain drove us in, the Ladies seem'd rather shock'd at this little adventure and were rather angry at having been obliged to wait tea for Miss Mynd ... Mr Pickering a Gentleman who dined here, had a little misfortune when he went with Mr Robinson to the boat after we had left them and tore his small clothes, which being black, the white shirt coming out cut rather a droll figure and Miss Mynd very good humourd'ly mended them for him. The party except Mr P. took their leave before Supper, and we were all very glad when the day was over, for except the little Boat scheme I never spent a more stupid one in my life.[4]

For the next few days Anne did her best to entertain the guests. They went shopping in Birmingham, visited friends, played cards and backgammon, played and sang to each other, and attended the 'dilettanti concert' (concerts put on by the Dilettante Society, formed to encourage music-making). Among the sights Anne took them to see was the altar window in St Paul's Church. The window, a painting on glass by her father's former employee Francis Eginton, after an original by Benjamin West, depicts the conversion of St Paul. Patty thought it not as good as one she had seen in Oxford. They visited Henry Clay's papier maché works where Patty's nose wrinkled in disgust: 'the smell of the pasting the Paper together and the Polishing is beyond any thing I ever smelt in my life.' There were illuminations in Birmingham to mark the Duke of York's birthday on 16 August so they 'walkd about the town' and did not return to Soho House until after midnight. Another day, disappointed by the lack of fireworks at Birmingham's Vauxhall (Plate 33), and in a petulant mood due to toothache, Patty sulked at Soho House while the rest of the party went to dinner at Doctor Withering's where, she maintained, 'they had a very stupid day'.

Anne, her father and the guests were planning a small expedition to Derbyshire, so on the evening of 25 August Mr Capper,[5] who was to join them, took Anne out for an experimental ride in his phaeton so that she could try it for comfort, as they thought it would probably give her more leg-room. Anne was so rattled and bounced about in the lightweight vehicle that Capper agreed to take her father's superior phaeton on the Derbyshire trip instead.

Next morning, Mr Boulton's phaeton and his carriage bowled up the Soho House drive, out through the gates, and set off on the open road for Derbyshire. In the phaeton were a well-cushioned Anne Boulton, escorted by Mr Capper, and in the crowded coach her Papa, the five Fothergill ladies, and Nancy Mynd. Another friend, 'Mr Wheatley' (possibly one of the Whateleys) also came along on horseback. They all dined together at Lichfield and looked round the Cathedral before going on to Derby, where they spent the night. Next morning they called on Dr Darwin at Radburn,

and he took us through his Gardin (and across a river in a boat that goes by itself) to another Garden full of all the common Weeds which he collects and is very fond of. At the end of this Garden he let us out to go and see the China Manufactory and promis'd to stay in his Summer House till our return. We were all delighted with the Manufactory, and saw a man mould a tea cup and saucer, and a Tea Pot, and the Painting the China etc. is vastly entertaining. We found the Dr in his Summer House on our return, and he then went with us to the Silk Mills with which we were also much entertain'd.[6]

Next stop was Matlock. The party re-grouped, with Anne Boulton, Mary and Patty in the phaeton, escorted by Mr Wheatley, and the 'old Party' following in the coach. Patty, not an easy girl to impress, was suitably awed by Matlock: 'I never was more struck than at the enterance of this Place, you have a view of the most beautiful rocks in the world with the River running at the Bottom.'

Boulton's own account of the trip records drily at this point:

> The sublimity of the lofty rocks, the beauty of the scenery, and the sprightliness of the company all conspired to delight and make all our flock of chickins kackle. No complainings were heard on our journey, no toothaches, nor fevers or asthmas, were known in our camp; but, like friskey kidlings, our virgins bounded over the rocks and asscended the highest torrs.[7]

The place where they had been hoping to stay, 'the Hall', was full, Patty recorded,

> so we were obliged to adjourn to the Temple, where we got our Tea and look'd at the Beds, and then went to Supper at the Hall. To Supper we sat down about seventy, and the style was so perfectly new to me I was quite charm'd with it. As the last comers we sat at the lower end of the Table, and did not make any acquaintance. After supper the tables were moved and the company all went to dancing but Mary was too much tired to join them, and we only saw two dances danced and then took our departure for the Temple where we slept.

On 28 August Boulton left his 'flock of chickins' to amuse themselves at Matlock while he went overnight to visit another old friend, Sir Joseph Banks, who lived about five miles away. After he had departed the rest of the party set off on another adventure, recounted breathlessly by Patty:

> [we] began our rambles which were very curious and I crawl'd up the Hills upon my Hands and Knees ... we took a Boat and went a quarter of a mile down the River between the Rocks, one of the most romantic places in the world ... Miss Howard [another guest at the hotel] had given us leave to join her party to see a Led Mine and Mary, Mr W. and myself accepted her offer. We went in the Boat as far as we cou'd and then walk'd by the side of the Rocks. At the enterance of the Mine the Gentlemen (of which there were four and two ladies besides ourselves) had Candles given them, but as we were not at first expect'd of the Party they had not provided for us. We walk'd three Hundred yards underground, and some times it was so wet we were obliged to walk upon a little board 2 Inches wide, but it was very worth while to go through this trifling inconvenience for the sight of so beautiful a Cavern. The light as we return'd opened upon us most beautifully. We return'd by a different road and had a most charming walk through a wood by the side of the Rocks. After tea we play'd at commerce with our own Party, and at night (as is the custom) after Supper the Tables were moved and we began dancing. This was rather uncommon for me, but I was asked to dance by a very smart Man (a Dr Simpson) I cou'd not possibly refuse. We return'd to the Temple at Twelve.

The next day Anne, Patty and Mary went in the open phaeton to the steep lead-mining valley of Bonsal, and the day following (after the rain had stopped) Anne and Mr Wheatley rode on horseback up a steep zigzag path, while Patty, Mary and friends followed on foot:

We had a most charming tho fatiguing walk and went much beyond the place we at first intended. The coming down was much more difficult than ascending, but fortunately we got very safe, and just in time for the dinner. Mary was very much tired and after dinner went to the Temple and took a nap, but I had promis'd to walk with Miss Howard which I did and went first with her and Mr Edgworth to see the Billiard Room – after which the Gentlemen (say Dr French, Dr Simson and Mr Clarke) joined us and we went across the water and walked opposite the Hall through a fine Wood by the Water side, when we [saw] the most beautiful clear spring I ever beheld. When we were returning Mr Wheatley met us and took us to the Temple to Tea and dress, which I did and when I came to the Tea Party I found Miss Goodenough and a Mr Samson Lloyd, a very agreable Man … After supper we danced as usual and as it was the last night we kept it up a good while and danced Over the Hills and Far Away which is one of the most romping dances I ever saw …

Leaving the sociable delights of Matlock behind, on 31 August they set off for Buxton. Once more Anne Boulton, Patty and Mary travelled together in the phaeton,

and a most beautiful ride we shou'd have had if it had not rain'd so violently as it did. We went through Darley Dale which is one of the sweetest places I ever saw, and it is reconed one of the finest rides in Derbyshire. We stop'd at Chatsworth which is about 12 miles from Matlock and the House belongs to the Duke of Devonshire but he resides very little in it. We saw the Gardens first which is quite in the Dutch style and the only one of the kind (they say) in this Kingdom. There are several fine cascades and one in particular that throws up the water ninety feet. There is also a curious Tree that by some Trap springs out water from all the Branches. The House is a very good one, but what it is most admired for is the carved work about it. In the dining Room it is particularly fine, and I think the Game that is around the Chimney Piece the most beautiful thing in the World. We saw the Chair our present King and Queen sat in at the Coronation – and were also shown poor Mary Queen of Scotts appartments when she was under confinement. There are no good Pictures in this House.

Having thus dismissed Chatsworth, they arrived in Buxton at eight p.m. but it seemed lacklustre after Matlock. Nevertheless, it made a good base from which to visit Castleton, where next morning they went into

one of the finest Caverns in England, unfortunately the Water came in so fast that the Guide wou'd not venture to take us further than the Boat: he said he could not answer for bringing us back safe. We dined at the Inn at Castleton and the People were all Dancing and singing it being the time of the Wakes. We got into the Post Chaise as soon as the Man had rested his Horses, and arrived at Buxton just in time to dress and go to the Play … we were very much entertained by the Performance of two Gentlemen, Mr Wade and Mr Carrol, the former Acted Captain Absolute in *The Rivals* and the latter Father Luke in the *Poor Soldier*.

There were further visits to caves, to another play, *Now to grow Rich*, and to a performance on the musical glasses, 'with which we were all much entertain'd'. On 6 September they left Buxton and turned the horses' heads towards home, via Uttoxeter, where they made a cross-country diversion to see a Mr Smith's farm. Determined not to miss out, Anne rode pillion behind their host's manservant, while the others rode singly.

Patty's descriptions of these various excursions conjure images of muddied skirts and shoes, manly arms offered to help over rocks and across streams and puddles, and maids shaking their heads and sighing at night over cleaning the bespattered gowns while the freshly primped ladies went chattering to the ball.

After the Derbyshire trip the visitors stayed on at Soho House until nearly the end of September. Often after dinner (which was usually between four and five p.m.) Anne and Patty walked in the gardens. On some evenings they had 'a great deal of singing. Mr Clavering sung the *Farthing Rushlight* and *Fol de Rol Fit* vastly well.' One evening, for a change after a hectic succession of dinners and dances, they 'staid at home and told Goast stories'.

It was as well that Anne enjoyed her Derbyshire adventure in 1793, for in the autumn of the following year she was to have an accident which would have made it much more difficult, even impossible.

The year 1794 started off busier than ever, for Matthew Boulton was to take office as High Sherriff of Staffordshire. Annie Watt wrote to Gregory: 'You will see by the papers that Mr Boulton is made Sherriff of Staffordshire & no doubt will make a great flash.'[8] The appointment certainly involved a fair amount of expense, since he was required to provide suits of livery for himself, 12 javelin men, a trumpeter and a bailiff. As High Sherriff he was expected to display armorial bearings, so he asked the College of Arms to prepare some for him. The arms have as their central element an anchor and two leopards' heads, probably reflecting Boulton's role in the foundation of Birmingham Assay Office, whose mark is an anchor. In the full coat of arms as it appears on items of family silver, the Boulton arms are quartered with the arms of Lowth, Babington and Robinson, reflecting his lineage and marriages. Although the Robinson quarter shows three bucks similar to those which appear on Elizabeth Montagu's arms, no genealogical evidence has been found to support the claim, made in the past, that Boulton's wives were distantly related to Elizabeth Montagu (*née* Robinson).[9]

While Boulton walked in chilly trumpeted procession to Stafford Assizes, Dr Withering was again wintering in Lisbon. This time he had taken his 17-year-old son William with him. They spent a mild winter in Portugal, taking excursions and collecting minerals, and returned to England in April 1794, following a scenic route home via Lyme Regis, the Isle of Wight, Winchester, Salisbury and Stonehenge (which William thought must have been 'erected by a very enlightened people to answer some great Astronomical purpose').[10] Arriving back in Birmingham they called first at Heathfield on 11 June to see the Watts, but to their dismay were met at the gate by Jessie Watt's funeral

FIG. 15 *The Boulton family arms as they appear engraved on a silver tea-vase now at Soho House. (Birmingham Museum & Art Gallery)*

procession coming away from the house.[11] Jessie had been ailing for some time. Various doctors had been consulted and cures tried. The child had not been able to go out much, but Dr Darwin thought it was good for her to keep occupied. He recommended a swing, which the Watts had installed in the laundry, games such as marbles and shuttlecock, and, obscurely, handbell ringing.[12] Thus confined, 15-year-old Jessie occupied herself (when not swinging or ringing the bell) by sewing, knitting and writing letters, but she had finally succumbed to tuberculosis.

By the time the Witherings senior and junior arrived home, James Watt junior had also returned, bringing with him to Heathfield a 15-year-old Sicilian boy as a servant.[13] James had moved on from France to Italy at the end of 1792, from where he wrote to his father: 'My curiosity abroad is fully satisfied and I have seen enough of other countries to be convinced that my own is far preferable to them all & to sit down contented in it for the rest of my life.'[14] In the New Year of 1793 he set off on the long journey home, taking a circuitous route to avoid travelling through France. James and his father patched up their differences and in 1794 James finally joined the firm of Boulton & Watt.

As the Boultons and the Watts welcomed back the prodigals, they said goodbye to another old friend. Joseph Priestley and his wife emigrated to America in the spring of 1794, joining their three sons who were already out there. The Priestleys had not lived in Birmingham since the 1791 riots, but remained in touch with their Birmingham circle and it must have been a wrench for Priestley to leave England, albeit for a country where he hoped to find greater intellectual freedom and tolerance. The Priestleys settled in Northumberland, Pennsylvania. They were followed a few weeks later by their good friends the Russells, another high-profile Birmingham family who had lost their home in the riots. William Russell was a fellow Guardian, with Matthew Boulton, of Birmingham Assay Office. He and his son Tom and his daughters Mary and Martha quickly ran into trouble when their ship was taken prisoner by French privateers in the Channel, just four days out of Falmouth. The Russell girls kept spirited journals of their four-month incarceration on board ship, enduring fleas, lice and revolting food but still managing to admire the sailors' dancing.

Eventually they were put ashore at Brest and spent the next six months in post-revolutionary Paris, where they embarked on a round of visits to museums, cathedrals and manufactories. They went shopping at the Palais Royal, where Mary's description of the shops echoed Matthew Boulton's of ten years earlier: 'the beauty and elegance of the shops was beyond description at night when they were all lighted up, it was past conception enchanting.'[15] They went to the theatre with Mrs Imlay (Mary Wolstonecraft, then living in the French capital with Gilbert Imlay and their eight-month-old daughter), and Mary Russell observed that at the Paris Opera 'the French heaven was I must confess much superior in taste and beauty to the English, tho' the English hell was far more terrific and dreadfull than the french'.[16] They attended a meeting of the National Assembly and concluded that most of the representatives taking part in the debate looked in need of a good wash (though conceded that it was generally judged unwise to appear on the streets looking too clean and smart). William Russell and his son went to an execution where, wrote Mary, they saw 16 people guillotined in 13 minutes.[17] Not until the summer of 1795 were the Russells finally able to set sail from Le Havre for America, where their keen eyes and pens took in and recorded everything they saw.[18]

The contrast between their lives and Anne Boulton's could hardly have been greater. Never one hundred per cent mobile, jumping down from a horse in the autumn of 1794 she had landed awkwardly and hurt one of her knees badly. Shortly after that she had slipped again and fallen down the coach steps in the dark, compounding the first injury. The knee was swollen and intensely painful and would not bear her weight. While her lifelong disability had caused her some awkwardness it had never really prevented her from getting about, but these two accidents and their painful aftermath now severely restricted her.[19] While Mary and Martha Russell explored Paris and excitedly scribbled their journals, Anne was virtually imprisoned on her couch at Soho House.

She occupied part of her time in the search for a housekeeper, for Nancy Mynd had now left following her marriage to Thomas Holbrook. With Anne laid up, she and her father really needed a reliable person and, not for the first time, they enlisted the help of Charlotte Matthews. Anne jotted down for her information what had been Nancy's duties: 'Miss Mynd took charge of the Household Linen, Mr Boulton & Mr M-B-s Cloathes, kept the keys of the Wine & fetched it up – Locked the Doors at night – kept the Accounts – Occasionally went to market – ordered the Meat on Thursday & saw it weighed.'[20] Soon, on Charlotte's recommendation, a Mrs James was engaged at 18 guineas a year including tea and sugar. They had a cook who was generally satisfactory, and the butler, Harper, was good at his job though inclined to steal the wine (to which Boulton turned a blind eye unless he got too bold). When Mrs James arrived from London in early December, Anne spent some time with her explaining her duties and the ways of the household, before introducing her to the rest of the servants. Two days later, to Mrs Matthews' intense embarrassment, Mrs James gave in her notice. She had decided to go back to London to learn to dress hair and live as a lady's maid, she said, and would leave as soon as she had recovered from the cold which she had brought with her. She did not like her sitting room at Soho House because it had a stone flagged floor (though Harper had put down a carpet for her) and also expected a private stillroom. Boulton acknowledged, 'It's true my House wants many Conveniences, and now it's my own I shall take an early opportunity of consulting Mr Wyatt in some necessary alterations.'[21] He had recently bought the freehold of his estate, after characteristically writing out a list of the pros and cons and deciding that if he did not, in years to come houses would be built up to the drawing room windows and the view spoiled.[22]

At the time Mrs James packed her bags and stumped off back to London to be a hairdresser, there seems to have been general unrest among the Soho House servants, for shortly afterwards Annie Watt told Gregory that all the maids had been sent packing.[23] The bibulous Harper stayed in post, for in February he and the Watts were in London with Boulton, who was ill: 'He does keep such a groaning you never heard anything like it, he sometimes does not receive much pity for he often eats and drinks what is very bad for him, his man Harper like Satan is constantly tempting him by setting before him food highly improper, then Mr B is sure to suffer [because] he cannot resist.'[24] After setting out for her son's disapproval some examples of Harper's menus (for he seemed to be choosing their meals without consultation), Mrs Watt concluded stoutly, 'The best place for him is Botany Bay'.

In May 1795 the Watts and Matt Boulton were back in London, where they met up with the Fothergills. There had been talk about a marriage between Matt and Miss Mary Foreman Fothergill ('Polly'), the third daughter of Boulton's late partner John Fothergill. Matt was not being overly co-operative in the matter. 'You know it was said the friends wished to make a match with Matt and her which he did not approve of,'[25] wrote Annie Watt to Gregory. It was not the first time the question had come up. A year or two earlier Boulton had sent his son a summary of the Fothergill women's fortune and expectations, showing that Polly had been left £15,333 in the will of Mr Foreman (possibly Charles Foreman, who had died in 1790; the Foreman and Fothergill families were related by marriage).[26]

In the same letter to Gregory, written after they got back to Heathfield, Annie told her son about a house guest at Heathfield, James Lind's sister:

> Miss Lind is still here and begs her complaints [sic] to you. She is not yet cured of her vainity and love of dress and show, it really hurts one to see such a being taken up with such things. Her figure & age makes it truly ridiculous, she always puts me in mind of the devil on two sticks when I see her tricked up as she does sometimes, and it makes her person a thousand times more remarkable. She has sense and yet is the most ignorant being about the common occurrences of life I ever met with. However with all her follies I think myself very much obliged to her, she is very attentive and obliging and is always ready to read to me which is always agreeable to me.[27]

While Polly tried (and failed) to capture Matt, that summer of 1795 Anne lay at the Dumergues' Piccadilly home with her legs up. In spite of bandaging and rest, the knee had failed to improve over the ten or more months since her fall. The Dumergues' home made a convenient place for London consultants to visit her. Two physicians were consulted, Henry Cline and a Mr Grant. The latter was, according to Fanny de Luc, 'a most eminent Surgeon, now removed from Bath to London'. Fanny related the story of a Mrs Fielding's daughter who had consulted him

> in a much worse State than Miss Boulton, from something very similar, & who had suffered years after years the most alarming relapses; she suffered so much that she was obliged to take Laudanum constantly & was carried to Bath in a Litter. Mr Grant saw her last year for a second time, examined her knee, did not recommend any thing for a fortnight, till he had sufficiently considered her case, then he prescribed with such judgement that he has made an absolute & most compleat cure of her.[28]

Cline and Grant came to Piccadilly and examined the 'poor unfortunate knee'. They concluded there was no actual damage to the joint and recommended a regime of plasters intended to reduce the inflammation. Anne hated what she called the 'stinking plaster'.[29] The basic ingredient of these 'plasters' was litharge, or red lead monoxide. Dr Withering wrote to Dr Edward Ash in 1798 of treatments involving lead which had produced bad side effects, including the case of 'a woman [who] had a pair of thick Legs swathed with plaister … after some time she had symptoms of … paralysis. She always complained much of the smell of her plaisters. Would not zinc make as good a basis for plaisters as litharge?'[30]

Anne wrote miserably of being confined to the Dumergue's drawing room, as she was unable to get up the stairs. Charles, Sophia and Nursey Nickey were the personification of kindness, but Anne was worried that when autumn brought the return of the entertaining season they would need their drawing room back; she thought it was time she returned to Soho. Mrs Nicholson had been so kind that Anne wanted to make her a gift of a fashionable gown. Explaining all this to her father, she added this injunction: 'I have only to request my letters may *not* be read to any of your party, for I am no *authoress*, only a miserable scribe.'[31]

Several of Miss Boulton's acquaintance had by now launched into print – there was Fanny Burney, of course, whose *Evelina* had taken society by storm in 1778 and who had followed it up with *Cecilia* in 1782 and would go on to write three more books (Plate 30); there was Mrs Montagu who was always writing about something; Anna Seward, the 'Swan of Lichfield' was busy with her pen; then there was Maria Edgeworth (Plate 54), daughter of Anne's father's friend Richard Lovell Edgeworth, who had been writing stories for her numerous little siblings for some years, and who in 1795 published a collection of them under the title *The Parents' Assistant* and another book, *Letters for Literary Ladies*; Maria later collaborated with her father on a much-consulted book, *Practical Education* (1798). In Birmingham, William Hutton's daughter, Catherine, had been writing since childhood. Her detailed account of the 1791 riots, in which her family lost their home, had been privately printed and circulated;[32] several of her magazine articles and novels were eventually published. Anne Boulton did not see herself joining the ranks of the literary ladies, but perhaps found a different route to self-expression through music.

Though she badly wanted to come home, Soho House was just then so full of visitors that her father was sleeping in her bed, so Anne went instead to see the Fothergills at Epsom. Her father suggested she ask Mr Cline whether sea-bathing might help the knee. A Mrs Stewart had told him Brighton was not so convenient a bathing place as Swansea or Southampton, but nevertheless it was popular with ladies. He went on to tell Anne about the severe bread and flour shortages in Birmingham and Lichfield, where the poor people were on the verge of starvation and he had been organising subscriptions to buy corn for them. He had given instructions that the bread at Soho House was to be made at least partly of cheaper wholemeal flour: 'for unless the opulent set the Example the poor of this neighbourhood are too fine mouthed & sausey to eat brown Bread – I intend every week to publish in Pearsons paper some observations upon the subject & endeavour to perswade the poor that Brown bread is more wholesome than White Bread ...' [33] In this, Boulton was following the lead set by George III, who insisted on the bread at his table being generally brown bread or potato bread, as an example to others.[34]

Instead of Brighton, Swansea or Southampton, in August 1795 Anne went to Ramsgate. She went into the sea reluctantly and hurried out again with chattering teeth. The water was bitterly cold. This would never do. Boulton wrote to her:

> [I] am sorry to find that you are so cold afterwards, however, it is not to be wonderd at when I consider what a Winterly Summer we have had. Moreover it would be more wonderfull if you were warm, as you say you do not wipe the Water off before you put on your clothes. I therefore beg you will cause the Water to be wiped off & then rubd with a dry Cloth & then put on a dry flannell Gown & all this should be done in less than half a minute if possible & then I doubt not but you will get warm again in a few minutes after you are dressed.[35]

He hoped that when Anne came home she would bring with her for company either the Epsom ladies (Mrs, Miss and the two Misses Fothergill, all apparently still on amiable terms with the Boultons in spite of Matt's rejection of one of their number as a potential wife) or else Charlotte Matthews, Mrs Vere and their two maids. The doctor had said Boulton had 'a large lodgement of Calculus in one Kidney' and he feared the proposed course of medicine, of which he had previous experience, would leave him feeling too low to be good company himself.[36] Anne and her father were still trying to resolve their staff problems, and had borrowed one of Charlotte Matthews's maids as a temporary measure. In the meantime Charlotte found them yet another housekeeper whom Boulton wanted at Soho as soon as possible:

> tell me when she can conveniently come so we may clear the way for her ... I am determind to avoid takeing any of the subordinate Maids from Birm[gm] as their Relations & connections are sure to crowd my House on Sunday & when I am absent. I therefore prefer Lincolnshire or any shire to this Neighbourhood. Dosey is a very good cook & Kitty, tho ugley, a good Chambermaid and Taberner a trifling foolish body, that is more likely to please a Master than a Mistress, but they are constantly quarrelling with each other & rude to my Daughter. I am therefore determind to have a new sett for I will have peace in Israel.[37]

He added that Dosey the cook's wages were currently nine guineas a year and Kitty the housemaid was paid six guineas a year. Harper had 25 guineas a year and paid for his own clothes. Joseph the coachman received a similar wage, but also had a small house for himself and his family; he too paid for his own livery.

Although getting on in years, and with some worrying signs that his health might be beginning to fail, Boulton remained as busy as ever. In the winter of 1796 he did not even get home for Christmas, for he, Matt and the Watts were in London for the court case over Boulton & Watt's engine patent (in which they were victorious). They spent Christmas Day with Charlotte Matthews at Croydon Lodge, from where he wrote to Anne, regretting his absence from home. It was bitterly cold in Croydon. Unable to get a chaise, Mrs Matthews and Gregory Watt had walked part of the way to a dinner on Christmas Eve, but in spite of having got very cold she had later insisted on sleeping in an unaired bed herself and letting Boulton have her own bed, 'with the accompaniment of a good fire and an Hydradown [eiderdown] quilt.' They were all warm and well, and cheerful fires blazed in every room of the house, keeping the outside cold at bay. A man in Croydon had told him the thermometer stood at eleven degrees below zero, and he was worried about his birds at Soho, asking Anne to

> immediately order the poor Turtle Dove & the pair of Carrier Pidgeons to be brought up to the House & put in one or two cages & hung up in the old Kitchen or somewhere out of the reach of ye Cat or otherwise they will dye. I know not which is the most Cruel to burn or to starve to death but think the latter as it is more lingering.[38]

How (apart from rescuing chilled turtle doves), or with whom, Anne spent her Christmas Day is not recorded.

9

'Elisium' at Soho

At the home of the turtle dove and the carrier pigeons, Anne watched as the gardens continued to develop. Each year, more plants were brought in. The shrubs which had been planted in 1788 were now well-established: 200 evergreen and flowering varieties, including a number of different rhododendrons, clothed the ground on either side of the Temple of Flora and in the plantation. At the same time 300 more herbaceous plants had been delivered for flowerbeds and borders. They had cost £7 3s. 10d. and the nurseryman instructed that if planted 'well varied and mixt, they will add much to the beauty of the Place, as well as furnish Miss Boulton with a Great Variety of choice flowers for Her Amusement in the Botanical system'.[1] One specimen of *rhododendron ponticum*, a shrub now considered little better than a weed, cost 9s., by far the most expensive item. Anne studied and sketched the plants and became familiar with their botanical and common names.

The garden was a constant source of interest to her father, too, but since the late 1780s he had been fired up with ambitious plans for improvements to Soho House itself. For almost as long as he had lived there, he had hankered after a grand house with two wings and a much bigger library; he had even made sketches of it in the past. In 1787 he talked it over with the architect Samuel Wyatt. The Wyatt family (from Weeford, near Lichfield) and the Boultons were old friends. Samuel's father, William Wyatt, had worked for the Robinsons, and was also the designer of the principal building at the Soho Manufactory in the early 1760s.

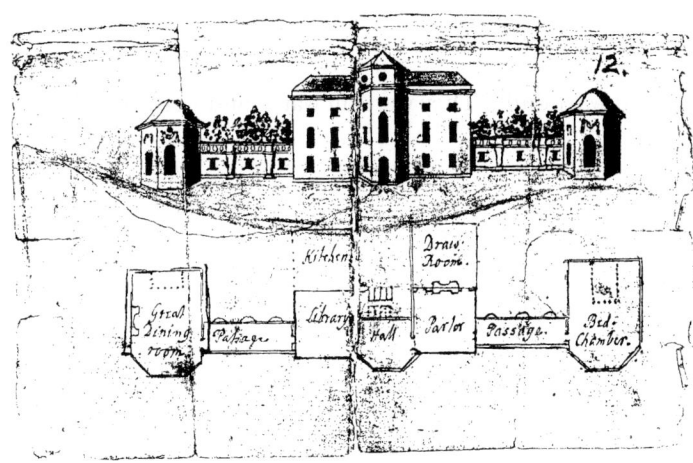

FIG. 16 *An early sketch of proposed alterations to Soho House, probably done by Matthew Boulton, n.d. (Birmingham City Archives)*

Various members of the family worked for Boulton, either at Soho or on other projects in which he had a hand, over many years. In his proposals for Soho House, after the discussion with Boulton in 1787, Sam Wyatt made the existing house the central element in a scheme with wings either side. The following year another architect, John Rawsthorne, drew up alternative plans and elevations in which the original house, redesigned with a new and imposing front, again became the focal point in the centre of a wide building, with single-storey wings either side containing rooms designated for 'Wet Chymistry, Dry Chymistry, Natural history, Botany-Green House, Astronomy'.

Work on the major alterations did not begin immediately, but some smaller improvements were made. In 1788 Sam Wyatt supplied a prefabricated wooden extension containing a bathroom, dressing room and water closet. The water closet was one of Joseph Bramah's new patent flushing water closets, costing £11 2s. 3d.[2] The bath, which was steam-heated and according to Boulton's notebook measured 8ft 3ins long x 5ft 9ins wide x 5ft 6ins deep,[3] had to be filled from an outside well. The well evidently did not produce a sufficient volume of water quickly enough to fill the bath at one go, for in a letter to Matt in 1793 Boulton, who was in London suffering with back-ache and feeling a warm bath would be just the thing to relieve it, remarked, 'I wish you would order my bath to be clean'd and half fill'd, and the day after to be fill'd up to the broad step, for the well will not supply all at once without mud.' He was setting out for home the next day, looking forward to a warm bath but planning to spend a night with the Herschels at Slough en route.[4]

Boulton was not overly satisfied with his wooden bath house but was too busy with the building of the Soho Foundry at Smethwick to give it much thought then. However, in 1794 he returned to thoughts of enlarging his home, and Sam Wyatt's brother, James Wyatt, drew up new plans. Again the old house was flanked by wings,

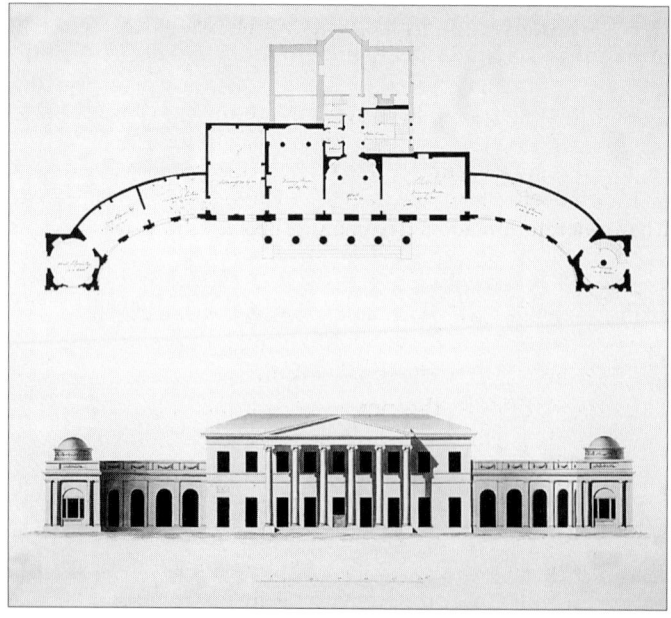

FIG. 17   *John Rawsthorne's proposal for the enlargement of Soho House, 1788. This scheme was not carried out. (Birmingham Museum & Art Gallery)*

FIG. 18 *James Wyatt's design for the new front elevation of Soho House, 1796. (Birmingham Museum & Art Gallery)*

but this time the original building was to be hidden behind a new, impressively pillared and pedimented block on the front to house a grand staircase. Boulton liked Wyatt's ideas and wrote to him, 'Your Ionick front with columns accords with my taste the best & yet it may be said to be an old fashion Front, as such were built 2000 years ago, but at the same time it may be said to have stood the test of Criticks & Time without amendment.'⁵ (He took much the same approach to silverware design, some of which James Wyatt also designed for him.)

Anne and Matt were evidently not too keen on seeing their familiar and comfortably-sized home thus transformed, for in a letter to Gregory Watt Annie Watt said the plans were 'not much to the likeing of his Son & Daughter, at present it is his Hobby Horse and he will ride it till he gets a new one.'⁶ Notwithstanding their reservations, the plans were approved and James Wyatt set about giving Soho House a neo-classical makeover. Boulton, lying in bed while he recovered from a leg injury, studied the plans and kept coming up with fresh ideas, among them the need to create a rear entrance for family use, to reduce the number of carriages driving up to the front door and the concomitant heaps of horse manure outside the best entrance, which made the gravel

> totally unfit for Ladies with satin shoes to walk out upon, which would not be the case if Ceremonial Visitors & great Folks only were to come to the Front: & the beauty of my place depends much upon my walks being clean & neat & my lawns green … Hence I am now become very desirous of having an entrance at the back-front … I have therefore made a new plan in Bed & send it to you herewith.⁷

In solving his 'back-front' problem, Boulton also solved the problem of the wooden bathhouse at a stroke, and to his great satisfaction, for by reducing the size of both his study and the housekeeper's sitting room the space he carved out was big enough to accommodate both the new rear entrance hall and a new bath and powdering room. In this small room the enormous steam-heated bath was re-installed.⁸

While he fiddled with the plans for the house, Boulton continued with improvements to the gardens. They were shaping up nicely, and as he surveyed his little park with its 'Garland of Flowers on one side & … an aqueous mirror on ye other'⁹ he could not resist jotting a little self-congratulatory verse in his notebook:

No Forest, but a Garden neat
An easy Walk, a resting seat
Made from the barren Wast by me
Who planted every Flower and Tree
To screen me from the NE Breese
And most of all my self to please.
Nor Knight nor Price nor Burk sublime
I ape, in Landskip, nor in Rhime.[10]

As usual, Annie Watt had views. She wrote to Gregory, 'Mr Boulton is going on in spending money. He is now narrowing his broad Gravel walks and has placed two Gigantic synphaxes [sphinxes] near the house. He is increasing the number of his carriages amazingly. Last night he got a new one with some kind of new screws, *springs* I mean. He has now a coach 2 post chaises a Yarmouth car and 2 kinds of Garden chairs. I believe he is gone crazy.'[11] The 'synphaxes' (Plate 35), along with three stone vases and transport, cost Boulton £47, with a further £8 14s. 7d. for three men's labour making and erecting their pedestals, organised by William Hollins, a local architect and sculptor who undertook a number of jobs for Boulton.[12]

One thing he really wanted was an imposing entrance to his estate, and in 1796 he had the gateway redesigned to complement the drive of 'Gothick arches made by Trees' which would suddenly open out to reveal to visitors an impressive vista of the Manufactory and park. Annie Watt told Gregory, 'Mr B is still going on with his improvements at a great expence. The grand entrance to his house is to go from the old apple man's stall where he has already placed a large bright green Gothick gate which cuts a most flaming dash.'[13]

Word spread far and wide about the alterations at Soho, and Fanny de Luc wrote to say how impatient she was to see all the improvements; the Herschels had promised her a lift with them next time they came to Birmingham. She had just been with the Queen at Windsor, where she had seen Madame D'Arblay (Fanny Burney) who had come to present her new novel, *Camilla*. Fanny's husband had come with her: 'he appeared to us very dejected, & considering the present state of his Country & of all others in consequence we esteemed him a sensible & feeling man from that cironstance, as for his wife she is all life & spirits as well as healthy.'[14]

Although James Wyatt had made a start on the building work, he was by now one of the most fashionable architects in the country and had more prestigious projects in hand, among them creating a series of landscape buildings for the Earl of Coventry's park at Croome, Worcestershire. In consequence he spent less and less time on Soho House and by late 1796 the house was swarming with quarrelling workmen, ineffectively supervised in Wyatt's absence by a Mr Heaton. It was just not good enough. Boulton complained to Wyatt: 'I have already paid a very large sum of Money to bring my dwelling house into the most uncomfortable state possible as the Winds Rain & Snow drives into it; & for want of the main Stack of Chimneys being built up to the top of the House it is constantly filld with Smoak by which my Books are spoiled my daughters health much injurd & my servants obliged to live out of Doors.'[15]

In the midst of all the chaos, 26-year-old Matt dropped the bombshell that he was thinking of moving out and getting a place of his own, not far away at Winson

Green. Boulton bewailed his son's plans to Charlotte Matthews, who promptly wrote to Matt urging him to at least discuss it with his father and give him the reasons for his decision, 'when he so anxiously wishes you to reside at Soho'.[16] She begged Matt's pardon for presuming to intrude but said her only motive was to conciliate any misunderstanding between father and son. Whether or not due to Charlotte's intervention, Matt stayed put at Soho.

Eventually his father grew so disheartened with all the delays and inconvenience and the general misery attendant upon having builders in, that in 1798 he abandoned much of the scheme and just concentrated on getting the main house and the new west wing reasonably habitable. James Wyatt's proposed new block on the front of the old house was also abandoned before it was begun, so that the main part of the house, dating from *c.*1757, stayed at much its original size, with its discreetly tucked-away staircase which still surprises visitors today. The old frontage was smartened up, however, with Samuel Wyatt producing a revised design in which the brickwork was clad with slate and stuccoed, and ionic pilasters and a modest pillared portico were added to give it a neo-classical feel.

Anne Boulton, who was at home more than her father, must have found the noisy and dusty invasion of builders even more wearing than he did. Coughing away the smoke, she kept a watchful eye on things when he was away, and the foremen and clerks of works soon learned to consult her before making any significant decisions. In June 1797 William Newbold wrote to Boulton at her insistence, to let him know that the roof framework was on and ready for the slaters to begin work. Work had been delayed by the fact that the walls had gone four courses of bricks too high and had had to be taken back, and the chimneys altered correspondingly.[17] William Hollins, who had already designed the visitors' tea-room, an aviary and the new entrance gates for the park, also worked on the Soho House improvements for a time and in 1798 wrote to say that Miss Boulton had instructed him to get her father's approval before finishing the bedroom adjoining the new library, where she thought there ought to be a new chimneypiece.[18]

Even after the curtailment of its planned alterations, Soho House was, like its owner, somewhat ahead of its time, with its steam-heated bath, its two 'Bramah' patent flushing water closets (one upstairs and one down), and most of all, its warm-air ducted central heating system. Boulton, who liked his creature comforts,

FIG. 19 *James Wyatt's design for the new 'back front' or rear elevation of Soho House, showing the new west wing, 1796. (Birmingham Museum & Art Gallery)*

had experimented with installing a central heating system in William Withering's house in Edgbaston a few years earlier, but the Witherings did not like the smell it produced and had it taken out again. Boulton, one of whose notebooks contains notes and diagrams on 'different ways of warming a church' which include both underfloor heating and double-glazed windows,[19] now devised an improved system for Soho House. A large coal-fired cockle stove[20] was installed in the cellar, connected to a network of ducting concealed within the walls around the house, leading to grilles in various rooms; through these a flow of air warmed by the stove could be directed to various parts of the house. While climbing slowly up the stairs to her own rooms, Anne had her toes warmed as warm air flowed out through holes in the risers on the staircase.

The alterations to the main house were more or less finished in 1798, including details like the smart new (albeit small-scale) arcaded and marble-pillared entrance hall (Plate 36) with its sculpture niches and fine mahogany and rosewood doors and door-casings to the principal rooms (still in place). There were new carved stone or marble chimney pieces in most rooms, and the former kitchen had been transformed into an elegantly pillared and vaulted dining room (Plate 37), a replacement kitchen being situated in the new west wing.

Work now began on the interiors, in which it is hard not to imagine Anne Boulton having a hand. The experience she gained in looking at paper and fabric swatches, sketches and furniture was to prove useful later. Though the rooms at Soho House were not large, they were to be modern and stylish. Cornelius Dixon, a well-known theatrical scenery painter who had also worked on the new British Museum and on Walpole's house at Twickenham, Strawberry Hill, was brought in as interior design consultant. Some of the walls were painted in plain colours and some were papered. The new pillars and pilasters in the dining room were artificially marbled. For the drawing room they chose a warm and sunny-looking scheme of creamy damask floral paper divided into panels separated by borders of plain deep yellow, edged with a narrow red and gold ribbon, all printed separately and pieced together on the walls; another paper was flowered and striped in pale grey and gold. Dixon ordered the papers from Lane & Co, paper stainers of New Bond Street, who promised to match any colour and size of stripes he chose to command.[21] The papers were delivered in short pieces – wallpapers were not yet printed on a long roll.

Whatever old furniture there had been in the house probably disappeared upstairs or into the servants' quarters, for the fashionable London cabinet maker James Newton was given the task of re-furnishing the main rooms. Bright new japanned and gilded furniture appeared in the ground-floor reception rooms. Benjamin Wyatt made a long mahogany D-end table for the new dining room, in sections so that it could be reduced or extended. The Watts were possibly planning to make the Boultons a gift of some table linen for it, for Gregory Watt wrote to his father (who was in Glasgow), 'I have enquired of Mr Boulton about his tablecloths. The dimensions I have obtained I beg you will communicate to my Mother – the length of the largest table including the two round ends is 16 feet, width 4'6". The table for 14 or any less N[umbe]r is 10ft 3inches.'[22]

To go round the table James Newton supplied 12 mahogany Gothic-back dining chairs and two carvers, all with red morocco leather-covered seats, costing in total

£37 10s. od. Two sideboards were made to fit in the alcoves either side of the chimney breast, their fronts curved to accommodate the pillars.

For the drawing room there were 12 black japanned and gilded elbow chairs at 42s. each, and sofa tables, mirrors and other occasional furniture. The sidereal clock, on a pedestal made for it by Newton, took pride of place. Upstairs, new beds, with dimity* covers and draped testers were supplied. To complete the room settings, Boulton jotted down on his London shopping lists such finishing touches as 'beautyfull sentimental prints'.

Throughout the house, windows were dressed in yards of white or buff calico and dimity, trimmed with flowered borders and fringes, except in the dining room where 55 yards of calico were splendidly marbled and glazed to replicate the artificial marbling on the pillars either side of the chimneypiece and the pilasters around the room. The marbling was 'entirely new & was fixd upon by Mr Dixon', wrote James Newton, in a letter informing Boulton that the packing case containing the dining room curtains was on its way from London.[23] The dining-room curtains, lined and trimmed with a crocus border, brown silk lace and ropes and tassels, including all materials and labour as well as rods, brackets, hooks and the packing case, came to £32 1s. 5d.[24] Floors were covered against the cold with Brussels carpet, carefully made up and fitted to the room plans. The overall appearance was rich, warm and comfortable. 'Soho is now nearly compleat and shines refulgent in all the grandeur of painting gilding Red Morocco & buff curtains,' wrote Gregory Watt.[25]

The plans for the alterations show the largest room on the second floor as Anne's bedroom, but it was on the north side of the house, and given her difficulties in managing stairs it seems more likely she would have actually occupied a smaller room on the first floor, next to her sitting room. For this tiny, sunny, feminine room (Plate 39) James Newton supplied curtains of fine white calico, trimmed with a green flowered border and green silk fringes, a small square sofa covered to match the curtains, two japanned elbow chairs, a fine satinwood writing table banded in rosewood and tulip wood, a work table, and two satinwood pole screens. In calculating his liability to pay duty on lights a year or two later, Boulton put down three for Anne's bedroom, one for her dressing room (the room she used as a sitting room) and three for the ladies' powdery and closet next door, giving Anne and her friends the best light to attend to hair, complexions and dress.[26] (Plate 40)

Between October 1797 and August 1799 Boulton spent a total of £506 19s. 3d. on new furniture and soft furnishings.[27] Meanwhile work went on to complete the new two-storey west wing of the house, which would include a much larger library on the first floor. John Phillp, a young man Boulton had brought from Cornwall and trained as a draughtsman (thought by some to be his illegitimate son[28]), produced designs for shelving for it (Plate 38). When it was finished the room in the main house which had been the library up till then became Matthew Boulton's bedroom.

Oddments remained to be completed, one of which was a painted floorcloth for the entrance hall. Floorcloths were a forerunner of linoleum. They were made of canvas, treated with size and painted, often in geometrical designs in colours which would sometimes mimic the colours to be found in decorative inlaid stone

---

* Dimity: fine cotton fabric, usually white, with a raised self-colour woven design.

floors in much grander houses, such as Kedleston Hall. The finished cloths, thickly varnished for protection, were tightly stretched and tacked down, and provided an easily-cleaned finish for floors where mud was likely to be trodden in from outside. The order for the Soho House floorcloth was placed by Cornelius Dixon in 1799 with Smith, Baber & Downing of Knightsbridge. The design, a large circular geometric centre, bordered with a brick pattern, was done by Downing, 'an artist of considerable merit' according to Cornelius Dixon. Yellow ochre is known to have been used for some floorcloths in the house, but it is not known what colours were used for the hall. It took a long time to complete, due to the intricacy of the design and the many coats of paint and varnish required to produce a tough surface, and Boulton complained about the delay to Dixon, who went along to Knightsbridge to check on progress. On hearing that Dixon had called at the works Downing wrote to him, explaining, 'The Pattern to compleat in the manner we are doing requires much time but when executed will be I think the Grandest of the kind ever laid on a Floor'.[29] In the event, it was nearly five years before the floor cloth, measuring 15 feet by 14 feet, was delivered, at a cost of £19 4s. 0d.

The full effect of the alterations to the house and gardens was duly admired by Fanny de Luc, who in 1801 came on a visit to Anne. Boulton was away on business and Fanny wrote to him from his own drawing room, 'Soho is more beautiful than ever & we every day regret that its charms remain so long unfelt by you during this delightful Season!' Fanny was writing instead of Anne, she explained, because Anne was just writing a hurried letter to Mary Fothergill which Gregory Watt, who was waiting to set off, would deliver for her. Anne had been feeling the effects of the hot weather, 'but it is now cooler & she is charmingly well this morning, and rejoicing most sincerely that you are doing all you can to confirm your own [health]!'. The two women had been to the theatre in Birmingham to see Mrs Siddons, but 'tho' her attractions are very great they have not been sufficient to fill the House yet'. Anne and Fanny had also tried out Boulton's 'new Warwickshire Walk' in his grounds, 'which was a great expedition for us both, & afforded us a very great satisfaction. She [Anne] got out of her Chair to pass the Flood Gate or the little bridge opposite to Mr Fords, & all the rest went as smooth as possible; that part of the Garden transports one in imagination to the most remote & sweet of retreats!' It would, thought Fanny, 'suit even our Romantick young Friends Mr & Mrs Moilliet, who have injoyed much of the Solitude of Malvern, as the most congenial to their feelings, tho' they rejoiced also to meet with you in their Journey … Mr Moilliet has just made his appearance at Soho this moment & says that he had the pleasure of leaving you well.' [30] The newly-wed Moilliets were Amelia, daughter of Boulton's friend James Keir, and her Swiss husband, Jean Louis (or John Lewis) Moilliet.

With its flowery park, its new decorations, its printed wallpapers, fringed and braided curtains, gilded mirrors and japanned furniture, accented by an array of silverware and ormolu from Boulton's own Manufactory and colourful china from his friend Josiah Wedgwood, Soho House was a richly decorative and welcoming house – no hint of austerity here, for all the cool rationalism of its neo-classical architectural details. William Herschel wrote, 'I find that the *Amusements* of the Town have no charms for you. It will make your Elisium, Soho, so much the sweeter. We shall be happy to see you in your way to that blissful Mansion.'[31] (Plate 45)

PLATE 21   *The house at Stoke-by-Nayland, Suffolk, once used by Revd. Samuel Parlby, where Matthew Robinson Boulton attended school from 1785-6.*

PLATE 22   *The Friends' Meeting House at Come-to-Good, near Trelissick, Cornwall. (Friends' Meeting House, Come-to-Good)*

PLATE 23 *Charles Dumergue (c.1739-1814), oil on canvas, c.1780, by Johann Zoffany (1733-1810). (Victoria Art Gallery, Bath and North East Somerset Council/Bridgeman Art Library)*

PLATE 24 *Sophia Dumergue, by Johann Zoffany, c.1780. (Victoria Art Gallery, Bath and North East Somerset Council.)*

PLATE 25 *Mrs Sarah Siddons.*

PLATE 26 *Sir William Herschel, by Lemuel Francis Abbott, 1785. (National Portrait Gallery, London)*

PLATE 27   'Transplanting of Teeth', cartoon by Thomas Rowlandson, 1787. (© The Trustees of the British Museum)

PLATE 28 *Elizabeth Montagu (above), by Thomas Cheesman, after William Evans, after Sir Joshua Reynolds. (National Portrait Gallery, London)*

PLATE 29 *Mary Linwood (right), water-colour by Richard Westall, 1799. (Leicester City Museums Service)*

PLATE 30 *(Left) Frances d'Arblay (Fanny Burney), by Edward Francesco Burney. (National Portrait Gallery, London)*

PLATE 31 *(Below) Miniature of Patty Fothergill. (Private collection)*

PLATE 32   *The Boulton family boat on Soho Pool, pen and ink drawing by John Phillp, 1796. Part of the Boulton family crest can be seen on the stern. (Birmingham Museums & Art Gallery)*

PLATE 33   *Vauxhall Gardens, Duddeston, Birmingham, according to Patty Fothergill 'of all stupid places the most so, and we had no fireworks'. Print of a drawing by E.H. New, 1837. (Birmingham Central Library, Local Studies and History)*

PLATE 34   *Temple of Flora,
Soho, watercolour by John
Phillp, 1794. (Birmingham
Museums & Art Gallery)*

PLATE 35   *Carved stone
sphinx, one of a pair bought
by Matthew Boulton for
the Soho House gardens
in 1795. (Birmingham
Museums & Art Gallery)*

PLATE 36 *The restored entrance hall, Soho House, showing the floorcloth reproduced from the design for the original. (Birmingham Museums & Art Gallery)*

PLATE 37   *The restored dining room, Soho House. The dining table was made for the room by Benjamin Wyatt in 1798.* *(Birmingham Museums & Art Gallery)*

PLATE 38   *John Phillp's design for shelving for Matthew Boulton's new library at Soho House. (Birmingham Museums & Art Gallery)*

10

'Her Leg or her Life'

The Soho House improvements saga ran as a sort of back-story to the lives of the family over some eight to ten years, and with their minds so taken up with building snags, furniture and fabric swatches, as well as with the general run of business, it seems almost surprising that they found any time to get involved with events outside the home, but Matthew Boulton was not one to take a back seat when opportunity beckoned. In October 1797 patriotic fervour was running high after the victorious naval Battle of Camperdown.[1] In towns and cities across the country, committees got together to organise fund-raising events in aid of the widows and orphans of the sailors killed in the battle. Boulton was not impressed with the Birmingham committee's plan to put on a small concert with a group of fiddlers, and took it on himself to write to Lords Aylesford and Dudley. With their influence he got the consent of several nationally-known singers and musicians to perform. The result was a GRAND CONCERT at the Birmingham theatre, followed immediately afterwards by a ball. With concert ticket prices between three shillings and seven shillings, and for the ball three shillings and sixpence, the evening raised £400 for the fund, well above the target figure of £300. Boulton was, he told Charlotte Matthews, 'one of the Masters of the Ceremony'.[2] The programme was much to his and Anne's taste, with plenty of Handel including an Oboe Concerto and several arias. It finished on a suitably triumphant note with Arne's *Rule, Britannia!* and *God Save the King*.[3]

There is no indication in the papers of whether Matt shared his father's and sister's love of music (though we know that he did not care for dancing), or whether he went to the concert, but in any case he had other things on his mind. Time was marching on. He had not been inclined to marry Polly Fothergill when it was suggested in 1795, but in 1798 he *was* contemplating marriage with someone, though in letters was irritatingly discreet about the lady's name. That late summer the Boultons all headed for spas – Anne and Matt to Scarborough, their father to Cheltenham, partly for the benefit of their health and probably partly to get away from the endless building work. Matt was bored at Scarborough and wrote to James Watt junior, 'you will easily conceive that the amusements of such a resort are not calculated to engross the mind in their pursuit, but I can assure you they are admirably well imagined to produce a complete torpor & to secure invalids against the baneful effects of mental exertion.'[4] While he was there his father wrote to him from Cheltenham on the subject of marriage. Matt filed the letter away, jotting on the outside of it, 'Advice upon matrimony, and offer of his assistance to promote my views in regard to the lady whom he has been informed is the object of my choice.'[5] Boulton was evidently delighted with his son's choice (how annoying that we do not know who she was!) and wrote:

> Pray do not blush to own that you are a man, nor disavow or suppress those virtuous passions which are so honourable to human nature and so conducive to the happiness of it, nor suffer your self to be turn'd from your purpose by the satirical laughs of envious batchelors; for such who have neither affection, love, or musick in their souls are fit for treasons, stratagems and spoils.[6] The purport of this is to express my hopes that you are disposed to marry; and, marry whom you please, you shall never feel that I disapprove your choice, because I am perswaded your own good sense and proper pride will prevent you from making choice of anyone whom you will not be proud of introducing to your friends ... If I can promote the attainment of your wishes (which I think is not improbable), you need only intimate the means.[7]

Again, nothing came of it, and eventually Charlotte Matthews wrote to Matt teasingly about his dilatory progress to the altar. Matt had remarked that on his return home he had found the ladies at Soho 'seemingly in as good spirits as I suppose a trio of forlorn single ladies living together can well be'.[8] Charlotte came back with a spirited riposte: 'As it seems a matter of surprise to you that single women *shou'd* enjoy good spirits, I think you betray great want of compassion not to join one in holy wedlock.'[9] But Matt remained silent – and single.

By August 1799 (the year in which their old friend and Anne's botany teacher William Withering died) Soho House was once more ready to receive important guests, among them the Russian Ambassador, Count Woronzoff, and his entourage during negotiations for Boulton & Watt to equip a new mint at St Petersburg. This meant a busy week for Anne, acting as hostess and providing songs and 'loyal musick' every evening, while a 'man cook' engaged by her father for the duration sent a steady succession of gourmet dishes to the dining room. The guests were shown around the Birmingham manufactories and taken to the theatre to see *Hamlet* and '*Blewbeard*' and on their last day Boulton pulled out all the stops for a visit ostensibly just to the Soho Foundry, not far away at Smethwick. He told Charlotte Matthews all about it in a long and triumphant letter.

At ten o'clock in the morning Boulton, Anne, the Count and his entourage had assembled on the canalside at Winson Green Wharf,

> where I had previously pland & arranged a Secret Expedition haveing provided 2 Compleat Seating Barges wth Coverd Cabins & 6 Sash Windows in each. One of them I sent a little forward out of sight with 2 Trumpetts, 2 French horns, 2 Clarinets, 2 German flutes, 2 Bassoons, 2 Hautboys & a large double drum.
> As soon as the Count & Co was seated in the Cabin he sayd, hark I hear Musick, the Windows were opend & the Swell increased as we drew near. He at length exclaimed this is delightfull & I am confident this is my dear friends plan. We passed the Band & saild into the Foundry, walked round, & re-embarked with the Band playing before us. In about 2 Hours we arrived at the Brades & saw one of our Engines Forging Steel, a Tilting Forge, grinding plates of Steel & Sad Irons, grinding Gun Barrells, Boreing them & also grinding Spectacle Glasses.
> After the interesting sight was over we adjourned to Mr Hunt's House where we found a large Table in the Parlour served with joints of Cold roast Lamb,

neat's Tongues, Pidgeon Pies with a variety of Pastry & Fruit which was also unexpected. The Band playd in the Hall whilst we dined & after Dinner had some Loyal Songs ...

We again entered our Boats & by the assistance of the Musick we increased the apparent population of the County immensely. After stoping several times to see Coal Mines, Iron Furnaces, Fire Engines & sundry works we at length entered the Regions of Darkness wch I dispelled by 100 Torches wch I had provided. New & immense Caverns opend as we proceeded, through which we often espied through openings the Inhabitants of ye Earth looking down upon us. The Band of Musick playing all the time & beautyfully echoed from the Salons of Erebus. [10]

It's difficult to resist the thought that Boulton got the idea of this 'royal progress' by barge along the canal from Smethwick to Dudley from Handel's *Water Music*, though nowhere does he mention what music this group of 13 musicians actually played – that was a minor detail; what mattered was to make a big impression on his guest, as indeed it must have, by the time he had gone through Dudley Tunnel and into the huge limestone working caverns under Dudley Castle Hill, with all those wind instruments ringing in his ears.

Though Anne (now aged 31) managed to get in and out of the boat on this trip, in spite of a variety of treatments her injured knee was still troublesome and the following month the inflammation flared up again. It was now some five years since the two accidents which were the original cause of the problem, and it is possible that by this time she had developed osteoarthritis in the joint. Boulton wrote to Charlotte Matthews,

my daughter is become a pitiable object for she has had patience to lye or sit upon a couch ever since I returned from London up stairs, & her knee exposed to a stream of cold water every hour, but all is not sufficient to subdue the inflammation. It has again been bled with leeches within this hour & is less painfull for the present, but it begins to lower her spirits, as very little progress is made towards a cure. Mr Minors the most eminent surgeon we have, attends her daily & recommends sea bathing ... unless I see some tokens of amendment tomorrow or next day I think I shall write to Dr Darwin to come over, for she must be set on her legs before she can go to the sea & if not soon it will be too late.[11]

The problem seems to have fluctuated in severity, for the following summer of 1800 a business contact, Thomas Lack (Secretary to Lord Liverpool) wrote,

I saw Miss Boulton on Sunday, and I can assure you it gave me great pleasure to see her rise with the greatest alacrity from her chair, when I entered the Room – she appears indeed to be much improved both in Health & Spirits – I wish I could say as much of our Friends at Epsom – The last Time I saw them Miss Fothergill in particular was very unwell & worn down; I hope however that the *Air* of Birmingham, the Gaiety of Soho will be of service to them. I should have great Pleasure in contributing my little mite to the Fund of Amusement, but I fear I have no Chance of a Holiday long enough to get so far as Soho for many Months. Though I cannot myself partake of the Hospitalities of your House, I hope you will allow me to contribute to them by the present of Half a Doe from Needwood Forest ...[12]

Still in search of a cure, a week or two later Anne went to Brighthelmston (Brighton) with the Fothergill ladies but instead of putting her back on her feet the trip dealt them all a blow, for while there Mrs Elizabeth Fothergill died.[13] After the funeral at Rottingdean, Anne and the remaining Fothergills returned sadly to the Fothergill home at Epsom. Sophia Dumergue wrote to Anne urging her to come to Piccadilly, where Mrs Nicholson promised to nurse her and a bed was made up in the back drawing room, ready and waiting for her. They were distressed to receive a melancholy letter from Anne from Epsom and Mrs Nicholson wrote to Boulton urging

> now my good Pappa Boulton, take my opinion, direct her to come to us as soon as possible, she requires advice for her knee, & I am very shure with her spirits, our House at this moment will I trust be more agreeable. All is ready for her, her Maid shall sleep in her room & no one thing that friendship can direct shall be wanting to make her comfortable, & in time Your Dear Daughter will return in good Health & make your mind easy.[14]

Obediently, Anne went back to London to stay with the Dumergues while she consulted Henry Cline and Mr Grant again about the on-going problems with her knee.[15] The extent of Boulton's anxiety can be understood when we read in a letter from him to Cline,

> I understand that it is currently reported at Birmingham, that some professional Man has said, my daughter must either loose her Leg or her Life. I therefore wish you would, at your leasure, write me such an ostensible letter as is consistant with truth & is properly calculated to check such a disagreeable Idea amongst my particular friends. I also wish to know the real joint sentiments of your Self & Mr Grant.[16]

Cline replied reassuringly a few days later that Anne's knee was much less painful and she was getting about with the aid of a stick. Mrs Nicholson also wrote to reassure Boulton and to tell him that it was

> determined by Mr Dumergue & Old Nick [herself] that from Piccadilly Miss Boulton *shall not* be removed till Mr Cline consents ... I beg you not to be in the least anxious, all shall be settled by us, & you shall be acquainted with the plan in time to have your best Coat on to receive my Patient ... She is anxious to return to you, but wisely sees the necessity of submitting entirely to Mr Cline's judgment ... Daddy [Charles Dumergue] visits her frequently in the Day, & if you will not tell, nor be jealous, very often gives a tender kiss. Little Laura is here constantly, Miss Boulton doats on her, she dined with us yesterday, & when we told her the Partridges came from you she said, good Pappa Boulton & very good Bird ...[17]

Boulton meanwhile wrote to the Fothergill girls, Patty and Polly, to offer his condolences on their mother's death and any help that he might be able to give them: 'let it be rememberd that you are not Friendless, that I feel myself desireous of being as kind as your *parent*, as affectionate as your *Lovers* & as sincere as your best *Friends*.'[18] He went on to thank them for all their care and attention towards Anne and added, 'Poor Nanney! She has long struggled with almost uninterrupted pain & though I have said little I have felt much.' To another correspondent he wrote that Anne 'hath been in a painfull Situation for two Years past by an inflam'd & swell'd Knee which has entirely deprived her of the Power of walking & obliges her to be carried up Stairs & down'.[19]

On 8 November Charles Dumergue wrote to Boulton to tell him 'your dear & amiable Daughter is getting better every day, dine[s] with us, Laugh[s] with & Play[s] wist with us'.[20] He told him that even if Anne were to stay with them for a year, it would be small recompense for the hospitality they had all of them, 'Christians & Beasts', received at Soho in the past. Anne had hotly denied having told her father that she was not making progress: 'Mr Watt & Mr Southern must have told you how well & cheerful she looks', protested Daddy Dumergue.

Boulton responded, tongue-in-cheek:

> Why the devil do you put your Self into such a damned passion my dear daddy? If you had red with attention my letter you would have found that I neither talked or thought of putting you to any Expence about my Daughter: because I know you are the last man in the World that would think of it, when your friends health or happiness is at stake. No, it was no expence I thought of, but it was my fears least the Comforts of my daughter should interrupt yours & your good Ladies, by depriving you so long of the conveniences & tranquil enjoyments of your own Mansion of peace: However if you choose to sacrifice at the alter of Friendship your own Comforts in favour of that dirty drab my daughter you must take the consequences ...[21]

While letters flowed back and forth between Pappa Boulton and Daddy Dumergue, Anne herself wrote to Charlotte Matthews,

> My plaguy knee has given me a great deal of pain lately. On Monday Mr Cline desired to have consultation with Mr Grant; they are to meet again on Saturday, so God knows when I shall get leave of absence. I almost despair of eating my Christmas dinner at Soho; fearful of alarming my Father, I have not yet informed him of this circumstance, but intend writing in a few days, when I hope to say I am better.[22]

On receipt of this letter Charlotte, with Mrs Vere and Mrs Mosley, went to drink tea with Anne. She was low-spirited, having been told by the physicians that her recovery was yet some way off. 'They wanted to put her on leeches and a blister* last time they saw her, but her spirits were weak and she cou'd not bring herself to consent to it,' Charlotte told Boulton; 'but if they wish it today when they see her, I believe she will submit. The inflammation had return'd, which was the reason of their desire to adopt that plan, but it is somewhat abated now. They, however, tell her she must not expect to be better till spring; this is, to be sure, most disheartening.'[23] The three friends had tried to cheer Anne up, playing cards with her and passing on all the gossip they could think of.

But there was better news after Cline and Grant's next visit. They put on another plaster and had planned to apply leeches three days later, but as Anne was improving Cline thought she could probably do without the leeches (which she hated). Charles Dumergue wrote to her father,

---

* Blister plasters contained an irritant which caused the skin to raise blisters which then ruptured and discharged – this was regarded as cleansing to the system.

> Messrs Cline & Grant came down to me last Saturday from your d^r Girl's room to tell me that they had found her so mutch better that they thought, as you was so anxious to see her, she might with safety undertake the Journey. My answer was, Gent[leme]n dont hurry her home if there is the Least Risque, for I will be darn'd if she more in our Way here, than a child just borne a month or a year is no more than a day. She gives no trouble & we love her: She knew all that, I was oblig'd to submit …[24]

In the end, Anne spent Christmas at Piccadilly, so she was unaware of events unfolding at Soho. Just before Christmas 1800 Boulton got wind of a planned wages snatch at the Manufactory; he and a posse of loyal workers armed with blunderbusses, cutlasses and other weapons, had lain in wait several nights, and finally caught the would-be thieves red-handed. On Christmas Eve he wrote to Anne: 'My dear Girl, don't be alarmd, I & all at Soho are perfectly safe & well, having had a better Nights sleep than usual and have the satisfaction of feeling that by my exertions the publick are freed from four wicked wretches that have long been a pest to it. They are all safely lodged within the cold and solitary Cells of Stafford Gaol.'[25] A night or two later the sleeping household at Soho was again roused by the sound of a blunderbuss firing; this time it was a nervy William Cheshire firing at what he thought were intruders, which proved in the light of day to be just the old gray pony grazing near the windows, frightened but unhurt.[26] Charles Dumergue wrote to congratulate his friend on his 'victory' but reproached him for even mentioning it to Anne:

> Dear Soul she wanted to take a post Chaise & set off Immediatly: but … I made use of my Veto. She had a bad day & a worse Night, but she is charmingly since the good news, Looks extremely well. Now upon another subject, & you will say (*Mêtez vous de vos affaires*), you wished to thank Mr Cline for his care, regardless of what you had wished to give him, I took the hint from what he told me in regard to Mr Grant, when I ask him what was the usual fees that it was two guineas for a Consultation & one for a common Visit in Consequence. I applied to my Friend Rush (who is, in as great practice as any in London) to inform me, as you was absent, how to thank Mr C in an handsom manner he told me £30 would be well paid … When I told him my Intention was to present him 50 guineas he said it was Princely. However your Daughter, wished me to give him £60 which I did Christmas Day, by a Draft. He is to make her a friendly visit one day next Week, as they have determined to make no alterations in the present treatment.

Anne herself added a note at the foot of the page: 'Mr Dumergue having left a little bit of blank paper I think I can fill it to good satisfaction by assuring you I continue mending, & I have been out two hours this morning – Laura was here yesterday when she desired to send a kiss to Pappa Boulton.'[27]

The excitement of thief-watching in a series of cold winter nights must have taken its toll on Boulton, who was now in his 73rd year (Plate 42), but this did not dampen his excitement at a celestial event in the New Year, namely the simultaneous appearance in the night sky of the planets Venus, Mars, Jupiter and Saturn. Though he had sold his original telescope to Alexander Aubert some twenty years previously, he retained an interest in astronomy and when the house alterations were finished he had a new instrument installed, supported on a base constructed in the roof space. A small flat well on the roof, concealed from ground level by the pitch of the surrounding slates, provided the perfect viewing platform. Up on the roof of Soho House with his eye glued to the telescope in January, planet-spotting, he went down with a heavy cold. Anne, who was looking forward to coming home soon, wrote to him reproachfully: 'the season is too severe for astronomical observations and we all petition you to lay aside the telescope 'till warmer weather. I have great confidence in Mrs Keen's medical skill & good nursing & with a little *prudence* on the part of her patient I trust I shall have the happiness to find you quite recovered before this day sevennight.'[28] (Mrs Keen, from Stafford, was yet another of Boulton's devoted female friends – so devoted that Matt had felt it necessary in 1798 to write to his friend Andrew Collins refuting 'tea-table talk' that he had 'taken the liberty of censuring her intimacy with Mr Boulton', though he conceded that he might have said that Mrs Keen's frequent visits to his father had 'occasioned some talk at Stafford'.[29])

In mid-January 1801 Anne finally left the kind Dumergues and Piccadilly. Well packed up by a fussing Mrs Nicholson against the cold and the jarring of the coach, she set off on the journey to Soho, taking three days over it instead of the usual two so as not to suffer too much from the jolting. On her arrival home her father wrote an immediate and emotional letter to Charles and Sophia Dumergue and Mrs Nicholson:

> My dear kind Creatures ... To my unspeakable Joy, my dear Daughter, after an abscence of 8 Months, arived at Soho last night about 6 o'Clock perfectly safe, but a little overcome with fateague & Joy. In about one hour she recovered her Self so as to be chatty & cheerfull, but not so far as to speak of either of the three bon Samaritans without sheding tears from the fountain of Gratitude, which I am perswaded will never be dryd up ...
>
> My Son accompanyd her to Meadenhead the first night, G Mynd to Oxford, Gregory [Watt] met her at Chappel House the 2d night and we all met at Soho ye 3rd where I hope we shall all remain in Comfort untill you three come & make us happy.
>
> I have been very much indisposed ever since I last wrote to you & have been much inclined to low spirits which the general state of politicks hath contributed to for I have some Money in Russia & a good deal in Denmark & Norway which is all in danger by the present mode of making war upon the private property of individual subjects. I think this Country never was in so precarious a state as it now is or soon will be in. I shall therefore prepare to till my own Land & grow my own Corn & if Invasion or any other evil should drive you from the Capital I beg youl come to Soho & divide the Brown loaf with me ... [30]

Thomas Lack, when he heard from Anne's father that she was back home and recovering well in her 'native air', added, in a letter mostly about coinage, 'I am happy to hear that Miss Boulton is arrived safe at Soho; I hope her *native air* (to which you know the most wonderful effects are ascribed) will completely restore her health, and I trust she does not forget that the first Time she resumes her Dancing, I am to be favoured with her Hand; I can venture to assure you that I shall be happy to be summon'd to Birmingham on so pleasing an occasion.'[31] This is the first affirmative mention of Anne and dancing in the papers, from which we may conclude that, although she had more than once eschewed dancing in the past, she had learned enough at her various schools to be able to enjoy it when her health allowed.

With Anne installed back at home, she and her father and brother picked up the threads of what passed for ordinary life in this extraordinary household, and finding themselves once more in need of a new housekeeper, put the word out among friends. Mary Linwood promptly sent a reference for someone she thought might be suitable. The woman was 'Mistress of what is requisite for the situation she offers for … wishes to know what is expected of her (hopes you've a good Cook), seems very pleasant in her manners – not a "fine lady"'.[32] However, she was too late. Anne had already found

> a very decent bettermost sort of a Woman, who seems well qualifyd for my place; except so far as relates to ye superintendency of Cooking, which is an art she is totally unacquainted with, at least the upper Regions of it, as she has never lived in any Gentlemans House, but has Boild her own Mutton & turnips. It is a dangerous matter I find to interfere in the department of the Ladies & the only way of governing them is to let them have their own way as I find I must do in the present case: but if it should so happen that the person you recommend should not get a place to her mind & that our new House keeper should not prove to our Mind (which I think is probable) I will take the liberty of writing to you again upon the subject.[33]

With the new housekeeper in post, in April 1801 Boulton went off to Cheltenham to take the waters. After two days he felt so feeble that he could scarcely reach the fountain, and decided that since he felt so much better on days when he did not drink the water, it would be better to drink it only every other day or perhaps even every third day, and enjoy good dinners in between.[34] The weather was good and he sent advice to Anne to have one of his chairs placed on the lawn at Soho, with a cushion and a footstool; she could then be carried to the chair and 'wheeled about upon the grass lawn without the least injury from shakeing: pray try it and do not loose the benefit of this fine spring Weather'.[35]

After a short stay at Cheltenham Boulton went on to London, where the Dumergues gave him a bed. Mrs Keen had been staying at Soho to keep Anne company, but now it was time for her to leave. She sat down at Soho House and wrote Boulton a thank-you letter in which she added various items of information she knew he would want to hear:

> Notwithstanding the dry weather your plantations look very well, the lawn has been watered frequently, we had a few showers on Thursday which I hope you wou'd benefit by on the road. I congratulate you on the amendment of your health and *sincerely* wish you a long continuance of it, I hope you will not repent taking the Doctors advice and staying another week at Cheltenham, he recommends it strongly to you to return by Cheltenham in your way home which I hope you will comply with.
>
> The Doctor and Mr Matt have been very busy in repairing your electrical machine as the Doctor is of opinion Miss Boulton may receive benefit from gentle Electricity, I believe they mean only to draw sparks without giving any shock. Indeed the Doctor has been most indefatigable, I have often been requested to give him his fees but I perceived it would not do as he seemed to think he

was only acting the part of a friend. Miss Boulton seems uncomfortable at these repeated obligations and has asked me to think of something she cou'd make him a present of. I observe he is very fond of the Rasin Wine Mrs Matthews bought you some time since, the only thing I can think of is that …

Your daughters knee has been much easier for some days past which she attributes to wearing some oiled silk that clothes it from her feeling the frequent changes of the weather …

A servant who lives in the capacity of footman with Mr Watt … came here to offer himself to supply Johns place. Your Son thought he was likely to suite you in every respect provided he cou'd wheel you round the garden, he made a trial with Joseph in the Chair but cou'd not succeed in getting him up the hill & [we] therefore hesitated about engaging him until we know your sentiment on this subject …[36]

Unfortunately, in spite of drawing sparks Anne's knee problems were far from over and, while staying at the Dumergues, her father met Mrs Zophany, wife of the artist Johann Zophany; Mrs Zophany knew all about bad knees. After their chat he wrote to Anne asking for

a distinct letter discribing your feelings & your Ideas of the present state of your knee or knees, & thereby enable me to consult Mr Cline or Mr Grant seperately or jointly, or perhaps seperately first, & jointly afterwards. I also wish to have their opinion whether repose at home or traviling to the Sea Side will be the best plan for you. For I assure you there is no trouble or expence that I should think too much to accomplish your Cure or Comfort. Your Brother says Dr Carmichael has advised you to try Electricity. There can be no objection to a trial but I conceive much depends upon the Strength & manner of applying it for if it tends to produce inflamation I presume it must not be perseverd in.

Mrs Zophany is upon a Visit at this Hospitable House & I last night had some conversation with her upon swelld, painfull & inflamed knees, which I understand she has had some experience of, but are now cured by Mr Rush, who applyd a Blister on each side of the Cap however this is a matter I can't give an opineon upon. I must therefore refer that point to the professional Gentlemen & if Dr Carmichael can suggest any thing that I should ask or say to either of ye Gentn aforemend it would be well to add it to your Letter.[37]

He add that there was a packing case on its way to Anne containing something she wanted:

Mrs Nicholson says there is a small Forte Piano sent to you about ten Days ago. The price of which is 30 Guineas but to dealers or to Mr Dumergue he takes off 4 Guineas. – She however paid £8 4s. od. wch with 20£ you pd her makes £28 4s. od. – I have also pd Mrs N £16 5s. od. for Grocery &c sent to Soho wch settles all money accts with her … Mr D has been with ye Queen at Kew this morng but no one there is allowd to mention anything about ye King. I fear he is in a bad way …[38]

George III had had a relapse early in 1801 and was suffering a medical regime of restraint, emetics, quinine and blisters. By May, though lucid at intervals, he was restless and exhausted, probably as much from the effects of his treatment as from the effects of illness.

FIG. 20 *'Dash', the Boulton family's pet dog, sketched by John Phillp c.1796. (Birmingham Museum & Art Gallery)*

After a month in Piccadilly Boulton returned to Cheltenham to take the waters for another two weeks, from where he wrote to Anne on 7 June. Promising her that the Dumergues and Mrs Nicholson had offered either to accompany her to the seaside, or to visit her at Soho, he wanted to know: 'Pray tell me who is now with you? Do my young Trees grow? Has James Duncan connected the pump wth ye Mint Engine? How does the Horses Dogs & Dash in particular go on? Is Mrs Morden in the Straw & how does she & the Child do. Is there any Birmgm News or Handsworth.'[39] Cheltenham was plainly hardly a rest-cure:

> As this is an Idle Place you will naturaly conclude I have been remis in not writing to you oftener; but the fact is, I have now got such an extensive acquaintance here that I am constantly interupted by Visitors or Visiting, or dressing, or drinking Water or Wine. Moreover I have many letters to read & to write. I receivd 24 on Sunday last & am therefore fully employd: however I propose to set out on Sunday & hope to be at home that Evening or Monday yet nevertheless I wish it not to be mentiond, otherwise I fear I shall be too much crowded with persons & business all at once. Your last letter of the 15th Inst has given me great pleasure particularly in being informed that you are free from pain, which blessing I pray God long to bestow upon you, to which I shall add every other Comfort & pleasure in my power – I have wrote to our Piccadillian friends what you say respecting a Marine Excursion, & I suppose they will pay us a Visit in Augt or so soon as the Golden Knocker begins to be a little tranquil – I shall order every part of the road round the Garden to be Rolld as smooth as possible that you may be induced to live in the open air as much as possible it being the next best thing to the Sea breezes. I also approve of the Swing & the Boat, but some very commodious means must be contrivd to place you in & take you out without the least risk, danger, or pain.[40]

A Thousand a Year

Matt Boulton's sudden notion, while the Soho House alterations were going on, of leaving and setting up his own establishment had perhaps been sparked by James Watt junior, who was planning to do the same thing.

After his return from Europe in 1794 James had joined the business at Soho, but after a year or so decided he could not live at Heathfield with his father and stepmother and began to look for somewhere else. Early in 1798 he moved into a cottage on the Soho Foundry site, jotting down in a notebook a list of 'Furniture &c at my house at Soho Foundry March 1798'.[1] The small house had two best bedsteads and bedding, a servant's bed, looking glasses, wash hand stands and a mahogany wardrobe. Downstairs there was a mahogany dining table and six chairs, and the parlour was carpeted. With an assortment of linen, china, silver, cutlery, glasses and kitchenware James was equipped to live, if not in luxury at least in reasonable comfort, and to entertain modestly. He spent a year there and then took a lease from Henry Piddock Whately on a house in Handsworth, called The Rookery, moving in on 1 July 1799. The house he left on the Foundry site was taken over temporarily by Boulton & Watt's engineer William Murdoch, now back from his long domicile in Cornwall; James left behind some of the furniture and other household goods for his use.

The Rookery was about a mile further on from Soho House along the turnpike road towards West Bromwich, on the opposite side of the road. When in 1801 James renewed the lease, he made another list, of 'Articles belonging to me at the Rookery'.[2] This house was bigger than the Foundry house, and the list covers saddlery and harness in the stable and coach house, garden and farming tools, silver plated tableware, crockery, linen, and glass. With two-and-a-half dozen large plates and similar quantities of other items for place-settings, he was clearly now able to entertain on a larger scale. A housekeeper, manservant, gardener, and labourer looked after the house and grounds. The local nurseryman, Thomas Pope, supplied plants and tools, and also did some work on the garden for a total of 59 days between 13 April and 29 June 1800, for which he charged £7 17s. 11d. James made notes of the dates when various fruits, vegetables and flowers were planted. Mrs Pope did some of his washing.

With a bigger house to furnish he seems to have bought items from friends, for there is a list of items purchased from various people, including a sofa cover from Anne Boulton, for which he paid her £2 5s. 0d. One of the Wilkinsons provided a chest of drawers for £11 8s. 0d., and his friend George Lee a 'Marseilles quilt'. The list of items for the house includes 'Portraits, say Genl[s] Washington & Bonaparte'.[3] These were perhaps wanted rather than obtained, as there is no price against them. With his home coming together, 29-year-old James settled down to a bachelor life at The Rookery. He was fully occupied with the Soho business.

The Boultons and the Watts lost one of their oldest and most trusted friends at the beginning of 1802 with the death of Charlotte Matthews, a woman who, in Boulton's eyes, combined every feminine virtue with good business sense. Her death was a special blow to Anne Boulton, for Charlotte had always spoken up for her, and had taken care of her in sickness and in health from time to time ever since her childhood. In her will Charlotte instructed that her real estate in London and Croydon was to be sold by her executors, Martha Vere of Berkeley Square, Edward Stewart and John Woodward. Martha was to have the organ from Croydon Lodge and any items of furniture she might like. The Fothergill girls, still unmarried, were to have Charlotte's books and a picture apiece. After payment of debts and some small bequests, the residue of the money was to be invested to provide annuities for Charlotte's sister, Elizabeth Griffiths, and Martha Vere. In a memorandum accompanying the will Charlotte instructed: 'It is my particular desire that in the event of my not recovering from my present Indisposition the Balance of Accounts in my hands due to Mr Boulton, Mr Robinson Boulton [Matt], Mr Watt, Mr James Watt and to the respective ffirms in which they are Copartners should be paid out of the Bills in my possession first coming due, and also Balances due to Martha Vere, Mary ffothergill, Mary Norman [correctly, Foreman] ffothergill and Martha Vere Fothergill.'[4]

At the time of Charlotte's death, Anne was being kept company at home at Soho by another long-time friend, Amelia Alston. The Alston family was originally from Scotland but Samuel Garbett had long ago brought 12-year-old James Alston to Birmingham with him to employ him in his Steelhouse Lane refining business. James went on to become a partner in a buckle and button making company in Birmingham, and was one of the Guardians of Birmingham Assay Office, so the family had had frequent contact with the Boultons over many years. James and his wife had three children, James junior, Charles, and Amelia (also known as Emily). They lived nearby at Winson Green, but still visited relations in Edinburgh from time to time. Amelia was a frequent visitor to Soho House, and an attentive friend and nurse when Anne Boulton was unwell. Like Anne she often spent time in London with the Dumergues, frequently carrying out shopping commissions and other errands for Anne while she was there. In 1803 she was in London and 'out of all patience with Miss Boulton's mantua maker and am just going to send a very angry note to her and the moment I have the gown it shall be sent off'.[5]

Following the news of Charlotte Matthews' death, Amelia wrote to Boulton in London to sympathise with him on the loss of his friend and to tell him that Anne was reasonably well apart from the pain of having had yet another blister applied to her knee. Anne was anxious that he should return home as soon as possible and recover from his grief at his own fireside, Amelia added.[6]

Close on Charlotte's death came that of another old friend, Dr Erasmus Darwin, the original inspiration behind the Lunar Society. Darwin had lost his eldest son, Charles, way back in 1778; 11 years later his second son, Erasmus junior, the boy who Matthew Boulton had once taken with him to Cornwall, drowned (whether accidentally or deliberately remains uncertain) in the river at the bottom of his garden, a tragedy from which his father never completely recovered. Only one son, Robert, now remained from Darwin's first marriage; Robert was married to Sukey Wedgwood and the first two of their six children had already been born.

Anne's health was much better by now, but in the spring of 1802 her father became quite ill for a time, possibly marking the onset of a prostate problem. Charles Dumergue spoke to Mrs Fitzherbert about it, and she kindly made arrangements for Boulton to have the use of the Prince of Wales's wheelchair; 'Prinny' himself was out of the country but Mrs Fitzherbert had no doubt that 'the Prince would feel great pleasure if his Chair contributed to your comfort in the smallest degree'. Maria Fitzherbert had been the Prince's mistress for a number of years and he had even gone through a form of marriage with her, clandestinely and illegally, in 1785. They had been back together – on and off – since the collapse of his marriage to Princess Caroline of Brunswick in 1796.

The wheelchair was duly crated up and sent to Soho, with instructions to unlock the wheels before use. Writing to tell Boulton of the arrangement, Mrs Nicholson signed off, 'You must be very good & do exactly as you are directed, and then I will come & give you 20 Kisses – Youl say what a temptation, kisses from an Old Woman, but recollect I am your obliged & very sincere Sally.'[7] Dumergue wrote with advice of his own: 'We think that you should sleep downstairs, have the Room called the Larder made in[to] a bed room, with a door made out of one of the Windows in order to go in your Bath with Ease & to be Wheeled out when you wish it …'[8] Trying to cheer up his old friend, Dumergue also wanted to know about Matt: 'How is the Grand Duke, is he not tayard [tired] of living single when there are so many aimiable Females in want of a mate. I think if you & I were only Forty we would risque once more to re-enter the great Societt.'[9]

Boulton was still unwell in September, but his spirits were lifted by a visit to Soho from the opera singer, Elizabeth Billington, and he invited his good friend Mrs Mary Keen over from Stafford to meet her. Mrs Keen could not come but wrote back: 'I thank you for your kind letter of invitation to hear Mrs Billington's fine voice, it made me very happy to find you was charm'd by the Enchantress, but believe me when I tell you, I had rather spend an hour with you than hear all the fine singing in the world.'[10] But though Mrs Billington provided an agreeable interlude, when Lord Nelson paid Soho a visit during his tour after the declaration of the Peace of Amiens, Boulton was still laid up and was obliged to receive the great man in his bed-chamber. In a faltering hand he pencilled in his diary 'Lord Nelson here'.[11]

At the New Year of 1803 the Dumergues sat down in Piccadilly to a dinner of venison sent by Boulton, and drank his health in a good burgundy. Mrs Nicholson, having received an unusually formal letter from him, wrote, 'just let me ask you why you stile me Madam, instead of your Sally – all the family took alarm & s'd have you offended Dear Pappa, take the hint & be no more fine, or I shall scold …'[12] He had asked her to get him a new quilt for his bed, and having looked round the shops she wrote that a good one would cost ten or twelve guineas; eiderdown was one guinea per pound weight, and the case was always made of silk. As he continued unwell, Mrs Keen and Mrs Nicholson both sent little delicacies in an effort to tempt his appetite, the latter urging: 'Keep up your Spirits be a good Boy

& do as you are advised, or I shall not give you so many kisses when we meet, I am a saucy old creature but you are used to my raillery God bless you *thou very best of Men* ...'[13]

By May he was much better, and as the Dumergues' ward, Charlotte Carpenter, had now married Walter Scott, Boulton invited the couple to come and see Anne, Matt and himself at Soho, an invitation which was answered by Scott himself. Scott, who clearly knew Boulton's reputation as a charmer, wrote:

> It was a wise man who said 'Trust not thy wife with a Man of fair tongue'. Now as I have very little wisdom of my own I am content to gather all I can get at second hand, and therefore upon the faith of the sage whom I have quoted, I should consider myself as guilty of great imprudence were I to permit Charlotte to wait upon you on her return or even to answer your kind letter to Mr Dumergue. That task therefore I take upon myself and you must receive my thanks along with hers for your very kind & flattering invitation to Soho. But independent of my just suspicion of a Beau who writes such flattering love letters to my wife, our time here ... lays us under an indispensable necessity of returning to Scotland as speedily as possible & by the nearest road. We can therefore only express our joint & most sincere regret that we cannot upon this occasion have the honor & satisfaction of visiting Soho & its hospitable inhabitants.[14]

All the London friends were relieved to hear of Boulton's steady improvement, and Amelia Alston, who was staying in town, may have been referring to Elizabeth Billington when she wrote, 'A certain Lady at the West End of the Town frequently boasts how often she hears from Mr Boulton. O fye Sir!! I hope that you will go on improving till we meet, when to outdo the aforementioned Lady you & I may Dance together. She I think only *aims* at singing a Duet with you.'[15] London was nervous that summer, for there were fresh fears of a French invasion following the post-Amiens resumption of hostilities, but Miss Alston had heard 'nothing of France nor of Frenchmen – and tho' our means of defence still advances, the public panic seems to have subsided for the present. I imagine Bonaparte has heard of your sons progress in the military art, and begins to waver in resolution.'[16] (Matt was currently a major in the First Battalion of the Loyal Birmingham Volunteers.) Miss Alston was looking forward to coming to Soho to see Anne and Boulton, and to 'that kiss which I shall so much preffer to a fraternal squeeze'.

In the autumn of 1803 Mrs Nicholson had some exciting news: her niece was getting married, to a banker 'who has behavd hansome beyond all I can tell you, when he addressed himself to her father his words were, talk not to me of fortune – your Daughter is all I ask, & if I obtain her, I consider myself the most happy of Men'.[17] She promised Boulton a list of the wedding clothes: 'I will give you a coppy as you are soon to dispose of a *Lady* also, I suppose it will be usefull to have the list.'[18]

It was true, as Mrs Nicholson had said, that Boulton was expecting to 'dispose of a Lady', and not before time, he may have felt, for Anne was now 35 years old. Suitors for her hand had either been thin on the ground or at least not thought worth mentioning in any correspondence, until September 1803 when Boulton wrote to his solicitor Ambrose Weston, 'My daughter is going to be married'. Peter

Ewart had also mentioned it in a letter to James Watt junior in July. Neither of them mentions the name of the prospective husband but from other evidence it appears he was Miss Boulton's 'indefatigable doctor', Doctor John Carmichael. Weston replied that he had already heard the news on the grapevine. He knew Boulton was keen to see Anne married and had previously written to him, ' … I imagine that your Daughter has no kind of apprehension of being *left dependent*. I hope *she* will *long continue dependent* upon *you*; unless a good husband should create another kind of dependence.'[19]

For their home, Anne and the Doctor were to have 'Scales House' – Thornhill House, a little to the north-west of Soho, whose four-acre grounds bordered Boulton's own estate (Plates 46, 47 & 55). It had been the home of the Scale family for some years, but by 1799 the Scales were reduced in number, John Scale was often away from home on business, and his mother found it lonely there by herself. Matthew Boulton, thinking the house would do for one of his children, had asked for first refusal should they ever wish to sell, so Scale offered it to him. [20] Boulton initially jibbed at the £2,000 valuation but after some negotiation settled on the house. However, when he offered it to Anne, she kept finding fault with the house, while the Doctor for his part seemed not the slightest bit interested in it. Unusually for Boulton where his daughter was concerned, he grew rather irritated by the engaged couple. Writing to Annie Watt in some exasperation, he laid out the whole saga:

> When you reflect upon all the circumstances attending Scales House, I am perswaded you will rather pity than blame me. I bought it at the instigation of my Son & kept it void near 2 years for him; but finding myself disappointed I expended near 2 Years rent more in improving & repairing it for Col. Mordent who also disappointed me in payments. My Son then renewd his intentions but afterwards declined it. I then let it to Mr James Watt who proposed to keep the projection in ye dining Room Square but as my daughter knew I intended to give her the House she recommended a Bow Window.
>
> Soon after, she & ye Dr communicated their intentions & wishes to me. I then begd Mr J Watt to relinquish it in their favour which he obligeingly did. She was perfectly well acquainted with the Situation, its Neighbourhood, its inconveniences, & then with my wishes to promote her happiness & make the place as Comfortable as possible at My Expence, as well as to obviate every inconvenience & unpleasant circumstance … My daughter now complains of the publick Houses being so near but I did not build them nor should I have increased the Dust but on the Contrary I should have blocked it out by Building Walls & Stables & planting Trees that would soon be talle ones, as to the 2 Trees I cut down they kept out the Air & light from ye Dineing room but not the Dust for they were Scotch firs without any branches below the Chamber Windows … I proposed to finish ye drawing room without the Warming Columns according to my daughters wishes but intended to put a Marble Chymney Piece in it & another in the Drawing [perhaps should be Dining] Room & then to plaster & finish ye Chambers plain.
>
> As to the House keepers Room with all the Cubberds Pantrys & Clossets I shall leave to my daughter as well as the tast & walks in the Garden in which I had principally considered her lameness & my own. However as she seems to have so contemptable an opineon of my tast & judgment I despair of giving satisfaction and as she has taken up many prejudices against it I wish she may find a place where she thinks she can be more happy whether it be a Farm

House a Cottage of Content or a Palace, for I have always been more anxious to promote the happiness of my Children than my own ...

PS I have all along observd a reluctance in the Dr to give me any opineon about the intended alterations in the House; & still more so to accompany me to the premises. To which add my Daughters numerous objections to the House, Grounds, situation, as well as to the Buildings not yet begun and the preference she gives to Greenfields & a Farm House. I am therefore desirous they should relinquish the place altogether, & endeavour to find another more to their own satisfaction. It shall make no pecuniary difference to them as I will try to purchase it for them.

If they go to Scales House against their Will they will always feel as if I had drag'd them there, & I also shall have the like Sensations. If she had given me in writing, as was proposed, a list of all the alterations she was desirous of, I would have executed them; but it is not agreeable to me to build up & then pull down again to gratify humour; & I think a little attention might have been paid to ye old proverb viz: not to look a Gift Horse in the Mouth.[21]

Boulton says early on in this letter that he had let 'Scales House' to James Watt junior and had subsequently had to ask him to relinquish it, but there is no evidence that James occupied the house at this time. His address from 1799 through to 1808 is at The Rookery. Possibly Boulton had offered him Thornhill as an alternative to The Rookery, and had then withdrawn the offer for the sake of his daughter and her intended husband.

In spite of the frustrations over the house, the prospect of Anne's marriage at least seemed to put Boulton back on his mettle, for by the autumn some of his old vigour had returned. Mrs Nicholson wrote to pass on the good wishes of his favourite singer, Mrs Billington, and his favourite actress, Mrs Siddons, to him and to Anne. Mrs Billington had told Mrs Nicholson that if he would only come to London, he would have '(I must not tell how many) kisses.'[22] Mrs Siddons likewise had said 'some very pretty things of you', and had also asked Mrs Nicholson to pass on a commission for a suite of steel jewellery to be made for her at Soho; it was to be a pair of arm pieces [bracelets] and a bandeau, not to be expensive but to look fine. 'Now pray is not Your Sally a good Ol Creature to tell you all these bits of news', said Mrs Nicholson.

The jewellery was duly supplied (as a gift, needless to say) and Mrs Siddons was delighted with it. She told Mrs Nicholson, 'Old as you are, she should be much more in love with you than any Young man'.[23] To Boulton himself the actress wrote effusively,

Never was any thing so beautiful, and so becoming. In short I'm afraid you will have to answer for awakening those sparks of personal vanity which ought now to be extinguished: nevertheless I thank you Dear Sir, a thousand and a thousand times and beg you will have the goodness to give orders for a *Clasp* for the Waist to answer the Bandeau &c. I wish one could have Necklace and Earrings too, for the effect is so Elegant and uncommon, though I don't know what one *coud* wear about ones Neck, that woud not look mean and wretched when compar'd to these beautiful Steel Ornaments but this I suppose is out of possibility. But the Clasp I shoud think *is* attainable, for which do not imagine I shall suffer your generosity to be taxed! *That I must be allowd to pay for*, and you will oblige me by letting me have it as soon as possible![24]

Anne had mentioned to the Dumergues that her father needed a new greatcoat, and Mrs Nicholson and Charles Dumergue knew exactly what he should have: silk, lined with flannel and well padded. 'Will you let me know if you think you should like it of Silk, it would be so light and so warm', said Mrs Nicholson, adding that as soon as she knew what he wanted she would order it, as Anne had more than enough to do at home, reading and writing letters for her father. The coat should be made big enough to button up Mrs Slade inside it with him, she added.[25]

For Christmas 1803 Mrs Nicholson packed up a little basket of delicacies which she directed to William Chesire, Boulton's personal clerk, to take to him direct in his room, for the contents were not for anyone else: 'You will enjoy & say not a word.'[26] She added, 'Your Dad [Charles Dumergue] is delighted that his *dear little Boy* is so well, your Sophia sends you 20 kisses – now be generous, & let my Dear Nanney partake, if you do you may double the number & make me the Debtor.' She also sent a cake, a brace of 'London fowls', some small gifts for everyone in the house, and briskets for 'my dear Dash' (the dog).

Doctor Carmichael's reluctance to look over Thornhill, or to discuss the alterations with Boulton, should have sounded warning bells. By 1804 the marriage was off. Boulton wrote confidentially to his son that Anne had been low-spirited and had finally confided in her father that she would like him to ask the Doctor about his true intentions, as he had shown a 'silent cold reserve towards her' for some time. Boulton had tackled the Doctor, who now seemed to wish to extricate himself from the engagement. Boulton thought his excuse, that he wanted to live in the town while Miss Boulton wanted to live in the country, and that therefore they should let the affair drop, was pretty lame, and told his son he thought Anne had been ill-used.[27]

None of the younger generation was making much progress towards matrimony. The suggested match between Matt Boulton and Mary Foreman Fothergill ('Polly'), for which Boulton had done some financial calculations in 1795, and Matt's own thoughts of marriage with an un-named woman in 1798, had both failed to materialise. Anne and the Doctor were no longer engaged, though he was still in medical attendance on her and her father. Likewise James Watt junior showed no signs of getting married, but some time after 1802 Polly Fothergill, having failed to capture Matt, set her sights on him.

Polly turned to Boulton for advice and again he did the sums. This time he put her original personal fortune at £20,000 but suspected that the value of the investments had fallen, and that she might also have reduced it considerably by over-generosity, something he thought she should reign in if she was now pledged to James. Boulton thought Polly's liberal disposition would tend to endear her to James rather than otherwise, but nevertheless suggested that it was time to act more prudently and put her future husband's interests before those of her sister. He recommended that whatever Polly's aunt, Miss Mary Fothergill, intended to give her should be given instead to Patty, in lieu of Polly herself giving money to Patty, so as not to either increase or, more importantly, further diminish Polly's fortune. 'I have no doubt but Mr J.W. will ultimately have a good Fortune from his Father but He & Mrs Watt may yet live many years & though J.W. is engaged in a profitable concern, yet nevertheless I think it would not be prudent for you to adopt an Expensive Establishment until he succeeds to a part of his Fortune,' Boulton advised Polly.[28]

How long and how hopefully Polly pursued the idea of becoming Mrs James Watt junior is not clear, and there is no reference to this 'engagement' in the Watt papers. The Watts in any case had other things on their minds. Gregory was seriously ill, and in November 1804, after a battle against tuberculosis during which his parents had carted him from spa to spa, he died. He was twenty-seven. He was buried in the cathedral at Exeter, their last port of call in the desperate search for a cure. Just a couple of years earlier Gregory had been travelling in Switzerland and Italy, sketching and sending home vivid descriptions of the scenery, including an ascent of Vesuvius during which he went down into the crater.[29] This talented young man, who excelled at Greek, mathematics and geology, but was also said to be modest, unassuming and genial, was deeply mourned by a wide circle of family and friends including his half-brother, James Watt junior, who to his credit never seems to have held his parents' evident preference for Gregory against the boy (Plate 43). James was sole executor of Gregory's will, which made provision for aunts, female cousins, Miss Boulton and the Fothergills to have lockets with hair; there were to be mourning rings for other friends. James wrote to his cousin Gilbert Hamilton about the rings: 'As I believe it is not a very usual mark of respect to the memory of friends in Scotland, it may be proper to mention that the Gentn wear them upon the little finger of the left hand and the ladies upon the forefinger of the same ...'[30]

In spite of rallies from time to time, Boulton's own health continued on an inexorably downward course, and some time during 1805 he went through a 'dangerous crisis', about which James Watt junior wrote to his friend John Furnell Tuffen:

> His fever was for some days very considerable and we have been kept in a state of much alarm. The additional assistance of Dr Darwin of Shrewsbury [Robert Darwin, son of Erasmus Darwin] was called & his opinion as well as that of Dr Carmichael afforded much ground for apprehension. However ... I have now the pleasure to inform you that either by their skill or the strength of his own constitution he has got the better of his fever and is gradually acquiring strength. He has been seen by none but his own family and medical assistants for the last three weeks and nothing can exceed the affectionate attentions he has experienced from the former ... The old gentleman is under a medical injunction not to attend to business for some weeks to come; of which however he will certainly make very light when absolute weakness no longer assures compliance. It is not in his nature to be penned up in his arm chair and resign the fasces of imperial sway to his successor. This he will not do whilst he is able to wield a pen or issue a mandate ...[31]

This illness must have been a cause of particular frustration for Boulton, for there were plans afoot for a Royal Tour of parts of England, and the Soho Manufactory was on the itinerary. Although George III's mental health was still somewhat fragile, and relations between him and the Queen were strained, they managed to achieve an outward semblance of civility and the King was popular. It was natural that Boulton himself would wish to show his sovereign round, but it looked as though Matt would have to conduct the tour, and Anne, too, would be expected to act as hostess. Royal visits then were just as stressful for the 'visitees' as they are now, and she was dreadfully worried about it. As a general rule nobody was allowed to sit in the presence of the King and Queen, and Anne could not stand for long. Fanny de Luc wrote to reassure her that they would understand:

> I only wish my dear friend Miss Boulton would make her mind easy, being persuaded that their Majesties will not expect from her anything above her Strength, having very probably heard, at least her Majesty, of her long & painful confinement, which Lord Dartmouth would also naturaly mention. And she may be certain that she will find all the Family uncommonly gracious & Kind, their manners are most bewitching & take off at once all possible aw[e] or fear, they are so perfectly *easy*. Lord Dartmouth was so polite as to answer my note to him & said he would take care His Majesty should be acquainted with its contents. Indeed with your Son, my dear Sir, every thing will go on perfectly well, & Miss Boulton will find some Friend to help her doing the honours in the House. *I am worse* than anybody even herself for I cannot Stand, for that reason I hardly ever go to the Terrace [the South Terrace of Queen's Lodge, Windsor, where the Royal Family and attendants regularly promenaded] or to Frogmore. By what I can collect here their Majesties are not to set out for tour till next Month, by which time your health, my Dear Sir, Please God may be still improved ...[32]

The following week Fanny wrote again, to say the King had told her father he was sorry Boulton was so ill, 'but his Son will do very well for me, for I intend to go, & tho' he is not well *I will see him*',[33]

But the King's sight was failing, and leeches had been applied to both inflamed eyes.[34] He was in great discomfort, and Fanny wrote,

> I am desired by my Father who returns this moment from the Castle, to inform you that our dear & good King has *given up* his intended Journey for the present, being alas! unable to receive any gratification from it; this may prove perhaps a relief to you, my worthy Friend, but I know your heart too well not to be certain that you will be sorry for the *cause*. My own heart aches for this dear King when I think of the *repeated Trials* he has undergone ... what will be the consequence of his present complaint in the Eyes, God only knows! His great mind seems to be prepared for anything, & his hopes are that *if Cataracts* he *may* recover his sight. He proposes setting out for *Weymouth* the 12th in consequence of which *if perfectly* convenient my brother & I might (when my Father goes) pay our respects at Soho, perhaps in a fortnight ...[35]

As Fanny had suspected, Anne probably heaved a private sigh of relief.

On 21 October 1805 the British fleet, under Admiral Lord Horatio Nelson, fought the Battle of Trafalgar. It was 6 November before Nelson's death became public knowledge in the newspapers and several days more before he was brought ashore. A great funeral was fixed for 9 January 1806 at St Paul's Cathedral. A day or two before it, the Dumergues, in common with many others, went to see 'that melancholy *spectacle* of Lord Nelson laying in State at Greenwich it is indeed an affecting sight ...'[36] When Fanny de Luc wrote with New Year greetings she said her own feelings were 'past expression' and described the King as 'much affected at the bad news', though in reality George III was no great admirer of Nelson, of whose private life he greatly disapproved.[37]

Barely had the muffled drums of Nelson's funeral procession faded when the country reeled again, from the death of the Prime Minister, William Pitt the Younger, on 23 January. The King was upset by this, and the subsequent political uncertainty in the face of the ongoing Napoleonic wars. Fanny wrote:

> Our good King is very *low* on account of the times & so is my Father, but he makes it a rule not to read the news Papers in general to avoid thinking much on politics; which the poor King cannot do! To day is the Queen's Birthday, my Father is gone to pay his respects at the Castle & the 9 o'clock Chapel but I don't hear of any *Gala*; we are to dine with the Ladies. I shall be sorry if the dear K loses his fondness for *Music*, I was in hope there would have been an Oratorio.[38]

Though, as James Watt junior had said, Boulton was not ready to 'resign the fasces', by the spring of 1806 he clearly felt it was time to put his affairs in order. He made his will, and gave much thought to how best to provide for Anne's future, writing to Ambrose Weston,

> I propose to set apart, in my Lifetime, as much Money, Land, Stock or good securities as will be sufficient to support my daughter handsomely, & comfortable, for as she cannot walk, she must have a Carriage; but whatever I may think proper to give her she must have the command of without being obliged to go to my Son for it, & it must be settled by an irrevocable Deed; but if she should Die without issue one half of her fortune should revert back to her Brother or his Family, & the other half to be at her own or her husband's disposal (with some modifications respecting her Children if she should have any). Thus I shall save to her the Duty upon Legacys & protect her from all Disputes with her Brother, who is not kindly disposed towards her.[39]

A deed of settlement was drawn up in June. The deed consisted of six gifts to Anne with a combined value of over £34,000. These included three per cent stocks currently said to be worth about £10,500, £8000 on mortgage to Henry Geast, the Sardon Estate, valued at £4,200, the Curborough Estate, valued at £1,300, the Coal Bank Farm at £1,600, a house and land 'lately occupied by Col. Mordant', £5,000, and '*Money* lent to Joseph Gibbins, Treasurer to the Rose Copper Co. & for their use, & is as safe as the Bank of England, £4,000'. Matt was to vest £5,000 from his father's residuary estate in his sister's trustees, James Watt junior, George Simcox and Nathaniel Gooding Clarke. Between them, these various investments and properties were to provide Anne, through interest and rents, with her future income: 'When this money is laid out in Land & out of its annual produce my daughter has paid all the Kings taxes *including* the property tax all the parochial taxes &c &c, she will not have more than a Thousand pounds or Guineas to spend upon herself, Serv[ts], Horses, Carriage, Repairs, &c &c.'[40] Under the terms of their father's will, Matt was also to pay Anne an annuity of £200 and £1,500 in cash to buy furniture.[41] In a codicil Boulton left Anne all his jewels, apart from the diamond ring given him by the Emperor Alexander of Russia, and a ring presented to him on the death of Nelson, which he left to Matt with instructions that they were to continue in the family as heirlooms. The house 'lately occupied by Col. Mordant' may have been Thornhill, for the colonel and his wife had been tenants there for a time.

Anne and her father continued to receive the support and companionship of their circle of friends, especially Amelia Alston. Amelia was often with Anne, but in the summer of 1806 she took time off to accompany her brother Charles to visit relatives in Scotland. They went by a roundabout route, taking in Chatsworth, Harrogate, York, Castle Howard and the Lake District, before crossing the border. Tourism in the remote and romantic Lake District was in its early stages, and Amelia wrote to her friends at Soho, telling them of a diversion to Buttermere, where Charles was determined to steal a kiss from 'the Maid of Buttermere' celebrated by Hazlitt and the other Romantics.[42] Charles, having satisfied himself that he was talking to the right 'Maid', duly paid his addresses:

> Charles resolv'd to see Mary of Buttermere, and further resolv'd to salute her if possible, he told me he wd give her a Guinea for a Kiss, accordingly a young woman made her appearance at the Inn, with nothing very striking in her appearance, after asking her a few general questions, Charles wth a voice of great emotion said 'are you Mary?' 'I am Mary.' 'Well Mary, before I left India I had made a resolution to come here to give you a Kiss.' Mary blush'd, Mary complied, and Mary's Father got the Guinea. The day was Heavenly (last Sunday), we sail'd upon the Lake, din'd at an innocent bit of an Inn and return'd to Keswick delighted – we walk'd by the Lake in moon light in the Evening and saw a Dozen Boats on it full of company ...[43]

After this excursion the Alstons continued on to Edinburgh, from where Amelia wrote again to pass on the good wishes of Mrs Walter Scott (the former Charlotte Charpentier, Dumergue's ward): 'I often see Mrs Walter Scott who always inquires after you, and always begs to be remembered to you and yours – Mr Scotts fame seems at the highest pinnacle as a Poet, and his excellent qualities as a man surpass his fine talents. They are a very happy pair and have four charming children.'[44]

Back at Soho, Boulton had reacted to Nelson's death by offering to strike a special commemorative medal. By the autumn of 1806 proof copies of the medal were ready and he sent a package of them to Fanny de Luc, asking her to ask her Father to show them to the King. 'I am now preparing Nineteen Thousand as presents from me to the Heroes of Trafalgar,' he wrote, 'and as the portrait is a tolerable likeness of the much beloved and immortal Commander I flatter myself they will be acceptable.' He asked her to make sure that all who handled the proof copies did so by the edges only, to avoid damaging the polish on the faces.[45] He and Anne wanted to know when Fanny was coming to Soho, for she had missed her usual summer visit due to organising a house move for her father and herself. De Luc himself replied that he had presented Boulton's 'little box' to the King at breakfast, and the King, the Queen and the princesses had all said 'how much they admired your feelings towards the memory of the *great man* and the *heroes of Trafalgar*', but due to his poor sight the King had been unable to distinguish any details on the medal. With regard to Fanny's visit he added, 'Don't, my dear Sir, call upon a Widower for his only comfort: I cannot spare my dear Fanny, she is my *whole*; her real friendship for you and your worthy Daughter, draws her to Soho very powerfully; if the *whole* could go together, as Miss Boulton mentioned it, the *whole* would very willingly move towards you; but I cannot, I have too much upon my hands that requires *home*. God bless you both.'[46]

A few days later Fanny wrote herself, with a little anecdote about the Nelson medal which she knew would please Anne and her father:

> I showed it this morning by the desire of a Lady to her Child, who is 2 years & three Quarters old, & almost immediately in putting his little head into his mama's Lap he said 'It is my God Father'. This child was Christened by the name of *Nelson* Sucklin very few days before the Great Hero left his Country *never* to *see it again*, & it is said that he mention'd as much in taking leave of his most intimate Friends, Colonel Sucklin being one of them, as well as his relations, for which reason I went on purpose to show the Medal, which gave them much pleasure.[47]

Fanny continued to live in hopes of being able to visit Anne and her father again and, having been alarmed at a bad report of Boulton's health from Charles Dumergue, she and her father opened a letter from Soho at the end of 1806 in trepidation, but it contained news from Boulton's man, William Cheshire, that their friend was improving. De Luc shed tears of relief at the news, but they were premature. At the New Year of 1807 Boulton was in great discomfort, and under the constant and watchful care of Dr Carmichael. William Cheshire wrote to tell Charles Dumergue that 'the faculty' (the doctors) would allow his master no visitors and had been trying to ascertain 'by the usual means' the actual cause of his urinary tract problems. 'You will be fully sensible what Mr Boulton's feelings must have been during this … scrutiny. It is intended to resume the investigation into the real cause of Mr Boulton's excruciating torments as soon as possible,' he wrote.[48] Anne was consumed with worry on her father's account: 'Miss Boulton's anxiety has considerably deranged her health: she has been confined to her chamber for the last 2 days.'[49] Boulton himself was restless and confused from the twin effects of pain and laudanum. William sent regular bulletins to Dumergue over the next week or so, which show that Boulton suffered further deterioration and then began slowly to improve again; meanwhile it was decided to seek a second opinion. Sophia Dumergue answered one of these letters with a letter to 'Pappa Boulton' in which she told him, 'My Father has been lately much with the Royal Family, & they one & all, *Queen, Princes* & *Princesses* have been very constant in their enquiries after your health, the first question was always "You must tell us how your Friend Boulton is."'[50] Mrs Nicholson had just come back from market with a little joint of lamb and some asparagus, which they were sending up to Soho to tempt his appetite.

It was March when the proposed letter seeking a second opinion went off to Henry Cline, the London physician who for so long had looked after Anne's knee. Dr Carmichael wrote to Cline outlining his patient's case and the treatment regime. Boulton, he said, had been having increasing pain and difficulty in passing water for the last two years. Periodically he passed small stones, leading Carmichael to suspect that there was a larger mass in the bladder. He experienced great pain on moving, whether sitting, standing or turning over in bed. He had refused a further internal examination. Warm baths sometimes relieved the pain, and sometimes he was given opium, which, however, had bad side effects. In spite of all this, his appetite was good, and he was drinking Madeira or sherry, well diluted with water.[51]

Replying to this, Cline commented that Carmichael had set out Boulton's case and treatment with 'much perspicuity', and that he approved of the treatment and had nothing more to add, other than applying suppositories in place of the opium by mouth.[52]

The Dumergues came to Soho for a short visit to see and cheer their old friend and returned to London anxious but hopeful. To add to the problems at Soho, Matt also became ill from some unspecified complaint, and for a time there was real concern about him, too. The faithful William kept the Dumergues abreast of developments at Soho House, writing sadly in April, 'I am much concerned to state that the gloom which overhung at the time of your departure from this once happy mansion is not yet dispelled, neither Mr Boulton nor his Son being any better.'[53]

By the following week Matt was out of danger but his father had relapsed again and was in extreme pain. William wrote to Dumergue,

> Although I have great confidence in Mr Boulton's constitution, by the gigantic strength of which he has so frequently been upborne from the bed of pain & sickness, yet I must confess that his appearance now alarms me, & I am apprehensive that it is nothing less than a real progression of his disorder which has produced his present lowness of spirits & the desire under which I now act, of communicating to you his doubts respecting the termination of his present relapse. I pray God we may be mistaken & that it may soon be in my power to send you better news. I should not have thought it proper to touch this tender string if my honourable master had not required it of me & his positive commands I ever have, & ever must hold sacred.[54]

Dumergue himself went down with a heavy cold at Easter; he could not shake it off and it had left him deaf, so in August he went to Muddeford, near Christchurch, for a rest. 'This place is very much retired, very proper for quietness & those coming in Search of Health,' he wrote to Boulton, thinking it might do him good, too.

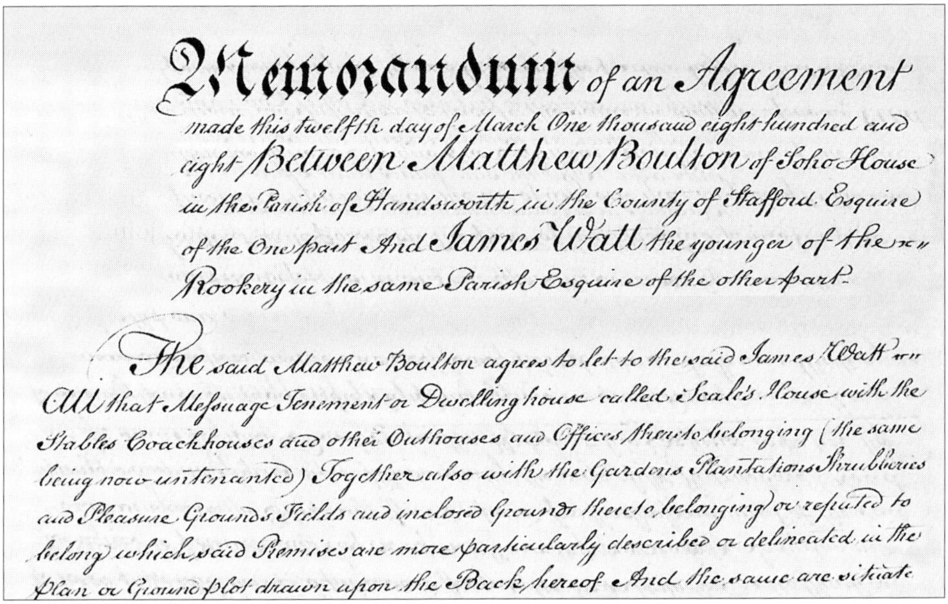
Memorandum of an Agreement made this twelfth day of March One thousand eight hundred and eight Between Matthew Boulton of Soho House in the Parish of Handsworth in the County of Stafford Esquire of the One part And James Watt the younger of the Rookery in the same Parish Esquire of the other part.

The said Matthew Boulton agrees to let to the said James Watt All that Messuage Tenement or Dwelling house called Scale's House with the Stables Coachhouses and other Outhouses and Offices thereto belonging (the same being now untenanted) Together also with the Gardens Plantations Shrubberies and Pleasure Grounds Fields and inclosed Ground thereto belonging or reputed to belong which said Premises are more particularly described or delineated in the Plan or Ground plot drawn upon the Back hereof And the same are situate

FIG. 21 *Part of the lease agreement between Matthew Boulton and James Watt junior for Thornhill House, 1808. (Birmingham City Archives)*

FIG. 22 *Drawing by George Bullock for James Watt junior, for a drawing room bookcase at Thornhill, 1809. The bookcase was intended to be built along the fourteen-foot wall facing the fireplace. (Birmingham City Archives)*

FIG. 23 *Drawing by George Bullock for the end wall of James Watt junior's 'little library' at Thornhill, later known as the little parlour or breakfast room. (Birmingham City Archives)*

'The air seems remarquably mild & the Roads admirable, so much so that in our Barouche … you would not be shooked [shaken] …'[55] Boulton did not feel up to the journey, but as he was a little better Anne and Matt did join them. From Muddeford they moved on to Bath. Dumergue wrote to Boulton from there in October that he was sorry that Anne must leave them soon: 'It is with a very sincere Grief I see the moment approaching of your dear & very aimable Daughter's departure from us, for a more worthy couse [cause] & precious object! – a Father! … For you my dear Friend we consent to part with her, for I do assure you she has been a Great Comfort to our Society, & my privation is the greatest, on my being unable to accompagny her as I had proposed …'[56] He thought Anne was better for the change of air and the bathing. So was Matt, whom they had left at Weymouth.

Though, as a result of the collapse of her engagement, Anne had not moved in to Thornhill House, her father had given it to her and she had several jobs done – a letter from Cornelius Dixon in August 1805 includes a watercolour drawing of the pump outside the kitchen window, elegantly encased in a neoclassical style plinth, which Dixon promised, 'if executed agreeably to the design then painted and sanded I make no doubt will produce a very good effect at a very trifling expence'.[57] The house needed an occupant, and James Watt junior returned to the idea of moving there from The Rookery. The lease (from Boulton) included permission for James to make and fence in a kitchen garden, and to re-paper rooms where necessary at Boulton's expense (the papering was done by George Bullock). He could convert the cow house to a chemical laboratory at his own expense and on payment of the additional insurance. The rent was to be £150 per annum.[58] (Plate 47)

Annie Watt went to see Anne, who declared she was happy for James to make alterations, with one or two provisos, as his stepmother explained:

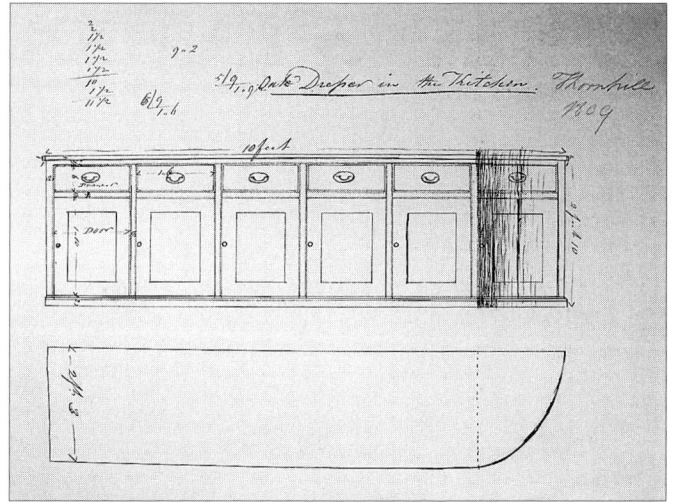

FIG. 24   *Sketch for kitchen cupboards at Thornhill, 1809. (Birmingham City Archives)*

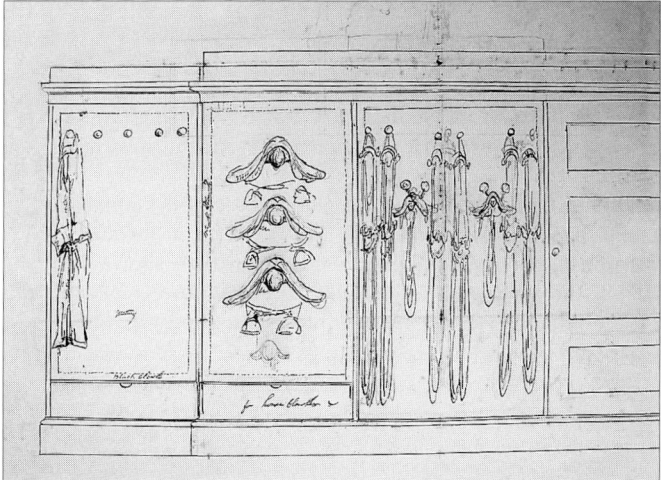

FIG. 25   *Sketch for fitting out saddle house at Thornhill, c.1809. (Birmingham City Archives)*

By your father's advice I shewed her your letter, that she might fully understand your plans. She said she would be very sorry if you was to give up the place, that as to any interference about the house she never once had thought of it except about puting nails in the dinning room and as for the grounds she had no wish but that you would not cut down any of the trees she had planted to serve as skreens to shut out some disagreeable object, that she had taken down 3 or 4 trees from that belt at the bottom of the hollow & could not conceive that any more should be taken out or that fruit trees should be planted in the room of forrest trees, that was all she had to request, that in no respect would she interfere with any plans of yours, she again repeated that she thought she should never life [live] at the place and had no fiar [fear] but you would take every necessary care of it, her wish was that if you take the place you would take sole charge of it within the exemptions I have stated ... It now remains with you to decide whether you go to the house or not, I will do the best I can to help you either ways. My opinion is once you was settled in it, all these little difficulties will never be thought of, *trees* excepted.[59]

On 25 March 1808 Anne handed over Thornhill's 46 keys to James (Plate 50), and he moved in.[60]

While James unpacked and sorted out the rooms at Thornhill, at Soho Matthew Boulton, unable to do anything else, fretted about his will, his daughter, and the state of his affairs. Ambrose Weston begged him to stop worrying:

You have made provision for your daughter, you have left memorials of friendship to some & given gratuities to others – and all the rest your son will have. What can you do or wish to do more that need create one hour's disquiet? It is very well if (without tormenting cares) you can invest your money in land to good advantage, & if you cannot your son may do it, when lands & money and all the concerns of this world will be looked down upon by you, without any other emotion than that of surprise that they should have ever appeared so important ... we ought to make the most of the little we have to come.[61]

Boulton was no longer in a position to make the most of anything. He slept fitfully, and when his mind was not completely dulled by pain and laudanum, he worried. William Cheshire wrote to Charles Dumergue in the summer:

After having for some time abandoned the hope of ever again seeing my afflicted Master I was much gratified to hear of his being better both yesterday & today & I was most agreeably surprised to receive a message from him this morning desiring me to wait upon him.

Among the anxious thoughts which press upon the mind of our valuable friend I have to inform you that he mentioned in the kindest & most affection[te] manner yourself & family, desiring me to drop you a line to offer you his sincerest good wishes which I do with great pleasure & should the remission of pain & good hope of the day gather stability, I shall communicate the good tidings to you most cheerfully.[62]

The *Subject*

In March 1809 Anne was staying in Bath with Matt[1] when she received a distressing letter from her father, begging her to come home. Boulton wrote to his 'Dearest Daughter', in what was probably the last letter he was ever to write, 'I shall not be hapy until I clasp you in my Arms for I am now very very miserable & therefore beg you will return to Birmingham … If you wish to see me living pray come soon for I am very ill.'[2] She hurried back to his side. Matthew Boulton lingered a few painful months longer. He died on 17 August 1809, just a week or two short of his 81st birthday.

James Watt and his wife were in Glasgow at the time of their old friend's death. James junior had prepared his father for the inevitable in a letter a few days earlier, when he described Boulton as being in 'very violent pain'.[3] Now, later in the day after the death, he wrote again:

> I saw him last night between 12 & 1 o'clock, when he was lying in a state of lethargic stupor and breathing very short and quick; his dissolution hourly expected, but did not take place until this morning about half past 9 o'clock. His son and daughter had been up all night and were both present: it was perfectly quiet and almost insensible, without any return of consciousness. Indeed nature was completely exhausted and the thread of life was spun out to the finest fibre. Miss Boulton had been up for two nights, and suffered much from anxiety and want of nourishment, and has since been in a state approaching to insensibility. Mr R. Boulton [Matt] had perfectly prepared his mind for the event, which he bears with firmness & composure.[4]

James added that the Manufactory and the Foundry had been closed as a mark of respect.

The same day he wrote to Ambrose Weston,

> Our venerable friend Mr Boulton has this morning paid the debt of nature. Since the last return of his pains about a week ago, a great change took place in his constitution and his stomach which had hitherto continued sound, refused to perform its function. Life has since gradually decayed from want of nourishment and he has lain in a state of lethargy, with slight interruptions of pain, until a little after nine this morning, when he expired in the midst of his family without the slightest struggle. Miss Boulton had been up for two nights, and had taken little or no nourishment and is much overpowered by the catastrophe, expected and inevitable as it was. I trust the attention of her friends and a little time will administer relief. Mr R. Boulton had long made up his mind for the event, which

he met with fortitude and composure ... When the whole of Mr Boulton's life is reviewed, it is no ordinary person whose exit we have reason to mark ...[5]

A post-mortem was performed by Mr Freer, who found

> one of the kidnies considerably enlarged and containing two stones: in the other kidney there were small pustules which it is supposed secreted the matter that caused the shivering etc.: there were two stones in the bladder, which are supposed to have forced themselves down from the kidnies, but the Prostate Gland was found less diseased than was expected, although both it and the bladder were injured. The principal seat of disease and pain appears thus to have been in the kidnies, where I apprehend it was removed beyond the reach of medical skill.[6]

Over the next few days James kept his father abreast of developments in Birmingham, informing him in one letter:

> Miss Boulton is much better and dines down stairs with her family. She however seems to suppress her Grief which prays upon her mind, and I am afraid does not communicate sufficiently with her female friends. Mr R. Boulton pays every degree of attention to her feelings and treats her with the utmost kindness & affection. I shall strongly recommend their leaving home as soon as the funeral is over.[7]

The service took place at Handsworth Parish Church, St Mary's, on 24 August. The next day James sent his father an account of the event. The weather had been good, he wrote, the procession was well conducted, the ceremony 'awful and impressive'. The procession opened with ten mourning coaches of friends, followed by the coffin borne by ten of the oldest workmen who had worked for Boulton for between thirty and fifty years, with ten others to relieve them when they got tired. James Keir and James Watt junior (representing his father) had carried the pall. Matt Boulton, as the chief mourner, was attended by his cousins Zack Walker and George Mynd, followed by some 40 agents and clerks of the business, 430 workmen and some 70 female employees, 'nearly all in mourning which they had voluntarily provided'. After them came the Soho House and Heathfield servants, all with crape hatbands. The whole procession, walking slowly two by two, proceeded from Soho House to the Church along roads lined with thousands of spectators. Bringing up the rear were the Boulton and Watt family coaches, and the coaches of those friends who were walking in the procession.

After the service the workmen, whose behaviour, said James, had been exemplary throughout, retired to various public houses where refreshments had been provided for them and drank a toast to Boulton's memory. Each was presented with a metal token stamped with his name and the date as a memento. Thereafter all returned to their homes and 'not a Soho man was to be seen upon the road for the remainder of the day'. Having previously told his father that Anne was suppressing her grief too much, James now added, 'Miss Boulton is better, but indulges her Grief too much. I hope Mrs Watt has written to her, as I rather think she has more influence over her than any other person.'[8]

James's description of the funeral was echoed by his friend John Furnell Tuffen, who also wrote to Watt senior, estimating that 'at least 10,000 persons' had lined the route; during the service *'Angels ever bright and fair'* had been sung by 'a Birmingham Lad who is considered to possess one of the finest voices in England'. Tuffen concluded, 'Thus my dear Sir has the Grave closed on one of our oldest & dearest friends, whose like, take him for all in all, we shall not see again!'[9]

Thanking James for his account, Watt observed, 'The ceremony seems to have been well devised & conducted, & it is pleasant to think the workmen behaved with so much sensibility & propriety ... Mr Boulton was too well beloved for any of his friends to have failed in those respects. Considering the publick life Mr B had led I think the whole a highly proper respect to his memory; but I pray that I may not be buried with so much parade, I have all my life hated show & ceremony, let it not follow me to the grave.'[10]

Matthew Boulton's will (whose total value is said to have been *c.*£150,000[11]) confirmed, as expected, the settlement he had made in trust for Anne in 1806. He left £100 each in trust to the General Hospital and the Birmingham Dispensary. A schedule of legacies with the will accounts for 30 bequests ranging from £10-£500, totalling £3,010. These are to servants, employees, friends and children of friends, including the Fothergills, Mrs Keen, Fanny de Luc, Amelia Alston, William Cheshire, Ambrose Weston, and Zack Walker's son Zacheus junior (the son of Boulton's sister Mary, who had died shortly after his birth in 1768). When Boulton made the will he had instructed that his niece Mrs Ann Davies, the former Nancy Mynd, subsequently Holbrook, was to continue to receive her £40 annuity, and that her sons by her two marriages were to have £20 a year each towards their education, but by the time Boulton died Nancy was already dead. Her aunt Helena Mynd's will of 1799 includes a codicil dated 1807 containing a bequest to the two sons of 'my late niece Ann Davies heretofore Ann Holbrook'.[12] To his nephew George Mynd, whose adolescent misdemeanours had caused him so much aggravation, Boulton left £500 – but it was to be deducted from the money George already owed him, unless Matt chose to 'forgive' any part of the debt.[13] The remainder of the estate went to Matt, his sole Executor, who was nominated 'to be my Successor if he shall think fit in all the Trades and Businesses in which I am concerned'.

With Matthew Boulton's death Anne lost 'the best of fathers' and possibly her best friend, certainly her champion. For a time she was overwhelmed. Ambrose Weston wrote to Matt,

> The great affection I had for your excellent father is now more than ever felt by me; *now* he is irreparably lost to us! You will, as I shall, dwell with peculiar delight on the recollection of his most amiable & respectable qualities, of which we shall have the higher an estimation when the painful consideration occurs, as it often will, that his place can never be filled up by another of the very same character, & so specially related to us; to you by nature & habit, & to me by fortunate circumstances of connection & a friendship so sincere & tender – we are irresistibly impelled to love those who love us...
>
> I have great pleasure in learning that your sister's good sense is acting its proper part in alleviating by degrees the grief, which she must have felt from such a distressing separation. Time & reflection will in the end calm & subdue her present feelings. Her consolations must come from within. Next to this source, you will be to her the best comforter, & in your brotherly Attentions to her, you will derive your own truest & most heartfelt consolations.[14]

There now began a new and unhappy phase of Anne Boulton's life. If the past few years had been marked with physical sufferings of her own and anxiety about her father's health, at least she had enjoyed their close companionship and the secure knowledge of his love for her. Now, without his father's presence to keep him in check, Matt seemed to become overbearing, while Anne's role became very much that of his housekeeper.

Marriage might have looked like a good way of escaping from this situation, but Anne, who was now 41 years old, had perhaps been put off by the Carmichael affair. At any rate, some time in 1810 she turned down with some vehemence a proposal from Sir Isaac Coffin, an American-born former Naval Commander. Anne's snub was recounted by Sir Isaac the following year when he wrote to James Watt junior to announce his forthcoming marriage to a Miss Greenly of Titley Court, Herefordshire. He gave the impression that Miss Greenly was very much his second choice: 'All this might have been prevented if Miss Boulton had given me credit for my *frank* intentions – rejected with scorn & indignation, I was under ye necessity of resorting to other means, as much may you say to the Lady. I shall regret to the latest day of my Life the loss I have sustained, & however strange it will appear to you, she will hold a lasting place in my Heart as long as I live.'[15]

James may have suppressed a smile at Sir Isaac's comment, for during 1810 the question of Anne's future had been very much on his own mind (Plate 51). He and Anne had been discussing marriage. That summer he hoped it would all be sorted out, in London. But first he had to get Anne down there, and Anne was accident-prone. Watt senior and Annie had gone to London at the end of May, expecting Anne to join them, but in mid-June Annie Watt wrote from London to James in Birmingham:

> I am much concerned Miss Boulton is still unable to begin her Journey, I was however glad to learn by a letter from Miss Alston yesterday that the foot was getting better. Mr Boulton is very anxious to know when it is likely his sister can set out, if not soon he talks of returning home, I wrote your fair friend urging her very much to return no more to Soho a single lady, you may add your forces to mine and try if we cannot prevail, I see many reasons for her doing so and some against it but the past can easily be done away with …[16]

At long last Anne's toe, which had been the cause of the delay, healed sufficiently from its unspecified hurt to allow her to make the journey. Instead of taking the Oxford mail coach she decided to hire a carriage to take herself, Miss Alston and a maid the whole way in greater comfort. They arrived in London the next day, safe but somewhat ruffled, having met with an accident in the chaise en route and being obliged to leave it at Oxford and travel the rest of the way by the mail coach, after all. Matt had taken lodgings for his sister at 35 Conduit Street.

One of the purposes of Watt senior's visit to London was to sit for a new portrait by Sir Thomas Lawrence. James junior had never liked Sir William Beechey's portrait of his father, but in order to avoid offending Beechey, his friend George Lee had agreed to say that the Lawrence portrait was for him.[17] When Watt senior got to London, however, Lawrence was too busy to start work on the portrait and instead, at Matt's suggestion, he reluctantly sat to a Miss Andras to have his profile done, observing gloomily to James, 'My face seems doomed not to have an exact copy taken of it'.[18] He was engaged in this 'tiresome job' when Anne and her companion reached town. Having had some conversation with her, he wrote to his son, in a letter which James annotated on the back, 'Miss B's difficulty with her brother. Thinks I should write to him'. Watt senior had written, somewhat obliquely: '… a certain person has informed Mrs W[att] that her brother seems to think that the affair is entirely broken off between her & her lover & that she cannot assume courage enough to speak to him on it, it seems therefore incumbent on the gentleman to come to an eclairissement with the Brother without further delay.'[19] He added conversationally that they had been to the opera with the Boultons, 'where we heard Catalani in full voice & saw a most gorgeous spectacle in the Vestal, though the Ballet excepting Vestris' dancing was completely ennuyante …'

James replied promptly to his father:

> It is not possible that Mr B. can suppose any alteration in my intentions, as he must have noticed the continuance of my attentions to his sister previous to his leaving home, and it is most probable that Miss A[lston] will have reported to him the continuance of them after his departure. The true state of the case I presume to be, that he has not yet reconciled his mind to our union, and he perhaps expects that by diverting her attention to other objects, he may delay, if not finally prevent it. I had hoped that a confidential communication between his sister & him might have removed all difficulties, but as this does not appear likely to take place, I shall write to him upon the subject in a few days and in the meantime have apprized her of my intentions in a letter by this day's post. I certainly feel extremely anxious that his difficulties & objections should be removed, as I am fully persuaded both of his affection for her and his friendship for me, and it would therefore be highly satisfactory to have not only his concurrence, but his approval.[20]

Following this, James did as promised and wrote to Matt, who annotated the letter,

'Urging a farther explanation to take place between my sister and self on the subject of his proposal to her. His sentiments and wishes in regard thereto.' James's letter read:

> My dear Sir
> As the conversation you had with your Sister, at my instance, left matters in a state which rendered farther explanation desireable, it has been much my wish and I am persuaded equally hers, that the subject should be resumed between you; but want of opportunity or of resolution on her part to introduce it, has she informs me, hitherto prevented it. I can readily comprehend the delicacy and difficulty she labours under, and feeling as I do the propriety of such communication not only that you may learn her sentiments fully from herself and that she may have the benefit of your counsel & advice upon a subject which so materially involves her happiness, but also that there may not be with regard to you any concealment of our wishes & plans, – it is with this view that I now, with her privity, address you to request you will embrace the first opportune moment of introducing the subject and of inducing her to disclose fully her sentiments and wishes. This from what I know of your affection for her and friendship for me I am convinced you will do, and I am equally persuaded it will lead to an unreserved confidence on her part.

It has from the first been my anxious wish and still is so, that my proposals should not only be in unison with your inclinations, but also that they should obtain the approval of your judgement. Of the former I have no doubt; and I have felt sufficiently the force of the objections that occurred to you, particularly of one of them, to have been equally desirous with yourself that they should be removed in your mind, and especially that upon the one alluded to every degree of information should be obtained which its extreme delicacy would admit of. Upon that point there has not been the most distant communication between me & your Sister, as I felt prohibited both by the injunction you had laid me under and the hope she had expressed to Mrs Watt that I knew nothing 'of it, as well as the peculiar difficulty that must have attached to the introduction of this topic by me independent of such considerations. I am satisfied however that she herself entertains no apprehension, and you may possibly have learnt from Mrs Watt that she also has none. Still I cannot but be anxious if there is a possibility of getting at more evidence that it should be done. I know not whether any thing may have passed between her & Mr Freer,[21] or whether his late attendance upon her may have enabled him to make any remarks. If so, they may have been communicated to you already, and if not you can take an early opportunity of ascertaining them & of acquainting me with the result. We can in such a case only proceed upon probabilities, and I hope these will appear to your sober judgement as amounting to no more than the ordinary risks of the sex.

If no obstacle arises from this or any other cause I have reason to hope that a longer delay will not be thought necessary than the period which respect for your father's memory prescribes. I should not indeed have felt a shorter one than she thinks of, inconsistent with that respect, but concede to feelings which originate in a motive I approve of.[22]

This sounds as though there was some kind of health-related question mark over the proposed marriage; the veiled terms in which it is couched suggest it was possibly a gynaecological or obstetric question. Perhaps it related to whether children were likely from such a marriage (Anne was 42, James 41), or whether any children might inherit Anne's disability, for James Watt suggested his son seek opinions from Mr Cline and the Birmingham surgeon Mr Mynors, both of whom had attended Miss Boulton at various times. If there was any correspondence about Miss Boulton between these three, it has not been found.

James's planned visit to London to join Anne and discuss all of this with Matt was brought forward unexpectedly by the funeral of Boulton & Watt's senior London agent, John Woodward, who fell from his horse early in July. The loss of Woodward was serious for the business and left both Matt and James preoccupied, so that, three weeks after the date of this letter, Matt had still not discussed the subject of his sister with James. The elder Watts had by now returned to Birmingham and from Heathfield Annie wrote to her stepson, 'pray bring Mr B to his senses before you leave town'.[23] His father, likewise, begged him to try to bring matters to a resolution. Early in August, leaving Anne behind in London, where she was receiving more dental treatment from Charles Dumergue, James and Matt set off back to Birmingham. The two men travelled together as far as St Albans and James thought this would give Matt an ideal opportunity to open the discussion but, '[he] has not yet opened his mouth to me upon <u>the</u> subject. Indeed his mind has been so much harassed & his health so indifferent that I could not press it; but have written to

PLATE 39 *Miss Boulton's restored sitting room, Soho House (shown right). The portrait reflected in the mirror is Mrs Mary Priestley, wife of Dr Joseph Priestley, by C.F. Von Breda. (Birmingham Museums & Art Gallery)*

PLATE 40 *'The Dressing Room' (below left), by Thomas Rowlandson, c.1790. (Birmingham Museums & Art Gallery)*

PLATE 41 *Martha Adcock (below right), one of the Soho House maids, drawn by John Phillp, 1797. (Birmingham Museums & Art Gallery)*

PLATE 42 *Matthew Boulton at seventy-three. Lemuel Francis Abbott, 1801. (Birmingham Museums & Art Gallery)*

PLATE 43 *Gregory Watt (1777–1804), son of James and Ann Watt. Engraved by Knight in 1806, possibly after a miniature of Gregory by Lady Beechey. (Birmingham City Archives)*

PLATE 44 *Wax portrait of John Phillp, by Peter Rouw, 1807. (Birmingham Museums & Art Gallery)*

PLATE 45 *Soho House and Park, engraved by Francis Eginton for Stebbing Shaw's* History and Antiquities of the County of Staffordshire, *1798. (Birmingham Museums & Art Gallery)*

![Thornhill House watercolour]

PLATE 46 *Thornhill House, watercolour by John Phillp. On the reverse is written: 'From nature, view taken about half past 8 o'clock in a fine evening June 1796.' At this time the house would have been occupied by the Scale family. From subsequent plans and later photographs it appears that by the early 19th century the bow extension on the right-hand side had been raised to the second floor. (Birmingham Museums & Art Gallery)*

The Plan or Ground Plot referred to by the foregoing Agreement.

PLATE 47   Plan of the Thornhill estate, from the lease agreement between Matthew Boulton and James Watt junior, 1808. (Birmingham Assay Office Charitable Trust/Birmingham City Archives)

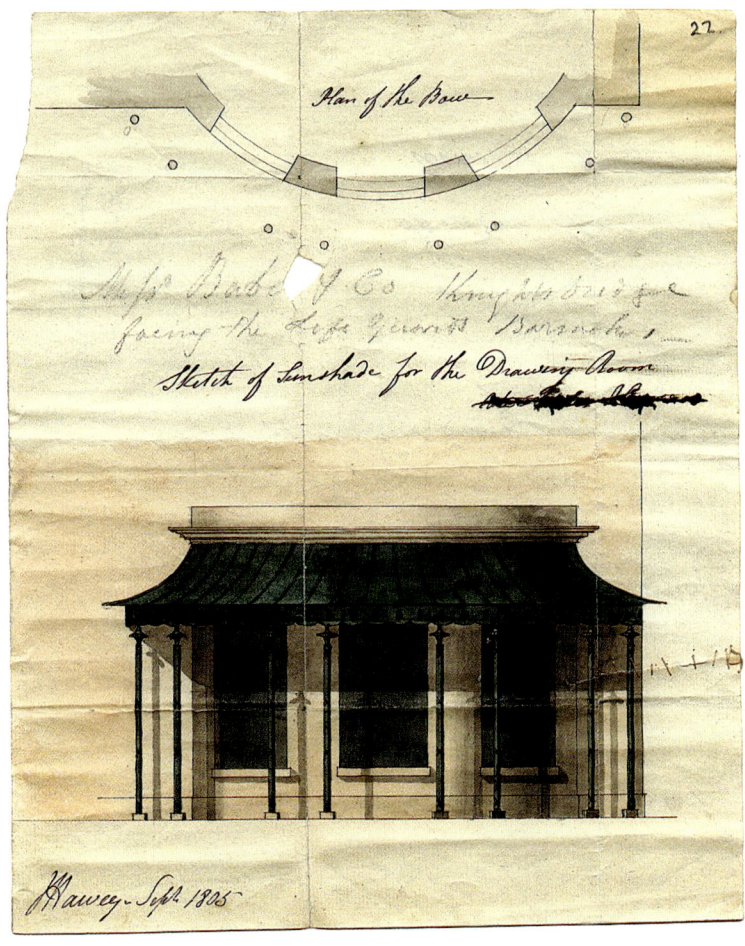

PLATE 48 *Design for a sunshade for the drawing room, Thornhill House, by Baber & Co. of Knightsbridge, 1805. (Birmingham Assay Office Charitable Trust/Birmingham City Archives)*

PLATE 49   *Thornhill House in 1890. (Birmingham Central Library, Local Studies and History)*

PLATE 50   *The keys of Thornhill House. (Birmingham Assay Office Charitable Trust/Birmingham City Archives)*

PLATE 51   *James Watt junior, by L. de Longastre, c.1805. (Private collection)*

PLATE 52   *Matthew Robinson Boulton, by Sir Thomas Lawrence and Sir Martin Archer Shee, 1828-31. (Birmingham Museums & Art Gallery)*

him about it since my return, which I suppose may produce an Answer. His sister has had a bad cold, from which she was not recovered when I left town.'[24]

Finally, on 27 August James (now back in London again) wrote to his father, a letter quoted here in full:

> The day previous to my leaving home Mr RB [Matt] broke silence on the subject of his sister, and stated in substance that although his objections remained as before, he did not think it right they should interfere with our plans, as both of us were *of age* to judge for ourselves.
>
> I enquired if he had availed himself of Mr Freer's recent opportunities of observation, to learn whether he had been able to form a more decided opinion upon the subject which had caused him before so much anxiety and which had necessarily excited a corresponding degree in my mind. He said he had not, as he did not conceive that any opinion Mr Freer could form without his Sister's knowledge would be of any service and he had concluded she was averse to having any queries proposed to her.
>
> I observed that this left the matter in a very unpleasant state as respected us all, but particularly involved upon me a degree of responsibility which I had hoped might have been avoided by his acquiring some further elucidation of his apprehensions.
>
> He then said that his Sister had spoken to him upon the subject of her Marriage Settlement and had stated my intentions to him, but as he did not clearly understand her explanation she had referred him to me. I replied, that the course to be pursued appeared to me very simple and already chalked out by his father's settlement on her. By it she was empowered to assign the proceeds of the land & funded property &c, which he had left to her, to any person with whom she might intermarry for the joint lives of herself & such person, and to settle one half upon him in the event of his surviving her, during the period of his life. That she was willing to make both these assignments in my favour, and that it was my intention in return to settle upon her a sum equal to half the proceeds abovementioned in the event of her surviving me. That I should propose to do this by Bond to Trustees for a sum to be vested in the funds or in real security whenever my decease took place, the interest of which should be paid to her during her life, and the principal then to revert to my heirs, or be disposed of in such other manner as I might by Will appoint. And that it was likewise my intention to make over to her the furniture of her house in the event of her surviving me, as an equivalent for the money she might bring me, which I understood to be about £3000, being the £1500 left her by her father's will and what she was before possessed of, or had since laid by. I added, that I should expect the power which was vested in her of determining the shares of children, to be assigned over to me, and reserve to myself as far as respected them the unlimited disposal of my own property.
>
> He asked what were my intentions with respect to the £12 or £14000, which he understood the settlement empowered her to make over to her husband. I replied that I had not been able to comprehend the meaning of that part of the Settlement but from its having said that the husband was to [?] mark down the Interest, I supposed it to be merely a power of raising money by way of loan to him upon the estates; and that not standing in need of such, it was not in my view then to avail myself of it. He said he thought the power of disposal was more absolute; but upon referring to the Abstracts of the Settlement, we could not unravel the meaning, and therefore agreed that I should consult Mr Jas. Weston upon it.

This I have now done, and he has given a cursory opinion, reserving a more studied one for his return from the Isle of Wight which will not take place before next Monday. He says that she can only bequeath £12000 to her husband in the event of none of their children living to be 21 years of age, and then upon the condition of his paying Interest for it whilst in the receipt of half the proceeds of the property, that is during his life. So that in fact it only enables him to dispose of the above sum after her death, if he has no children by her: a power, which in my view of it, is scarcely worth the claiming.

There is a farther sum of £2000, which she may give the absolute disposal to her husband, or to any other person by the above deed of Settlement.

You will perceive from what I have said, that during Mr Weston's absence no progress can be made, and I hope Miss B will defer her return until she has received full explanation of this abstruse document, the merit of which is entirely given by Mr Weston to the late Mr Boulton, as he says the conditions were entirely of his dictation.

After this, the necessary papers may be drawn out & submitted to Mr RB's approval, and I have a plan in view in the interim for obtaining information upon the point alluded to in the commencement of this letter, but wish nothing to be said about it, or the remaining contents, until I see you ...[25]

James Weston had taken over the legal work for the Boultons and Watts following the death of his brother and partner, Ambrose Weston, in January 1810. James Watt junior saw James Weston a day or two after writing this letter to his father, and ascertained that, as far as he could gather, 'the £12,000 can only be given in the event of there being no children who attain the age of 21 years and upon the condition of the Interest being paid by the husband during life, that is so long as he is in the receipt of one half of the proceeds of the property; which in point of effect differs little from what I before supposed to be the intent.'[26] Finally James Weston produced an abstract of the terms of Boulton's settlement to his daughter, and James wrote to his father that they proposed to draw up a new one: 'I find the power of determining the shares of Children is *not* transferable, which is to me a very unpleasant feeling and repugnant to every idea I entertain upon that subject.'[27]

Anne returned home in September following some kind of accident to one of her eyes. William Cheshire wrote to Miss Alston, who had stayed behind in London, to tell her that Miss Boulton had arrived home safely and viewed her recent accident 'in the light of a most fortunate escape – the preservation of so invaluable a blessing as sight after having been placed at extreme hazard cannot be too gratefully acknowledged ... the cure of the wound is proceeding as fast as can be expected and without any material uneasiness ...'[28] William added that he was writing for Anne as she could only see with one eye at present, 'which sympathizes with the imprisoned orb'. She came home to the smell of new paint, something she hated, for Matt was having work done about the house.

Amelia Alston had been Anne's constant companion during her stay in London and Anne must have confided in her about her proposed marriage to James Watt junior, for Amelia now took it upon herself to write to Matt in November, in a letter endorsed by him, 'her wishes for my Sister's change of name to take place'. Pleading a previous engagement, Amelia turned down an invitation from Matt to visit Soho, but added:

should it ever be her [Miss B's] wish & yours that I should once more become an inmate under that roof where the happiest of my Days has been spent, with infinite pleasure will I obey the Summons – at the moment I make this declaration, I cannot help hoping that any future invitation given by yr Sister will no longer be under the name of Boulton (a name ever dear to me). My Dear Sir will you pardon my mentioning so delicate a subject, but I have so thorough a conviction that her happiness depends on it that I cannot help wishing most sincerely that an event may not be far distant, which ... [torn out] when I left her must have occur'd ... This is a stupid Epistle.[29]

By Christmas it had all gone quiet. The subject of marriage between Anne Boulton and James Watt junior seemed to be closed. Annie Watt, who though she had often spoken critically of Matthew Boulton and his wife had a genuine affection and respect for their daughter, watched Anne anxiously, and on St Valentine's Day 1811 she finally spoke out, in a letter to her stepson:

I cannot any longer refrain from informing you, indeed my heart reproaches me for haveing so long delayed it. I see with the most sincere regret the great unhappiness your cold and distant conduct causes to a friend of ours. The great change has been remarked by all of us ever since she returned from London, nor can we divine any sufficient cause. Seeing I may say the misery she was living in, I offerred my service to speak to you. She had formed an idea that for some reason unknown to her you had changed your sentiments in regard to her. My offer she rejected & said on no account would she consent to your being ? ..., knowing how much you was opprest with business. Thus things went on. Your manners to her was the barometer by which her spirits rose or fell & if it had not been for the great regard she feels for you, a regard of a much longer date than perhaps you are aware of, ... for years ago finding there was no chance of that regard being returned she strove to repress it, but you not many months ago recalled what had so long lain dormant & she I believe at this instant feels a warmer interest about you than ever she did for any other person, and had it not been for that she long ere this would have left her brother's house and it is only on your account that she now submits to his haughty over bearing & unkind manner.

He I know at first strove to raise up a thousand objections from a pretended friendship to you both. They arose I am certain from a very selfish motive that was to retain her as a superintandent of his household for he has said since he cannot live alone. He told your father she by wishing to marry had over turned all his plans. She may thank God & her father that she can live with comfort with out being his housekeeper. How differently would that good old man have acted could he have but seen what you lately proposed realized. It was the last work of his heart to see his daughter happily married & you I believe of all men would have been the man of his choise. I cannot now for one moment think you mean to withdraw from your engagements that gave pleasure to all the friends of both. Tell her but so and she will be satisfied, but while she is in doubt she is most miserable.

When you went away she was very unhappy about your health & she requested you to write, which you promised. You have now been gone three weeks & she has not received one line. I think your own feelings will tell you it is very unkind. Thus I have wrote with out the knowledge of any person & if our dear friend was to know of it she would not forgive me but I could not see her health &

spirits getting worse daily without letting you know in whose power I am certain it is to remove every thing that gives her pain. She is in no hurry to be married. Put her but out of suspense and for any time she will bear with the unkindness of him who ought to be to her as a father. Farewell in hopes of seeing all the bright prospects return that last summer saw before us, and that all the wild fears that arose from self vanish.[30]

If James did write or speak to Anne about marriage again after this, if they had ever so much as touched hands briefly or exchanged a kiss, there is no record of it. They remained friends, nothing more.

The picture which emerges from everybody's letters, of Anne and James going about their normal lives, attending the opera or concerts at Vauxhall with family parties, visiting the dentist, shopping, dealing with business, and above all keeping up appearances, as though nothing of particular significance was being decided that summer, is one of extraordinary tension and control, though no doubt more was spoken than written. Even James Watt senior, though he and his wife were evidently in favour of the marriage, devotes far more space in his letters to his son to crops, weather, and his apple trees, than he does to the subject of his heir's marriage. Why the two did not marry, when it is clear that they wished to do so, remains a puzzle. As Matt himself had pointed out, although he was not personally in favour of it (and nowhere does he seem to have explained his objections in writing) they were of an age to decide for themselves. Whether money, and the financial implications of any children they might have, lay somewhere at the bottom of it is not clear but it may have been one inhibiting factor. The possibility, or indeed wisdom, of Anne becoming pregnant may also have had something to do with it.

Whatever the practical reasons, both were denied – or denied themselves – the opportunity of long-term and closer companionship.

Leaving Soho

To what extent the proposed marriage of Anne Boulton and James Watt junior was common knowledge among their friends, or whether it was all kept quiet, it is not possible to judge. The only ones who mention it in letters are those who were consulted at the time: Annie Watt, Amelia Alston and James Weston. Life seems to have gone on as usual at Soho House, with no hint of the emotional drama being played out. Anne played on a new pianoforte, delivered by Broadwood in November 1810 shortly after her return from London. She instructed John Mosley to nag Brunswick & Co. to speed up the return of her white swan's-down tippet, which she had left with them in London for cleaning. Visitors came and went, especially the Keens and the Alstons. In the summer of 1811, probably at the urging of her Piccadilly friends, Anne stayed with the Dumergues, who were 'affectionately kind to her'.[1] From there she and Miss Alston went on to Worthing, where they joined the Westons, including James Weston's wife and children, and Ambrose's widow and children. James Weston, who was commuting between Worthing and his legal practice in London, wrote to James Watt junior (who was in Herefordshire) telling him about their 'very pretty Society', adding, 'They are within 2 doors of each other and want only your & Mr Boulton's Company to form a compleat Circle. I believe Mr B [Matt] is expected, as to yourself I leave you to guess.' His wife, Jane, had been with him in London for a day or two but was returning to Worthing alone tomorrow – 'she & I are so fashionable as not to travel together', he commented facetiously.[2]

Anne spent some of her inheritance on a new vehicle of her own. In November 1811 she took delivery of a smart landaulet,* built for her by Elliott & Holbrook of Westminster. With a capacious trunk built in at the back to take her parcels, and its protective covers of green baize and oilskin, it cost her £327 0s. 6d., to which was added the cost of a pair of four-year-old bay horses (£210), and harness, horsecloths and all the other incidentals, making the total cost of the equipage £613 13s. 10d.,[3] a sizeable expenditure when compared with the average price of a small family car in the mid-20th century. Thus equipped, she could get about without having to consult Matt's convenience.

Two small personal account books survive from this period of Anne's life, one covering the years 1815-21,[4] and the other 1825[5] only. The obvious gaps may perhaps be explained by the instruction on the front of the 1815-21 volume,

---

* Landaulet: a small version of a landau, a four-wheeled enclosed carriage with a removable front cover and a back cover that can be raised or lowered.

'To be burnt', which, although not carried out in this case, may have been with some others. In these little books Anne kept records of her personal expenditure. Some of the entries are matched by surviving loose bills, but there are others for which bills are not found elsewhere, particularly medical expenses. In 1815, for example, she spent a total of £29 1s. 4d. on medicines and medical attendance. Five consultations with a Dr Baillie cost a total of five guineas, two with a Dr Johnstone two guineas, and two with a Dr De Lys two guineas. She paid Charles Dumergue two guineas for dental treatment. 'Daddy' Dumergue had died in 1814, so this treatment must have been carried out by his nephew, Charles, who was evidently continuing his dental practice. Mr Cline received a guinea, perhaps for a call in London to check on her knee. Mr Freer, a Birmingham physician, was paid £6 13s. 6d., and there was 10s. 10d. for 'hartshorn magnesia', possibly an indigestion remedy, and £4 0s. 0d. for Savory & Moore, who made up pills and medicines. She paid a guinea for the loathsome leeches.

Leeches apart, Anne did enjoy herself, too. In the same year she records expenditure of £3 4s. 6d. on 'Amusements'. These included tickets to concerts and plays, a ticket to see a 'Panorama' and the 'Picturesque Theatre', entrance to an exhibition (unspecified) and the accompanying catalogue, and a visit to a museum and 'Wests Pictures' – possibly an exhibition of the work of Benjamin West. She bought a 'Bonaparte Picture' for one shilling. 'Dolls Toys & Battledores' at 13s. 10d. were perhaps bought as presents for children of friends, or may have been for poor children – Anne records a number of gifts to poor women and children in her accounts. Incidentals during the year include 'flower roots' at 3s. 3d., and a 'Wellington medal' at 3s. 6d.

For her own use she spent a total of £91 3s. 6d. on clothing that year. She made a list of 'Heads of Expences of Wardrobe 1815' which gives the following information:

	£	s	d
Shoes	4	17	6
Stays	3	6	0
Stockings	2	14	8
Gloves	3	5	10
Flowers & Feathers		19	0
Ribbons	7	3	2
Thread, pins,Tape &c	1	18	7½
Shawl, scarfs, Handkerchiefs	6	7	6
Sattins & crape	6	3	9
Lace	26	2	1
Hat & Bonnet	3	14	0
Mrs Thomas, Miss Cooper,			
Burrage bills	6	7	6
Worked Flounces	5	16	8
Muslin, Cambric, Flannel &c	10	15	9
Hair dressers	1	5	6
2 Gold Pins		3	0
Silk purse		2	6
6 pair white tassels		5	0
lost		3	7½

The total for gloves covers 22 pairs of various kinds including 'long white' and 'double' gloves. The flowers, presumably artificial flowers, included white and yellow roses, and the scarves and kerchiefs were in pink, green and white, and green and brown. Anne had over 25 yards of 'worked flounce' in three orders from Catherine Cooper, a dressmaker in South Molton Street, London, who made clothes for her over a long period. The un-named maid who helped her to dress and looked after the clothes was paid £9 6s. 1d. for the year. The accounts do not tell us a great deal about Anne's clothes, though it is apparent from fabric entries over the years covered by the books that apart from black and white she favoured colours in the red-pink-crimson-lilac-lavender range. Hats include both straw and fabric bonnets, a black fur hat in 1818, and turbans (including a turban bought for Miss Alston in 1819). Anne spent more on her wardrobe in 1815 than in any other year recorded in the 'Own Account' books.

Matt meanwhile was looking for a less ephemeral investment, and that year he bought Tew Park, on the edge of the Oxfordshire village of Great Tew. The estate included a run-down part-17th-century mansion, together with a lodge, cottages, a park, plantations, tenanted farms, and a small hunting estate, an acquisition which led James Watt junior to describe Matt drily as 'the Lord Expectant of Great Tew' (Plate 52).[6] He began gradually to refurbish and refurnish the mansion, but with the Soho business needing his constant attention in Birmingham, Tew Park was for recreation and investment – not until the next generation would the Boulton family look upon it as home.

Annie Watt had cast Matt as the selfish villain of the piece in the affair of his sister and her stepson, but in spite of that he seems to have been capable of generosity, for over the next year or two there are affectionate letters from various ladies, family friends, thanking him for hospitality and for gowns, silk and other gifts. In 1815 Amelia Alston reciprocated with a gift of her own: 'a very large, very yellow, very dashing Indian silk handkerchief'; she added the hope that he would never have to pay the 'tax on Bachelors'.[7]

Matt had no intention of paying such a tax. Now in his mid-40s, he had a bride in his sights: 19-year-old Mary Anne Wilkinson, a niece of Joseph Priestley's late wife, Mary. Young Mary Anne's father, William Wilkinson, was the brother of 'Iron-Mad' John Wilkinson, and had been in charge of the family's Bersham works in north Wales, where James Watt junior had spent part of his time as a trainee before going to Switzerland in 1784. William Wilkinson had appointed James guardian of Mary Anne and her younger sister, Elizabeth Stockdale Wilkinson, on his death in 1808. The two girls went to a school at Chester for a time but, like Anne Boulton's schooling, their education seems to have been an on-off affair, though a look through Mary Anne's personal bills reveals an interest in music, with the purchase of arias from *The Marriage of Figaro* and *Messiah*, an Italian song collection and piano arrangements of Beethoven trios. She also bought complete acts of operas including *La Clemenze di Tito* and *The Magic Flute*. There are also bills for artists' materials, paint brushes and so on.[8] On the face of it, apart from their age difference she and Anne Boulton should have had a lot in common. After their father's death both Mary Anne and Elizabeth stayed at Soho House from time to time, and sometimes with the Watts at Heathfield.

The nature of Matt Boulton's interest in Mary Anne was plain enough to some and is to be deduced from a letter which 'Daddy' Dumergue wrote to Matt in April 1814, not long before he died. It is annotated by Matt, 'invitation to Miss Wilkinson' and begins, 'Mon cher Petit Robin'. 'Daddy' explained that some expected guests had been obliged to postpone their visit, leaving a bedroom available, and:

> ... on a dit a nos dames dans Salisbury Square que Vous veniès En ville sous peu, comme il est possible que vous ayez l'inclination de profitter de cette occation de faire voir cette Babilone a votre Désagréable Pupille, & que, amoins que vous ne lui donniés votre nom Elle ne pourrait pas loger dans la meme Maison: mes femmes me charge d'insister, quoi que contre mon Gré que vous ameniéz Mlle Wilkinson prendre possetion de la Chambre destinée au D[emoise]lles Brandt, & nous vous permettions de la venir voir quelques fois.[9]

Annie Watt had had her suspicions all along, but the first inkling that most of Matt's friends got that marriage was in the air came in a letter from James Watt to John Furnell Tuffen in December 1816. 'Mr Boulton is at last about to marry Miss Wilkinson,' he wrote. As James Watt junior was Mary Anne's guardian Matt would presumably have had to ask his consent to marry her as she was still under twenty-one. Watt senior added that Anne Boulton and Miss Keen were visiting Bath and Cheltenham.[10] The visit must have lasted at least three weeks, for Anne recorded expenses for the trip of £131 19s. 3d., including £57 17s. for house rent, and 'Bath pump & woman 3 weeks' at £1 os. od. She had spent 10s. 6d. at the chalybeate well and 19s. at the saline well,[11] though from what Watt could gather she did not seem to have derived much benefit from the waters.

Whether or not Anne and her companion knew about the impending marriage before they left home, Tuffen was astonished at Watt's news:

> I always admired Mrs Watt's penetration but did not credit her prediction that Miss Wilkinson would be the future Mistress of Soho, this however I now learn is decided, and the marriage will I presume speedily take place, as I understand the Settlements are executed. Convinced as I am of Mr Boulton's sincere regard, it would have been more flattering to my *amour propre* to have known this from himself than another, but with his constitutional reserve this was not perhaps to be expected ... I hope this projected Wedding will not compel my friend James [James Watt junior] to change his residence. Bath will certainly be much more cheerful to Miss Boulton than a lonely house in the country.[12]

In March 1817 Matt married his '*désagréable pupille*'. The newlyweds went off to Harrogate for a short honeymoon. Watt wrote to Tuffen that since their return to Soho they had had many visitors, but that Matt had now left his bride and his sister together at Soho House and had gone on his own to Tew, where he was having a cottage repaired for their use:

> As soon as Tew is habitable they propose to go there for a short time & from thence to London etc. Further this deponent knoweth not! James is still unprovided with a house. Miss Boulton says she will not take that from him which he is in [Thornhill]; but has not yet been able to find one for herself, though she is in quest of one. Her health is not very good, though she has had no particular illness lately. I agree with you in your observations on my Son's way of passing his life, unfortunately he has no person to leave his fortune to who merits it![13]

Tuffen told Watt he had received a piece of bride cake, 'with a card of Mr & Mrs B's compliments. I would much rather have had one friendly line from him ... I presume from his merely fitting up a small house at Tew he intends Soho to be his home ...' [14]

Leaving Anne Boulton and her new sister-in-law alone together at Soho House was not the most tactful thing for Matt to have done. They were not on friendly terms. Anne, having been disappointed in her hopes of marriage to James Watt junior in 1810-11, largely due to her brother's objections, had probably resigned herself to life as a spinster but at least had some status in her role as mistress of Soho House. To be usurped by a slip of a girl nearly thirty years her junior must have been galling, and relations became tense and strained, notwithstanding the maintenance of an appearance of civility in public. In June they were all putting on a front in London together, with Annie and James Watt, for the official opening of Waterloo Bridge. It was a grand spectacle, wrote Watt to his son; water and land were 'covered with well dressed spectators. The Regent was well received and cheered ... Mrs Watt & I had places by the Miss Rennies & Mrs & Miss Boulton. Messrs Boulton & Barber were on the water. The weather is now exceeding hot, from 80° to 84° in the shade.' [15]

But Anne was very unhappy. Just as Watt's friend Tuffen had suspected, she had begun thinking about moving out of Soho House even before Matt's marriage. Tuffen predicted that Anne 'would never occupy the house at Thorn Bank [Thornhill]. It would therefore be very idle for my friend [James] to give it up on a principle of false delicacy towards her.' [16] He thought she would be better off moving to Bath or Brighton, where she regularly spent time. She does not seem to have gone to Bath or Brighton in 1817, but she did go to Stafford, probably to visit the Keens, and she did pay a visit to Tew Park. Travelling expenses (but not dates) for the two journeys are in the 'Own Account' book. [17]

James was certainly well-established at Thornhill (where he described the drawing room and bedrooms as warm and cheerful, but the dining room as rather cold [18]), but knowing Anne's desire to get away from Soho he felt uncomfortable about staying there, and began to look around for somewhere else. Shortly after they had all returned from the Waterloo Bridge event, Anne called on Annie Watt at Heathfield. In the course of their conversation she told her friend that it was not possible for her to remain at Soho House 'without coming to an open rupture'. [19] She had heard that James knew of a house at the Foundry, but as Annie Watt pointed out, it was very small. Anne thought that as long as it was not right in the middle of the Foundry site she might go there herself, for four, six, or even twelve months as a temporary expedient, if she could be sure of having Thornhill at the end of that time. Annie was very concerned about this suggestion which she thought quite unsuitable, and told Anne she was sure James would be willing to vacate Thornhill if Anne would be willing to move into it furnished with his things, as there would not be room for them in the little house at the Foundry. Anne was diffident about turning James out, and said that, after all, she would wait another few months to give him chance to find somewhere more suitable.

Annie cast around for diplomatic solutions to the situation which would be acceptable to Anne. She told James about a house she knew of in Birmingham which was available to let for a year. 'If you was to take that house and let her have it till you could find one that you could go into with comfort, do you think it would be right to make her that offer, that is to say if the house is to be got & it to appear it was your[s] but was to[o] small for your books &c &c and as there was a chance of more than one good house being to be had in the Parish you would be glad to wait a little longer.'[20]

FIGS 26 & 27   *Two views of Heathfield House, designed for James and Annie Watt by Samuel Wyatt, 1787-90. (Local Studies Department, Birmingham Reference Library)*

James, who was in London, was increasingly bothered by Anne's situation and the difficult position in which it put him, though he was not surprised. He wrote to Annie, 'I am much concerned to learn from your letter that Miss Boulton finds herself so little at her ease at Soho, though it is what I expected would happen, and I must regret that I did not follow the impulsion of my own judgement in giving up the house previous to the arrival of the new mistress.' Her reluctance to move in to Thornhill with his furniture in it would inevitably delay her move from Soho House, because, although he was willing to go and live in the little house at the Foundry, he had nowhere to put his furniture. He wondered if his books, fossils & wines could be stored temporarily at Heathfield, until he found a suitable house in Handsworth or Harborne. He wanted a house which would enable him to entertain his friends as he had been used to doing, and had his eye on a couple but was not yet sure whether they were available, or on what terms. Come what may, Annie was to 'Assure Miss Boulton that in any event any measures shall be taken as to insure her possession of her own house in 3 months from [now] at the latest and it shall be as much sooner as may be in my power.'[21]

On 8 August Anne went over to Heathfield in the landaulet to spend the evening with Mr and Mrs Watt, who showed her James's letter. Annie did not see how James, willing as he was to move, could leave Thornhill in less than three months. Anne said she had not meant to suggest he should empty the place, and that he could leave his furniture there for a while, although eventually she would want to put in her own. The Watts said they could not accommodate James's wine or fossils at Heathfield – the cellars were too small for their own wine stocks, and Watt's fossil room floor could not take any more weight, so 'Miss B. agreed to give these articles lodging also, as to the books you & her must settle about them when you meet'.[22] Watt and Annie had tried suggesting various houses to Anne, but 'as no place hereabouts which could be named seemed to be satisfactory to her, Mrs W. strongly recommended to her to go to Bath, Clifton or some other watering place until you could give her possession. She is certainly very unhappy where she is.'

That evening, when Anne got back to Soho House, she hastened to correct any misapprehension, in a letter to James which makes it clear that she no longer felt at home there:

My dear Mr Watt,
You perhaps may not pardon the application that has been made to you, but I trust you will listen to the motives and do me the justice to believe it was far from my wish to put you to the slightest inconvenience respecting the removal of your Furniture, Books, wine etc. I am extremely sorry to perceive there has been a total misunderstanding for I never made the least objection to their remaining where they now stand for any length of time you please, and that I may not appear quite the fickle, selfish being you must at present consider me, I have come to the resolution of troubling you with these few lines, to endeavour to account for my conduct, and at the same time to assure you, I do not wish that you should remove from your present house until you can find another more suitable to you, than the one I *now* understand you are fitting up – it was in consequence of this report that I applied to Heathfield to know your real intentions, that I might be guided by them in looking for a temporary abode for myself, two of my friends having told me they were informed by Mrs Watt that

you meant soon to leave Thornhill, and were preparing a house to go to. This I mentioned to Mrs W, who then said the house she alluded to was at the Foundry, but that you wished to get Hampstead, or Oxhill ... When you kindly offered in the Spring to give up Thornhill, I never doubted but ere this I should have met with another situation in the neighbourhood to suit me, and you are well aware of my intention to have done so, but a fruitless search has been the result of all my inquiries. I have looked at some small houses that are to let, one lately occupied by Mr Bett's father at Winson Green, but like all the rest of that size it affords no accommodation for my horses or carriage which would be extremely inconvenient for me to do without. My *visit here* has been prolonged far beyond the term I originally proposed to myself, and if there existed no other cause the state of my health would make me anxious to get settled in some home of my own. At the same time my dear Sir I must repeat that if it be more convenient to you to continue at Thornhill beyond the period mentioned in your letter to Mrs W, I beg & intreat you will do so, whether it should be for six, twelve months or more, only say so and I will dispose of myself accordingly.

I cannot close this without expressing my *earnest* hope that what has now past will not lower me in your estimation, or interrupt that friendship begun in happy infancy, and which I trust will never cease but with my life – in that persuasion I still subscribe myself, Yours most faithfully and affectionately, A. Boulton.[23]

James was touched by the tone of Anne's letter about what he called their 'mutual difficulties', and arranged to see her as soon as he returned from a business trip.

For the rest of 1817 and the beginning of 1818 both Anne (described by Annie Watt as 'unhappy & unwell'[24]) and James Watt junior looked around for somewhere else to live (separately) – Anne so that James could stay at Thornhill, James so that he could leave it. Both rejected various houses on various grounds. In the end, wrote Watt senior to his son, Anne resolved not to move from Soho 'until she does so once for all'.[25] But only a day or two later she felt so desperate that anything seemed preferable to remaining at Soho – even John Whately's house, The Rookery, which she had previously rejected. She asked Watt to find out if it was still available. 'It appears to me that one cause of Miss B's coming to this solution is the disagreeable predicament in which she cannot help finding herself at Soho, which may be increased by Mrs B's confinement if it takes place there,' wrote Watt to James.[26] With his letter to his son, Watt senior enclosed one which he had received from Anne, for she had not been well enough to brave the cold wind across the common to Heathfield for a week or two. Her brother and pregnant sister-in-law were away, but expected back at any moment as she hastily scribbled the note:

I must therefore trouble you with a few lines, the purport of which you will perhaps do me the favour to transmit to your Son. I understand by a letter I received from Mrs Watt yesterday, that an offer of The Rookery had been made to him for one year, which he has declined – I can only say, that should it be his *decided wish* to continue at Thornhill another twelvemonth I will endeavour to take The Rookery for the same term, provided I can have his determination through you or any other channel immediately, for in all probability Mr Whately will try to dispose of his house as soon as possible. I have only time to add that as far as lies in my power I am desirous and willing to do whatever is most likely to contribute to your happiness & his – and with the most sincere attachment I beg you to believe me my dear Sir, ever faithfully & affectionately yours, A. Boulton. Excuse this hasty blotted scrawl as I am expecting the London party to arrive every moment.[27]

To be on the safe side, Watt arranged that all further correspondence on this subject should be passed to Anne via Annie Watt's sister, Janet McGrigor, who was staying at Heathfield, 'for she [Miss Boulton] is so watched by Mrs B, who is now come home, that my going would occasion many impertinent questions ...'[28] But in the end, Anne still could not face The Rookery – she turned it down again, and also did not think it suitable for James any more (nor did he).

By May 1818, with the birth of the Boultons' first child now imminent, James felt he absolutely must vacate Thornhill, although he still had nowhere else to go. He offered to meet Anne either at Soho House, or at Thornhill if she thought they would have less interruption there, to hand over the keys.[29] There was little chance of them obtaining five minutes' uninterrupted conversation at Soho House, said Anne, so she accepted his invitation to call at 'what shall I call it, *ill-fated Thornhill*'.[30] Perhaps she felt awkward about the difficulty he was in – at any rate, they agreed that Anne should have possession of her house by the end of the third quarter, and she steeled herself for her sister-in-law's confinement and a few more months at Soho House.

The first of Matt and Mary Anne Boulton's seven children,[31] Anne Robinson Boulton, was born on 5 June 1818. Anne Boulton became the baby's godmother, but James Watt junior declined Matt's somewhat diffident invitation to him to be godfather.[32] The choice of Miss Boulton as her new niece's godmother was probably made on the grounds that it was the proper thing to do, and perhaps also partly as an olive branch. Anne ordered what may have been a christening gown and bonnet for her niece-god-daughter from a shop in St James's Street, London. She seems to have jibbed at the price, for the supplier, Mrs Bell, wrote to her somewhat frostily:

> Madam, I can assure you that my charge for the Infants Mantle & Bonnet is as reasonable as any person could make such articles, receiving the costly materials they are made of. It is my invariable practice to be as moderate in my charges as possible – nevertheless a reasonable profit I am confident you will not object to; and I declare that I have only put a fair profit on the articles. In order however to please, and considering that the Amount will be early remitted to me, I shall have no objection to allow a discount of 5 per cent.[33]

Mrs Bell's bill, for 14 guineas, was paid in October (less the 14 shillings).

Not having found anywhere to live locally to his liking, James decided the best thing to do was to take a house near London, as he had to spend so much time there anyway, so early in October 1818 he wrote to Matt to tell him that he was surrendering Thornhill to Anne and moving south. He told Matt he had pressed the house on Anne several times, both before Matt's marriage and since, and she had declined it 'through motives of kindness to me',[34] but it was now clear that her removal from Soho House should not be postponed any longer. James also wrote to his father, who was with Mrs Watt in Tenby, explaining why he now felt it had become so urgent:

In making this communication [to Matt] I omitted all notice of the causes of his sister leaving his house, but he in his reply stated his regret that the efforts of himself *and of his wife* to render her situation comfortable had not been successful, and alledged some grievances against her, into which, as well as to what related to the efforts of his wife, I judged it best not to enter, but said I knew his sister to be sensible of his kindness towards her since his marriage ...

Yesterday Mrs B, whom I had not seen since my arrival although she had made one call here, came to me and complained of my not seeing her etc., which led to a pretty full communication of my sentiments upon her conduct to Miss B., and much protestation on her part of her intentions being misconceived and her conduct misrepresented, and expressions of her regret at the consequences about to ensue. As her coming to me at all, or offering any explanation was more than I expected, I felt in consequence disposed to act the peacemaker, and accompanied her back to Soho and had a conference with Mr B., to whom I stated frankly, but with as much moderation as possible, what had been my opinion of his wife's conduct, as well as the explanation she had given and my desire that all parties should be reconciled and an Act of Oblivion passed, to which he readily assented, but as might be expected not without some comments upon his sister and some vindication of his wife. I next saw Miss Boulton who readily acquiesced in the propriety of my recommendations, retaining however her intention of immediately leaving the house, but wishing me to continue to occupy hers & she would go to London. This I, of course, declined, and left the two Ladies together, in the expectation that an amiable explanation would take place. However, it appears that like all peacemakers, I failed, and that a scene of great violence ensued, which led to mutual complaints to Mr Boulton, who of course sided with his wife. In this state of matters Mr Barker and myself interposed our mediation, and a treaty of peace was effected, to continue in force so long as Miss Boulton remains in the house & as much longer as the parties chuse.[35]

At eight o'clock next morning Anne wrote a hurried note which she sent over to James at Thornhill:

My dear Mr Watt, will you do me the favour to say if I can see you *sometime* this morning, and at what hour it will be most convenient – I should have taken my chance to finding you soon after breakfast but should not wish to stumble upon another member of this family with whom perhaps you may have an engagement – if you can, I hope you will comply with my request, for you can form no idea of the load of misery you have most unintentionally brought upon me. In great haste believe me ever most truly your affectionate A.Boulton.[36]

James sent his reply back with the servant:

My dear Miss Boulton,
I believe it is better that I should call upon you at Soho, and I will do so as soon as I can after breakfast, as I am at this moment expecting some persons here. Mine has been the usual lot of peacemaker, that of making matters worse than I found them [*crossed out:* and of involving myself in disputes I have been most anxious to avoid] but I shall be still most anxious to do every thing in my power to tranquillize your mind, and remain affectionately yours, J.Watt. [37]

James's parents were staying in Herefordshire, and Watt senior wrote to his son, 'I thank you for the details of the fracas at Soho which is no more than I expected would have taken place upon an eclairissement. I think you are perfectly right in persisting in your intention of giving up the house, though I am very sorry you feel yourself obliged to do so.'[38] He was not, however, happy at the thought of James living in London, so it did not happen. John Rennie wrote to James that he was sorry he had given up the idea of moving south (where he would have been nearer to Rennie), but that he had 'acted right as a dutifull son ought' in acceding to his father's request to him not to go. [39]

As the problem grew bigger, so did the solution. In desperation James took a ten-year lease on Aston Hall, a huge Jacobean house about two miles from Soho House and Thornhill, with a 95-acre park, lake, walled garden and flower garden (Plate 53). It was far bigger than he really needed and, even after shutting up part of the house, the part he proposed to occupy needed some work on it before he could move in, but at least a decision had been made. 'I hope now that you will have plenty of room in your Home and will take a Partner & fullfill the intentions of your Creator,' wrote Rennie.[40] Anne wrote to thank James. She badly wanted to talk to him, 'and if you will say when you are likely to be disengaged, I will call at Thornhill, for I would rather see you there than here. As you mentioned that you were going to enquire about Grates, I must remind you that there are two in your present abode which I beg you will not hesitate to remove whenever it suits you without considering my accommodation, as I can easily find substitutes to answer my purpose until I go to Town.'[41]

Early in December James wrote a note to Anne and enclosed with it the keys of Thornhill, including the keys of his private drawers and bookcases. He paid Daniel the gardener up till Christmas and left him in charge of the dog, asking Anne to instruct her servants that the animal was not to be beaten.[42] Then, taking a last look round the place which had been his home for ten years and making a mental note of what furniture he would take away in due course, he went off to the Watt family's country estate at Doldowlod[43] in Wales. For the next few months, while Aston Hall was made ready for him, James divided his time between Wales and his father's house, Heathfield.

In readiness for the move Anne invested about £20 in some odds and ends of cutlery, crockery, a rolling pin and four warm bed quilts.[44] A few days before Christmas 1818 she left the house where she had been born and moved into Thornhill.

Mistress of Thornhill

When the deep Brunswick green-painted front doors of Thornhill House closed behind Anne Boulton in December 1818, standing in the narrow hall with its staircase winding up and around above her head, among the boxes and cases, she must have heaved a sigh of mingled relief and apprehension as she untied her bonnet. At least she was away from the tensions at Soho House, but the move from what had been a happy childhood home to what she herself had called 'ill-fated Thornhill', with its associations of disappointment, cannot have been easy for a 50-year-old woman in indifferent health. She laid in a large stock of meat (there are bills for over 175 pounds in weight altogether of beef, mutton and veal between 16-24 December, costing just over £5 11s. 8d. in total, and suggesting not only company but perhaps some distribution for the poor), together with five guineas-worth of groceries (including sugar, nutmeg, allspice, cloves, ginger, cinnamon, sweet almonds and currants, all of which sound like the makings of seasonal fare), and lamp oil and soap,[1] but just how she spent that Christmas is not recorded.

FIG. 28 *Pen and ink drawing of the front door of Thornhill House, c.1820. (Birmingham City Archives)*

If Anne wrote many letters during her Thornhill years (and probably she did, for there are regular entries for postage of letters among her bills), or if she received many, they have not come to light. Most of what can be reconstructed of her lifestyle during this period has to be deduced from her personal and household accounts. These she kept meticulously, making it possible now to look at expenditure on clothes, travel, books, furniture, house maintenance, the stable, the garden, food, housework, and regular charitable donations of a guinea a year to the Handsworth National School, the Handsworth Book Society, the Handsworth Penny Club, the Committee for the Enlargement of Handsworth Church, the Birmingham Dispensary, and the General Institution for the Instruction of the Deaf and Dumb.

As is to be expected, most of the expenditure on items such as furniture, tableware and other household goods comes in the earlier years, while expenditure on consumables (food, fuel, candles) and items which would wear out (clothing, household linen) is spread across the entire period. Towards the end of the series of bills, the system of separate wrappers which Anne employed to keep her different classes of bills filed begins to break down and to become more random.

Although numerous bills have been saved, some evidently were not, for the annual balance sheets produced for Anne, recording income and expenditure, show higher expenditure figures than can be accounted for from the loose bills and entries in cash books. The balance sheets also provide information on her income, not only from the rents, dividends and mortgages which her father had set up for her in his settlement, but also from fees paid for grazing at Thornhill and sales of fencing timber, pea-sticks and faggots from the small estate. For example, in 1821 income from such sources and also the sale of some old chimney pots amounted to £15 2s. 0d. Annual income from all sources including interest is generally between £2,000 and £5,000, well above the thousand pounds a year which Matthew Boulton took pains to ensure that his daughter would have to live on. This allowed Anne, after making essential payments including the maintenance costs of her tenanted farms, to invest a substantial amount in modifications to her house as well as high-quality and stylish furnishings.

Thornhill House, described by Charles Pye as 'secluded from public view by a lofty brick wall',[2] was a solid-looking three-storey building, with a square front (Plate 49). A rather ungainly deep full-height bow was tacked on to the north-north-east wall, rather like a turret with a flat roof, and on the opposite side there was a shallow single-storey bow window. It was one of those houses where the rooms inside perhaps look better than the outside. There was a wing at the back which housed the kitchen and other domestic offices. The house was assessed for tax on 35 windows, an annual tax liability of £23 16s. 6d..[3] Some further idea of its size can be gathered from the list of keys which Anne had handed over to James Watt junior in March 1808 when he moved in.[4] When Anne wrote out the list there were 16 keys for the ground floor, ten for the 'chamber story' and seven for the 'attic story', as well as a group for the stables, coach house and gates, and for various cupboards and passage doors.

The ground-floor keys are for 'three parlours', which would have been the drawing room, dining room and breakfast room. The latter room (c.11 feet by 14 feet) was on one side of the front door. This was the room which James had called 'the little library', and which George Bullock had lined with bookcases for him. On the other side of the front door was the drawing room, approximately 19 feet 5 inches square, with a shallow bow window on the south-south-west side; there were two flat 'blind' windows on the front (east-south-east) wall, a wall covered on the inside by more bookcases. The largest room, the dining room, which extended into the deep bow, measured 27 feet 4 inches by 17 feet 11 inches, and was on the north-north-east side of the house, which was probably the reason for its being, as James had said, rather cold. The plan shows what appear to be two pillars in the dining room opposite the fireplace. These may have been 'warming columns' heated by warm air to provide some background warmth; Matthew Boulton had considered installing warming columns in the drawing room when he was planning to give the house to Anne and Dr Carmichael, but at Anne's request had not done so.[5]

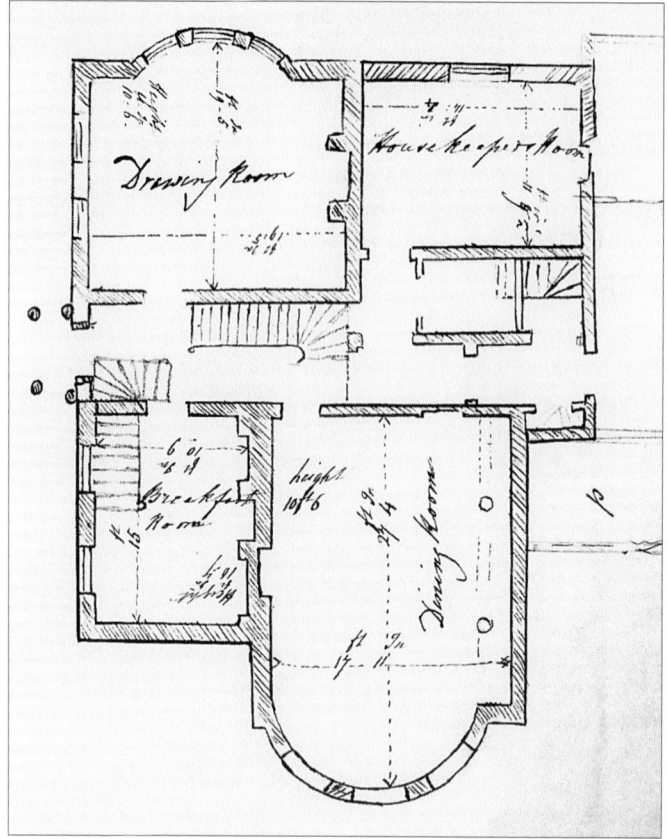

FIG. 29 *Ground-floor plan of Thornhill House, c.1820. (Birmingham City Archives)*

At the back of the house was the housekeeper's room, which had its own door into the kitchen. The kitchen and other offices at the back, including the pantries, dairy, larder, brewhouse, and cellars, could also be reached from the rear hall. The brewhouse, with its maiding tubs and scrubbing boards, was where the laundry was done, brewhouse (or 'brew'us') being a word commonly used in Birmingham, and perhaps elsewhere, for the laundry or wash-house. The actual brewing of ale may have been done in the cellar, for the inventory[6] shows the mash tub, casks and other brewing equipment to have been down there. The ground-floor plan shows steps leading down to it from a small area at the side of the housekeeper's room. The list of keys for the outbuildings shows that there was a coach house, a harness room, and stables with a room over them, which could be used for a bedroom for one manservant if required. Other 'outside' keys included the stable yard gates, road gates, the gardens (perhaps a walled garden and garden stores), and the hen pen.

Upstairs, the 'chamber story' had three bed-chambers, a dressing room and a water closet. The chambers, or bedrooms, were the 'small front chamber' over the breakfast room, the 'large front chamber' over the drawing room, and the 'bow chamber' over the dining room. The 'back chamber', above the housekeeper's room, may have served as a dressing room to the 'large front chamber', which is marked on the plan as the 'best bedroom'. In the 'attic story' were the 'back

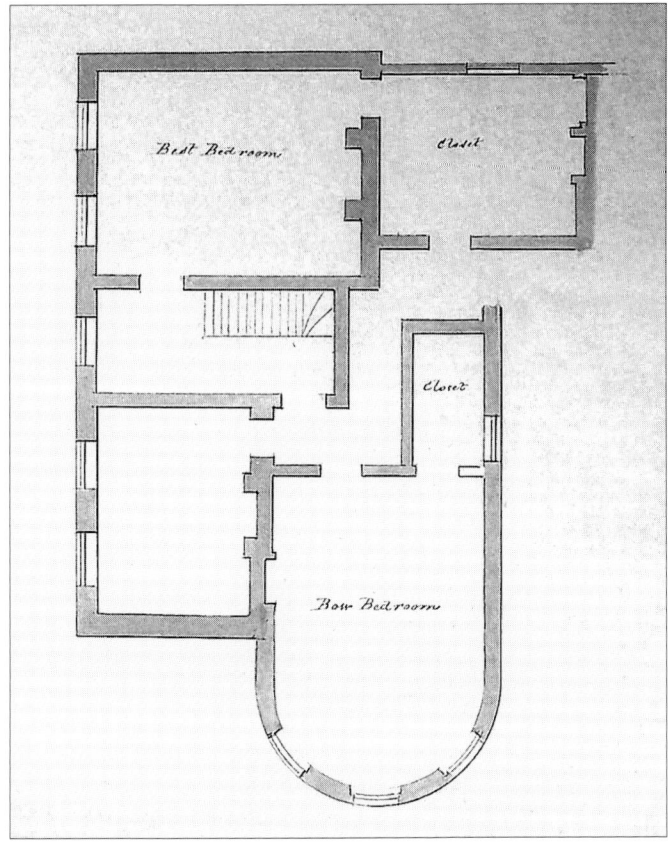

FIG. 30 *First-floor plan of Thornhill House, c.1820. (Birmingham City Archives)*

attic', 'bow attic and small front attic', 'middle front attic', and 'large front attic'. Some of these were quite expensively furnished and possibly used for guests, and some were probably servants' accommodation, though Miss Boulton did not have a large household and not all of the servants lived in.

Whether some of James's servants stayed on for a short time when Anne moved in, or whether Anne's maid came with her from Soho House is not clear, but in March 1819 she advertised for servants in *Aris's Gazette*. According to Anne's tax assessments she had three male servants, on whom she paid tax of £11 3s. od. per year.[7] The tax assessment does not necessarily imply that the menservants lived in, though in this case it is probable that they did. They are likely to have been the footman, coachman and gardener (who lived with his wife in a cottage somewhere in the grounds, or possibly in the lodge). Anne also had three female servants: a cook, upper servant and housemaid, some of whom may have lived in. In addition to these 'house' servants she perhaps had a lady's maid, for a servant always travelled with her when she went to London, Brighton or elsewhere. In the 1820s tax was not chargeable on female servants. The servants were usually engaged for a year at a time, though some stayed only a few weeks. When servants left, Anne generally advertised in *Aris's Gazette* for their replacements, such advertisements being placed anonymously with replies directed to the newspaper's office.

There are records of the names of some of the Thornhill servants at various times, but their jobs are not always identified. The men include James Sneyd (coachman), Stephen Edwards (probably his successor), Richard Smith, Stephen Cove, Samuel Griffin, John Wright, Edwin Walker and John Collins. Joseph Rollston came in 1826; his wife Mary gave Anne a receipt for his quarter's wages of £5 10s. 6d. in April 1826.[8] John Wright joined the small staff in 1829 at 19 guineas plus two suits of livery, a dressing jacket and garters, and a guinea for tea. His livery description suggests he was the footman. The gardener from 1824 was Thomas Davenport. He was paid £3 14s. od. per month and was allowed a quart of beer a day, but no ale. Once a quarter his cottage rent of £3 5s. od. was deducted from his month's wages, so Thomas and his wife had a thin time in rent months unless they had saved enough to tide them over. Mrs Davenport occasionally did some work for Anne in the house. In March 1826 Davenport received an overdue bonus of £1 1s. od. 'a cording to a Greement due the 26th of Jany last though it is at your opshan'.[9]

Female servants over the years included Ann Middlecote, 'Penelope', Hannah Taylor, Mary Sneyd (perhaps the coachman's wife), C. Masters, Elizabeth Moseley, Margaret Winn, Lidia Cordwell, Ann Buggins, Harriet Herbert, Mrs Hicken, Mary Wood, Mrs Thompson, Elizabeth Jones, and a Mrs Brown. The latter was recruited from London – her travelling expenses of £3 os. 6d. were paid in August 1824; her annual salary was to be 30 guineas,[10] but she only stayed for about three months. Which of these women worked as upper servant, cook, housemaid or lady's maid is not clear, though higher wages would have been paid to the cook and upper servant. Mrs Thompson was paid £18 per year and her tea found.[11] The servants' wages generally range from about £10-£35 per year, with the annual outlay on wages from 1819-25 being between £75-£98.[12] Thereafter it drops dramatically, to under £40 per year, though whether this is due to incomplete records or to Anne employing fewer servants is not known. Annual expenditure on livery for the coachman and footman is generally between £20-£40.

Anne had had past experience of assessing potential staff at Soho House, and made herself lists of the duties required of the different servants, and questions to ask them at interview. With any candidate Anne wanted to know:

> In what places have you lived & how long in each?
> What did the Establishment consist of?
> How long since you quitted your last place?
> What were your reasons for leaving it?
> What wages had you, and what clothes?
> Are you married or single, and what age?
> Do you understand brewing, marketing, etc?[13]

She may have copied some of the lists of duties from a housekeeping manual, for they include some duties not applicable at Thornhill. For instance, the list of butler's duties includes 'cleans his masters Shoes & Clothes and prepares for his Masters Toilette'. Other butler's duties include cleaning and replenishing the candlesticks, serving breakfast, washing the tea-things, cleaning plate and answering bells, dressing the lunch and dinner trays, decanting wine, arranging the sideboard and the dinner table, waiting at the dinner table, and last thing at night, checking that all windows and doors are secure and fires and lights have been left safe. He was also to manage the brewing, deliver and convey messages, draw the servants' ale and direct the regular cleaning of the cellars.[14] It may be, however, that Miss Boulton did not have a servant with the title of butler at all. There is no mention of a butler's clothing among the servants' livery bills (which list only clothes for the footman and coachman), and Anne's list of the footman's duties seems to cover most of the butler's functions.

The footman's livery consisted of black velveteen breeches, white shirt, cashmere waistcoat, livery coat with gilt buttons, and, for outdoors, a caped greatcoat and a black hat with a gold band. These were supplied annually. He was forbidden to keep any of his clothes in his pantry and was to dress upstairs, presumably in one of the attic rooms. He was a busy man. His jobs included opening all the shutters in the morning and checking that all doors, shutters and windows were securely fastened at night. He 'rubbed' the furniture, mahogany doors and tables in the three reception rooms (no oil to be used on the rosewood and only cold drawn linseed oil on the mahogany). He cleaned the lamps and candlesticks, attended to the fires, cleaned the ladies' shoes, went out with the carriage, answered the bells after one o'clock, answered the door, waited at dinner, brought in the coal, cut the bread and butter for tea, lit the lamps, helped clean the windows and shake the carpets, cleaned his own pantry and washed the glasses. Some parts of the footman's job description have been written out in greater detail:

> The Glasses and tea things are always washed up as soon as done with & put by – there are two bowls, one for glass & the other for the tea things, which must be used for their own separate purposes as well as the different sorts of cloths. Remember always to fill the Tea Urn with water before you put in the heater. Never leave a candle burning in the pantry. The Lamp in the inner passage is always used when there is company. In putting out the lamp recollect the plug must be pulled up to prevent the oil overflowing. The oil is emptied every day out of the pillar lamps & used for the Hall lamp.[15]

The brewing vessels, which were kept in the coach house in winter and the cellar in summer, were to be washed out the day before they were wanted. The cellar was to be cleaned once a month. The male servants were allowed one pint of ale and the women half a pint at dinner and supper, the footman drawing it from the barrel. The footman was to take the spoon drawer upstairs at night, having first counted the contents. Visitors' servants were allowed to sit in the warm laundry, but were on no account allowed in the footman's pantry. The footman was expected to assist the coachman in the stable when the carriage came in at night, and was also in charge of the horses' oats, which he issued to the coachman once a fortnight. Anne noted that 'for a horse not in full work a peck of oats is sufficient for a day'.[16] For all this the footman was paid about £19 a year, but Anne added firmly, 'No tea allowed except on Sunday morning' and 'No perquisites'.[17]

Miss Boulton's household was small, so the servants had literally to be maids or masters of all work, and there is a lot of overlapping on their lists of duties. All of them performed tasks which they might not have been expected to perform in a larger establishment. The Thornhill cook had to be up early – cleaning the candlesticks before breakfast is on her list, as well as cleaning her pantry and larder every day and the meat hooks twice a week. She was to:

Keep a cloth for meat & wipe it every morning. Kitchen dishes are washed immediately after dinner, parlour dishes in an evening. Take charge of the poultry. Brick oven always used for baking bread & iron one for pastry. Clean latter once a week. Feathers are kept in paper bags. Assist at the wash until it is got up. Riddle the cinders & use to back the fire. Occasionally help to make beds. Wipe all tins every Friday & clean once a fortnight. No fire under boiler except Sat. a.m. Clean flags at back door every Sat. Kitchen and pantry shutters close before dark. Back door locked. Get the men's breakfast. Clean bacon room. Broth to be made from the boiled meat, save the bones for kitchen soup. Occasionally go to market. When out return before supper & never go out without leave.[18]

Although there was a room at Thornhill called 'the housekeeper's room', the 'upper servant' seems to have fulfilled the role of housekeeper, but the job title perhaps reflects the fact that she was expected to undertake tasks which housekeepers in larger houses might have considered beneath them. She breakfasted at 8a.m. in the summer and 8.30a.m. in winter. After breakfast she gave out what was needed for the day. She went to market occasionally, saw the meat weighed when it was delivered, examined the meat in the larder every morning and kept a tight control over waste in coal, meat, bread, butter, candles, lamp oil and other consumables. From time to time she inspected the pots and kettles for cleanliness. She saw to it that the parlour was ready for breakfast and the drawing room ready for company. She helped to make the large beds, and saw that the tray was properly sent in for morning visitors. In the footman's absence she answered the door. She gave out clean linen on Saturdays and received dirty linen in exchange: 'The great wash is once a month, the kitchen clothes are washed every fortnight by the cook.'[19] She made the starch and assisted at the wash, saw to the laundry fire and assisted at the getting in of the linen. Regular payments of one shilling or one-and-sixpence a day to a Mrs Worthington and a Mrs Cottrell for washing and ironing suggest that outside help was also needed on washdays.

Like the footman, the upper servant kept a watchful eye on visitors' servants: 'When there is company men servants dine in the kitchen & sit before & after dinner in the laundry … No men servants except those belonging to the house to be admitted into the Housekeeper's Room.' When Miss Boulton had guests to dinner the ladies would retire to the drawing room after dessert, leaving the gentlemen to their port, and when at last the gentlemen left the dining room the upper servant saw the candles put out and the dessert taken away. The treasured dessert service and best china were always washed up under supervision in the housekeeper's room. Making preserves, pickles and pastry, and helping to prepare dinner when there was company were also on the upper servant's job description.[20] And after a long day, it was part of her job to check that the footman had securely locked the doors and windows for the night.

The housemaid was at the beck and call of all the others, cleaning the whole house except the kitchen and pantries which were the domain of the cook. The quantity of different kinds of brushes, mops and soap which the household got through annually (over £2 most years on brushes which individually did not usually cost more than a few pence, and between £5-£8 most years on white, yellow and mottled soap, buying it by the pound), conjures up images of a succession of housemaids, sleeves rolled up, scrubbing vigorously with reddened hands. The footman probably delegated some of his furniture maintenance tasks to the housemaid, for she also looked after the drawing room and breakfast room furniture; the chairs were all to be 'well rubbed twice a week', suggesting buffing with a soft cloth rather than the frequent application of polish. The housemaid made the fires, prepared the drawing room for company, helped with the cooking when there was company, washed the best china, and was generally to 'give every assistance within your power'.[21] She waited at table and answered bells in the absence of the upper servant or footman, and indeed must 'endeavor to supply his place indoors'. Repairing linen formed part of her duties, so she was to 'Sit down and sew as soon as the chambers are finished', but before doing so must be neatly dressed. She cleaned the laundry, helped to wash, starch and iron linen and dresses, and helped the footman to clean the windows. When necessary she was to assist in 'putting up furniture' (this probably refers to curtains). Down on her knees early in the mornings she cleaned the grates ('put a cloth over the hearth first'), and at night closed the sash windows before it grew damp and turned down the sheets, before falling wearily into her own bed. Above all, Anne hoped, the housemaid went about her duties with her mistress's mantra echoing in her head:

> Do every thing at the proper time
> Keep every thing in its proper place
> Use every thing for its proper purpose
> And never think any part of your business too trifling to be well done.[22]

The coachman looked after the carriage and horses, as well as the pigs and the poultry. He cleaned the pigsties and stables, swept the yard every morning and thoroughly cleaned it once a week. Occasionally as necessary he helped in the garden, filled the coal hole, helped to shake carpets, assisted in brewing, wheeled the garden chairs about, and sometimes even waited at table. The carriage was always to be cleaned before breakfast, except on mowing mornings. The horses were to go out every day. An unmarried coachman perhaps slept in the room over the stables, and probably took his meals in the kitchen. One of the rules he had to abide by was: 'Ask leave when you want to go out & be home by nine o'Clock.'[23]

We know from the correspondence between Anne and James Watt junior during 1817-18 that James had bought much of his own furniture, because the problem of what to do with it was one of the things which had delayed him moving out. Anne was prepared to live with James's furniture for a while, so did not immediately begin redecorating or buying much new furniture of her own (though what woman would not have re-arranged the rooms on coming into a furnished house? A bill for two guineas from Edward Townsend for 'shifting furniture' and other jobs in February 1819 seems to confirm this.[24]). Anne's earliest bills for Thornhill are for items bought from Birmingham suppliers, including beds (£11 10s. 2d. from Thomas Day) and bedding (four warm bed quilts, £1 17s. 6d.), bought in December 1818 at the time she moved in. In her first months at the house, apart from small essentials like a clothes' line and pegs (15s. from E. Parker), an ironing blanket from Richard Cadbury (19s. 3d.), and brushes and saucepans, most of her household purchases were of incidentals such as looking glasses, a mahogany knife box (£1 9s. 0d. from Thomas Hensman), a fashionable fender (£1 4s. 0d. from

James Busby), and a wash-hand table and stand (£2 5s. od. from George Horton). She perhaps had some old furniture smartened up – a bill from W.E. Whitehead is for 'furniture japanned buff and white' (15s. 3d.).

James finally moved the last of his things from Thornhill to Aston Hall in the summer of 1819. This was not long before his father's death, an event which prompted him to enter on a long-term project to see memorials to Watt senior erected in various places. Anne would later contribute £100 to the fund for a Watt monument by Sir Francis Chantrey in Westminster Abbey, telling James, 'Words can ill express my feelings … but remembering as I ever must do with pride and grateful affection the friendship and unceasing kindness I always met with from him that is *gone* I trust I may be allowed to participate in the general sentiment of enthusiasm …'.[25] After the funeral Watt's widow Annie sealed up her husband's garret workshop at Heathfield. It would not be re-opened for another 64 years, when the contents were listed; they were eventually removed to the London Science Museum before the house was demolished in the 1920s.

Although Anne had not immediately embarked on large-scale purchases of furniture, she does seem to have begun looking around for what she might want. A four-page list, probably written by James Watt junior's friend John Furnell Tuffen,

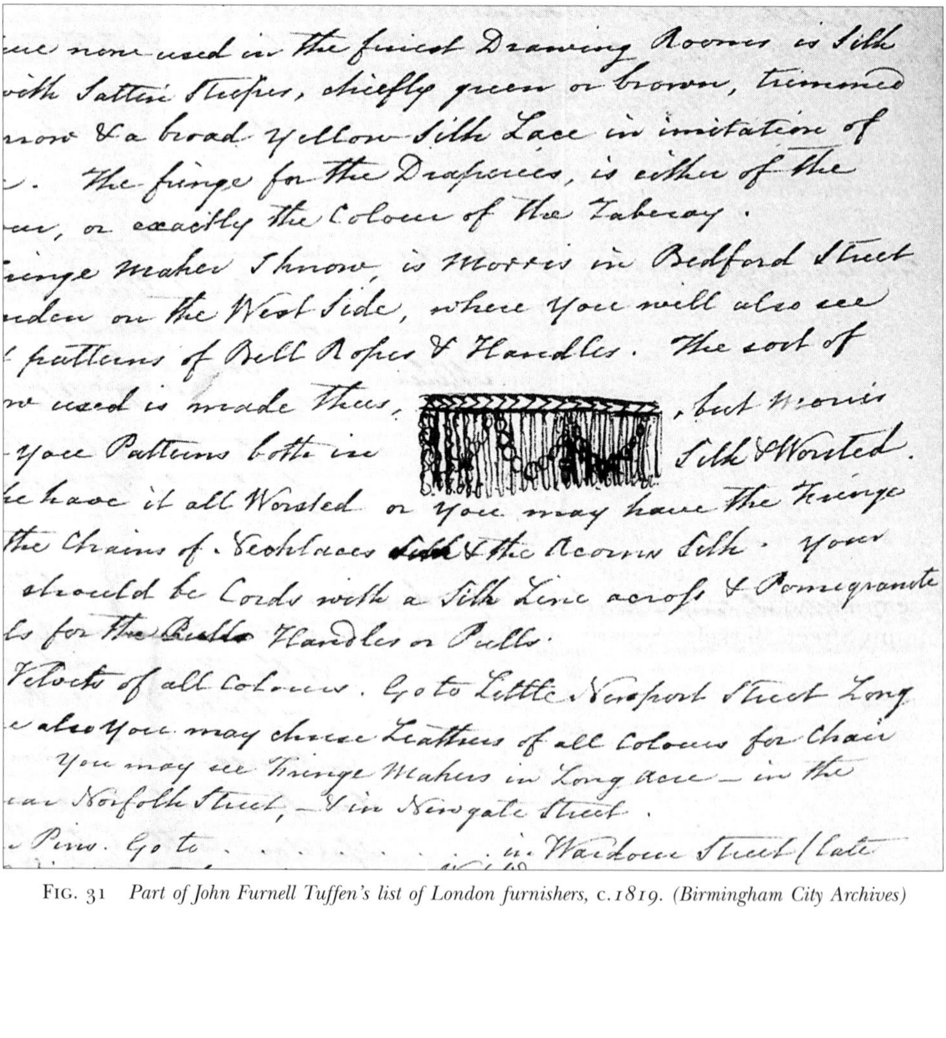

FIG. 31   *Part of John Furnell Tuffen's list of London furnishers, c.1819. (Birmingham City Archives)*

sets out where in London she might see the latest in furniture of all kinds (at this period the term 'furniture' included not just pieces such as tables and chairs, but what we would think of now as soft furnishing and also equipment such as tableware). The list is undated, but refers at one point to 'the late Mr Bullock', which puts it some time after George Bullock's death in 1818. Tuffen, who had a house in Park Lane, London, was evidently well-up on furnishings. His list is full of ideas for the woman intent on a stylish home, and worth quoting at length:

> To look at Silk Furniture go to Roberts & Co a Silk Mercer in Chandos Street Covent Garden, near Bedford Street. Also Cooper in Pall Mall. The furniture now used in the finest Drawing Rooms is Silk Taberay with Sattin Stripes, chiefly green or brown, trimmed with a narrow & a broad Yellow Silk Lace in imitation of Gold Lace. The fringe for the Draperies, is either of the same Colour, or exactly the Colour of the Taberay. The *best* Fringe maker I know is Morris in Bedford Street Covent Garden on the West Side, where you will also see the newest patterns of Bell Ropes & Handles. The sort of Fringe now used is made thus [drawing], but Morris will shew you Patterns both in Silk & Worsted. You make [may] have it all Worsted or you may have the Fringe Worsted & the Chains of Necklaces silk & the Acorns Silk. Your Bell Lines should be Cords with a Silk Line across & Pomegranite Silk Tassels for the Handles or Pulls.
>
> For Cotton Velvets of all colours go to Little Newport Street Long Acre, & there also you may chuse Leathers of all Colours for Chair Seats. You may see Fringe Makers in Long Acre, in the Strand near Norfolk Street, & in Newgate Street.
>
> For Curtain Pins go to ... [name omitted] in Wardour Street (late Marlar & Co) it is on the left hand or West Side as you enter the Street from Princes Street. There is in Wardour Street on the Right hand, or East Side, a famous Chair Maker. You will also find some well pattern'd Chairs in Marybone Street Piccadilly, on the South Side of the Street nearly opposite the end of Warwick Street.
>
> For Paper Hangings Duppa in Oxford Street near Hanover Square, [also] ... In the Strand near the Adelphi, ... In Cheapside on the South Side about halfway from St Pauls, they are persons of good Taste & have some elegant things, ... In St James's Street for the new sort of Flock Papers in imitation of Cloth, ... Bond Street West side, close to Bedford Street. Crease & Co No.7 Great Newport Street have some Paper Hangings that will wash, from 4d. to 11d. per yard.[26]

The list (which in places advises 'make use of J.F.T.'s name') also recommends for carpets and floor cloths, Richards & Co. of Chiswell Street, at the corner of Finsbury Square, or Watson & Co. of Bond Street, and for 'Chintz Furniture' a Mr Avery in Tavistock Street, Mr Miles on the north side of Oxford Street, and un-named shops in Bond Street and Southampton Street. Stevens on the south side of Piccadilly 'a few doors from the top of the Haymarket', Tatham & Bailey in Mount Street, Berkeley Square, and Baker in Margaret Street, Cavendish Square, are all recommended for 'upholstery & Cabinet Goods', the latter because 'I understand he was a principal assistant to the late Mr Bullock'. Two 'Persons in Princes Street Coventry St' make 'Cabinet Goods in the French Stile'. For 'old china' Fogg in Warwick Street is recommended, and for 'Earthen Ware & Porcelaine &c' Wedgewood [sic] & Co in York Street St James's Square, Spode at Newcastle House, Portugal Street in Lincoln's Inn Fields, and Mortlock & Co on the south side of Oxford Street. Fenders, grates and kitchen furniture may be had from Summers on the west side of Bond Street and Jewitt [?] in Queen Street, Lincoln's Inn Fields.

Brown & Co. of the 'new road near the End of Tottenham Court Road' supply scagliola (items made in imitation of marble).

In addition to all these household items, the list includes shops recommended for straw bonnets, artificial flowers, shawls, dresses, lace, shoes, 'the new sort of Counterpanes for Servants Beds', 'good & cheap muslins of all sorts', boxes, prints, ornaments and other items. As an afterthought, Smith & Co of Knightsbridge are suggested for floorcloths – this is the successor to Baber & Downing, the firm which had supplied the Soho House hall floorcloth in 1803 and a sunblind for the Thornhill drawing-room window in 1805 (Plate 48).

Tuffen also took the opportunity, while he was on a visit to Soho House, to measure up the mirror over the fireplace, possibly in the dining room, and reported to Anne that it was 56 inches high by 51 inches wide. Facing it on the opposite wall was a bigger one. Tuffen gave the combined prices of the two as £87 13s. od. and asked Anne to keep the information to herself.[27]

With Tuffen's helpful list to hand, some time just before or after she moved to Thornhill and probably while she waited for James's furniture to disappear, Anne studied thoughtfully a list of all the rooms, showing which were to be papered and what furniture was needed for them.[28] The list is attributed to Matthew Boulton, which would date it to before 1809. Certainly the writing resembles his, but there are both similarities and inconsistencies between it and Miss Boulton's writing. The listed rooms are numbered but there is no accompanying plan to show where they are; however, they tie in better with the Thornhill plan than the Soho House plan, and most of the furniture listed can be traced through Anne's bills and on through the contents auction which took place after her death, so it would make perfect sense for Anne to have written it herself, c.1818-19, though this is by no means certain.

She bought some furniture from local makers, such as a Spanish mahogany butler's tray, a mahogany work table on turned legs with castors, a mahogany chest of drawers with columns and mahogany knobs, and a mahogany pot cupboard, all supplied by William Ryley of Handsworth for a total of £21 19s. 4d.[29] Thomas Hensman of Birmingham supplied a number of items over the years, including altering a cabinet and making a new plinth of zebra wood with a brass fretwork gallery round the top, for £2 16s. 6d.[30]

For larger furniture purchases Anne went to London. She was a customer of James Wellsted of Molyneux Street, off Bryanston Square. In November 1819 he sent an estimate for making a dining table, sideboard, 12 chairs, a wardrobe, a bedstead, a Pembroke table and some further chairs, which were costed at a total of £139 18s. od.[31] She bought several items from Gillows of Oxford Street, including a pair of rosewood card tables on reeded legs for 18 guineas in October 1820[32] (they fetched £7 10s. od. at the auction of Thornhill's contents after her death[33]), and five stained rosewood chairs to match some earlier ones, at £4 15s. Gillows also supplied a mahogany three-drawer dressing table with stout reeded legs and castors for seven guineas in 1824,[34] and some curtains.

Goods bought in London, whether furniture, fabrics, clothes or wine, were generally transported to Birmingham by Pickfords, or by John Jolly's Fly Boats, or by John Whitehouse & Sons. The two last-named used the canals and worked between London and Birmingham's Crescent Wharf, using carts for the last short stage of the journey up to Thornhill. Carriage charges depended on weight, the bulkiness or fragility of the item, and distance: to transport 'a cabinet from London' weighing two hundredweight, two quarters and seven pounds (2cwt. 2qu. 7lb.) in 1824 cost 10s. 3d.[35] By the end of the 18th century there were several options for transporting goods between Birmingham and London. Entirely by water the cost was 2s. 6d. per hundredweight or £2 10s. per ton; a combination of water transport between Birmingham and Oxford and road transport between Oxford and London worked out at 6s. od. per hundredweight or £6 per ton. Both alternatives were cheaper than transport entirely by road, which cost 8s. 6d. per hundredweight, or £8 per ton.[36]

With James's furniture out of the way, Anne began thinking about redecorating and refurnishing. She decided to concentrate at first on the principal rooms – the drawing room and the dining room.

The new dining room colour scheme was predominantly pink and red, colours chosen to warm up a chilly room. A bill for colouring the walls in 'Dutch pink & Venetian red' in August 1819[37] seems to mark the start of work on this room. The following year the décor was modified slightly, for Cornelius Dixon came from London and charged three guineas for 'altering the Margins on Walls of Dining Room and shadowing & lighting ditto'.[38] While he was on site he also repainted the woodwork in the 'boudoir' and marbled a chimneypiece.

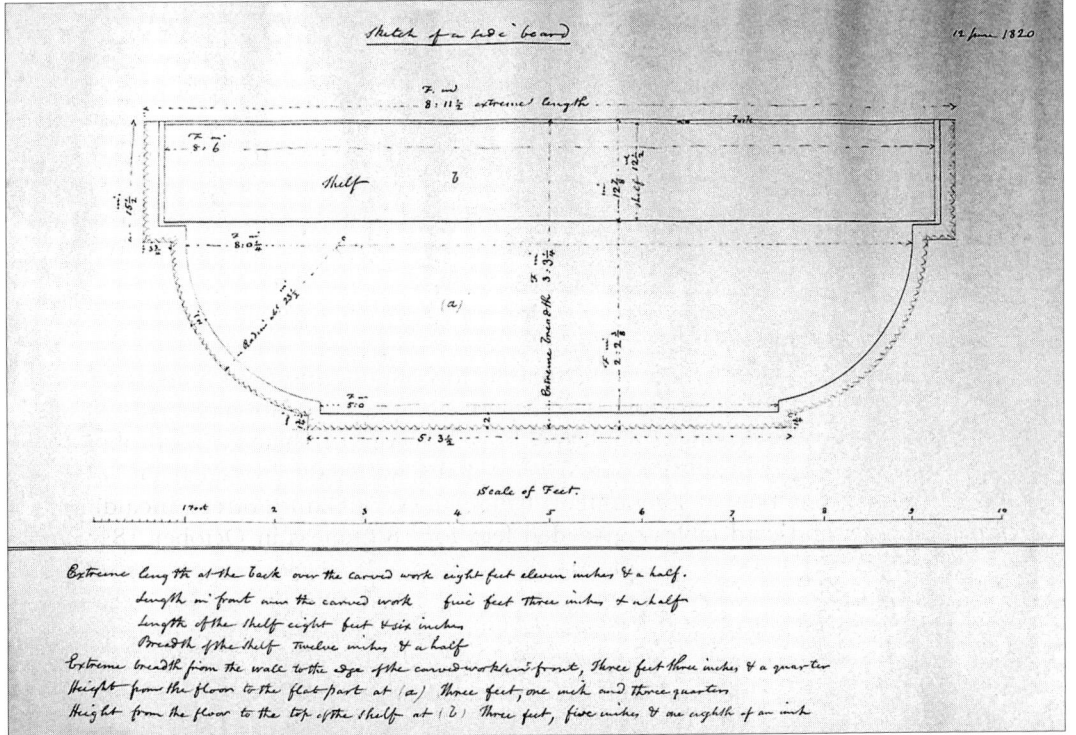

FIG. 32   Plan by James Wellsted of Molyneux Street, London, for a sideboard which he subsequently made for Miss Boulton, 1820. (Birmingham City Archives)

For the dining room the list made by Anne or her father included 'a Temporary Carpet of Green Bays or Cloth', twelve chairs, '3 Tables with Claws to form a Dineing Table', a sideboard, and 'window curtins with a Brass Rod'. The new furniture which Wellsted had quoted for, which broadly matches this, was delivered in the spring of 1820. The London interior designer Richard Bridgens, who was doing some other work for Anne, called at the Molyneux Street company to check on its progress, and thought the dining table looked rather narrow, but Wellsted told him firmly that that was how Anne wanted it, and besides it was too late to change it.[39] The dining table was actually a set of Spanish mahogany tables on four carved pillars and castors. Going by the list it was probably a set of three, with a longer central section on two pillars, and two smaller extensions each with a central pillar. Put together their total length was 14 feet 6 inches, 18 inches longer than Wellsted's original estimate, with a width of 4 feet 6 inches.[40] Bridgens admired the mahogany sideboard which Wellsted had made to go with the table. Almost nine feet long, it had a projecting front which was straight in the centre and curved at each end, giving it a slightly cropped semi-circular shape. Its six reeded tapered legs were ornamented with carved lions' heads at the top. [41] To go round the table there were 12 mahogany chairs with carved backs, reeded legs, and 'patent spring seats' with red morocco covers.

The Pembroke table which Wellsted made was despatched by Pickfords after the rest; he apologised for the delay, explaining that he had been waiting for the wood to be well-seasoned.[42] Anne seemed to be in two minds about keeping it, for Wellsted later offered to take it back. From Thomas Dowbiggin of Mount Street, Grosvenor Square, she bought 'a handsome Mahogany Sarcophagus with carved paw feet French polish'd' in 1823 for £24 13s. od. This was possibly a cellaret, for it was in the dining room.[43] Richard Bridgens had charged for designing a cellaret in late 1822, when he also produced designs for dining-room curtains. These may have been made up by Gillows, for two undated estimates for supplying curtains for three windows, bordered with crimson cloth and gold lace, may be for the dining room, to go with the red colour scheme. Both with deep fringes and silk tassels and cords, the two slightly different specifications are priced at £118 12s. od. and £85 8s. 4d. respectively.[44]

The dining room's 'temporary carpet' was replaced in 1821 by James and Robert Rickards of Finsbury Square, London (one of the suppliers recommended by Tuffen). The new carpet was a Brussels weave with a neutral background, patterned in shades of crimson and scarlet, made to the dining-room floor plan. It cost £28 9s. 7d., plus a further £3 17s. od. for a 'superfine worsted hearth rug to suit ditto'.[45] The carpet was described in the later auction catalogue as 'very elegant' and 'in the best state of preservation', and fetched £8 os. od.

For company, the Thornhill dining table was elegantly laid with china, glass and silver. Much – but not all – of the silver came from the family firm, naturally, but was accounted and paid for nevertheless, though one hopes Anne's brother allowed her a discount. Unspecified silverware from M.Boulton & Plate Co. was invoiced at £123 3s. 11d. in May 1819.[46] In 1823 they supplied a further £43 14s.-worth which included two oblong waiters with leaf feet, silver borders and silver shields (£7 os. od.), three pairs of oblong salts, gilt inside (£4 14s. 6d.), an oval sugar basin (£4 os. od.), a matching oval cream ewer (£2 5s. od.), an oblong cheese toaster (£6 6s. od.), a dozen silver table forks to match the existing ones (£13 5s. 4d.), and a dozen plated table forks £2 12s. 6d. All of these were engraved with the Boulton arms, an engraving charge of £4 2s. od. Later there was a further engraving charge of £2 1s. od. for adding the arms to a teapot, coffee pot, two snuffer trays and a bread basket.[47] Silver on the Thornhill table also included a set of 18 dessert forks, £15 9s. 1d. from the firm's London agent, Richard Chippindall.[48] From Rotton & Son of London came a further consignment of cutlery costing £17 5s. od.[49] The cut glass decanters sparkled in the candlelight and wore necklaces of silver chain from which hung silver and mother-of-pearl labels for Holland, Madeira, Brandy and Sherry, £2 4s. od. for four labels.[50] Mary Rollason, a china and glassware retailer of Birmingham, who counted Miss Boulton among her regular customers, supplied two pint decanters with large 'globle [sic]

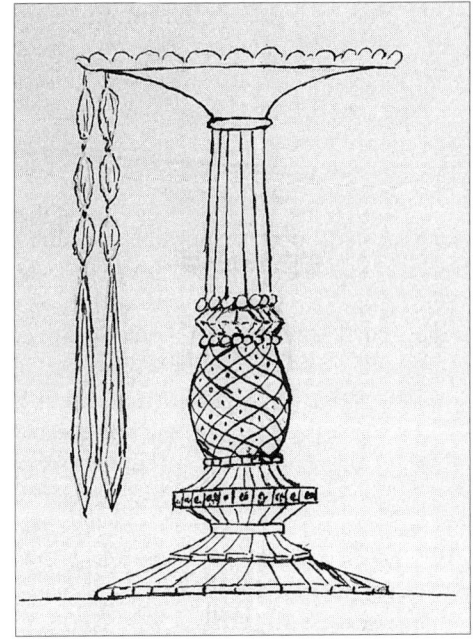

FIG. 33 *Drawing of a pedestal or candlestick with pendants for Thornhill, c.1820. (Birmingham City Archives)*

stopper flutes with polish'd mouths', at £1 8s. od.[51] and an assortment of glassware costing £3 3s. 11d. which included 18 tulip claret glasses (£1 5s. 6d.) and one 'rich cut glass jug' (18s. od.).[52]

Anne liked decorative china. Her own inventories show that there were different and colourful china services for breakfast, tea, dinner and dessert, and a quantity of earthenware. Most of Mary Rollason's bills are not very informative and are just made out for 'china' (there is one for half a dozen egg cups at 6s. od.[53]), but from a J. Bedford came four pink china dishes in two sizes, embossed with flowers, in April 1820 (£1 6s. od.),[54] and from Sarah Bedford & Co of Birmingham (possibly the same shop) butter boats, a dish and cover and a hash dish in blue china (£1 6s. od.).[55] The Bedfords also supplied 24 dinner plates in a bluebird design and some matching dishes in 1824 (£3 5s. 6d.) and sundry other pieces of the bluebird pattern over a period.[56]

But perhaps the pride of Anne's table was the dessert service – the one which must always be washed up under supervision in the housekeeper's room – which she bought at H. & R. Chamberlain's Worcester Royal Porcelain Manufactory's New Bond Street showroom, a set of 24 plates in the 'Chantilly' shape, with a lilac border and flowers. These cost her £9 12s. od. with a further 3s. for the packaging, and must have been borne back to Birmingham with extra care.[57] With the bill Chamberlains quoted for some additional items to match, including a centre piece, two end dishes, four squares, four shells, two hearts and two cream tureens, in total £15 12s. od. with a further £8 8s. od. for a pair of ice pails if required, and added a note that they were 'very glad to find Miss Boulton is pleased with the plates'.[58] A year or two later she bought 24 cups and saucers, with two plates, a basin and a sugar bowl in the 'Baden' shape, pattern number 938, from the same place (£18 16s. 6d.).[59]

When she came to consider her drawing room, Anne decided it was time for a major re-styling. According to the list the room was to have 'a handsome paper', and for its bow windows three Venetian blinds and three curtains on brass rods. Furniture for the room was to include '12 Chairs & some of them Lownging Chairs, one Sopha', and 'a drawing Room Table & a set of small drawing room Tables 4 wch slide under each other', as well as two fire screens, two looking glasses, a marble table and 'a handsome Carpet'.[60] Most of these items, including 16 chairs rather than 12, were in the room at the time of the auction sale after Anne's death, along with two Broadwood pianofortes for which no bill has been found.

The drawing room got a lot of sun and Baber and Co of Knightsbridge had supplied a design for an external sunshade or awning for it back in 1805.[61] If that design was carried out then, it may have been getting a bit shabby by the time Anne moved in, for in November 1819 the same firm (now Smith & Baber) sent instructions on how to measure the bow correctly for a new sunshade (Plate 56).[62] Richard Bridgens produced alternative designs for the drawing room and a verandah, for which he charged £8 2s. od. in September 1820 (Plates 57 & 58).[63] Bridgens' verandah proposals look more substantial than simply an awning or sunshade, though the structure is light and pretty, perhaps with cast iron pillars and ornamentation round the top; stands for potted plants are shown beneath the canopy.

Bridgens suggested two alternative colour schemes for the drawing room, one in shades of brown and buff, the other in green and amber. He painted an exploded view of the room showing all four walls in the brown and buff scheme (Plates 59 & 60). The bow windows are shown dressed with a deep draped brown pelmet ornamented with a gold-coloured braid, over full-length plain buff curtains with brown borders at the bottom. The fireplace has a tall gilt-framed mirror over it, and is flanked by fitted cabinets with shelving for books and ornaments above. The wall opposite the fireplace is shown with a matching cabinet with a brass gallery round the top. Bridgens suggested it might be used to support another mirror: 'upon the Cabinet opposite the chimney piece you can if you at any time wish it, place a glass by removing part of the brasswork.'[64] This suggests that the Bullock bookcases which James had had fitted on that wall had been removed, perhaps to Aston Hall, though the two 'blind' windows remained concealed. Against the wall by the door are a buff-covered sofa and a pole screen. The overall effect would have been rich and warm. The alternative green-and-amber scheme shows the windows dressed in pale amber curtains with green fringes and draped green pelmets. Bridgens thought this would have 'a light cheerfull effect'[65] and if adopted recommended 'let there be green and amber in the Carpet' (Plate 61). The doors he proposed to be 'in imitation of rose wood, but not too dark, and the moulding gilt. The Cabinets should have a little brass work to relieve them, or all rosewood will look heavy in a Drawing room.' When Anne had decided which of the two colour schemes she preferred, added Bridgens, he would send her the tints for the walls and a pattern for the borders which he recommended at skirting board and ceiling levels.

FIGS 34 & 35   *Sketches from Gillows showing two alternative curtain treatments for Thornhill, c.1820. (Birmingham City Archives)*

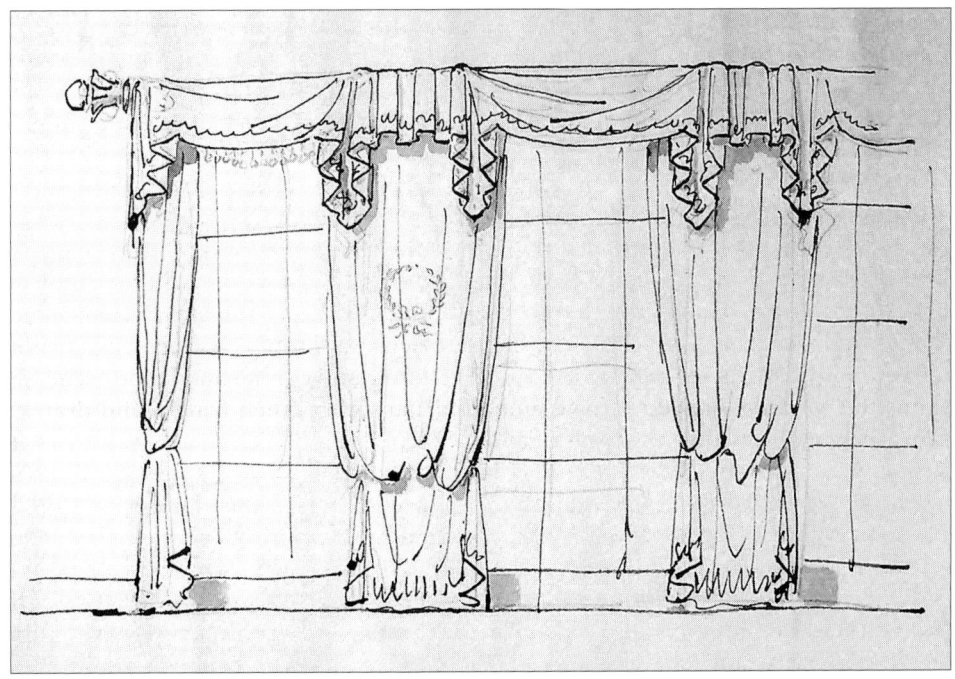

It is not clear whether Bridgens' ideas for the drawing room décor were carried out in 1820, or if so which colour scheme was adopted. Certainly some wallpaper in a 'moss sprig on fawn colour'd ground' was supplied that year by G. Morant of New Bond Street (Ornamental Painter & Paper Hanging Manufacturer to Their Royal Highnesses the Dukes of Sussex & Cambridge).[66] This cost £3 10s. 0d. for seven pieces, and sounds as though it would co-ordinate with either of Bridgens' colour schemes. An undated memorandum in Anne's hand summarises a Gillows estimate for 'French curtains of russet cloth' finished with gold-coloured silk lace and fringes. It comes to £59 14s. 5d., and may be for the drawing room;[67] it probably refers to an undated Gillows sketch showing the four curtains. A tassel hangs from every curtain ring; two of the curtains are shown hanging straight and the other two gathered up with ornamental pins.

Whether or not the drawing room was redecorated and refurnished in 1820, it was in any case an expensive year, for Anne's purchases of furniture (£430), soft furnishings (£130), tableware (£218) and repairs and redecorating (£249) took her year's expenditure up to over £1,973, the highest it reached during her years at Thornhill, which must have necessitated drawing on some of her capital.

Perhaps because of this, spending was reigned back in 1821 and 1822 to top up the reserves and gather strength for the next onslaught. In 1823 much more extensive changes certainly were made to the drawing room by Rickman and Hutchinson of Birmingham, who produced new designs. For the designs, working drawings and superintending the work they charged £15 0s. 7d., based on five per cent of an outlay of £300 12s. 9½d.[68] (Plate 62)

The new designs show the three windows in the bow bare of curtains and separated by neoclassical-style pilasters which continue on the fireplace wall. They are coloured in blue, though whether the room was actually decorated in blue is not known (there is a bill of £2 10s. 0d. for a pair of dark blue and gilt porcelain vases from Louis Fleschelle of New Bond Street, but this hardly seems enough evidence on which to base an entire colour scheme). John Newbould charged £50 17s. 10d. for painting and glazing in the drawing room but the bill does not specify the colour. Before it was painted the room was re-plastered and a new marble chimney piece and new bell-pulls were installed. Three separate 'outside shade blinds' were fitted over the bow windows, so either Bridgens' verandah was removed, or more likely it had never been constructed. The windows were re-glazed with plate glass. Including some of the furniture Anne spent a total of £353 12s. 6d. on the room.[69] Again her annual expenditure shot up, this time to nearly £1,558. In the same year Thomas Dowbiggin in London supplied a set of curtains for three windows; these were possibly for the drawing room too, for it would have been rather soon to replace the dining room curtains. They were 'trim'd with Crimson silk Velvet Gimp & fringe' and with materials, labour, curtain poles, carriage and packing cost a total of £27 9s. 4d.[70] For the re-furbished drawing room Dowbiggin supplied 16 solid rosewood chairs with richly carved backs, reeded legs and cane seats, at £52 16s. 0d., plus £6 16s. 0d. for the seat cushions in 'fine brown linen' (the chairs sold for £35 4s. 0d. at the auction).[71]

The frames of the drawing-room blinds were repainted two years later by John Newbould, who regularly did redecorating for Anne. The frames, all the gates and doors, the chicken pen and five garden chairs received two coats of 'best Brunswick

PLATE 53   *Aston Hall, Birmingham, now a museum. It was built by Sir Thomas Holte between 1618-35. James Watt junior lived there from 1818-1848. (Birmingham Museums & Art Gallery)*

PLATE 54   *Maria Edgeworth. Maria visited James at Aston Hall in 1820, writing 'Mr Watt has fitted up half of it so as to make it superbly comfortable …'* (A Study of Maria Edgeworth, *by Grace Oliver (1882)*

M.rs Maria Edgeworth

PLATE 55 *Watercolour by John Phillp, c.1795, looking towards Handsworth from the stables at Soho House, with Thornhill House in the distance, far right. (Birmingham Museums & Art Gallery)*

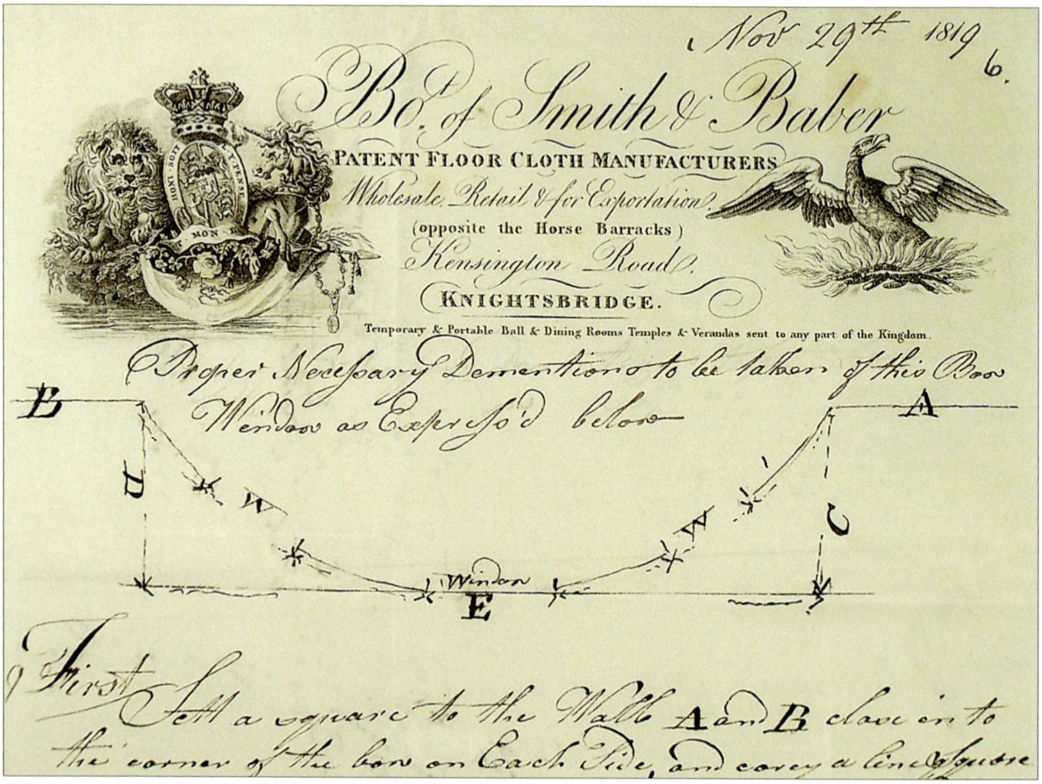

Nov 29th 1819
6.

B⁰ of Smith & Baber
PATENT FLOOR CLOTH MANUFACTURERS
Wholesale, Retail & for Exportation.
(opposite the Horse Barracks)
Kensington Road.
KNIGHTSBRIDGE.
Temporary & Portable Ball & Dining Rooms Temples & Verandas sent to any part of the Kingdom.

Proper Necessary Dementions to be taken of this Bow
Window as Express'd below

B

A

D

W

C

W

Window

E

First Sett a square to the Walls A and B close in to
the corner of the bow on Each Side, and carey a line of square

PLATE 56 *Part of Smith & Baber's directions for measuring the bow window at Thornhill. (Birmingham Assay Office Charitable Trust/Birmingham City Archives)*

PLATES 57 & 58 *Richard Bridgens' drawings of alternative proposed sun canopies for the drawing room windows, Thornhill, 1820. (Birmingham Assay Office Charitable Trust/Birmingham City Archives)*

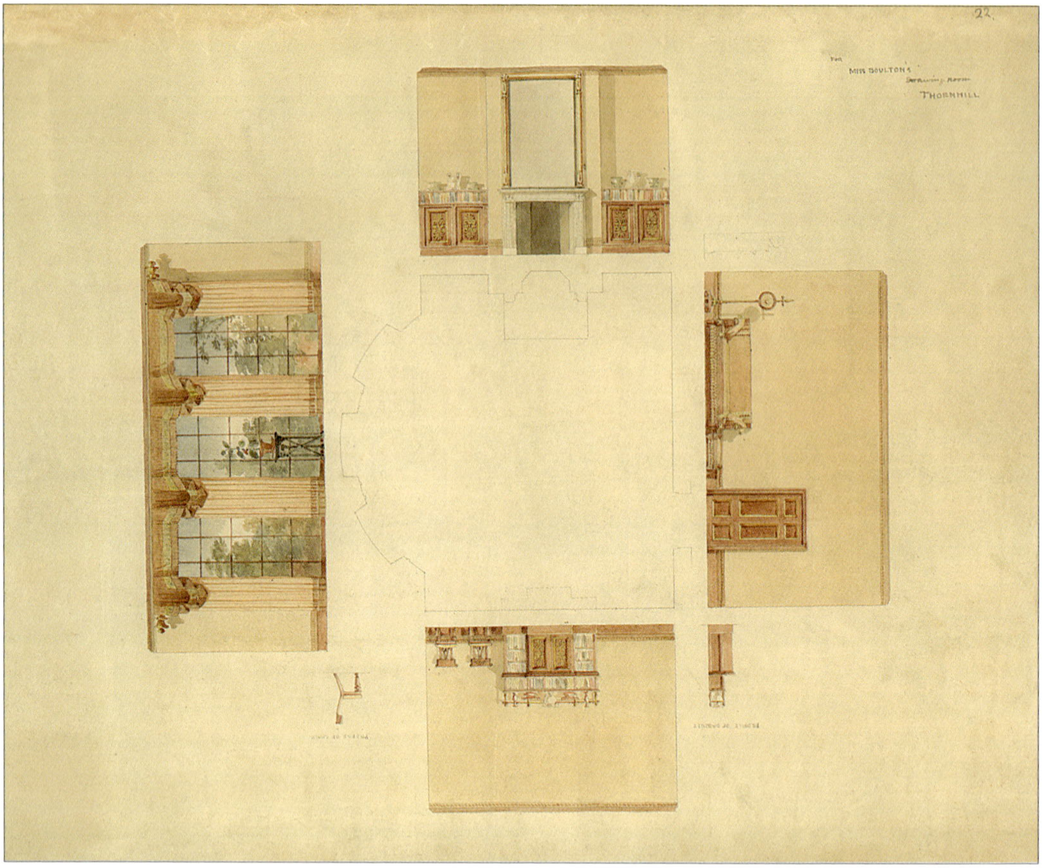

PLATE 59 *Richard Bridgens' drawing showing all four walls of the drawing room, Thornhill, c.1820. (Birmingham Assay Office Charitable Trust/Birmingham City Archives)*

PLATE 60 *Detail of the drawing above, showing the bow window treatment. (Birmingham Assay Office Charitable Trust/Birmingham City Archives)*

PLATE 61 *Richard Bridgens' alternative treatment of the drawing room bow window. (Birmingham Assay Office Charitable Trust/Birmingham City Archives)*

Design for alterations at Thornhill

TRANSVERSE SECTION.

PLATE 62 *Rickman and Hutchinson's treatment of the drawing room bow window, Thornhill, 1822. (Birmingham Assay Office Charitable Trust/Birmingham City Archives)*

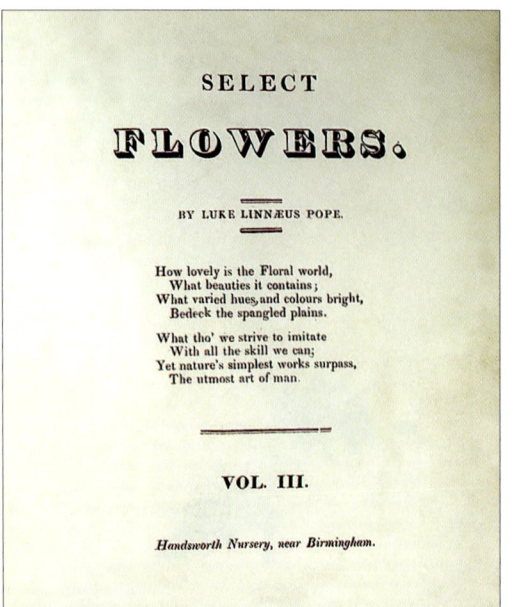

PLATE 63   *Front page of Luke Linnaeus Pope's* Select Flowers, *a hand-drawn and coloured collection of flowers, 1820. Luke Pope supplied many of Miss Boulton's plants. (Birmingham City Archives)*

PLATE 64   *'Andromeda polifolia nana', by Luke Pope, one of the plants in Miss Boulton's garden at Thornhill. (Birmingham City Archives)*

PLATE 65   *'Auricula van Georgiana' by Luke Pope. (Birmingham City Archives)*

PLATE 66   *Sir Francis Chantrey's memorial to Mrs Mary Anne Boulton, Matthew Robinson Boulton's wife, in the Church of St Michael & All Angels, Great Tew, Oxfordshire. Mary Anne is buried at Handsworth Parish Church, Birmingham.*

PLATE 67 *Sir Richard Dyott (c.1590-1659), great-great-great grandfather of Anne Boulton. (Private collection)*

PLATE 68 *Lady Dorothy Dyott (c.1605-1672), great-great-great grandmother of Anne Boulton. Text on the portrait reads 'sole daughter and heir to Richard Dorrington Esq. of Stafford'. (Private collection)*

PLATE 69 *Matthew Dyott of Stichbrook (1620-1698), great-great grandfather of Anne Boulton. (Private collection)*

PLATE 70   *Donegal House, Bore Street, Lichfield, built by James Robinson in 1730.*

PLATE 71   *Detail from Samuel and Nathaniel Buck's South West Prospect of Lichfield (1732), showing (centre foreground) Bowling Green House and the Bowling Green, with trees round the perimeter fence. Bowling Green House was for a time the home of Luke Robinson junior. (William Salt Library, Stafford)*

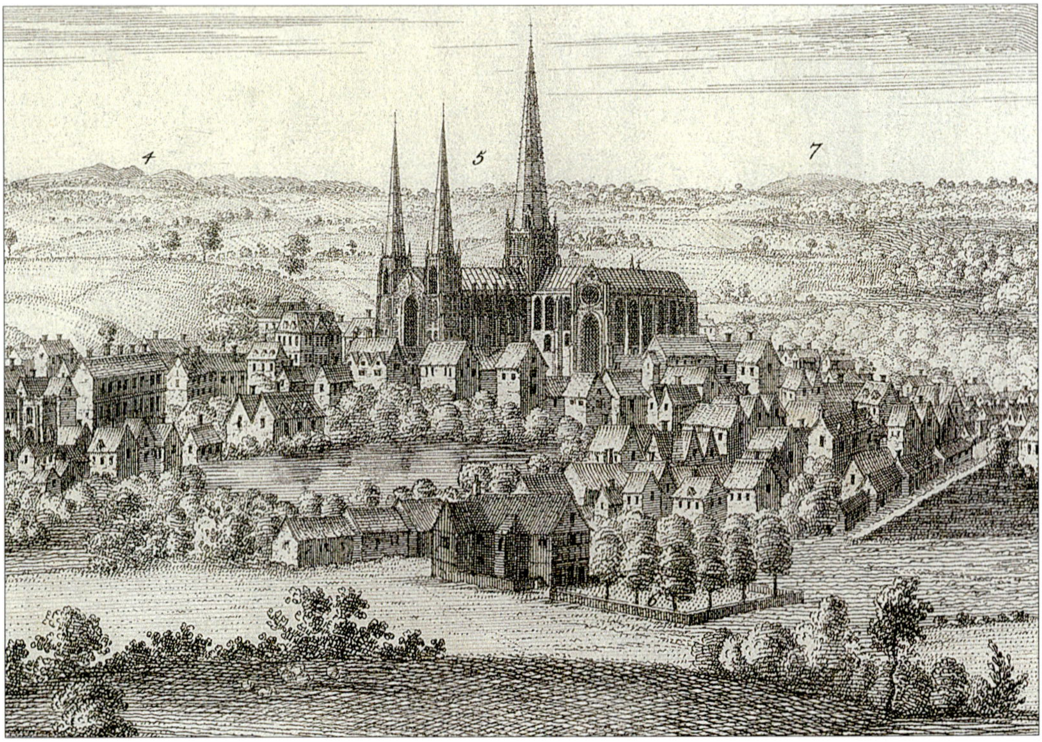

Green', which with some rain spouts and door frames painted in white, came to £11 10s. od.[72]

With most of the budget being devoted to the dining room and drawing room, the breakfast room seems to have received relatively little attention. It is not clear whether the bookcases with which James had had it lined remained, but Anne's breakfast room list includes two book cases 'with a writing Table to draw out', two curtains and a looking glass.[73] There is a plan of the room but no designs or bills which can be identified specifically with this room, nor is it mentioned in the auction catalogue.

The main bed-chambers were all papered. It is not known which room was Anne's bedroom. The 'Bow Bedroom' is the largest, but the bedroom over the drawing room, with an adjoining closet or dressing room, is labelled 'Best Bedroom' on the floor plan; this may have been reserved for guests. According to Anne's list the 'Front Chamber S.E. next the Road & faceing Soho over ye Breakfast Room' was to have a bed, bed curtains, four chairs, a table, looking glass, Venetian blinds and 'a Carpet for the whole Floor'. The list for the bedroom over the drawing room includes a looking glass, curtains and Venetian blinds, a bed and six chairs ('some easy'), and 'a Carpet to cover the Whole Wilton not Gaudy'. The 'new room' sounds smaller, for it was to have three chairs, a curtain, a table and glass and a 'press bed'. The 'Bow Bedroom' had a bed, wardrobe, three window curtains and blinds, six chairs, 'common carpet all over', a dressing table, 'fancy table', two glasses, and '2 best wash hand stands'. The adjoining dressing room was to have a further table, a glass, two chairs and a Venetian blind. Much of the bedroom furniture seems to have been painted judging from the auction catalogue, which does, however, list several 'lofty 4-post bedsteads' with carved mahogany pillars in the first floor and some of the attic bedrooms.

FIG. 36 *Drawing of a chair for Thornhill, c.1820. (Birmingham City Archives)*

FIG. 37 *Richard Bridgens' design for bed curtains, probably for the 'white bed' at Thornhill, c.1820. (Birmingham City Archives)*

Bridgens supplied a drawing for curtains and a cornice for the 'white bed', possibly the bed in the 'first chamber' described in the auction catalogue as having a gilt cornice and dimity hangings. The same bed had a straw paliasse, a 'capital curled horse hair mattress, a 'prime white goose feather bed', and a 'handsome Marseilles quilt'.[74] There was a pair of painted bedside cupboards, mahogany bed steps lined with cloth, a painted dressing table with three drawers and a swing dressing glass. A painted wash-hand stand stood in the corner, equipped with the necessary earthenware. Mary Rollason supplied an 'Arcade' ewer and basin and a matching foot bath, large jug and soap stand and tray for a total of £4 16s. 0d.[75] Nearby stood a mahogany folding napkin horse, over which hung the towels.

Some of the attic rooms may have been furnished for guests and some for servants. The large 'Bow Room attic' had a bed, carpet, two curtains, chairs, and 'one center Glass wth Curtains like Window', presumably intended to give the impression of another window and reflect more light into the room. The attic over the front room was to have two beds, a carpet, a looking glass, five or six chairs and a dressing table. One of the attic bedrooms contained, in addition to the bedroom furniture', a 'capital blunderbuss with bayonet'; this was perhaps for the use of the footman, another of whose jobs may have been to be ever-ready to defend the household at any hour of the night. The weapon sold for 14s.0d. at the auction.

How the Thornhill kitchen was equipped when James Watt junior lived there is not known, beyond the fact that somewhere in it there was a ten-foot run of built-in cupboards with drawers and a worktop, sketched probably by James in 1809.[76] Anne may have given some thought to the ideal arrangements for cooking after she moved in. A nice little sketch and plan survives of the Dumergues' kitchen range, with its fireplace, ovens, and a shelf of pots and pans with items hanging beneath it, together with another sketch which may be Anne's plan for the Thornhill kitchen range. With the grate in the centre, it has a 'steam kitchen' and hot closet on one side, with a cupboard for coal beneath, and on the other side an oven and a 'stew hearth'.[77] This may be the arrangement installed in 1820, for a bill that year for 'stoves, ovens etc.' (£32 1s. 6d.) from John Slater suggests a replacement of whatever had been there before.[78]

For the kitchen and for servants' use there was inexpensive but serviceable earthenware tableware, much of it from Mrs Rollason or Sarah Bedford (both in Birmingham), including brown jugs and a black coffee biggin. The kitchen was also equipped with a comprehensive array of pots and pans, saucepans, patty pans, baking tins, biscuit cutters, jelly moulds, a 'hedgehog mould', tea-trays, rolling pins, skewers, an iron tea-kettle, sundry knives, a strong black tin fish kettle, graters and gridirons.

The food bills for Thornhill, though numerous, are probably incomplete. Nevertheless they provide some useful clues to diet and expenditure on food. Most of the Birmingham food shops, the grocers, fishmonger, butchers, soap and candle suppliers, whose bills are on file are in or near Bull Street in the town centre, which was clearly the heart of the provisioning quarter.

Fish featured frequently on Anne's menu, including 'Severn salmon' or 'London salmon' at 2s. 6d. per pound, lobsters (around 1s. 8d. per pound), oysters at

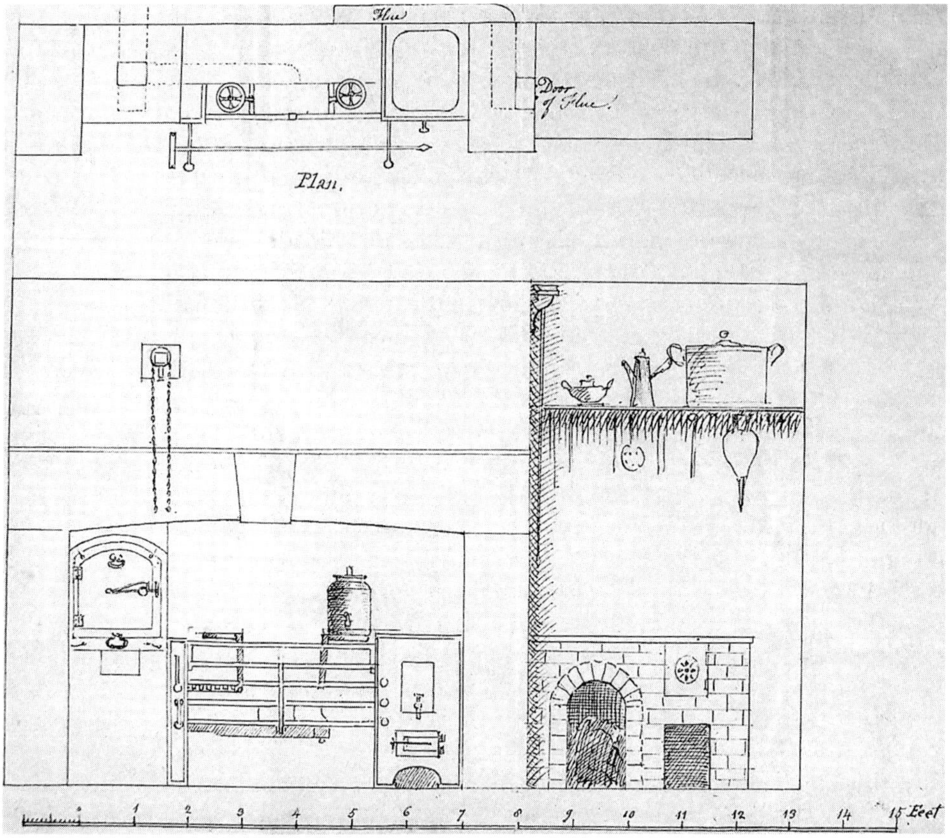

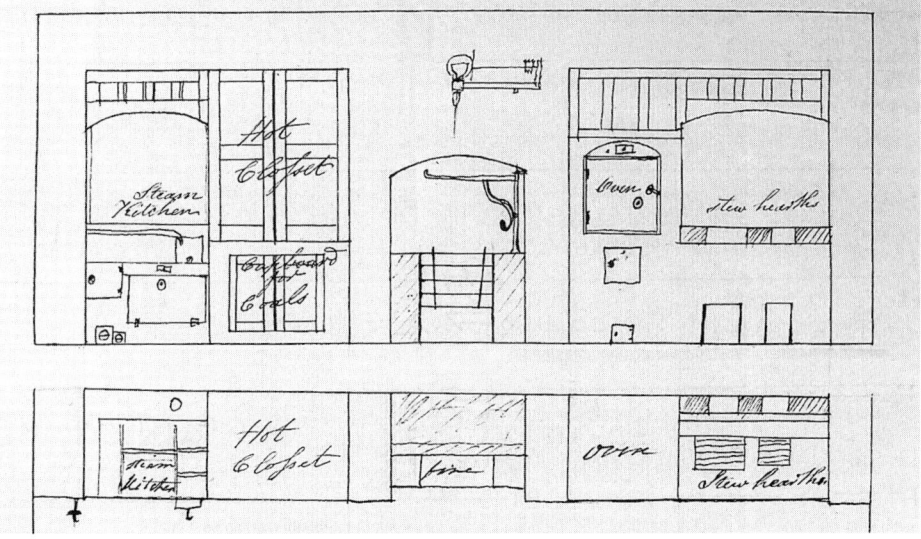

FIG. 38 *'Miss Dumergue's kitchen', pen and ink drawing. (Birmingham City Archives)*

FIG. 39 *Pen and ink drawing and plan of a kitchen range, possibly for Thornhill, possibly done by Anne Boulton. (Birmingham City Archives)*

around 2s. for 60, sole at 1s. 4d. per pound, and cod at 11d. per pound. There
are fewer loose bills for meat, but regular purchases of meat are shown in the
household cash books where they are entered from the 'butcher's book', presumably
a notebook in which the weekly orders were written and priced. Meat purchases
include chicken, duck, turkey, beef, lamb and veal. In addition to bought-in meat
there were always a couple of pigs being fattened up for the table at Thornhill.
Dairy produce included regular purchases of whole cheeses weighing anything
up to twenty pounds, mostly at prices under 1s. per pound. Eggs, cream and milk
purchased are recorded in the cash books rather than in loose bills.

The house brewed its own ale and the regular purchases of malt and hops are
some of the largest of the housekeeping bills, usually amounting to over £30 per
year and sometimes very much more. The 'Ale Cellar Book' for 1821 records:
'Remaining in Cellar from 1820 158 Gallons of ale viz 2 Barrels 54 Gallons each
and 2 Barrels 25 Gallons.' The total brewed in 1821 was 540 gallons, with similar
totals for succeeding years. On 21 March 1821 Anne noted that '12 Strikes of Malt
made 108 Gallons of Ale'.[79] Brewing must also account in part for the large amount
of sugar in the bills, totalling between £10 and £20 a year and featuring quantities of
up to fifty pounds' weight at a time, of various kinds. Preserves including raspberry
jam, 21 pots of redcurrant jelly, blackcurrant jam and apricot and plum jams were
made in 1819 and accounted for about twenty pounds' weight of sugar purchased
that year. Groceries, including tea and coffee from John Cadbury in Bull Street, and
flour, spices, dried fruit and other items, come to between £16 and £30 per year.
Wine and spirits, including sherry, brandy and gin, are generally more modest at
around £4-£17 a year, except for 1822, 1825 and 1827 when Anne bought larger
quantities including, in 1825, a hogshead of sherry in London for £47.

Lighting and heating were expensive. Plain wax candles were used for the kitchen
and chambers, and better quality 'Kensington moulds', costing around £10 0s. 0d.
for 12 dozen, for the reception rooms. Anne bought candles from her local shops,
from Thomas Mallett in Lichfield, and on most of her visits to London. A candle
bill of 1823 from Eusebius Say & Greenhill of 27 Jermyn Street gives some idea
of the wide range of candles available, listing

> Genuine Wax Lights, Fine Genuine Wax Lights, Fine Carriage Lights, Fine Wax
> Night Lights to burn in Water, Fine Wax Pieces, Finest Sperm Lights, Finest
> Composition Lights, Sealing Wax & Bougie, French Floating Wicks, Japan &
> Glass Burner for ditto, Genuine Spermaceti Oil, Fine Whale Oil, Flambeaux &
> Bottle Wax, Mould Candles on an Improved Principle, Store Kitchen & Stable
> Candles, Turkey Lights for Reading by, Rush & Night Lights …[80]

The bill also contains helpful advice on how to get the best out of them:

> Candles should be kept perfectly clean, cool and dry, not snuffed too low, leaving
> the Wick about half an inch long, and that no part escape the Snuffers, as it
> produces what are called Thieves, causes them to gutter, and not give so good a
> light. Moulds in particular burn better if lighted where required for use and not
> moved about, the flame being liable to blacken the outside. Wax, Spermaceti &
> composition candles should on no account be snuffed, but the Wick turned a
> little on one side with the point of the snuffers & the large top that frequently
> accumulates will disappear.

Cheaper rushlights were used in the cellar and outhouses, and oil lamps in some rooms (including an impressive-sounding Lotus pillar standard lamp which was refurbished by Samuel Parker of the Bronze & Iron Works, Argyll Street). Regular supplies of candles and sperm oil for lamps added another £20-£25 a year to the housekeeping bills. The fires at Thornhill, including the kitchen, laundry and brewery stoves and boilers as well as the reception and bedrooms, were kept going with thirty to forty tons of coal a year, costing on average 12s. 6d. per ton.

Altogether, the surviving bills for food, drink, fuel, and lighting at Thornhill range from a high of £447 15s. 10½d. in 1820 to a low of £266 10s. 9d. in 1829, averaging out at just over £355 a year. Actual figures, assuming there were bills which have not survived, would have been a little higher. The wide range is probably explained by the amount of entertaining in any given year (for which there is no information) and the amount of time Anne spent away from home on prolonged visits to London, Bath and elsewhere.

The grounds at Thornhill extended to about four acres. Having taken an active interest in the gardens at Soho House, Anne set about planning a new garden. Until the last few years she kept the garden-related bills filed separately, listing tools bought or mended, lime and manure delivered and spread, seeds, plants, and other items.

James Watt junior had established the kitchen garden while he was living at Thornhill, and a succession of gardeners continued to maintain it. The regular bills for vegetable seeds indicate a varied vegetable diet for the household, which must have been almost self-sufficient in vegetable production since there are few bills for bought-in vegetables apart from the occasional bag of potatoes. Vegetable seeds or seedlings were planted every season to provide a succession of crops through the year, with several varieties being grown of many vegetables. They included 'erly taters'; spinach; cos lettuce; early, York, dwarf, Savoy, and red cabbage; Brussels sprouts; borecole; green and purple-sprouting broccoli; cauliflower; Strasbourg, Deptford and Spanish onions; endive; early frame, early Charlton, Prussian and Blue Imperial peas; Windsor, long pod, scarlet runner and dwarf runner beans; sweet fennel; white radish; dwarf and green marrows; melon; cucumber; carrots; parsnips; turnips; beetroot; leeks; celery; and mustard and cress. Vegetable seed bills in an average year worked out at about £2. The apple trees and currant and gooseberry bushes which James had planted were well-established by the time Anne moved in. Melons were grown in a hotbed in a frame, other early vegetables in cold frames. If James's greenhouse was still in use it would have further widened the variety of flowering plants and fruit and vegetables which could be grown.

The pleasure garden consisted of lawns and grass walks which were kept short and neat with scythes and rolled regularly, for which Thomas Toye charged 3s. 6d. a time. To give the landscape some height, Weymouth pines and mountain ash trees were planted. To provide privacy and divide up some areas of the garden there were hedges of beech, hornbeam, holly, hawthorn, laurel and privet. Anne paid £12 19s. 3d. in 1819 for mixed hedging plants to get the hedges started, and added others subsequently, sometimes buying little box hedging plants by the yard (3s. 4d. for

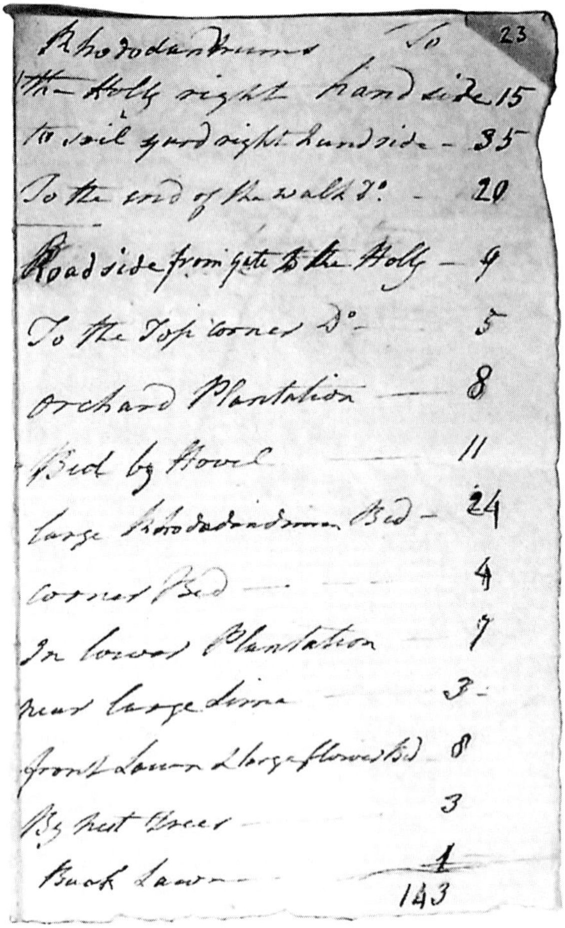
Rhododendrons To 23
the Holly right hand side 15
to soil yard right hand side - 35
To the end of the walk D°. - 20
Road side from gate to the Holly - 9
To the Top corner D°- 5
Orchard Plantation — 8
Bed by Hovel 11
large Rhododendron Bed - 24
corner Bed 4
In lower Plantation 7
near large lime 3
front Lawn & large flower Bed 8
By hot house 3
Back Lawn 1
143

FIG. 40 *Part of Miss Boulton's list of rhododendrons required for various sites at Thornhill. (Birmingham City Archives)*

ten yards). Against this green backdrop she had borders and beds of fashionable rhododendrons planted, calculating that she would need 143 rhododendrons to fill the areas she had in mind. Varieties mentioned in bills include *r. odorata, r. ponticum, r. spectabile, r. rosea, r. rosea hirsuta,* and others. Flowering shrubs planted included *kalmia augustifolia* and *k. rubra, daphne cneorum,* yellow, orange, white and pink azaleas, lilacs, *genista spinosissima, andromeda casinifolia, a.polifolia, lignum vitae,* red dogwood, and guelder rose. There were rose-beds featuring moss roses and china roses, with varieties including rose *Duc de Tuscany,* standard *Wellington,* standard *White Provence,* standard *Celestial* and 13 'fine named roses of sorts'. The flower-beds burst forth each spring and summer, scented and richly colourful with double daffodils, double yellow and red tulips, primroses, cowslips, foxgloves (memories of Dr Withering), daisies, mignonette, stocks, hollyhocks, anemones, sweet Williams, snapdragons, Canterbury bells, phlox, campanulas, ranunculus in variety, thalictrum, double scarlet lychnis, double nasturtium, double dahlias, double scarlet anemones, larkspur, peonies, daphnes, carnations, gentian acaulis, and geraniums, some of them 'quite new'.[81]

The plants and seeds were supplied by local firms, seedsmen such as John Forbes, James Hunter or Thomas Smallwood, and the flowering plants and shrubs by nurserymen including the old-established local firm of Luke Pope & Son whose land bordered part of the Thornhill grounds, and whose current incumbent went by the splendidly appropriate name of Luke Linnaeus Pope (Plates 63-5).

On the garden equipment inventory,[82] in among the spades, rakes, forks, hoes, shears, scythes, watering cans, axes and numerous other essentials, is some fishing tackle; it was bought from John Crowder in Union Street, Birmingham, in 1820 and included a 'strong hickery fishing rod' (11s. od.), '2 best strong patent lines' (2s. 6d.), '1 bank reel' (2s.), '4 pike hooks & wires' (6d.), '1 doz. Gut hooks' (1s.), and some split shot.[83] Was this for the gardener's use? There is no sign on the plan of a fish pond in the grounds.

Trawling through the accounts, it is noticeable how often repairs feature – not just the building repairs which are an inevitable part of all house maintenance over the years, but repairs to items which today would be more likely to be thrown away and replaced with new. Garden rakes get new handles or new tines, buckets, saucepans, frying pans and sieves are new-bottomed, tubs and barrels have new metal hoops and new tops and bottoms. Such work is generally carried out by local tradesmen who are used regularly, including the cooper Thomas Smith and the braziers Edward Baker & Son. John Newbould, who did most of the painting around the house, regularly attended to the garden frames and also charged 3s. 6d. for '1 cart plate wrote Ann Boulton Thorn Hill Staffordshire' in 1824. This would perhaps be for a delivery cart, for the Thornhill grounds produced regular 'crops' of pea-sticks, faggots and timber which were sold to supplement Anne's income from investments and rents.

An Enduring Taste for Bonnets

And what of Anne herself, the hub around which this household revolved and for whom the garden bloomed? Her personal bills reveal a taste for luxurious fabrics, lace collars, feathers and flounces, French flowers and French frills, shades of pink, crimson, scarlet, and lavender, and ribbons enough to rival the much-mocked Miss Landell. In Birmingham, Richard Cadbury of Bull Street and William Newton of Temple Row supplied most of her muslin, linen, bombazine, lutestring and 'Welch flannel', and she used local seamstresses to make them up.

But Anne's smartest clothes came from London. Her regular dressmaker, Catherine Cooper in South Molton Street, made her a number of garments in 1819 including a lilac gauze gown (£1 15s. od.) and a pelisse of claret cloth (ten guineas). In 1821 Miss Cooper altered a pink satin dress for her and made other items including a 'puce sarsnet* dress' and a muslin dress. The bill, including fabrics, laces, thread, hooks and eyes, buttons, ribbon, and '20 silk acorns', comes to £12 1s. 5d. A lace handkerchief from Mrs Cooper cost 3s.6d. From Marrs, off Oxford Street, Anne bought an India sprig muslin dress costing £1 11s. 6d. A dozen French cambric handkerchiefs cost £2. And from the very grand Madame Maradan Carson & Cie of 12 Princes Street, Hanover Square, she bought '*Un manteau de satin noir double de Florence cerise ... avec pelerine etc.*', costing £8 os. od.[1] Another French-sounding couturier, M. Triaud of Bolton Street, Piccadilly, supplied a '*Oiseau gros de Naples* Evening Dress with d[itt]o trimming & blond lace' at £10 19s. od. plus 10s. for the box, together with 'a Paris net cap with flowers & ribbon' at £2 4s. od.[2] Perhaps to help her get into the dresses, Anne bought a pair of corsets from a Miss Vivian in Mount Street for £1 11s. 6d. and a 'supporter' for 17s. od., and from a Thomas Hitchman stays (£1 1s.), and a pair of 'confiners' (15s. od.).

About the house Anne wore modest muslin caps, bought in the main from Birmingham shops, and costing around 7s.-12s. each. Out and about it was a different story. An 'elegant gauze Turban' was bought from Routledge of St James's, London, in 1819 and cost her £1 8s. 6d. In 1820 she paid three guineas at Otway, Outhwaite & Otway of St James's for a spectacular-sounding 'rich French white sarsnet bonnet, richly ornamented with satin, French blonde lace, with rich French carmine bunch of flowers'. A 'gros de Naples material bonnet trimmed with satin,

---

* Sarsnet: a fine soft silk fabric used for linings and lighter garments.

flowers &c' cost £3 13s. 6d. in 1823, with a further 2s. 6d. for its box. Perhaps she felt, like Catherine Hutton, that 'there is a style, a manner, in a London hat which our untutored hats in the country cannot equal,' – though Catherine might have looked askance at all the flowers and ruffles, for as a younger woman she had ordered from her own London milliner 'a fashionable, plain, black riding hat, without either feathers or lace'.3

Anne's ageing (and never very reliable) legs were clad, according to the weather and the occasion, in stockings of silk, cotton, gauze or wool. In her kid- or silk-gloved hands she carried a Tiffany fan and in summer a green parasol with an ivory handle (18s. from E. & M. Rann of Bradford Street, Birmingham). In the winter she kept her hands warm inside a muff. Two white swansdown muffs bought for 3s.4d. in Birmingham in the winter of 1824 may have been Christmas presents for Anne's nieces, or may have been for Anne and her friend Ann Keen (daughter of her father's old friend Mrs Mary Keen).

Stylish clothes called for appropriate jewellery. Anne had inherited some of her mother's jewellery and her father had given her other pieces, but in 1820 she bought herself a pair of emerald earrings costing one guinea from Theophilus Richards, the Birmingham jeweller who also supplied Matt's wife, Mary Anne Boulton, with a number of items. In 1823 Anne took an amethyst brooch to the London jewellers Rundell, Bridge & Rundell, and had them re-set it as a bracelet clasp for her, a job which cost a guinea. And on the same day that she bought that evening gown from Triaud in Bolton Street, Piccadilly, she bought accessories to go with it from Madame de Thier, who shared the same premises. She picked out a pair of gilt bracelets, a purse, a fan and a cloak clasp, costing altogether £4 13s. 6d.4 She left plumes of feathers, presumably for evening head-dresses, with Adcocks in Cavendish Square for cleaning.

The fashionable hair styles of the 1820s called for frizzy curls at the forehead, peeping out from under the bonnet, and women wore 'fronts' of artificial or real hair to achieve the desired effect. Anne paid 16s. 0d. for a front of 'superfine and natural curled hair' from Francis Trufitte of New Bond Street in 1826, perhaps replacing a cheaper one bought in 1821 from Vickery's of Tavistock Street. The reverse of the 8s. bill reads:

Vickery's Real Bear's Grease
RESTORES
Hair where it has fallen off through violent Fevers, &c. &c.
STRENGTHENS
Hair thin in its Growth, or debilitated by Sickness
INCREASES
In Length or Thickness all Hair which is Short or Thin
SOFTENS
Hair of the hardest and coarsest Texture
NOURISHES & BEAUTIFIES
With a luxuriant Growth, all Hair to which it is applied5

A later bill from Vickery's for altering a front (2s. 6d.) tells us on the back that

> ### VICKERY
> Patent
> ### HEAD DRESS MAKER
> Has the honor to acquaint the Public, that he has engaged
> Assistants
> Of Peculiar Excellence in the Art of Hair Cutting;
> He has also to announce, a Superior Assortment of Ladies'
> Head Dresses, and Gentlemen's Perukes, Toupees, and
> Scalps, made to imitate Nature,
> And adapted to all the Purposes of Court, Opera, Ball,
> theatre, and Elegant Dress Parties.
> Also, a Variety of Perukes made expressly for Gentlemen,
> whose Hair will not keep in Dress.
> These Articles are at very moderate Prices.
> Families and Boarding Schools attended by excellent
> Hair Cutters[6]

Anne's shoes are a matter of some interest, because of her disability. From infancy her parents had had her left shoe made with a thick, built-up cork sole to try to compensate for her limp, a problem possibly due, as we saw earlier, to a club foot. A dozen or so shoe bills survive from Anne's Thornhill years, all but one of them from London makers. She shopped for shoes regularly at E. Millin of 6 Berkeley Square.

Well-to-do women's shoes of this period were generally of brocade, satin or some other fabric, their very fragility being a kind of indicator of class compared with workaday leather. Anne's shoes include dainty pumps, shoes and slippers, many of them in 'Prunella', a kind of fabric with a silky sheen. She also bought 'spring clogs', boots and galoshes for wet weather. All of the bills are for odd shoes, or for shoes specified separately as being for the right foot or the left foot, for example: '2 cork left shoes £1 4s. 0d. 2 r.foot shoes pumps, 10s. 6d.' from Millin[7]; and from the same shop, '1 Prunelle cork shoe, 12s. 0d.; 1 right shoe Prunelle, 5s. 3d.; 2 cork Denmark satin shoes £1 4s. 0d.; 1 ditto boot, 16s. 0d. 2 Denmark right shoes 10s. 6d.'. With a box, this bill totals £3 9s. 3d.[8] From the same shoemaker in 1825 Anne bought '2 Prunella slippers double sole 11s.6d.; 1 large prunella slipper 5s. 3d.; 1 d[itt]o single sole 5s.3d.; 2 cork shoes £1.4s.0d.; 2 clogs 5s.; 1 galosh, 5s. 9d. 1 double sole Prunella 5s. 9d.'[9] Ann Lloyd supplied one Denmark satin shoe, one kid galosh and one prunella shoe, totalling 8s. 9d., in 1825. Some of the shoes probably rubbed: Anne's personal account books include entries for corn plasters and corn salve.[10]

How did Anne spend her time? While preoccupations with husband and children took up most of a married woman's time, the middle class spinster's life could be one of considerable industry and some variety. Witness Anne Boulton's near contemporary in Birmingham, Catherine Hutton, who at the age of 89 wrote down what she had done with her life. Catherine seems to have been a living testament to the old adage that 'a woman's work is never done'. The Huttons, though of similar social standing to the Boultons, were not as wealthy and she made her father's and brother's shirts and most of her own clothes 'with the exception of shoes, stockings, and gloves'. Her busy needle stitched and embroidered counterpanes, curtains, chair covers, patchwork quilts 'beyond calculation' and 'upwards of one hundred wallet purses'. She made pastry and confectionery, writing, 'I laud the makers of puddings and shirts; I have formerly made abundance of both, and made them well'. She kept house for her father, sang and played to him on the guitar every night from music she had copied out herself, and nursed both him and her mother during their declining years. She both devoured and wrote books: 'I have been a reader from three years old to the present day, and I have read innumerable English books and many French ... I have written nine volumes which have been published by Longman and Co., and three which have been published by Baldwin and Cradock; and I have written sixty papers which have been published in different periodicals.' She amassed large collections of pictures and prints of English and foreign costume, was an avid autograph collector, and wrote numerous letters herself. She tended the garden, and drew and painted flowers, birds, and butterflies. She 'walked much, and danced whenever I had an opportunity', and rode both side-saddle, and on a pillion behind a servant. She had, she tells us, 'ridden in every sort of vehicle, except a wagon, a cart and an omnibus'. She had visited 39 counties in England and Wales, had been to London 26 times, and to watering places 26 times. Catherine concludes this account: 'Is it enough? It is ... I never was one moment unemployed when it was possible to be doing something.'[11]

Miss Boulton did not leave the kind of first-hand account of her activities which Miss Hutton left, but many of Miss Hutton's occupations (apart from the writing of books and articles, which Anne had eschewed) would have been familiar to her, and the means of carrying them out are all to be found among her bills. Sitting in her drawing room in the evenings, Anne sewed or read, or perhaps played the piano. Her interest in music was long-established so it is surprising that no bills for sheet music have been found for the Thornhill years, but perhaps she already had a sizeable collection; she had certainly bought many pieces while still living at Soho House. There were two Broadwood pianos in the drawing room at Thornhill when the contents of the house were sold after Anne's death, and Anne's personal account books record payments for tuning a pianoforte in 1819, 1820, 1821 and 1825, two or three times a year at 2s. 6d. a time. Whether, when she moved to Thornhill, she brought with her the Broadwood pianoforte which had been delivered to Soho House in 1810, or whether she bought a new instrument in 1819 and another later, there is no indication. There was certainly still a pianoforte at Soho House in the 1820s, which Mary Anne Boulton and the children played.

Though perhaps becoming a little short-sighted (for in 1817 she bought a reading glass costing £1 12s. od.), Anne read a fair amount. Her reading matter ranged from the local newspaper, *Aris's Birmingham Gazette* to London papers including the *Morning Post* and *St James's Chronicle*, and journals including the *Quarterly Review* at 6s. per issue. She collected a partwork, *Graphic Illustrations of Warwickshire*, published in eight parts at 12s. 6d. each.

From the Birmingham booksellers Robert Wrightson, and Beilby, Knott & Beilby, she bought books of practical information including *Cooks Oracle* (9s. 0d.), *Mason's Self Knowledge* (11s. 0d.), *Hawes' Gardener* (8s. 0d.); *Simpson's Cookery* (8s. 0d.), and *Buchan's Domestic Medicine* (13s. 0d.). She bought literature and history including the works of Walter Scott (11s. 3d. for three volumes), *Childe Harold* (3s. 9d.), *The Lady of the Lake* (3s. 9d.), Aikin's *Elizabeth* (£1 11s. 0d. for two volumes), Debrett's *Baronetage*, 2 vols. £1 8s. 0d., Debrett's *Peerage*, Doddridge's *Expositor* (£3 13s. 6d.); Macknights *Epistles* in four volumes (£2 10s. 0d.), *Cowper's Private Correspondence* (8s.), *Blair's Sermons* (five volumes, £1 5s. 0d.), and *Elizabeth R* (7s. 6d.). And in January 1829 she paid a bill of £1 5s. 0d. for children's books including Helmes' *Cortez & Pizarro* (11s. 0d.), which she had probably given as Christmas presents to some of her nephews or nieces, for whom she also bought toys from time to time (£2 7s. 3d. in 1825). She had items bound, including three volumes of the *Paris Spectator* at 6s. 0d., and two volumes of sketchbooks, nicely done with gilt backs, at 4s. 8d. Whether the latter were books of Anne's own sketches there is no indication; if so, it would be good to know if they survive anywhere.

In London Anne went to Hatchard's in Piccadilly and to John and Arthur Arch, booksellers in Cornhill, where James Watt junior was also a regular customer. At Hatchard's in 1821 she bought works of history including 'Crabbe, *Elizabeth*, and *Rokeby*', totalling £2 4s. 0d., receipted 'for father & self, T.Hatchard', and also Russell's *Letters* and Johnson's *Dictionary*, totalling £7 14s. 6d. From the Arches in the same year came *Rasselas* (11s.), Boswell's *Life of Johnson* (£2 12s. 6d.), Milton's *Poetical Works* in seven volumes (£5 13s. 6d.), *Lady [Mary Wortley] Montagu's Works* (£3 4s.), Hayley's *Life of Cowper* (£3), eight volumes of the *Spectator* (£5 8s.), five volumes of *British Drama* (£5 10s., perhaps reflecting a love of theatre – theatre and concert tickets appear regularly in the 'Own Account' books), and a Bible (£5 10s. 0d.). The Milton volumes were damaged in transit back to Birmingham and the lettering on the binding of the *Spectator* volumes and Lady Montagu's works were not as Anne had specified: a note from Arch offers to replace them and repair the Milton if Miss Boulton will return them. Anne's interior designer Richard Bridgens supplied 18 numbers of 'Italian Costume'. The bill for this is docketed 'prints' – these were perhaps published as a partwork but may have been supplied for framing.

Something else which kept Anne occupied for some time was the study of a rather arcane system of mnemonics, Richard Grey's *Memoria Technica*, or *New Method of Artificial Memory*, first published in 1730. The edition she used was printed in Wolverhampton for W. Lownds of Fleet Street, London, in 1790. This extremely complicated system was designed to help readers remember dates and other facts. It appears to be rather more difficult to master than simply memorising the straightforward facts. What led Anne to it is a puzzle. In her notes on a table of the six 'ages of the World before our Saviour's time' she puts the Creation of the World at 4000 B.C. This had once been an accepted idea, but it seems a strange notion to be harboured by a daughter of the Enlightenment, whose father and his friend Erasmus Darwin had long ago concluded that the earth was millions of years old, and the fact that she was learning how the system worked does not necessarily mean she believed it. The *Memoria Technica* worked like a code, with a number value for each vowel, consonant and diphthong sound, so that strange-looking words could be constructed and memorised, which translated into dates.

Anne's father had once commented that 'as she cannot walk she must have a carriage', and when she moved to Thornhill she brought with her from Soho House her own landaulet and pair of horses. Apart from the day-to-day costs of keeping the vehicle, she was assessed for carriage tax at £12 per annum, together with tax on two horses of £9 9s. od. per annum.[12] The carriage doors were emblazoned with the Boulton family crest which her father had obtained when he became High Sheriff of Staffordshire in 1794. The use of the arms was another taxable privilege which cost Anne an additional £2 8s. od. a year.

In cold weather, her pair of smart bay horses trotted about the town in fine quality red blankets appliquéd in yellow cloth with her monogram AB (£1 3s. od.)[13] The coachman's livery consisted, like the footman's, of a greatcoat and waistcoat with embroidered buttonholes, velveteen breeches, stockings, boots, and a top hat decorated with gold braid.

Aside from the tax, livery and wages, keeping carriage horses was no small expense: annual bills for fodder, shoeing, veterinary attention and harness range up to £160. In one of her account books Anne jotted down the information that there were 45 pounds of oats in a strike, four bushels or a strike of oats in a bag, the usual weight of a bag was nine stone, and ten bags should last a pair of horses 16 weeks.[14]

Anne's original disability had never really prevented her from getting about, though she had been severely restricted by the knee accident in 1794 and its aftermath, but that had either long since improved or she had learned to live with it, and with the flexibility afforded by running her own carriage she continued to enjoy visits to London for shopping most years, and to Bath, Cheltenham or Brighton to meet up with friends, take the waters and bathe, and enjoy the social scene. Living apart from her brother and sister-in-law seems to have effected some sort of reconciliation between the three of them, and when Matt took his family to Tew Park she sometimes visited them there. In the autumn of 1819 she went to London, a return journey via Daventry and Dunstable which cost a total of £24 4s. 2d. including ostlers, toll gates, eating en route, and 5d. which was lost. Lodgings in London for seven weeks came to a further £29 8s. od. During this visit Anne indulged in some serious shopping (this was when she ordered some of the furniture from Wellsted). The Soho clerk, her cousin Zaccheus Walker junior, wrote to let her know that some goods she had ordered in London had arrived safely. Zack was keeping an eye on Thornhill for her and added

> I have advanced two guineas to Cookey, whose funds were wasting as fast as her cheeks are filling, but that has been the only application hitherto made for money by any of the servants. They have kept frequent fires in different parts of the house, and had succeeded very well in keeping out the winter enemy, damp, until this last fit of ultra wet weather, which, until yesterday, baffled their best efforts. In addition to the humidity arising from the general state of the atmosphere, your bow-room attic admitted the snow and rain, and we have been obliged to employ Barnes's men and a slater to stop the leak, which seems accomplished perfectly for the present, but may probably require further investigation in the course of next summer. The servants seem all very anxious for your return, being tired of each other's company and longing for their mistress and more occupation.[15]

Zack went on to tell Anne: 'The "Lord of Aston" [James] is fitting up his stately Hall and other apartments with pictures, busts, &c &c &c of his ancestors and friends, in which labours he seems to be completely absorbed ... The "Squire" [Matt] is gone to Tew, first to receive rents, and afterwards to shoot pheasants ... I suppose he will be absent about another week, having left all the nursery at home.'[16]

Relations must have improved considerably between Anne, Matt and Mary Anne, for in September 1820 while Anne was back in London with her friend Amelia Alston, she interviewed a potential cook for Soho House. Amelia, who sat in on the interview, wrote to Matt to give him their impression of the woman, a Mrs Maclauren:

> She seems a straight forward tidy body, very respectable in her appearance tho neither young nor handsome. She says she does not profess to understand made dishes but can do anything from receipts [recipes], and was in the habit of cooking for Lord Colchester and his friends when his Lady did not accompany him into the country ... among one of Miss Boulton's first enquiries was to know if she was fond of Children – *there* the Aunt appear'd. Mrs M seems most desirous of giving satisfaction and she really appears capable of doing so. Should this find you at Soho will you have the goodness to tell Mrs Boulton that I have sent a dozen of silk stockings to choose from ... We dine this day with Miss Dumergue, we meet the Drummonds when the meeting will consist of *one* half Dozen *Spinsters*. I long to see your Darlings, of whom Miss Boulton often talks ...[17]

A couple of years later Amelia passed on information about another cook who was under consideration at Soho. This one was said to be 'constitutionally nervous', a condition Amelia put down to her having been employed in Wales, with a Welsh-speaking staff who made her 'extremely provok'd at them speaking only Welsh' so that she had 'great difficulties'. She was 'an admirable cook, but temperamental.'[18]

In the summer of 1821 Anne and Miss Keen went to London to shop for clothes. This time they travelled by the Oxford coach, the two ladies riding inside and two servants on the outside, for which the combined fare was £4 0s. 0d. They stayed overnight at Oxford on the way down, and at Woodstock on the way back, which cost just over £1 plus meals. Lodgings in Bond Street for four weeks and a day cost them £26 2s. 0d., with a further £2 18s. 0d. for laundry, fires in the drawing room and kitchen, and a broken dish.[19] The total cost of the trip, including travelling, was £69 4s. 0d. King George III having died the previous year (on Anne's 52nd birthday, 29 January 1820), preparations were well advanced for George IV's Coronation procession on 19 July, but the two ladies, perhaps not relishing the thought of the crowds, left the capital before the event. Shortly after they returned home Anne's coachman, James Sneyd, was taken ill with 'inflammation of the lungs'. He died at Thornhill later that month. Mr Hodgson the surgeon attended the sick man and charged £4 14s. 6d. for his services, a bill paid a year later.[20] James Watt junior mentioned the coachman's death in a letter to his niece Agnes Miller, who commented, 'Miss Boulton will be sorry about her Coachman, I suppose he answered her very well and I know she does not like new servants, besides what grief his poor wife will be in'.[21]

In 1821, as in other years, Anne bought subscription tickets to concerts, probably in Birmingham; in London she went to the theatre and to exhibitions, though her account books give no information on what performances or exhibitions she saw. There were London visits and a trip to Tew Park in 1823, and a visit to London and then on to Brighton in 1826, where Mrs Keen attended a china sale and bought on Anne's behalf a large dinner service costing £37 7s. 9d.[22] This may possibly be the blue and gold china dinner service of nearly 150 pieces which fetched £12 0s. 0d. at the Thornhill contents auction.[23]

But new china was not the uppermost thing on Anne's mind. While in Brighton she must have been feeling uncertain about her health, for she was moved to make an informal Will. Dated 15 November 1826, it begins, 'If I should not have an opportunity of making a Will I address this my last request to my beloved brother with perfect conviction that it will meet with his ready compliance.'[24] Among the bequests was one to Mary Anne Boulton, her sister-in-law, of an emerald brooch once given to her by Matt. She took the document home with her and quietly put it away in a little red trunk with her other papers.

In September 1828 Anne and Miss Keen set off once more for London, taking a roundabout, sightseeing route via Worcester and Malvern before heading south. They spent two weeks at Malvern, where their lodgings and meals cost them £10 4s. 6d. and putting up the horses cost £8 13s. 6d.[25] While in Malvern Anne became unwell, and Miss Keen had to send for a doctor, and again at Worcester. The doctor declared that there did not appear to be

> any organic disease but want of strength at present is the principal part of Miss Boulton's complaint, and that by a constant attention to diet with regular hours and exercise he hopes she will soon recover. He says she may safely ride about twenty miles a day, which will be serviceable to both Mistress & horses, we therefore propose beginning our travels to day, and hope in due time to get a peep at some of our good friends.[26]

The two continued on their journey at the prescribed rate of 20 miles a day and arrived in London on 8 October, where they had difficulty finding accommodation. After trying two hotels which were full, they managed to get rooms at Scaife's Hotel in Lower Brooke Street. Six days there cost them £10 0s. 0d. including rooms for themselves and two servants, their meals (all itemised), chamber lights and laundry. As most of their London friends seemed to have gone to Ramsgate, there was not much incentive to stay long at Scaifes, which Anne found noisy, and on 14 October Miss Keen wrote to Matt to let him know they had left the hotel and had taken lodgings with a Mrs Gilbert at 6 Wilton Street, Grosvenor Place, at £4 8s. 0d. a week. Mrs Nicholson had urged them to go and stay with her in Piccadilly, as Sophia was away, but 'invalids always feel most comfortable in a house of their own & your sister is certainly much too feeble to enter into parties ... If you should come to London Miss Boulton hopes you will find us out as we are very near the Park where we ride most days, indeed the weather has been most beautiful since we have been here.'[27]

The two ladies returned from London at the end of November and once more took up residence at Thornhill. Miss Keen did some of the household shopping and generally looked after her ailing friend and kept her company. By the spring of

1829 Anne was much better and able to think about buying plants for the garden. She also bought various fabrics, for both household and personal use, and had a few jobs done about the house. And she made one major purchase: in May 1829 she took delivery of a new carriage from Obadiah Elliott of Westminster, ordered the previous November when she and Miss Keen were in London. Bought for £331 5s. 6d., and described in the bill as 'a Handsome Fashionable Chariot', it had

> a modern shaped body with easy steps, painted rich deep crimson lake relieved & fine striped lighter ditto and highly varnished, arms painted in first style on doors; lined inside with drab cloth and lace to choice, squabbed red morocco and quilted; best plate glass, real Venetian blinds, crimson silk curtains with brass ends and fastenings, silk lines and tassels; a handsome barouche seat and boot in front, trimmed and squabbed to present fashion, boot panelled and japanned and made to lock; matching rumble seat for servants; handsome circular dress lamps; fitted cap case; the whole finished in first style of Elegance.[28]

A 'Handsome Fashionable Chariot' is a brave kind of purchase, a purchase full of optimism and the promise of jaunts and high-spirited escape, but one of its first outings would be to a funeral.

At Soho House, Mary Anne Boulton gave birth to her seventh child, Mary Ann, on 23 May. On 7 June Mrs Boulton died of puerperal fever. They managed to fit in the baby's christening on 10 June, a week before the funeral on 16 June. By that time Miss Boulton had bought (from William Newton in Temple Row House) mourning wear including 'best patent crape, black silk hose, muslin, mourning gauze, lustring etc.'. The fabrics were hurriedly made up by a local dressmaker, M.Allen, and Anne's remaining dress fabric purchases that year, from William Newton and from Richard Cadbury of Bull Street, were all in black.

The Soho Manufactory and Foundry were closed till after the funeral at Handsworth Church. The procession, along roads lined with spectators, consisted of eight mourning coaches and 16 private carriages, the hearse bearing Mary Anne's coffin being drawn by six black horses. Though his wife was buried at Handsworth, Matt had a monument to Mary Anne sculpted by Sir Francis Chantrey and placed in the Church of St Michael and All Angels at Great Tew (Plate 66). The inscription speaks of her 'Rare mental endowments, elegant attainments, amenity and grace ...'

After Mary Anne's death the care of the children was taken over by her sister, Elizabeth Stockdale Wilkinson, known to them all as Aunty Bessy. Matt's son, nine-year-old Matthew Piers Watt Boulton, wrote to his father in August 1829 to say that he and his eight-year-old brother Hugh William had been good boys in their father's absence. Matt and Aunt Bessy and the younger children were in Leamington Spa; young Matthew Piers Watt and Hugh William were at home practising their music and learning to jump fences. After church on Sunday the two boys had been to Thornhill and found 'Aunty was much the same'.[29] (Little Matt's name represented an easing of tension between his father and James Watt junior; for though James had declined to be godfather to Matt's first child in 1818, when the upsets between Miss Boulton, her sister-in-law and himself were all too raw to be ignored, he had agreed to be Matthew's godfather in 1822; Annie Watt told Mrs Boulton that her stepson would be 'much gratified by having the Name of Watt joined with Matthew Boulton. I pray the dear Infant may long live

& enjoy the great Qualities of his Eminent & Worthy Namefathers.'[30]) Anne was one of the baby's sponsors.

By October the Boulton children were being looked after at Soho while Matt was in Brighton, where he received a letter from Miss Keen; describing Anne as 'languid', she said they were about to take an airing.[31] With her own letter she enclosed one from a Dr Johnstone, who wrote to Matt that he had seen Anne several times 'on account of a higher degree of excitement than usual, accompanied with some degree of fever'.[32] On the morning of 10 October he had found her rather better, 'tho' there is still a considerable degree of nervous excitement & failure of memory. If there is any change of such a nature as I conceive you would wish to be apprised of, I shall not fail instantly to communicate it'.[33] On 16 October Miss Keen sent Matt a further bulletin on 'our dear invalid'. She thought there was not much change, though Anne's spirits were not quite so good; this she put down to the gloomy weather, but they were about to take an outing in the carriage and Miss Keen was certain that Anne would be 'refreshed & better when she returns from her ride'.[34] 'The noble Boys & dear smiling Baby are well, they were all here yesterday morning,' she added. Matt's friend, the Birmingham solicitor George Barker, also wrote to him to say that Anne was much better, 'her fever nearly gone, her mind calmer but not stronger'.[35]

After these reassurances it must have come as something of a shock to Matt to receive a second letter from Barker dated 26 October. Matt docketed the letter, 'Announcing the paralytic seizure of my Sister & Dr Johnstone's opinion of her situation.'[36]

Anne's situation was not good. Barker wrote:

> It is with great pain I communicate to you the unexpected and distressing change which has taken place in your Sisters health. Dr Johns letter fully explains what has occurred and what in her present state, in talking the matter over with Mr Watt, we have thought it best for me to write to Mr Mosley by tonights post inclosing his & the Doctors letter & requesting him to forward them by an express messenger to you.
>
> I left Mrs Barker at Thornhill about an hour ago & your sister was then asleep, the latest information was to be communicated to Mr Watt which he will send in a letter he had previously written to Miss Wilkinson & which will come with this. I am afraid these tidings so unexpected will be felt by you severely tho I cannot but hope that you will in some degree be prepared for any event. Miss Boultons health has been long obviously & gradually declining, and the attack about a fortnight ago seemed to leave everything at risk. On Saturday she passed our house apparently in every respect much better, and I find every body about her, for the last four or five days, has been quite astonished to see her so much better; had not the impression of her amendment existed amongst us all, I should have written to you again. Poor Miss Keen keeps up pretty well but is much distressed.[37]

Three days later, in the early hours of Tuesday morning, 13 November 1829, Anne Boulton died at Thornhill. She was sixty-one. Later that day her cousin John Robinson, one of the Soho staff, wrote to the faithful John Mosley in London (these two men, together with the Soho cashier William D. Brown, had looked after Anne's financial affairs in Birmingham and London ever since her father's death): 'It is with most sincere regret I have to announce to you the event we have been daily expecting, the death of I may say *our* much esteemed friend Miss Boulton. She died this morning about 3 o'clock, apparently suffering no pain whatever.'[38]

Anne was buried near her father and sister-in-law in the Boulton family tomb in the crypt of Handsworth Parish Church on 20 November.[39] There is no memorial stone or tablet to her at Handsworth, though her name is included on a family plaque at St Michael and All Angels at Great Tew.

It was Aunt Bessy who found the little red trunk containing that document which Anne had written out three years earlier, in case she 'did not have an opportunity to make a Will'. In it, she had left a sum of £1,000, plus one hundred pounds a year, to Ann Keen 'to whose affectionate kindness I am indebted for so much of the comfort and happiness of my latter years'. Mary Anne Boulton never got to wear the emerald brooch which Anne had left her. To Amelia Alston she left £200 with mourning and a 'handsome ring', and asked that her goddaughter Miss E.A. Barker be given a hundred guineas for the purchase of a harp or a grand piano. Another of the 'half dozen spinsters', Miss Carmichael, was to receive her diamond locket. Anne left to her 'much esteemed friend Mrs Watt … a piece of plate or any other article she may prefer in remembrance of AB to the value of three hundred guineas.' Her niece and god-daughter Anne Robinson Boulton received her diamond earrings, diamond brooch and a ring set with brilliants 'containing my beloved ffathers hair'. Her second niece Katherine Boulton received her pearls and other jewellery, the Indian shawl given to her by her father, and 'the small gold repeater belonging to my dear Mother'. A blue enamel watch and a ring went to Elizabeth Stockdale Wilkinson. Other friends were to have various mementoes or sums of cash, and each of her servants was to have one year's wages, plus a further £20 each for the two longest-serving. The land she had purchased in Curborough and Handsworth, and the residue of her fortune, she left to 'my dear Brother to whom I now bid a long and last farewell'.[40]

Epilogue

After Anne Boulton's death in 1829 her brother Matthew Robinson Boulton sold the contents of Thornhill at auction in 1832. The sale raised a total of £490 1s. 1d. Apart from valuing the items for sale, preparing the catalogue, advertising and commission, the auctioneer's fees included valuing the property for rental. After the sale the house was let to tenants for a time, until in the late 19th century it became Handsworth Technical College. It was demolished in 1900.

Soho House still stands and is now restored and furnished with some of Matthew Boulton's own furniture; it is run as a museum by Birmingham Museums & Art Gallery, as is James Watt junior's later home, Aston Hall. The Soho Manufactory was demolished in the 1860s. Parts of the Soho Foundry remain, including possibly the small house in which James Watt junior lived before he went to The Rookery. James Watt's house, Heathfield, was demolished in 1927.

Anne's brother, Matthew Robinson Boulton, died in 1842. Four of his seven children did not marry: Anne Boulton's god-daughter *Anne Robinson* (1818-1907); *Hugh William* (1821-47); *Montagu* (1823-49, killed at the siege of Mooltan in India); and *Lionel* (1826-30). Of those who married, *Katharine Elizabeth* (1819-90) married James Patrick Muirhead, a descendant of James Watt's mother. They had six children.

Matthew Piers Watt Boulton (1820-94) married Frances Eliza Cartwright of Aynho, Northamptonshire, in 1845. Frances's father seems not to have been too sure about his daughter marrying into 'trade' and wrote to her brother asking him to find out what he could about Matthew's circumstances: 'I presume good, if not great. But these things are often exaggerated … I might say he has acted very properly so far & decently & sensibly. The materials are good, but they want a little rubbing and polishing – Peel was the son of (as he boasts) a cotton spinner.'[1] There were two daughters of the marriage. After Frances's death, M.P.W. Boulton married Pauline Gleissberg, by whom he had four children. Several of M.P.W. Boulton's children did not marry; none of them had any children.

Matthew Robinson Boulton's last child, *Mary Ann* (1829-1912), married John Robb. They had two sons. The last descendant of their second son, Frederick, was Major Eustace Robb who died at Tew Park in 1986.

James Watt Junior was the only one of James Watt's children to survive his father. James died in 1848, unmarried and childless. The Watt estates in Birmingham and Wales then passed to James Watt Junior's niece, Agnes Gibson (née Miller), and thence to her children who adopted the name Watt and became Gibson-Watt.

Of Anne Boulton's close friends, James's stepmother Annie Watt died in 1832. Sophia Dumergue died unmarried in 1831, leaving the house in Piccadilly to Mrs Nicholson, 'my more than Mother', for her lifetime. Mrs Nicholson herself died in 1839 leaving her estate to her nephew, Stephen Barber. Amelia Alston died in 1833. In her will she left mementoes including a diamond ring containing Anne Boulton's hair, a mourning ring of Mary Anne Boulton, her 'beautiful Bronze medal of the late great Mr Boulton', and 'the night shade that belonged to our dear our mutual lamented friend Miss Boulton', to various friends. No information about Ann Keen's later life has been found.

Family Connections

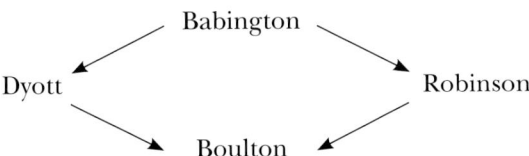

However well or poorly it has fared, one generation of a family does not exist in isolation; it is, one way or another, the product of its ancestry. In order to try to establish some social and economic context for the family into which Anne Boulton was born in 1768, further genealogical research has been done which has produced some additional detail about her family background. The information given in this Appendix takes us from the early 17th century up to the death of Matthew Boulton's first wife and that of his father, both of which occurred in 1759. The family tree constructed from this information follows the Appendix. Some notable questions remain to be answered when more evidence comes to light.

Several different Boulton family trees exist.[1] Like most family trees, they become increasingly conjectural the further back they go, between them claiming links to an exotic and improbable mix of ancestors from Richard III to Lady Godiva. They all converge, however, on the two figures of Rev. Zachary Babington, Chancellor of Lichfield, who died in 1613, and Sir Richard Dyott, who died in 1659. Both were from families of ancient lineage. In this Appendix I have dealt with them, and other families involved, a family at a time, beginning with the Babingtons. As there are Zachary Babingtons in several generations, in the following pages they have been numbered to help distinguish them from one another.

Babington

The Rev. Zachary Babington [I], Chancellor of Lichfield, married Thomasina Lowth. At the time of Zachary's death in 1613 his home was Curborough Hall, a mile or two north of Lichfield.[2] Zachary [I] and Thomasina's son, William Babington, married Helen Littleton of Pillaton Hall. William and Helen eventually made their home at Curborough Hall, and were succeeded there by one of their sons, another Zachary Babington [II], who with his wife Katherine (née Alden) lived at Curborough for a time, and was there when it was assessed for tax on 13 hearths in 1666.[3]

Zachary [II] and Katherine Babington had four sons: John (d.1706), Zachary [III], Alden and Alden (names of children who had died were often re-used), and four daughters: Eleanor, Mary (d.1688), Katherine and Dorothea. The eldest son, John Babington, moved into Curborough Hall, perhaps on his marriage. John and his second wife, Mary Hawkes (d.1716), had a son, Zachary [IV], and four daughters, Dorothy (d.1760), Mary (1694-1734), Katherine, and Elizabeth.

With John Babington and his wife installed at Curborough Hall, John's parents, Zachary [II] and Katherine Babington, moved to what was probably a smaller house at Whittington, a village south-east of Lichfield; they were still there at the time of Zachary's death in 1688. The house is illustrated in Stebbing Shaw's *Antiquities of the County of Staffordshire*;[4] only the weathered gate pillars of it, dated 1673, now remain. The Babington memorial is in the Parish Church of St Giles at Whittington.

Zachary Babington [II] of Whittington seems to have been a man of some wealth, judging from his will, dated 9 December 1687.[5] Under its terms, Katherine received her husband's estates in Whittington and elsewhere for the remainder of her life, and also 'a moiety' from her late father's will of rent income from a house built since 'the late dreadfull ffire in London', occupied by a tenant merchant. After Katherine's death this 'moiety' was to pass to her younger son, Zachary [III], 'according to his Grandfather Alden's will', while the majority of the estate was then to go to her eldest son, John. He was to pay his sister Katherine £5 per annum out of estate rents; Katherine was also to receive a one-off payment of £50. Zachary Babington [II] also left £200 to 'my grand child Dorothy Dyott that lives with me', and £5 each to his 'Daughter Babington', 'Daughter Dyott',

FIG. 41   *Zachary Babington II's house at Whittington (left of centre). (Stebbing Shaw:* History and Antiquities of the County of Staffordshire *[1798])*

and a third daughter whose name is illegible. Zachary's widow Katherine was appointed sole executrix; her sons John and Zachary [III] were to be overseers of the will, their father 'not doubting but that they will both and each of them faithfully assist their dear mother ... she and myself having been kind parents to them'.

The inventory of the Whittington household which accompanies this will lists furniture, textiles and other items (including 'one clocke with chimes' and four looking glasses) in the great parlour, hall, little parlour, four bedchambers, kitchen and brewhouse, plus corn, hay, cattle, sheep, pigs and 'two yoke of Oxen', in all valued at £249.

Dyott

Zachary Babington [II] mentioned the Dyotts in his will, and turning now to this family, Sir Richard Dyott (d.1659) was a member of King Charles I's Privy Council at York, and Steward of Lichfield from 1621-1641 (Plate 67). According to his memorial in St Mary's Church at Lichfield, because of his loyalty to the King he 'suffered frequent imprisonment by ye late usurping powers with much resolucion & great humility'. Sir Richard married Dorothy Dorrington of Stafford (Plate 68). They had six sons, several of whom served in the Royalist cause. One of these sons, Matthew (1620-98), is referred to in the Boulton pedigree as 'Matthew Dyott of Stichbrooke' (Plate 69), and it is with him that the Babington and Dyott family trees come together.

Matthew Dyott married Zachary [II] and Katherine Babington's daughter, Mary, the sister of John Babington, on 20 June 1655.[6] Mary is the 'Daughter Dyott' mentioned in Zachary Babington's will. Under the terms of the marriage settlement for the pair, drawn up between Matthew's father, Sir Richard Dyott, and Mary's father, Zachary Babington [II] , a day or two before the wedding, Zachary provided his daughter with a dowry of £600, in return for which Sir Richard Dyott sold to Zachary Babington, John Alden and Richard Floyer, lands and properties in the Lichfield area. Sir Richard also gave Matthew and his bride for their home the 127-acre Stichbrooke Estate between Curborough and Lichfield, which had been in the Dyott family for some three generations.[7]

Matthew and Mary had a large family; baptism or burial records have been found in the registers of St Chad's, Stowe, and St Mary's, Lichfield, of nine children, including a daughter, Dorothy, probably the 'grand child Dorothy Dyott that lives with me' who is also mentioned in Zachary [II]'s will. Their other children include John, Zachary, Matthew, Richard, Catherine, Anne, Mary and Elizabeth; the latter was baptised at St Chad's Church, Lichfield, on 7 April 1670.[8] Matthew Dyott's wife Mary died and was buried at the same church on 13 July 1688,[9] and Matthew Dyott himself in December 1698.[10] In his will Matthew Dyott left property and land in Stowe Street, Lichfield, and estates at Stichbrooke, Curborough and Elmhurst to his son, John, who was to settle any debts and pay the remaining legacies. These included an annuity of £20 to John's brother Matthew for life, and an annuity of £5 to his other surviving brother, Zachary. Matthew Dyott senior's daughter Elizabeth was to have an annuity of £10, and his other 'wellbeloved daughters' Dorothy, Catherine and Anne annuities of £5 each.

Though there is a lot of land in Matthew Dyott's will, the inventory accompanying it suggests a simpler lifestyle at Stichbooke than Zachary Babington [II] enjoyed at Whittington: furniture, hangings and other goods are listed in the hall, great parlour, kitchen, four bedchambers, a garret, brewhouse and yard, totalling £37 9s. 10d. The goods include a warming pan, pewterware, racks, spits, jack and weights in the kitchen, a clock with weights, one looking glass, napkins, tablecloths, counterpanes and bed hangings. The appraisers added a note that they had not seen and therefore could not value six gold rings and some silverware, said to be in the custody of Mrs Dorothy Dyott.[11] As Matthew Dyott's mother had died in 1672, the identity of this woman is uncertain. The tendency of different branches as well as different generations of families to use the same Christian names repeatedly gives rise to many problems of identification.

In February 1699, two months after her father Matthew's death, Elizabeth Dyott married John Bolton (or Boulton – the 'u' seems optional at this period). They were both 29 years old. Before her marriage Elizabeth may have been living at 10 Bird Street, St Mary's, Lichfield – there is a record of a spinster of the right name and age living there in the household of a Charles Haworth in 1695.[12] But the marriage took place, not in Lichfield but at the Church of St Mary Savoy in The Strand, London.[13] Why this should be so is unclear. There were Dyott relations in London, to whose care she may have been entrusted before the wedding; or possibly there was family opposition in Lichfield to the marriage. Elizabeth was the woman about whom Matthew Boulton of Soho wrote to his daughter Anne in 1785, after she had reported meeting a Mr Dyott: 'I know not if you know that he is a relation of ours, but I must turn your Eyes further back than you can see to shew you the degree of Affinity. My Grandmother was a Dyott (viz my Fathers Mother) & was born at Litchfield.'[14]

Boulton

Elizabeth Dyott's husband, John Bolton, the great-grandfather of Miss Anne Boulton, is an elusive figure. He is described as 'of Lichfield' in various family trees, but Samuel Smiles, Matthew Boulton's 19th-century biographer, says that John Bolton came from Northamptonshire 'in which county Boultons or Boltons have been settled for a long period, and where there are records of many clergymen of the name'.[15] The latter statement is certainly true, but none of the clergy listed under these names in an index of Northamptonshire clergy appear to have any connection with the Lichfield and Birmingham Boultons/Boltons.[16] Smiles says that John Bolton settled in Lichfield towards the end of the 17th century. However, the International Genealogical Index lists as Elizabeth Dyott's husband a John Bolton who was baptised at St Mary's Church, Stafford, on 10 October 1670.[17] In the Church Register his parents are named as John and Frances Boulton. The Lichfield Freemen's Roll lists a John Bolton becoming a Freeman of the Company of Taylors on 7 January 1700.[18] The Lichfield Poll Books for 1710, 1714, 1718 and 1721 show a John Bolton voting at various times for Walter Chetwynd (Whig), and Richard Dyott and John Cotes (both Tory).[19] His qualification for voting is given as 'ffreehold lands in the County of the City of Lichfield'.

Neither John Bolton's burial record nor his will has yet been found, which would help to answer a number of questions. He was certainly still alive in 1741 because that year his brother-in-law, John Dyott of Lichfield, made provision in his will for his sister, John Bolton's wife Elizabeth, and her children. Elizabeth was to have two annuities for life, one of £10 and one of £5, money which he stipulated was to be 'for her own sole separate and private Use wherewith her Husband shall not intermeddle nor shall the same be subject to his Debt Controul or Engagements'.[20] The International Genealogical Index lists the death of a John Bolton in Northampton in 1750; the same entry names as his spouse an Elizabeth 'Dyett' of Stichbrooke, b.1642. Her place of birth is right, but the date makes no sense; she must belong to a previous generation and could not have been the wife of John Bolton – though there is no record of a daughter among Sir Richard Dyott's children. A search at Northampton County Record Office yielded only one John Bolton buried in 1750, a single man in the parish of Yelvertoft, whose will leaves all his estate to his siblings; again, there is no discernible connection with the Lichfield Boultons. A John 'Bouton' senior of Sandford Street, Lichfield, was buried at St Michael's, Lichfield, on 19 March 1759, 'aged 89';[21] if the absent 'l' is a clerical mistake, this would fit with a baptism date in 1670, but there is nothing at present to confirm his identity.

We do know that John and Elizabeth Bolton had at least six children: Matthew (baptised at St Mary's, Lichfield, on 30 March 1700), John (b.1703) and Henry (b.1704), both said to be dead 'some time since' in 1769,[22] Catherine (baptised at St Mary's, Lichfield, on 12 January 1706), William (b.1710, still living at Lichfield in 1769), and Richard (baptised at St Mary's Lichfield on 28 September 1711,[23] in business as a wig-maker in Birmingham in 1769[24]). William was singled out in his Uncle John Dyott's will, receiving £50 plus a £10 annuity for life. His brothers and sisters and cousins were all to have £3 annuities. All the annuities were to come from rents on lands around Lichfield (John Dyott had no surviving children of his own).

Notwithstanding all the Lichfield baptisms, Dickinson in his 1936 biography of Matthew Boulton suggested that the family moved to Birmingham early in the 18th century, and that John Bolton used his wife Elizabeth's fortune to establish a business of some kind.[25] However, judging from the wills quoted earlier, Elizabeth does not appear to have had a great fortune (she received an annuity of £10 from her father, most of whose estate went to her brother, John Dyott, whose own will, referred to above, was dated 27 February 1741). Smiles says it was John and Elizabeth Bolton's firstborn, Matthew (who will be referred to henceforth as Matthew Boulton senior), who made the move to Birmingham,[26] where he is said to have been apprenticed to a stamper and toymaker.[27] 'Toys' in this context were not children's playthings but small decorative accessories for adults, such as chatelaines, buckles, watch-chains, snuff boxes, vinaigrettes and so on. The button and 'toy' trade was a rapidly growing one in the mid-18th century, offering the prospect of a good living. Birmingham, which during the 18th century became known as 'The Toyshop of Europe', was already an established manufacturing town, a busy, dirty, noisy, money-making place in stark contrast to Lichfield, which saw itself as more genteel, with an intellectual, literary, musical and social scene revolving round the Cathedral and the likes of Samuel Johnson, David Garrick, and Anna Seward.

On 21 June 1723, 23-year-old Matthew Boulton senior married Christian[a] Peers or Piers, said to be the daughter of Daniel Peers/Piers of Chester, at Birmingham Parish Church, St Martin's in the Bull Ring.[28] Here we hit another obstacle. Research into Christian[a]'s background has not so far produced any information. The name Peers/Piers occurs in registers of various parishes around Chester but so far no record of a Christiana Peers's baptism has been found at the right date. If, as her obituary notice in *Aris's Gazette* claims, she was 96 at her death in 1785,[29] she must have been born *c.*1689, which would make her some 12 years older than her husband, and 34 when they married and began a large family.

Matthew Boulton senior and Christiana had at least eight children, not all of whom survived infancy. The first, a son they named Matthew after his father, was baptised at St Philip's in Birmingham on 31 March 1724 and buried on 4 March 1727. Next came Elizabeth (1726-28), then another Matthew (1728-1809), then John (*c.*1730-73), Mary (1731-68), Catherine (baptised 26 April 1735), and James (born and died in 1736). Other births mentioned on various family trees, which may or may not be correct, are Thomas (born 1733), Martha (born 1737), Jolus, and Anne (born *c.*1739).[30]

The second Matthew Boulton on this list was the pioneer industrialist and father of Miss Anne Boulton. At the time of his birth, the family was living at their place of business in Whitehalls Lane (later re-named Steelhouse Lane) in the town centre, but in 1731 they moved to Snow Hill, three doors down from their friends the Garbetts.[31]

Nothing is known about Matthew Boulton's early childhood and little about his education. Among the mass of papers which he kept, there are relatively few dating from before 1760. One or two notebooks; a book of copy letters from the business he carried on in Birmingham with his father; the occasional personal document: these are the meagre resources for a study of his young man's life. It is as though there had been a great clearing-out, a discarding of the past. Samuel Smiles, presumably relying on the account of Boulton's grandson, says he attended a school in Deritend (then a hamlet on the south-east edge of the town) run by the Chaplain of St John's Chapel, Rev. John Hausted.[32]

St John's was a chapel of ease to Aston Parish Church.[33] The Guild of St John had run a school since its earliest years, in its priest's house and guildhouse. This building is still standing; it is now known as the Old Crown Inn. By the time young Matthew Boulton went to school the Guild of St John had been long dissolved, and its school had been replaced by the King Edward VI Grammar School in New Street, founded in 1552. Hausted's Academy was presumably independent of the chapel, and indeed his obituary notice in *Aris's Gazette* describes him as 'Master of a Private School, remarkable for his great Abilities as a Divine and for his Learning and unwearied Diligence in the Instruction of the Youth committed to his Care'.[34] Dickinson suggests that Matthew Boulton was educated at Hausted's Academy because the King Edward VI School was in 'a semi moribund state' at the time.[35] Hausted died at his house in Moor Street in 1755. The house was demolished in 1909 to make way for Moor Street Station, along with one lived in for a time by another old friend of the Boulton family, the printer John Baskerville.[36]

FIG. 42   *Detail of William Westley's 'Plan of Birmingham survey'd in the Year 1731', showing the area of Snow Hill and White Hall or Steelhouse Lane where the Boulton family lived and ran their business before the building of the Soho Manufactory in 1762-4. (Local Studies Department, Birmingham Reference Library)*

Matthew Boulton's education was probably fairly typical of the time. The range of information young people were expected to assimilate, either at school or at home, can be gauged from an advertisement for a new book in *Aris's Birmingham Gazette* of 3 February 1755:

This day was published
Price one shilling, neatly bound,
(being a proper Press fit for a Christmas Box or a New Years Gift)
A MUSEUM FOR YOUNG GENTLEMEN and
LADIES, or, a Private Tutor for little Masters and Misses
Containing a Variety of useful Subjects, and, in particular,

1. Directions for Reading with Elegance and Propriety
2. The antient and present State of Great Britain, with a compendious History of England
3. An Account of the Solar System
4. Historical and Geographical Description of the several Countries of the World; with the Manners, Customs and Habits of the People
5. An Account of the Arts and Sciences
6. Rules for Behaviour
7. Advice to Young Persons on their entering upon the World with short Rules of Religion and Morality
8. Tables of Weights and Measures
9. Explanation of Abbreviations used in Words and Dates
10. A Description of Westminster Abbey, St Paul's Church, with the Tower and Monument in London
11. The Seven Wonders of the World
12. Prospect and Description of the [?] burning Mountains
13. Dying Words and Behaviour of Great Men, when just quitting the Stage of Life; with many other useful Particulars, all in a plain familiar Way for Youth of both Sexes

Interspersed with Letters, Tales and Fables, for Amusement and Instruction, and illustrated with Cuts, being a Second Volume to the pretty Book for Children.
Printed and sold by J. Newbery, in St Paul's Church Yard, R. Baldwin, Paternoster Row ...

Thus equipped to face the world, young Boulton left school and went into his father's business in about 1742 at the age of fourteen. Little is known about the early years of the firm, which Matthew Boulton senior must have set up some time after completing his apprenticeship, and possibly after his marriage. In time he must have employed a number of people, for a former employee in a letter to Boulton senior's grandson many years later refers to time spent in the workshop in 1737 and to 'your grandfather's old workmen, some of whom had serv'd in the

Warrs of Queen Ann & George 1st [who] seem'd to take delight in telling me the story's of their youth'.[37]

Matthew Boulton junior evidently took to his father's business readily, and showed an inventive turn of mind. He is credited with having invented inlaid steel buckles, which proved such a fashion hit that they were exported in large quantities to France and re-imported as the latest French novelty.[38] Boulton himself may not have been responsible for claiming this credit, for in a 1765 letter from Boulton & Fothergill to a customer the writer comments, 'Buckles inlaid wth pearl & steel were originally invented & made by the Ancestors of our Boulton'.[39]

In 1746 Matthew Boulton's Grandmamma Bolton, Elizabeth (née Dyott), died. She was buried at St Chad's, Lichfield, on 17 August that year.[40] Whether his grandfather, John Bolton, was still alive, and if so where he was living, is not at present known, as discussed above, but the fact that Elizabeth is listed in the Parish Register as 'Mrs Bolton' rather than 'Widow Bolton' suggests he may have been.

Robinson

Although Matthew Boulton and his parents were now well-established in Birmingham, the family's Lichfield links remained strong, and were about to become stronger through union with another notable Lichfield family, the Robinsons.

Going back to the mid-17th century, William Robinson was a mercer. The Lichfield Freemen's Roll records his admission to the Company 'of ye Mercers and Apothecarys' on 10 January 1677.[41] In 1695, aged 42, he and his wife, Sarah (38), and six of their children, William (14), Luke (13), James (nine), Sarah (11), Mary (five) and Hannah (one) were living at 17 Sadler Street ('alias Market Street'), Lichfield.[42] In his will in 1708 William left his house to his widow, and money for William, Luke, James, another son, Joseph (born 1696), and Hannah. He seems to have had high hopes of Joseph, for he stipulated that Sarah was to

> maintaine my said Sonn Joseph with all things necessary fitt and convenient for him till he comes to his said age of one and twenty years and if my said Son be fitt to goe to the University my said Executrix shall maintaine him there soe that the said sume of one Thousand pounds shall come clear to my said son Joseph when he comes to his age of one and twenty years.[43]

William senior's widow, Sarah Robinson, moved into her eldest son William's house in Cathedral Close, Lichfield. In 1724 Sarah's second son, Luke, married Dorothy Babington (the daughter of John Babington and his second wife, Mary Hawkes). Both Luke and Dorothy's fathers were long dead by then, William Robinson in 1708 and John Babington in 1706, and it was in any case a second marriage for Luke (he had married his first wife, Sarah Wright, at St Michael's, Lichfield, in 1706, and Sarah had died childless in 1722[44]).

The marriage settlement for Luke and Dorothy was therefore drawn up between Luke himself, Dorothy's brother Zachary Babington [IV] (then living on the Packington estate which he had inherited from his father, John Babington), and Zachary and Dorothy's brother-in-law, Theophilus Levett (her sister Mary's husband). Zachary provided a bond for £1,000. Luke, being 'not at present capable of settling any Messuages Lands Tenements or Hereditaments upon her the said Dorothy Babington', provided £2,000 in cash for the marriage settlement, the £3,000 total to be used to buy lands and property. In the event of Luke and Dorothy's deaths before their children reached the age of majority, the money was to be administered on their behalf by Zachary Babington [IV] and Theophilus Levett. If Luke and Dorothy should die childless, the money was to go instead to Luke's elder brother, William Robinson, and his heirs. (In the event William himself died in 1725, a year after his brother's marriage and two years before his mother, Sarah.) Dorothy Babington is described in the marriage settlement as being possessed of a 'considerable personall Estate' which included ready money, securities, household goods, watches, rings, old gold, linen 'and severall other things', and the settlement stipulated that she was to retain personal control over these items and that Luke was not to have any power over them.[45]

Luke Robinson and Dorothy Babington were married at St Mary's Church, Lichfield, on 17 May 1724.[46] Luke was 41 and Dorothy probably in her early thirties. They were to have eight children, only three of whom survived.[47] The children included three pairs of twins. The first two were born in 1725, a day apart; one, a daughter, was stillborn and the other, John, died in 1728. A second pair, both girls, was born in 1727; again, one was stillborn. The surviving twin, Mary, was baptised at St Mary's on 7 September 1727. Next came a stillborn son in December 1728. A third pair of twins, both boys, was born on 20 June 1731 and baptised on 17 July. One of the boys, William, died aged eight weeks; the surviving twin was Luke junior.[48] The last child to be born to Luke and Dorothy Robinson was Mary's sister, Ann, who was born on 3 November and baptised on 30 November 1733.[49]

In 1727, three years after Luke and Dorothy's marriage, Luke's mother, Sarah Robinson, died. Sometimes wills provide a distant echo of admiration expressed, fabrics fingered, promises made: in her will Sarah left her daughter-in-law Dorothy 'my Velvett Hood and Scarfe', and to Jane, the wife of her third son James, 'my Sattin Gown and petty coat'.[50] She also left £200 each to two young grandchildren, John, son of Luke, and a granddaughter 'lately borne and not yet Christened'.[51] John died in 1728 in his third year; the not-yet Christened granddaughter was Mary Robinson, who would become the first wife of Matthew Boulton.

In 1730 Luke's younger brother James Robinson, who was his mother's sole executor and residuary legatee, built a fine town house adjoining the Guildhall in Bore Street, Lichfield (the house is known today as Donegal House; now Grade II listed, it is used at present as a Tourist Information Centre (Plate 70)). Like his father and two of his brothers, James was a mercer. Luke, James and Joseph became freemen of the Company of Mercers and Apothecaries in 1706, 1710 and 1714 respectively.[52] After James's death in 1744 his widow, Jane Robinson, continued to run the business, and in 1760 left the shop fittings and stock, with the house in Bore Street, to her son Joseph as long as the house was lived in by a member of the family in the mercer's trade. Jane also directed that the family were to have mourning out of the stock in trade. Other bequests included silverware and jewellery.[53]

Luke Robinson took a lease on a house in Bore Street, exact location unknown but not far from his brother James. Here he and Dorothy and the children made their home. Luke also had a lease on another house called Bowling Green House.

This one we can pinpoint, though it is no longer there. There had been a bowling green in Lichfield, west of the Friary, since the 17th century – it is shown, with the associated house, on Samuel and Nathaniel Buck's south-west Prospect of Lichfield (1732), somewhere near where the present-day *Bowling Green* public house stands (Plate 71). These property leases from St John's Hospital were for three lives – those of Luke senior, his wife Dorothy and his son, Luke junior.[54]

Boulton=Robinson

On 9 February 1749, at the age of 21, Matthew Boulton the younger of Birmingham married 22-year-old Mary Robinson at St Mary's Church, Lichfield.[55] Babington blood flowed in both their veins. Mary's grandfather, John Babington, and Matthew Boulton's great-grandmother, Mary Babington, were brother and sister, the children of Zachary Babington (II) of Whittington.

Mary Robinson was a good catch. In 1737 at the age of ten she had inherited part of the estate of her godmother and cousin, Elizabeth Bailey.[56] Luke Robinson also made a handsome marriage settlement for his daughter. The marriage settlement included £3,000 and the Babington estate at Curborough. Mary's mother Dorothy, already wealthy at the time of her marriage, had inherited Curborough on the death of her brother Zachary Babington [IV] in 1745, along with the other Babington estates at Whittington and Packington a little further south.

Luke Robinson senior died in the year of his elder daughter's marriage to Matthew Boulton, and was buried at St Mary's, Lichfield, on 29 October 1749.[57] He and Dorothy had evidently made good use of their £3,000 marriage settlement. Luke's will includes land and property in the city of Lichfield and in five parishes in the three counties of Stafford, Warwick and Derby. Mary was left just £10 by her father, 'she having had her portion on marriage'; Luke's new son-in-law Matthew Boulton also received £10. Mary's sister, 16-year-old Ann Robinson, was to receive £3,000 at the age of twenty-one. Luke junior received his father's estates in Yoxall, Elmhurst, Hanbury, Chorley and Burton-upon-Trent. Luke senior's widow, Dorothy, was to have the remainder of his estates for life, including a 'dwelling house held by lease of St John Baptist Hospital, Lichfield' which after her death was to pass to young Luke (presumably the house in Bore Street).[58] In addition, Luke Robinson senior left £300 to four trustees, the interest to be given annually on Christmas Day to the poor of St Mary's parish.

Where the newly-married Mr and Mrs Matthew Boulton lived is not so far known. The three daughters they are known to have had were all baptised or buried in Lichfield. None of the girls survived long: Dorothea Babington Boulton was baptised at St Mary's, Lichfield, on 30 January 1750,[59] and buried at St Giles, Whittington, on 15 May 1750.[60] Anne or Anna Boulton was baptised at St Mary's, on 2 May 1753.[61] The following day her sister Maria Boulton was buried at St Chad's Church, Stowe, Lichfield.[62] As Matthew Boulton was working with his father it would seem logical to assume they lived in Birmingham, but a bill for medicines in 1749-50 is from Edmund Hector, a Lichfield apothecary. Totalling £6 8s. 6d., it includes various tinctures, pills, cordials, camomile flowers, draughts, emulsions and 'large opening mixtures'; the maid had a 'wine vomit' and somebody had 'an Hysterick Mixture'.[63]

From an early age Boulton junior had an inquiring mind, and was attracted to scientific ideas, so the 'hysterick mixture' may have led him to look into the subject. He recorded his findings in one of his early notebooks. 'Hystericks', he notes,

> is supposed to arise from disorder of ye Womb. An hysterick Paroxysm begins wth a Sense of Coldness creeping up ye Back & afterwards spreading over ye whole Body then ensues a headach & sometimes a palpitation of ye Heart with a Fainting from wch ye Patient soon recovers sometimes after ye Coldness. There succeeds a remarkable heat wch brings on ye above symptoms. Hysterick womn feel a sense of Cold in ye Crowne of ye Head & this is ye Chief Diagnostic of ye disease the real cause is in ye animal Spirits & ye nervous system. For ye cure during ye Paroxysm ... Volatile Spirits help to wake ye Patt [patient] out of ye Paroxysm as allso tickling in ye sols of ye Feet ...

After a list of symptoms including 'Suffocation of ye Womb' he goes on:

> Convulsions of ye musiles of ye larynx shortens[?] ye wind pipes & prevents ye air passing into ye lungs. Hence it is tht Hysterickal Womn feel constriction in ye throte as if strangled.

Recommended remedies (which sound more likely to induce 'hystericks' than cure them!) include bark, peony roots, lily-of-the-valley leaves, mistletoe, powdered human cranium, 'tooth of Sea Horse', peacock's dung, and 'Elks Claws is good'.[64] It's difficult to resist wondering which particular female in Boulton's life gave rise to this line of research.

Bills and notebook lists of expenditure give us some idea of payments made in these early years. In January 1757 he recorded the payment of a guinea for a New Year's gift for his wife, and gave her two guineas to pay for some stays. Mary received regular sums of between 2s. and 10s.6d. from her husband. He spent 9s. on a pair of shoes, 3s. having a pair mended, and paid a Mr Jackson £9 for 'my stopt Watch wth a Second Hand'. He gave 5s.6d. to H. Boulton (possibly his uncle, Henry Boulton). He paid a guinea for 'Vergil', his subscription to Baskerville's celebrated edition of the Roman poet, and was plainly bent on doing some serious reading: other books purchased included Chambers' Dictionary in two volumes (£4 13. 8d.), four bound volumes of *The Tatler* (10s. 6d.), Italian and French dictionaries (10s. 6d.), Clares *Instructions on Bookkeeping* (2s. 6d.), Pope's *Essay on Man*, a Classical Dictionary in two volumes, nine volumes of the works of Shakespeare, 14 volumes of Swift, three volumes of Locke, and several works on the subject of electricity. In March 1757 there are five payments for 'Electricity', ranging from 1s. to 14s. 6d., though it is not clear what these are for.[65] Bills include two from Mary Froggatt for Mary Boulton; in January 1758 she spent 16s. 8d. on millinery which included muslin, 'making duble ruffles' and 'clearstarching the thing'.[66] In April there was a further 13s. 11d. for a silk handkerchief, two pairs of mitts (one pair were 'work mitts'), some green ribbon and other items. Thomas Aris billed Boulton for more books, bought between 1754-57. These include '*Boadicia*', and Hogarth's *Analysis of Beauty*, while from another bookseller, Richard Bailye, Boulton bought works by Dryden, Boorhaave, Johnson, Addison, Voltaire and others, and back volumes of the *Gentleman's Magazine* for 1734, 1754 and 1755, totalling £6 7s. 0d.[67]

In 1759, after ten years of marriage, Mary Boulton died. The cause of her death is not recorded. As she lay in her open coffin before the funeral, her 31-year-old husband looked down at her, then went to the writing table, took quill and paper and began to write. When he had finished, he made a copy of what he had written. One he placed in the coffin with Mary. The other he filed away. It is endorsed, 'Upon seeing the Corps of my dear Wife Mary many Excellent Qualitys of Hers arose to my Mind which I could not then forbare acknowledging Extempory with my pen & depositing it in her Coffin, of which this is a Copy.' It gives some indication of the quality of their relationship and is the only truly personal document we have relating to this marriage:

> If Sincerity to all & Flattery to none
> If a good natur'd Hand; & Compassionate Heart
> If being truly affectionate & dutyfull to her Parents,
> If a sincere Regard to her Brothers & Sisters
> If Loveing to Excess her weeping Husband
> If Bearing many Children, & endureing many Pains & illnesses, with Patience under her Eye
> If preserving fair Virtue around her unpolluted Bed
> If passing through Life without one Black Spot upon her Fame
> If these things can endear a Wife to a Husband
> Thou wert dear to me.
> If these things are worth the Remembrance
> Thou shalt not be easily forgot.
> If these things can recommend thee to the throne of Grace,
> Thou shalt find Mercy & Happiness in Heav'n.
> And O almighty & Eternal God, who art the Creator & Governor of this & all other Worlds, & who knowest the Secrets of all Hearts, look down with Mercy & Pity upon thine afflected Servant, give me Comfort & a Sure Confidence in thee, support & strengthen me under all the infirmitys of Nature, but above all preserve me throughout the remainder of my days, pure & as free from Sin as my departed Blessed Wife hath liv'd & forgive me good God all my Trespasses & offences ever committed against her; as I forgive all her little Trespasses against me. Receive her Gracious Lord as one of thine Elect. Receive her I beseech thee most mercifull God into thine Heavnly, Glorious, & Eternal Kingdom, where the Blessed are ever Singing Hallalujas to Him that was: that is: & is to Come, to the Lamb that was slain, but liveth for ever. Farewell Farewell.[68]

The line about 'bearing many children' is interesting and makes one wonder whether there were in fact more children of this marriage than those recorded, especially given Mary's family history of twins. Three children in ten years would hardly have seemed 'many' in the 18th century, but exhaustive searches of parish registers have failed to reveal any more.

Mary, her coffin covered in a black velvet pall, was drawn on a hearse by black horses to St Giles' Church at Whittington on 20 August 1759.[69] At the same time, the church bell was tolled at St Mary's in Lichfield. A band of mourners followed in black cloaks. Altogether over 145 yards of black fabric of various kinds (crape, silk, shalloon,* dimity, broadcloth), 22 yards of black ribbon, 37 pairs of various

---

* Shalloon: a lightweight woollen worsted fabric.

FAMILY TREE

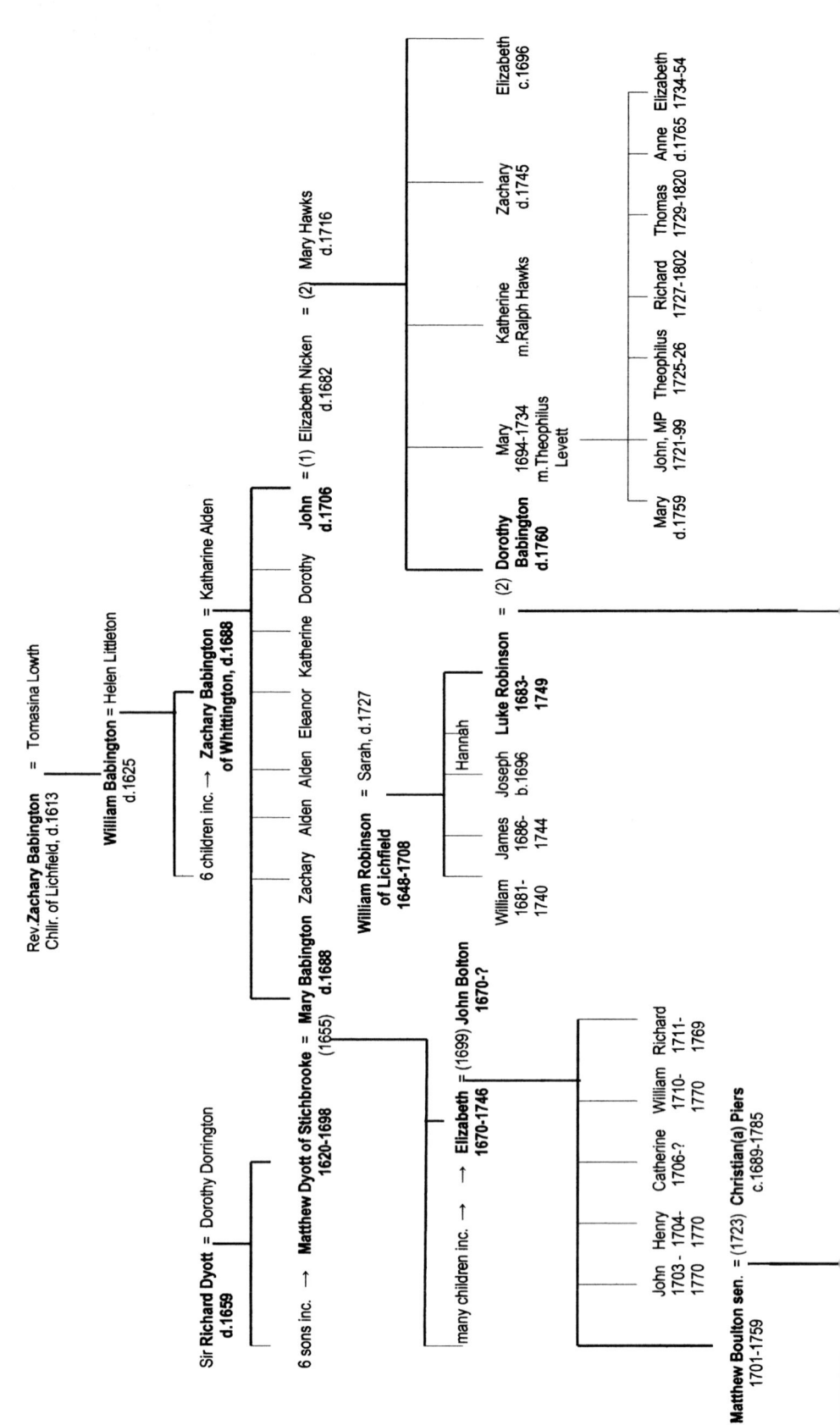

Rev.**Zachary Babington**
Chllr. of Lichfield, d.1613 = Tomasina Lowth

William Babington = Helen Littleton
d.1625

6 children inc. → **Zachary Babington** = Katharine Alden
of **Whittington, d.1688**

Zachary Alden Eleanor Katherine Dorothy **John** = (1) Elizabeth Nicken = (2) Mary Hawks
d.1706   d.1682   d.1716

William Robinson = Sarah, d.1727
of **Lichfield**
1648-1708

William James Joseph **Luke Robinson**
1681- 1686- b.1696 **1683-**
1740   1744   **1749**

Hannah

Sir **Richard Dyott** = Dorothy Dorrington
d.1659

6 sons inc. → **Matthew Dyott of Stichbrooke** = **Mary Babington**
1620-1698   **d.1688**
                                    (1655)

many children inc. → → **Elizabeth** = (1699) **John Bolton**
1670-1746   1670-?

John Henry Catherine William Richard
1703- 1704- 1706-? 1710- 1711-
1770   1770   1770   1769

Matthew Boulton sen. = (1723) **Christian(a) Piers**
1701-1759   c.1689-1785

Dorothy
Babington
d.1760 (2)

Mary
1694-1734
m.Theophilus
Levett

Katherine
m.Ralph Hawks

Zachary
d.1745

Elizabeth
c.1696

Mary
d.1759

John, MP
1721-99

Theophilus
1725-26

Richard
1727-1802

Thomas
1729-1820

Anne
d.1765

Elizabeth
1734-54

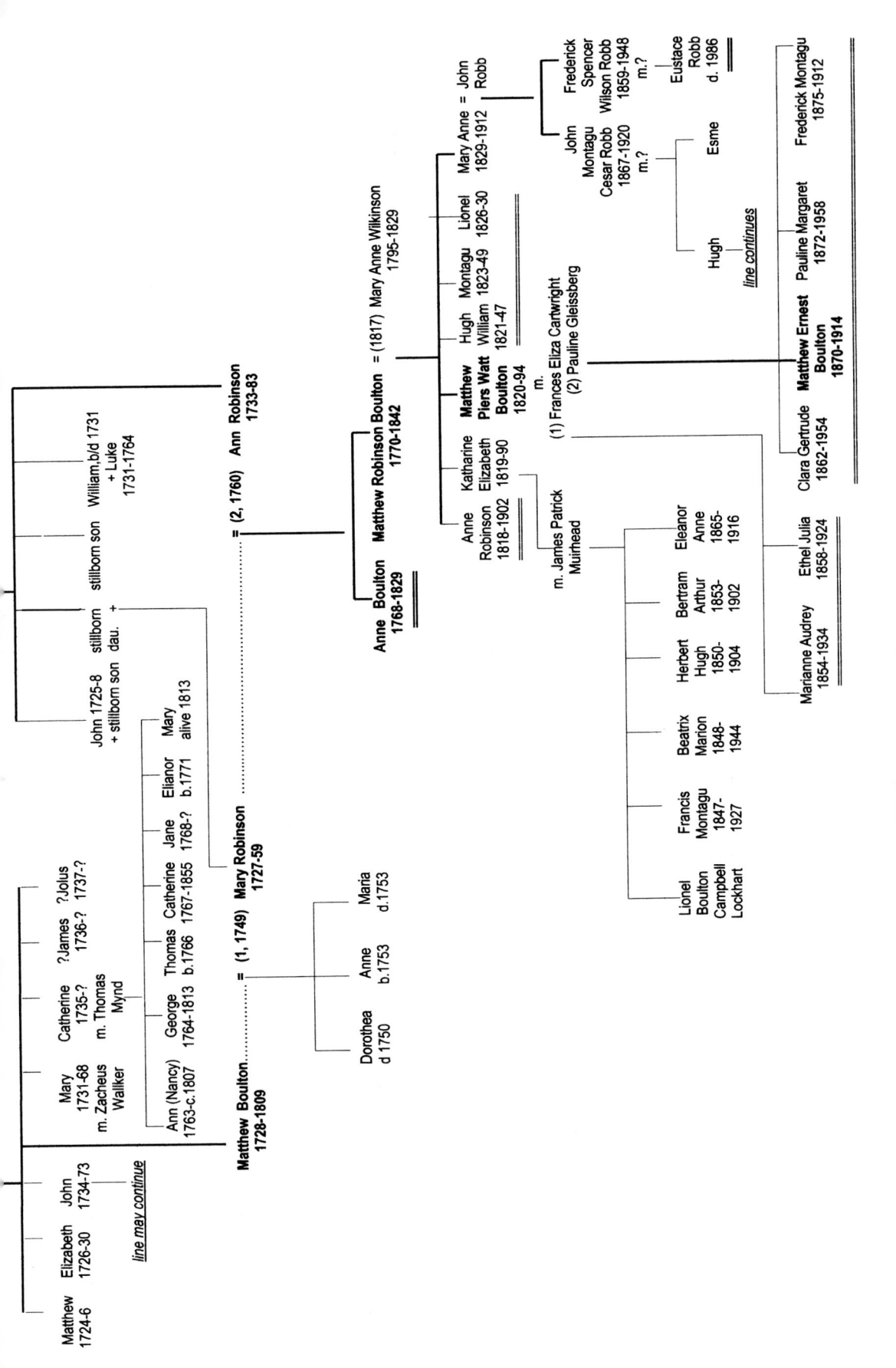

kinds of gloves, black hatbands, black gauze handkerchiefs and black scarves were supplied for the funeral which, with fees for opening the vault at Whittington, and provision of hearse and horses, accounted for funeral costs of over £47 in a larger bill from John Barker.[70]

Scarcely had Matthew Boulton buried his wife when his father, Matthew Boulton senior, also died, and was buried at St Chad's, Stowe, Lichfield, on 23 September 1759.[71] Again John Barker supplied the funeral, a much smaller affair totalling £21 0s. 1d.[72] Why Boulton senior was buried at Lichfield is unclear. At the time of his death (cause unknown), he seems to have been living in retirement at Sarehole, Birmingham; either he or his son was the tenant of Sarehole Mill for a time (the receipts for the half-yearly rent are among early bills), but the family was still strongly rooted in Lichfield. Thus in the space of a few months Matthew Boulton lost his 32-year-old wife and his 59-year-old father, and possibly also – though this is by no means certain – his grandfather, 89-year-old John Bolton. Less than a year after Mary's death, Boulton married her sister, Ann Robinson.

Notes

Abbreviations and Sources

Most of the documents quoted from are in the Archives of Soho in Birmingham City Archives. These come in three groups under the general headings MS 3782 (Matthew Boulton Papers), MS 3219 (James Watt Papers), and MS 3147 (Boulton & Watt Papers). Any references beginning with these numbers are therefore to documents in Birmingham City Archives. Where other primary sources are quoted I have included an indication of where the documents are to be found.

The following abbreviations have been used for frequently-used names: MB = Matthew Boulton; Mrs AB = Mrs Ann Boulton; Miss AB = Miss Anne Boulton; MRB = Matthew Robinson Boulton; JW = James Watt; JWj = James Watt junior.

Chapter 1 – Friday's child

1   MS 3782/13/38/7, Miss Anne Boulton-Matthew Boulton, 9 Sep. 1792.
2   Boswell, James, *The Life of Samuel Johnson, LL.D.* , Vol.I (London, 1793), footnote to p.457: 'Mrs Burney informs me that she heard Dr Johnson say, "An English Merchant is a new species of Gentleman." He, perhaps, had in his mind the following ingenious passage in "The Conscious Lovers" [Sir Richard Steele, 1772], Act iv. Scene ii. where Mr Sealand thus addresses Sir John Bevil, "Give me leave to say, that we merchants are a species of gentry that have grown into the world this last century, and are as honourable, and almost as useful, as you landed folks that have always thought yourselves so much above us …"'.
3   MS 3782/Bills 1760-68, Mrs Mary Ironmonger, various chaise hire bills, 1760.
4   MS 3782/Corresp. of Mrs Ann Boulton/1, MB-Ann Robinson, Oct. 1759.
5   MS 3782/Corresp. of Mrs Ann Boulton/6, MB-Ann Robinson, Dec. 1759.
6   MS 3782/Corresp. of Mrs Ann Boulton/11, MB-Ann Robinson, Mar. 1760.
7   MS 3782/Mrs Ann Boulton/9, MB-Ann Robinson, 1759.
8   MS 3782/Mrs Ann Boulton/5, MB-Ann Robinson, Dec. 1759.
9   MS 3782/12/55, MB-Dorothy Robinson, n.d.].
10 MS 3782/Bills 1760-1768, W.Bailye, 3 Oct. 1759-22 May 1760.
11 Parish Register of St Giles, Whittington; Stafford Record Office, microfiche F4834/1/3.
12 MS 3782/12/103, receipt dated 23 Jun. 1760.
13 MS 3782/Miscellaneous Bills 1760-1768.
14 Will of Dorothy Robinson, 1755. Public Record Office Prob.11/929.
15 MS 3782/12/103, two receipts for payments from Luke Robinson via William Wyatt, one dated 7 Apr. 1759 for £40, 'being half a years Interest of three thousand pounds', and one dated 7 Apr. 1760 for £80, 'being one years Interest of three thousand pounds', both signed by Ann Robinson.
16 Parish Register, St Mary's, Rotherhithe.
17 Old Testament, Leviticus chap.20, v.21: 'If a man shall take his brother's wife, it is an unclean thing.' The Church regarded this as applying equally to marriage between a man and his deceased wife's sister because marriage to a sister-in-law (regarded as the man's actual sister by virtue of the first marriage) was deemed consanguineous.
18 Fry, John, *The case of marriage between near kindred particularly considered with respect to the doctrine of scripture, the law of nature and the laws of England* (1756), published by J. Whiston and B. White, 2s. Boulton obtained a 50 per cent discount on the published price for his 'bulk order'. Bill, MS 3782/Miscellaneous Bills 1752-1760, J. Whiston & B. White, 22 April 1760.

19   MS 3782/Letterbook 1780-81/62, MB-Richard Lovell Edgeworth, 20 Nov. 1780.

20   MS 3782/Bills 1760-68, Henry Paulin-Mrs AB, 26 Jun. 1760.

21   'Love ribbon' was a type of stiff gauze ribbon in which the weft was made from 'singles' – twisted single filaments of hard-dyed raw silk (that is, silk which has not had the natural gum sericin removed from it), rather than from 'doubles' which were constructed of two or more threads twisted together. My thanks to Huw Jones of the Herbert Art Gallery and Museum, Coventry, for this explanation.

22   MS 3782/Miscellaneous Bills 1760-68, Elizabeth & Hannah Concher, 17 Jul. 1760.

23   MS 3782/Miscellaneous Bills 1760-68, Thomas Welch & Son-MB, 26 Jul. 1760.

24   MS 3782/1/8, Thomas Hurst-MB, June 1760.

25   MS 3782/1/9, Thomas Hurst-MB, 3 Jul. 1760.

26   Parish Register, St Giles, Whittington; Stafford Record Office, microfiche F4834/1/3; Luke Robinson buried 24 Sep. 1764.

27   MS 3782/Matthew Boulton/Letterbook 1780-83, MB-William Matthews, 31 Aug. 1781.

28   MS 3782/Mrs Ann Boulton/14, MB-Mrs AB, 1763.

29   MS 3782/Miscellaneous Bills, George Donisthorpe 1763 (receipted 9 Jan. 1773).

30   MS3782/House/Miscellaneous Bills 1760-68, Elizabeth Sabet's account 1763-68.

31   MS 3782/Mrs Ann Boulton/105, Mary Darwin-Mrs AB, 10 Oct. 1765.

32   MS 3782/12/60, John Fothergill-MB, 14 Dec. 1765.

33   MS 3782/Mrs Ann Boulton/17, MB-Mrs AB, 10 Feb. 1764.

34   MS 3782/Mrs Ann Boulton/16, Catherine Boulton-MB, 13 Feb. 1764. Catherine's use of the word 'cousin' as a general term denoting a family member would have been quite antiquated at this time.

35   MS 3782/Mrs Ann Boulton/19, MB-Mrs AB, 15 Feb. 1764.

36   MS 3782/Mrs Ann Boulton/18, MB-Mrs AB, 12 Feb. 1764. The *George Inn* was in Aldersgate Street.

37   MS 3782/Mrs Ann Boulton/16, MB-Mrs AB, 9 Feb. 1764.

38   MS 3782/Miscellaneous Bills, Ann Bentley for Mrs Jefferys, 12 Aug. 1760.

39   MS 3782/12/103/68, 1764.

40   *Ibid.*

41   *Ibid.*

42   *Ibid.*

43   Charles Simpson (1732-1796) in *Johnsonian Gleanings*, iv.161.

44   Will of Luke Robinson, junior, 1764. Public Record Office, Prob. 11/929. Dorothy Robinson's and Luke Robinson junior's wills were both proved at the same time in 1767, some years after both deaths.

45   MS 3782/12/60, John Fothergill-MB (Lichfield), 24 Sep. 1764.

46   MS 3782/1/37, Boulton & Fothergill letterbook, MB-J.L. Baumgartner, 9 Mar. 1765. Baumgartner seems to have lived in Birmingham earlier so Boulton had probably known him for some years; the baptism of Baumgartner's daughter Susannah is recorded at St Philip's Church on 10 Sep. 1756.

47   MS 3782/1/48, J.L. Cantrel-MB, 18 Mar. 1765.

48   MS 3782/13/53/26, Benjamin Franklin-MB, 22 May 1765.

49   Transcript in the Westwood Papers of a letter said to be from 'Letter Copy Book 1765', no longer to be found. Birmingham City Archives.

50   MS 3782/12/60/20, John Fothergill-MB, 3 Nov. 1765.

51   MS 3782/12/72/1, John Scale-MB, 11 Nov. 1765.

52   MS 3782/1/37, J.Fothergill-J.Motteux, 18 Nov. 1765.

53   MS 3782/Mrs Ann Boulton/24, MB-Mrs AB, 18 Nov. 1765.

54   MS 3782/Mrs Ann Boulton/25, MB-Mrs AB, 20 Nov. 1765.

55   MS 3782/Mrs Ann Boulton/26, MB-Mrs AB, dated 24 Nov. 1765 (actually 25 Nov.).

56   MS 3782/Mrs Ann Boulton/28, MB-Mrs AB, 1 Dec.1765.

57   MS 3782/Mrs Ann Boulton/29, MB-Mrs AB, 8 Dec. 1765.

58   MS 3782/MB/Correspondence 1758-73/64, John Baskerville-MB, 9 Dec. 1765.

59   MS 3782/12/60/43, John Fothergill-Mrs A.B., 16 Dec. 1765.

60   MS 3782/12/60/47, John Fothergill-MB, 22 Dec. 1765.

61   MS 3782/12/108/3, Notebook 1765.

62   MS 3782/Mrs Ann Boulton/22, MB-Mrs AB, 7 Nov. 1765.

63   MS 3782/Mrs Ann Boulton/30, MB-Mrs AB, 14 Oct. 1766.

64   pers.comm. Rosemary Harden, Museum of Costume, Bath, to Shena Mason, 25 Sep. 2004.

65   [MBP Box 430, Hugh Whishaw's bill, 20 Jun. 1767-5 Mar. 1768].

66   MS 3782/12/60/265.

67   Birmingham rate books, cited in Robinson, Eric: 'Matthew Boulton's Birthplace and his Home

at Snow Hill: A Problem in Detection', in *Transactions of Birmingham Archaeological Society*, Vol.75 (1957).
68 MS 3782/12/60/265.
69 *Ibid.*
70 MS 3782/12/71/8, John Motteux-MB, 2 Oct. 1766.
71 MS 3782/12/60/265.
72 MS 3219/4/1, MB-JW, 7 Feb. 1769.
73 MS 3782/Matthew Boulton/Letterbooks/Letterbook 1766-68/10, MB-Johann Zumpe, Jul. 1767.
74 Members of the Lunar Society over the years included Dr Erasmus Darwin of Lichfield (grandfather of Charles Darwin); Dr William Small; Josiah Wedgwood; John Whitehurst of Derby (a clock and scientific instrument maker and early geologist); Dr William Withering, a botanist, chief physician at Birmingham's General Hospital, who put his botany at the service of medicine, developing the use of digitalis from foxgloves as a treatment for dropsy and heart complaints; Thomas Day and Richard Lovell Edgeworth, both idealists and educationalists; Samuel Galton, the Quaker gunmaker, who was Charles Darwin's other grandfather; James Keir, the chemist and metallurgist; Dr Joseph Priestley, a Yorkshire weaver's son and multi-linguist whose astonishingly wide-ranging mind had already led to him writing books on light, optics, electricity, chemistry, and gases and airs; as well as another botanical physician, Dr Jonathan Stokes, and another chemist, Rev. Robert Augustus Johnson. From 1775 when he joined Boulton as a business partner, James Watt, too, would become a key member of the group.
75 MS 3782/MB/Letterbook 1766-68, MB-Francis Garbett, Jan. 1768.
76 MS 3782/MB/Letterbook 1766-68, MB-John Motteux, 15 Jan. 1768.
77 MS 3782/MB/Letterbook 1766-68, MB-Richard Levett, 6 Feb. 1768.
78 MS 3782/MB/Letterbook 1766-68, MB-Ebbinghaus, 6 Feb. 1768.
79 MS 3782/MB/Letterbook 1766-68, MB-(——), 2 Mar. 1768.

Chapter 2 – Doctors
1 MS 3782/House/Miscellaneous Bills, Mary Greaves' bill, receipted 6 Oct. 1769.
2 MS 3782/6/6/51 Household Bills 1768-80, Henry Bunney to MB, 18 Jul. 1768.
3 MS 3782/13/53/141, Erasmus Darwin, notes on baby care, n.d.
4 MS 3782/13/53, Erasmus Darwin-MB, 19 Jun. 1769.
5 *Ibid.*
6 Boswell, James, *London Journal*, p.133.
7 MS 3782/Mrs Ann Boulton/37, MB-Mrs AB, 3 Mar. 1770.
8 MS 3782/Bills 1769, John Platt-MB 2 Mar. 1769, receipt for £81 1s. 6d. for '14 Tons ¾ of a Hund. of Blue John'
9 *See* note 7 above.
10 MS 3782/Mrs Ann Boulton/40, MB-Mrs AB, ?9 Apr. 1771.
11 *Ibid.*
12 MS 3782/Bills 1770, R. Williams-MB, 18 Apr. 1770.
13 MS 3782/13/53/45, Elizabeth Montagu-MB, 31 Oct. 1771.
14 MS 3782/Mrs Ann Boulton/64, MB-Mrs AB, 16 Aug. 1777.
15 MS 3782/12/60/50, John Fothergill-MB, 3 Apr. 1771.
16 MS 3782/MB/Correspondence 1758-73/195, John Hunter-William Small, 5 Apr. 1771.
17 MS 3782/12/81/4, John Whitehurst-MB, 6 Jun. 1771.
18 Alistair Thompson F.R.C.S., consultant orthopaedic surgeon, Birmingham Royal Orthopaedic Hospital, to Shena Mason, pers. comm. 17 May 2002.
19 MS 3782/MB/General correspondence 1781/81, John Hunter-MB, 11 Jun. 1781.
20 A sidereal clock measures the time between one appearance of a star on the observer's meridian and the next; this form of time-measurement is more accurate than the solar mean time which is used for everyday time-keeping. Sidereal time is used where absolute accuracy is vital, for instance in space exploration.
21 MS 3782/Mrs Ann Boulton/43, MB-Mrs AB 11 Apr. 1772. The pet-name for Anne, which Boulton uses more than once, may derive from a popular musical play, *The Maid of the Mill*, by Isaac Bickerstaffe, first produced in 1765 and based on the storyline of Richardson's *Pamela*.
22 MS 3782/Mrs Ann Boulton/44, MB-Mrs AB, 18 Apr. 1772.
23 MS 3782/Bills 1769, Roger Eykyn-MB, 6 Apr. 1769.
24 MS 3782/Bills 1769, various including Christopher Greatrex, Mr Hector, and Harriman of London.
25 MS 3782/Bills 1770.
26 MS 3782/Mrs Ann Boulton/46, MB-Mrs AB, 23 Jan. 1773.
27 I am indebted to Dr Marcel Roethlisberger of the University of Geneva for information on Jean Etienne Liotard and his work, pers.comm. 14 Jun. 2003.

28 Probably a 'Teresa', or light gauze scarf worn on the head, over the indoor cap. (Thanks to the Museum of Costume, Bath, for this definition.)
29 MS 3782/Mrs Ann Boulton/49, MB-Mrs AB, 4 Feb. 1773.
30 MS 3782/12/MB Correspondence 1758-73/174, J.Duval-MB, 19 Nov. 1770.
31 MS3782/12/72/10, John Scale-Mrs Ann Boulton, 25 Mar. 1773.
32 MS 3782/Mrs Ann Boulton/47 MB-Mrs AB, 2 Feb. 1773.
33 MS 3782/Mrs Ann Boulton/49, MB-Mrs AB, 4 Feb. 1773.
34 MS 3782/Mrs Ann Boulton/48, MB-Mrs AB, n.d.
35 MS 3782/Mrs Ann Boulton/61, MB-Mrs AB, 29 Apr. 1777.
36 MS 3782/Mrs Ann Boulton/64, MB-Mrs AB, 16 Aug. 1777.
37 MS 3782/Mrs Ann Boulton/63, MB-Mrs AB, 12 Aug. 1777.

Chapter 3 – Lessons

1 MS 3782/1/24/193, Robert Edwards' bill for Miss Anne Boulton, April 1775, £1 13s. 6d.
2 MB-Lord Dartmouth, 22 Mar. 1777, Dartmouth MSS, Historical Manuscripts Commission, Vol II.
3 MS 3782/12/108/5, Notebook 6, 1771.
4 MS 3782/12/108/7 Notebook 1772.
5 [MBP 290/20, n.d.] List of books with drawing of bookcase. A bookcase similar to this, with a Boulton provenance, appeared in a Roberson of London sale catalogue in the 1920s.
6 MS 3782/Bills, 1775.
7 Gregory, Dr John, *A Father's Legacy to his Daughters* (1774).
8 Rousseau, Jean-Jacques, *Emile*, Book V, 'Sophie'.
9 Rousseau, Jean-Jacques, *Emile*, Book V, 'Sophie': 'Watch a little girl spend a day with her doll, continually changing its clothes, dressing and undressing it, trying new combinations of trimmings either well or poorly matched. Her fingers are clumsy, her taste is crude, but already a tendency is shown in this endless occupation. Time passes without her knowing it, hours go by, even meals are forgotten. She is more eager for adornment than for food. "But she is dressing her doll, not herself," you will say. Of course; she sees her doll, she cannot see herself; she cannot do anything for herself, she has neither the training, nor the talent, nor the strength. So far she herself is nothing, she is engrossed in her doll and all her coquetry is devoted to it. This will not always be so; in due time she will be her own doll.'
10 Swift, Jonathan, 'On the Education of Ladies', in *The Prose Works of Jonathan Swift*, ed. H.Davis, 1939-74.
11 Photocopies of the 300-page MS of James Keir's *Dialogues on Chemistry between a Father and His Daughter* (1801) are in the Westwood Papers, Birmingham City Archives.
12 *See* Reilly, Robin, *Josiah Wedgwood* (London, 1992), pp.171-2.
13 From an unidentified letter by Matthew Boulton, cited by Phillada Ballard in *Soho House Gardens*, research report for Birmingham Museums & Art Gallery, 1992.
14 MS 3782/12/81/11, John Whitehurst-MB, 30 Oct. 1775.
15 MS 3782/General Correspondence 1774-79/166, Henry Pickering-MB, 24 Mar. 1777.
16 Hutton-Beale, Catherine, *Reminiscences of a Gentlewoman of the Last Century* (Birmingham, 1891).
17 MS 3782/MB/General Correspondence 1774-9/146, Mrs Gandry-MB, n.d., 1777.
18 *Ibid.*
19 MS 3147/1_11B&W/3/MB 1777/3/1/11, MB-JW, 22 May 1777.
20 MS 3782/MB/General Correspondence 1774-9/112, Mrs Terry-MB, 24 Jun. 1777.
21 MS 3782/MB/General Correspondence 1774-9/142, Mrs Terry-MB, 26 Dec. 1777.
22 MS 3782/House/Miscellaneous Bills 1771-84, Mrs Terry's account, 31 Jul. 1778.
23 MS 3782/12/60/130, John Fothergill-MB, 2 Feb. 1778.
24 MS 3782/6/6/1220, D. Williams, 3 Oct. 1774. Bill for 6 months' instruction in writing, copy book, pens and ink, 19s.
25 MS 3782/12/108/13, Notebook 14, 1778.
26 MS 3782/Mrs Ann Boulton/106, Ann Watt-Mrs AB, 1 Sep. 1777.
27 MS 3782/Bills 1779, J. Davenport & Farrant, Tavistock St, London, 24 Dec. 1778.
28 MS 3147/1_11B&W/3Corresp./MB 1779/3/3/2, MB-JW, 20 Jan. 1779.
29 MS 3782/Mrs Ann Boulton/67, MB-Mrs AB, 5 Mar. 1779.
30 MS 3782/Mrs Ann Boulton/68, MB-Mrs AB, 23 Apr. 1779.
31 MS 3782/17, Notebook 'Holland',1779.
32 *Ibid.*
33 MS 3782/Mrs Ann Boulton/69, MB-Mrs AB, 8 May 1779.
34 MS 3782/Mrs Ann Boulton/70, MB-Mrs AB, 10 May 1779.
35 MS 3782/Mrs Ann Boulton/71, MB-Mrs AB, 13 May 1779.
36 Ms 3782/Bills 1771-1784, Mrs Terry, account to MB, 1 May 1779.

37 MS 3782/Mrs Ann Boulton/72, MB-Mrs AB, 18 May 1779.
38 MS 3782/Mrs Ann Boulton/75, MB-Mrs AB, 2 Jul. 1779.
39 MS 3782/12/60/178, Miss Fothergill-MB, 18 Jul. 1779.
40 MS 3782/Mrs Ann Boulton/77, MB-Mrs AB, 29 Jul. 1779.
41 *Ibid.*
42 MS 3782/Mrs Ann Boulton/78, MB-Mrs AB, 14 Aug. 1779.
43 MS 3782/12/93/6, Elizabeth Montagu-MB, 10 Sep. 1779.
44 MS 3782/General Correspondence/295, Mrs Terry-MB, 25 Oct. 1779.
45 MS 3219/4/4/6, Ann Watt-JW, 13 Nov. 1779.
46 MS 3219/4/4/8, Ann Watt-JW, 28 Nov. 1779.

Chapter 4 – 'Holding the Ballance of Love even'.

1   MS 3219/4/4/1, Ann Watt-JW, 21 Sep. 1779.
2   MS 3219/4/4/2, Ann Watt-JW, 4 Oct. 1779.
3   MS3219/4/4/6, Ann Watt-JW, 13 Nov. 1779.
4   MS 3219/4/4/5, Ann Watt-JW, 1 Nov. 1779.
5   MS 3219/4/4/7, Ann Watt-JW, 21 Nov. 1779.
6   MS 3219/4/4/9, Ann Watt-JW, 5 Dec. 1779.
7   MS 3782/12/93/7, Elizabeth Montagu-MB, 22 Nov. 1779.
8   MS 3782/12/65/41, J.Keir-MB, 20 Nov. 1779.
9   MS 3782/Mrs Ann Boulton/82, MB-Mrs AB, 13 Jan. 1780.
10 MS 3782/General Correspondence 1774-79/303, H. Pickering-MB, 5 Dec. 1779.
11 *Ibid.*
12 *Ibid.*
13 MS 3782/MB/Letterbook 1780-83/73, MB-George Mynd, 15 Aug. 1781.
14 MS 3782/Bills of John Scale 1768-91/610, Winson Green School, Christmas 1782.
15 *Aris's Gazette*, 20 Dec. 1779.
16 MS 3782/12/65/44, J.Keir-MB, 11 Dec. 1779.
17 MS 3782/12/65/50, J. Keir-MB & J.Watt, 22 Nov. 1779.
18 MS 3782/Mrs Ann Boulton/81, MB-Mrs AB, 25 Dec. 1779.
19 Playbill for the Theatre in New Street, 24 May 1779.
20 MS 3782/Mrs Ann Boulton/82, MB-Mrs AB, 13 Jan. 1780.
21 MS 3782/Correspondence 1780/4, Mrs Wilkes-MB, 18 Feb. 1780.
22 MS 3782/12/93/8, Elizabeth Montagu-MB, 12 Apr.1780.
23 MS 3782/Bills 1780, Shelley & King, 1 Jun. 1780.
24 MS 3782/Bills 1780, Thomas Hoyland, 23 May-1 Jun. 1780.
25 MS 3782/Diary 1782.
26 MS 3782/Correspondence 1780/36, Mr Stretch-MB, 22 May 1780.
27 MS 3782/Mrs Ann Boulton/86, MB-Mrs AB, 5 Jul. 1780.
28 MS 3782/Mrs Ann Boulton/87, MB-Mrs AB, 6 Jul. 1780.
29 MS 3782/Mrs Ann Boulton/88, MB-Mrs AB, 7 Jul. 1780.
30 MS 3782/12/93/16, Mrs Wilkes-MB, 10 Jul. 1780.
31 Ms 3782/12/93/16, Elizabeth Montagu-MB, 10 Aug. 1780.
32 MS 3782/Letterbook 1780-81, MB-Thomas Day, 16 Oct. 1780.
33 MS 3782/12/72/33, John Scale-MB, 28-29 Aug. 1780.
34 MS 3782/Mrs Ann Boulton/90, MB-Mrs AB, 14 Sep. 1780.
35 MS 3782/Mrs Ann Boulton/80, MB-Mrs AB, 3 Oct. 1780.
36 MS 3782/12/72/34, John Scale-MB, 21 Sep. 1780.
37 MS 3782/Mrs Ann Boulton/80, MB-Mrs AB, 3 Oct. 1780.
38 MS 3782/12/72/20, John Scale-MB, 8 Feb. 1778.
39 MS 3782/Mrs Ann Boulton/92, MB-MrsAB, 9 Nov. 1780.
40 MS 3782/Letterbook 1780-81, MB-Mrs Ann Watt, 4 Oct. 1780.
41 MS 3782/Letterbook 1780-81, MB-JW, 13 Nov. 1780.
42 MS 3782/6/14/1-2, inventories of Cosgarne, 1781 and 1782.
43 MS 3782/Letterbook 1780-83, MB-JW, 11 Dec. 1780.
44 MS 3782/Letterbook 1780/70, MB-Mrs Wilkes, 5 Dec. 1780.
45 MS 3782/ Letterbook 1780/71, MB-Mr Stretch, 5 Dec. 1780.
46 MS 3782/MB/House/Miscellaneous Bills 1771-84, Mrs Wilkes-MB, letter and bill, Dec. 1780.
47 Hemlow, Joyce, *The History of Fanny Burney* (1958), p.145.
48 *See note 46.*
49 MS 3782/Letterbook 1780-81/91, MB-Peter Capper, 17 Jan. 1781. Probably Peter Capper 'formerly of Birmingham' who died in Bath in May 1786 aged 73 (monument inscription, Bath Abbey).

50 MS 3782/Mrs Ann Boulton/97, MB-Mrs AB, 19 Apr. 1781.
51 MS 3782/Mrs Ann Boulton/98, MB-MrsAB, 24 Apr. 1781
52 MS 3782/Mrs Ann Boulton/95, MB-Mrs AB, 4 Apr. 1781. 'Lutestrings', or 'lustrings' were plain silks with a shiny finish, worn during the summer.
53 MS 3782/Mrs Ann Boulton/99, MB-Mrs AB, 3 May 1781.
54 MS 3782/Bills 1781, Barton & Nelthorpe, 1 May 1781.
55 MS 3782/Mrs Ann Boulton/99, MB-Mrs AB, 3 May 1781.
56 MS 3782/13/38/1, Miss AB-MB, 18 May 1781.
57 MS 3782/Correspondence 1781/83, Mrs Wilkes-MB, 11 Jun. 1781.
58 MS 3782/12/72/82, Ann Watt-MB, 28 Jun. 1781.
59 MS 3782/Correspondence 1782/20, Mr Stretch-MB, 14 Mar. 1782.
60 MS 3782/Correspondence 1782/20, Mr Stretch's account, 4 Jan. 1782.
61 MS 3782/Correspondence 1782/BP 255/257, Mr Stretch-MB, 19 Aug. 1782.
62 MS 3782/Bills 1771-84, Mr Stretch's account, Dec.1783.
63 MS 3782/Letterbook 1780-3, MB-William Matthews, 21 Jun. 1782.
64 MS 3782/Diary 1782.
65 MS 3782/12/93/16, Elizabeth Montagu-MB, 10 Aug. 1780.
66 MS 3782/12/93/22, Elizabeth Montagu-MB, 28 Sep. 1780.
67 Quoted in Scott, Walter S.: *The Bluestocking Ladies* (London, 1947).
68 MS 3782/13/38/3, Miss AB-MB, 5 Nov. 1782.
69 MS 3782/12/61/47, S.Garbett-MB, 5 Dec. 1782.
70 MS 3782/12/60/204, Miss E.V. Fothergill-MB, 12 Nov. 1782.
71 MS 3782/12/107/ Diary, 1782.
72 MS 3782/House/Bills 1771-84, Mrs Moore-MB, 14 Dec. 1782.
73 Susan Constable, Shoe Heritage Officer, Northampton Museums and Art Gallery, to Shena Mason, pers.comm. 17 May 2005.
74 Ballard, Phillada *Soho House Gardens* (1992).
75 MS 3782/12/60/208, Mary Fothergill-MB, 19 May 1783.
76 MS 3782/Bills 1783, Brunton & Forbes, 9 Apr. 1783.

Chapter 5 – 'An amiable Female character'

1   MS 3782/12/61/50, Samuel Garbett-Mrs Barker, 13 Jul. 1783.
2   *Ibid.*
3   MS 3219/4/123/Letterbook 1, JW-Joseph Fry, 22 Jul. 1783.
4   MS 3782/12/60/209, Elizabeth Fothergill-MB, 18 Jul. 1783.
5   MS 3782/ Letterbook 1780-83/269, MB-Elizabeth Fothergill, 2 Aug. 1783.
6   Parish Register, St Giles Church, Whittington, Lichfield Record Office.
7   MS 3219/4/123, Letterbook 1, JW-Joseph Fry, 16 Sep. 1783.
8   MS 3782/12/67/87, Charlotte Matthews-MB, 20 Aug. 1783.
9   MS 3782/12/108/38, Notebook 1783 'Ireland'. The verse, in Italian, French, Latin and English, reads: 'In this house you will find/everything that one could wish/wine, bread, fish, meat/coaches, horses, chaises, harness.'
10 MS 3782/12/57/1, MRB-MB, 3 Sep. 1783.
11 MS 3782/12/57/2, MRB-MB, 6 Oct. 1783.
12 MS 3147/3/7/25, MB-JW, 19 Dec. 1783.
13 MS 3782/Bills 1771-84, Mrs Moore-MB, 25 Dec. 1783.
14 MS 3782/Bills 1771-84, Richard Conquest-MB, 6 Jan. 1784.
15 MS 3782/Bills 1771-84, Davenport & Farrant, 15 Jan. 1784.
16 MS 3147/3/8/8, MB-JW, 28 Jun. 1784.
17 MS 3782/14/76/2, MB-Miss AB, 19 Jun. 1784.
18 MS 3782/14/76/5, MB-Miss AB, 17 Jul. 1784.
19 MS 3782/12/61, S.Garbett-MB 29 Jun. 1784.
20 MS 3782/14/76/2, MB-Miss AB, 19 Jun. 1784.
21 MS 3782/MB/General Correspondence 1784/51, MB-William Withering, 5 Jul. 1784.
22 MS 3782/14/76/ 3, MB-Miss AB, 23 Jun. 1784.
23 MS 3782/MB/General Correspondence 1784/54, William Withering-MB, 20 Jul. 1784.
24 MS 3782/MB/General Correspondence 1784/43, William Withering-MB, 25 Jun. 1784.
25 MS 3782/MB/General Correspondence 1784/51, MB-William Withering, 5 Jul. 1784.
26 MS 3782/14/76/ 4, MB-Miss AB, 5 Jul. 1874.
27 MS 3782/14/76/5, MB-Miss AB, 17 Jul. 1784.
28 Mary Knowles-Dr William Withering, 30 Apr. 1783. Royal Society of Medicine MS534/63.
29 *Ibid.*

30 Royal Society of Medicine, MS534/68/69, Lady Catherine Wright-Dr William Withering, 20 Jan. 1785.

31 Royal Society of Medicine, MS534/79/80/81, Lady Catherine Wright-Dr William Withering, 11 Aug.1785.

32 Royal Society of Medicine, MS534/88/89/90, Lady Catherine Wright-Dr William Withering, 5 Dec. 1787.

33 The copying press was originally developed by Watt to cut down on the amount of writing required at the Soho Manufactory. The machines were subsequently marketed widely. Watt developed a slow-drying ink with which letters were written on normal paper. The letter was then overlaid with a sheet of special absorbent translucent tissue paper and the two were pressed or rolled together, producing a mirror-image 'blotting' of the original on the tissue. By turning the tissue over, the text could be read clearly from the other side. Many such copy press documents survive in the Soho Archives; on some the ink has faded, but many are still legible.

34 MS 3219/4/5/84, Ann Watt-JW, 26 Sep. 1784.

35 MS 3219/4/123/10, JW-Dr James Lind, 26 Dec. 1784.

36 MS 3782/12/57/5, MRB-MB, 15 Feb. 1785. John Rennie was a civil engineer who worked on several Boulton & Watt projects including the Albion Mill.

37 MS 3782/14/76/10, MB-Miss AB, 3 Mar. 1786.

38 MS 3782/12/57/6, MRB-MB, 25 Mar.1785.

39 MS 3219/6/2/136, MRB-JWj, 7 May 1785.

40 MS 3219/4/5/14, Ann Watt-JW, 21 Feb. 1785.

41 MS 3219/4/123/171, James Watt Private Letterbook 1782-89, JW-William Matthews, 13 Mar. 1785.

42 MS 3219/4/123/, James Watt Private Letterbook 1782-89, loose fragment of a letter, JW-unidentified, but presumably MB, n.d.

43 MS 3219/4/87/21, W.Matthews-JW, 28 Mar. 1785.

44 Bur. 23 May 1785 (Parish Register of St Philip's, Birmingham); *Aris's Gazette*, 23 May 1785.

45 MS 3782/12/57/120, MB-Joseph Banks, 5 Sep. 1804.

46 MS 3782/14/76/6, MB-Miss AB, 14 Jun. 1785.

47 Sutcliffe Smith, J., *The Story of Music in Birmingham* (1945).

48 John Pixell, *A Collection of Songs, with their recitatives & Symphonies, for the german flute, violins etc.*, n.d., list of subscribers' names; John Pixell: *Odes* (1775), list of subscribers' names. Both in Birmingham University Special Collections.

49 Lines, Denise, *Capel Bond and his Six Concertos in Seven Parts*, unpublished BA Dissertation, Colchester Institute, 1986. Also 'A forgotten Gloucester composer', in *Gloucester Citizen*, unattributed article, 2 Aug. 1955. Music festivals in aid of the General Hospital were organised from 1759 onwards, with liberal helpings of Handel and also works by local composers including the Birmingham postmaster-cum-Cathedral organist, Barnabas Gunn, Jeremiah Clarke, and the Coventry Cathedral choirmaster, Capel Bond, who directed the 1768 festival and a number of other early performances. The Birmingham music festivals eventually became established in a regular pattern as the Birmingham Triennial Music Festival, which continued into the 20th century and for which new works were regularly commissioned from leading composers, including Mendelssohn's *Elijah* (1846) and Elgar's *Dream of Gerontius* (1900).

50 Dr Gregory, John *A Father's Legacy to his Daughters* (1774).

51 Swain, Margaret, *Embroidered Georgian Pictures* (1994).

52 MS 3782/14/76/7, MB-Miss AB, 6 Aug. 1785.

53 *Ibid.*

54 MS 3782/14/76/8, MB-Miss AB, 17 Aug. 1785.

55 *Ibid.*

56 *Ibid.*

57 *Ibid.*

58 *Ibid.*

59 MS 3782/MB/General Correspondence 1785/68, Rev. Parlby-MB, 1 Sep. 1785.

60 MS 3782/12/57/9, MRB-MB, 18 Oct. 1785.

61 *Ibid.*

62 *See* note 59.

63 MS 3782/14/76/9, MB-Miss AB, 5 Oct. 1785.

64 MS 3219/4/5/30, Mrs A.Watt-JW, 24 Sep. 1785.

65 *Ibid.*

66 MS 3782/MB/General Correspondence 1785/91, Miss M. Linwood-MB, 11 Nov. 1785.

67 MS 3782/MB/General Correspondence 1786/23, Rev. Parlby-MB, 14 Feb. 1786.

68 MS 3782/12/57/10, MRB-MB, 16 Mar. 1786.

69 MS 3782/12/57/11, MRB-MB, 1 May 1786.
70 MS 3782/Miscellaneous Household Bills 1785-88, A. Kirkman-MB, 21 Jun. 1786.
71 MS 3782/13/142/1, J. Harris-Miss AB, 30 Jan. 1787.
72 MS 3782/14/83/17, Miss Boulton's Italian exercise book, n.d. ('My books are in my room' and 'The Italian language is sweeter and more charming than English, but the English language is more energetic and stately than Italian').
73 MS 3782/14/76/11, MB-Miss AB, 9 Sep. 1786.

Chapter 6 – Fly, fly from Calypso!

1   MS 3782/14/76/12, MB-Miss AB, 10 Nov. 1786.
2   MS 3782/14/76/15, MB-Miss AB, 20 Dec. 1786.
3   MS 3782/14/76/13, MB-Miss AB, 26 Nov. 1786. 'Bags' = bag-wigs.
4   MS 3782/14/76/16, MB-Miss AB, 31 Dec. 1786.
5   MS 3782/14/76/15, MB-Miss AB, 20 Dec. 1786.
6   MS 3782/13/36/1, MB-MRB, 24 Dec. 1786.
7   MS 3782/13/36/2, MB-MRB, 4 Jan. 1787.
8   MS 3782/13/38/4, Miss AB-MRB, 21 Apr. 1787.
9   *Ibid.*
10 MS 3782/13/38/6, Miss AB-MB, 16 Apr. 1792.
11 MS 3782/14/76/16, MB-Miss AB, 31 Dec. 1786.
12 MS 3782/13/38/4, Miss AB-MRB, 21 Apr. 1787.
13 MS 3782/13/36/3, MB-MRB, 23 Jan. 1837.
14 MS 3782/13/36/4, MB-MRB, 4 Mar. 1787.
15 MS 3782/12/57/15, MRB-MB, 20 Mar. 1787.
16 MS 3782/12/57/15, MRB-MB, 20 Mar. 1787.
17 MS 3782/13/36/5, MB-MRB, 29 Mar. 1787.
18 MS 3782/13/36/6, MB-MRB, 5 Apr. 1787.
19 MS 3782/12/57/16, MRB-MB, 27 May 1787.
20 MS 3782/13/36/7, MB-MRB, 8 Jun. 1787.
21 MS 3782/13/36/10, MB-MRB, 21 Sep. 1787.
22 MS 3782/14/76/20, MB-Miss AB, 5 Oct. 1787.
23 MS 3782/MB/Correspondence 1787/160, Mlle De Lassert-MB, 22 Oct. 1787. Matt was accepted by the De Lasserts 'as a child of our house, apart from the fact that the happiness he has of being your son, gives him a thousand rights to our attention and our best welcome, he is moreover an excellent boy, sweet, good, and now speaking French very well.'
24 MS 3782/13/36/13, MB-MRB, 2 Nov. 1787.
25 *Ibid.*
26 MS 3782/12/57/152, MB-F.Reinhard, 26 Aug. 1788.
27 MS 3782/13/36/26, MB-MRB, 2 Nov. 1788.
28 *Ibid.*
29 MS 3219/6/1/45, JW-JWj, 24 Sep. 1788.
30 MS 3782/13/36/26, MB-MRB, 2 Nov. 1788.
31 MS 3782/13/36/27, MB-MRB, 18 Dec. 1788.
32 *Ibid.*
33 *Ibid.*
34 MS 3782/13/36/28, MB-MRB, 23 Feb. 1789.
35 MS 3782/MB/General Correspondence 1789/55, Fanny de Luc-MB, Mar. 1789.
36 MS 3782/12/57/155, F.Reinhard-MB, 10 Apr. 1789.
37 MS 3287/12/57/157, F.H.Reinhard-MB, 13 Jun. 1789 (in French).
38 MS 3287/12/57/158, F.H. Reinhard-MB, 13 Jun. 1789 (in French).
39 MS 3782/13/53/96, Julie Werngner (Baroness Wangenheim)-MRB, May 1789. Translation: 'Write to your father, tell him frankly that you love a girl who is too honest to form a secret liaison with you, tell him that his plans for you will not be upset; God preserve us from wishing to insist that you marry me immediately; no my friend, if you believe you will be happy with me, travel for a couple of years longer as your father wishes, I will remain faithful to you…'.
40 MS 3782/13/36/30, MB-MRB, 26 Jun. 1789.
41 MS 3782/13/36/37, MB-MRB, 12 Nov. 1789.

Chapter 7 – Live Transplants

1   MS 3782/MB/General Correspondence 1787/35, M. Linwood-MB (Soho), 8 Mar. 1787. Includes draft of letter from MB-JA de Luc.
2   MS 3782/MB/General Correspondence 1787/46, M.Linwood-MB, 28 Mar. 1787.

3   MS 3782/MB/General Correspondence 1787/59, M. Linwood-MB, 21 Apr. 1787.
4   MS 3782/MB/Letterbook 1783-88/84, MB-William Matthews, 20 May 1787.
5   MS 3782/MB/General correspondence 1801/344, Charles Dumergue-MB, 31 Oct.1801.
6   MS 3782/MB/General correspondence 1803/407, Mrs Nicholson-MB, 1803, n.d.
7   MS 3782/13/36/8, MB-MRB, 29 Jun. 1787.
8   MS 3782/12/56/6, Sir Joseph Banks-MB, 14 Feb. 1787.
9   MS 3782/13/36/9, MB-MRB, 30 Jul. 1787.
10 MS 3782/12/67/79, Charlotte Matthews-MB, 25 Jul. 1794.
11 MS 3782/12/67/104, Charlotte Matthews-MB, 3 Aug. 1787.
12 MS 3782/14/76/19, MB-Miss AB, 30 Sep.1787.
13 MS 3782/14/76/20, MB-Miss AB, 5 Oct. 1787.
14 MS 3782/14/76/22, MB-Miss AB, 29 Jan. 1789.
15 MS 3782/MB/General Correspondence 1789/128, Mrs Nicholson-MB, 28 Jul. 1789.
16 MS 3782/MB/General Correspondence 1789/133, Charles Dumergue-MB, 3 Aug. 1789.
17 MS 3782/13/36/33, MB-MRB, 29 Jul. 1789.
18 MS 3782/13/36/35, MB-MRB, Oct. 1789.
19 *Ibid.*
20 MS 3219/6/2/B/130, MB-JWj, 26 Dec. 1789.
21 MS 3782/14/76/10, MB-Miss AB, 5 Mar. 1786.
22 MS 3782/12/72/84, John Scale-MB, 9 Jun. 1791.
23 MS 3782/General Correspondence MB/203, MB-Charles Dumergue, 18 Aug. 1791.
24 MS 3782/General Correspondence MB/203, MB-Charles Dumergue, 18 Aug. 1791.
25 MS 3219/4/39, JWj-JW, 23 Aug. 1792.
26 MS 3219/4/40, JWj-JW, 4 Sep. 1792.
27 MS 3782/13/38/5, Miss AB-MB, 1 Apr. 1792.
28 MS 3782/14/76/25, MB-Miss AB, 8 Apr. 1792.
29 Public Record Office Prob. 11/1217, Will of William Matthews, 1792.
30 MS 3782/13/38/5, Miss AB-MB, 1 Apr. 1792.
31 MS 3782/14/76/26, MB-Miss AB, 22 Aug. 1792.
32 MS 3782/14/76/28, MB-Miss AB, 22 Sep. 1792.
33 *Ibid.*
34 MS 3782/13/38/7, Miss AB-MB, 9 Sep. 1792.
35 *Ibid.*

Chapter 8 – 'Sublime' Matlock

1   MS 3782/14/76/29, MB-Miss AB, 25 Jan. 1793.
2   MS 3219/7/1/6, Annie Watt-Gregory Watt, 27 Apr. 1793.
3   Diary of Patty Fothergill, 1793 (private collection).
4   *Ibid.*
5   Possibly Peter Capper junior of Bath, who died on 26 Nov. 1793 aged 48 (memorial inscription, Bath Abbey, which describes him as 'many years a member of the British Factory at St Petersburg in Russia').
6   *See* note 3.
7   MS 3782/13/36/106, MB-MRB, 'Journal of the Sohoites', 1-2 Sep. 1793.
8   MS 3219/7/1/12 Annie Watt-Gregory Watt, 15 Feb. 1794.
9   Dickinson in *Matthew Boulton* (1936) claimed that Matthew Boulton's wives were related to Mrs Montagu, but Mrs Montagu's Robinson pedigree, as published by her great-niece Emily Climenson in *Elizabeth Montagu* (1906), traces her ancestry from the 14th century but does not appear to show any link with the Lichfield Robinsons, nor does their genealogy appear to show any link with Mrs Montagu's. Mrs Montagu's will (PROB. 11/1346, 1800) gives no help with this question, either. In it she leaves the majority of her estate to her nephew Matthew Montagu, her plate (presumably including the silver dinner service made for her by Matthew Boulton) to his wife Elizabeth, annuities to her friends Elizabeth Carter and Hester Chapone, and various other bequests to friends, nieces and nephews, and servants. Mrs Montagu died childless, her only child, John, having died in 1744 at the age of 15 months. By order of his mother's will he was exhumed from his Yorkshire burial place and re-interred at Winchester Cathedral with his parents.
10 MS 4.2/1-12, William Withering junior's journal, 1793-4, Birmingham University Special Collections.
11 *Ibid.*
12 MS 3219/7/1/11, Annie Watt-Gregory Watt, 25 Dec. 1793.
13 MS 3219/7/1/13, Annie Watt-Gregory Watt, 24 Mar. 1794.
14 MS 3219/4/13/45, JWj-JW, 22 Dec. 1792.

15 MS ZZ324:660357B, Diary of Mary Russell,Vol.II, Birmingham City Archives.
16 MS ZZ324:660357C, Diary of Mary Russell, Vol. IV.
17 *Ibid.*
18 *See* Jeyes, S.H. *The Russells of Birmingham*, 1911. Also the Diaries of Mary, Martha and Tom Russell, Birmingham City Archives.
19 MS 3782/12/68/98, MB-Charlotte Matthews, 23 Nov. 1794.
20 MS 3782/12/68/101, note by Anne Boulton on Charlotte Matthews-MB, 2 Dec. 1794.
21 MS 3782/12/68/106 MB-Charlotte Matthews, 17 Dec. 1794.
22 MS 3782/12/111/(150), 'Considerations upon the propriety of buying Soho', n.d.
23 MS 3219/7/1/18, Annie Watt-Gregory Watt, 2 Jan. 1795.
24 MS 3219/7/1/21, Annie Watt-Gregory Watt, 24 Feb. 1795.
25 MS 3219/7/1/24, Annie Watt-Gregory Watt, 29 May 1795.
26 MS 3782/13/36/52, MB-MRB, 13 Jan. 1791.
27 MS 3219/7/1/24, Annie Watt-Gregory Watt, 29 May 1795.
28 MS 3782/MB/General Correspondence 1800/398, Fanny de Luc-MB, 26 Nov. 1800.
29 MS 3782/13/38/8, Miss AB-MB, Jul. 1795.
30 William Withering to Dr Edward Ash, 12 May 1798, Royal Society of Medicine Archives.
31 MS 3782/13/38/8, Miss AB-MB, ?Jun. 1795.
32 Miss Hutton's account of the 1791 riots was eventually re-published by R.K. Dent in *Old and New Birmingham* (1878).
33 MS 3782/14/76/30, MB-Miss AB, 9 Jul. 1795.
34 *See* Hibbert, Christopher *George III, A Personal History* p.55 (London, 1998).
35 MS 3782/14/76/31, MB-Miss AB, 9 Aug. 1795.
36 *Ibid.*
37 MS 3782/12/68/154, MB-Charlotte Matthews, 24 Nov. 1795.
38 MS 3782/14/76/33, MB-Miss AB, Christmas Day 1796.

Chapter 9 – 'Elisium' at Soho

1   MS 3782/Household Bills 1788/Letter, James Hunter-MB, 18 Apr. 1788 and bill, Brunton, Forbes & Co., 18 Apr. 1788.
2   Soho House Archaeological Report, Hereford Archaeology Unit, 1990.
3   MS 3782/12/108/72, Notebook 1796.
4   MS 3782/13/36/105, MB-MRB, 11 Jul. 1793.
5   MS 3782/12/85/131a, MB-James Wyatt, 7 Jul. 1796.
6   MS 3219/7/1/19, Annie Watt-Gregory Watt, 5 Jan. 1795.
7   MS 3782/12/85/131a, MB-James Wyatt, 7 Jul. 1796.
8   *See* Note 3.
9   MS 3782/12/108/70, Notebook 1795.
10 *Ibid.*
11 MS 3219/7/1/26, Annie Watt-Gregory Watt, 10 Nov. 1795.
12 MS 3782, Bills, Edward Gray Saunders-MB, 8 Aug. 1795 and W. & J. Hollins-MB, 25 Sep. 1795.
13 MS 3219/7/1/28, Annie Watt-Gregory Watt, 13 Apr. 1796.
14 MS 3782/MB/General Correspondence 1796/211, Fanny de Luc-MB, Jun. 1796.
15 MS 3782/12/85/134, MB-James Wyatt, 18 Nov.1796.
16 MS 3782/13/13/17, Charlotte Matthews-MRB, 5 Nov. 1796.
17 MS 3782/MB/General Corresp. 1797/128, W.Newbold-MB, 5 Jun. 1797.
18 MS 3782/MB/General Corresp. 1798/67, W.Hollins-MB, 30 Apr. 1798.
19 MS 3782/12/108/88, Notebook 1801.
20 Cockle: a stove with a totally enclosed fire, used to heat the air with which it comes into contact. The cockle is fitted with fins which increase its surface area and thereby the volume of air which can be heated. Such an apparatus needs to be installed well below the level of the area to be heated (e.g. in a cellar), and is fed by cold air drawn in from outside. Once heated the air is funnelled into a series of flues or ducts around the building. It would only be possible to install such a system during major building or re-building work. *See* City of Hereford Archaeology Unit Report on Soho House (1990), pp.103-11.
21 MS 3782/MB/General Corresp. 1798/113, Lane & Co-Cornelius Dixon, 3 Jul. 1798.
22 MS 3219/7/49/16, Gregory Watt-JW, 31 Aug. 1798.
23 MS 3782/MB/General Corresp. 1799/259, James Newton-MB 24 Aug. 1799.
24 MS 3782/House/Miscellaneous Bills 1795-1802, James Newton 22 Aug. 1799, sent to Charlotte Matthews, 9 Nov. 1799
25 MS 3219/7/49/16, Gregory Watt-JW, 31 Aug. 1798.
26 MS 3782/12/107/31, MB diary, 1803.

27 MS 3782/MB/House/Correspondence 1805, James Newton-William Cheshire, 4 Apr. 1805.
28 There seems to be no conclusive evidence of a father-son relationship between Matthew Boulton and John Phillp, who Boulton brought to Soho from Cornwall; Phillp's mother, Mrs Elizabeth Fletcher of Falmouth, occasionally asks to borrow money from Boulton to help her husband get established in a business, and writes to thank Boulton for his care of her son [MS3782/4/41/342,29 & 165, 1795, 1796 & 1801], but nowhere does she suggest that he has any responsibility in regard to the boy. Phillp, who made a number of drawings and watercolours of the Soho estate, lived at Soho House, though not apparently with the family, for some time. He made an unhappy marriage and committed suicide in 1815, news communicated to his mother by Matthew Robinson Boulton in a letter dated 18 July 1815 [MS 3782/MRB Private Correspondence 1815/61-62, MRB-Elizabeth Fletcher, 18 Jul. 1815, and 3782/13/10/77, Elizabeth Fletcher-MRB].
29 MS 3782/MB/General Corresp. 1799/50, Thomas Downing-Cornelius Dixon, 7 Feb. 1799.
30 MS 3782/MB/General Correspondence 1801/196, Fanny de Luc-MB, Jun. 1801.
31 MS 3782/MB/General Corresp. 1793/129, William Herschel-MB, Jul. 1793.

Chapter 10 – 'Her leg or her life'
1   The Battle of Camperdown (11 Oct. 1787) was between the English Fleet under Admiral Duncan and the Dutch Fleet, which was on its way to join the French Fleet for a planned landing in Ireland.
2   MS 3782/12/69/67, MB-Charlotte Matthews, 20 Nov. 1797.
3   *Aris's Birmingham Gazette*, 20 Nov. 1797, concert programme.
4   MS 3219/4/87, MRB-JWj, 8 Sep. 1798.
5   MS 3782/13/36/133, MB-MRB, 19 Sep. 1798.
6   'The man that hath no music in himself ... is fit for treasons, stratagems, and spoils': Shakespeare, *Merchant of Venice* Act V.
7   MS 3782/13/36/133, MB-MRB, 19 Sep. 1798.
8   MS 3782/13/13/116, MRB-Charlotte Matthews, 23 Feb. 1800. The 'trio' were Anne Boulton, Charlotte Matthews and possibly Amelia Alston.
9   MS 3782/13/13/23, Charlotte Matthews-MRB, 25 Feb. 1800.
10 MS 3782/12/69/161, MB-Charlotte Matthews, 7 Aug. 1799.
11 MS 3782/12/69/177, MB-Charlotte Matthews, 22 Oct. 1799.
12 MS 3782/ Thomas Lack 1797-1836, Thomas Lack-MB, 23 Aug. 1800.
13 MS 3219/4/16/6, JWj-JW, 4 Oct. 1800.
14 MS 3287/MB/General Corresp. 1800/322, Mrs Nicholson-MB, 7 Oct. 1800.
15 MS 3219/4/16/8, JWj-JW, 11 Oct. 1800.
16 MS 3782/MB/General Corresp.1800/345, MB-Henry Cline, 23 Oct. 1800.
17 MS 3782/MB/General Corresp.1800/339, Mrs Nicholson-MB, 22 Oct. 1800.
18 MS 3782/12/60/218, MB-the Misses Fothergill, 29 Oct. 1800.
19 MS 3782/MB/General Corresp.1801/4, MB-Eliza Carles, 2 Jan. 1801. Mrs Carles was in a debtors' prison in Bath; Boulton sent her £20 towards her £370 debt and was trying to organise some further help for her. Mrs Carles replied expressing concern for Anne's predicament and praising Mr Grant the physician who she said was very well respected in Bath.
20 MS 3782/MB/General Corresp.1800/371, Charles Dumergue-MB, 8 Nov. 1800.
21 MS 3782/MB/General Corresp.1800/399, MB-Charles Dumergue, n.d.
22 MS 3782/13/13/28, Miss AB-Charlotte Matthews. 10 Dec. 1800.
23 MS 3782/12/70/37, Charlotte Matthews-MB, 13 Dec. 1800.
24 MS 3782/MB/General Corresp.1800/429, Charles Dumergue-MB, 22 Dec. 1800.
25 MS 3782/14/76/52, MB-Miss AB, 24 Dec. 1800.
26 MS 3782/14/76/43, MB-Miss AB, 27 Dec. 1800.
27 MS 3782/MB/General Corresp.1800/436, Charles Dumergue-MB, 27 Dec. 1800.
28 MS 3782/13/38/10, Miss AB-MB, 15 Jan. 1801.
29 MS 3782/13/9/50a, MRB-Andrew Collins, 11 Mar. 1798.
30 MS 3782/MB/General Corresp. 1801/34, MB-Charles Dumergue & Mrs Nicolson, 20 Jan.1801.
31 MS 3782/ British Coinage Vol.1, Thomas Lack-MB, 5 Feb. 1801.
32 MS 3782/MB/General Corresp.1801/106, Mary Linwood-MB, 24 Mar. 1801.
33 MS 3782/MB/General Corresp.1801/110, MB-Mary Linwood, 6 Mar. 1801.
34 MS 3782/14/76/45, MB-Miss AB, 1 May 1801.
35 MS 3782/14/76/44 MB-Miss AB, 24 Apr. 1801.
36 MS 3782/MB/General Corresp.1801/158, Mrs Mary Keen-MB 11 May 1801.
37 MS 3782/14/76/46, MB-Miss AB, 12 May 1801.
38 *Ibid.*
39 MS 3782/14/76/48, MB-Miss AB, 7 June 1801.
40 MS 3782/14/76/49, MB-Miss AB, 19 Jun. 1801.

Chapter 11 – A thousand a year

1   MS 3219/6/35, James Watt Junior's notebook 1798-1801.
2   *Ibid.*
3   MS 3219/6/37, James Watt Junior's notebook 1799.
4   PROB 11/1368, Will of Charlotte Matthews, 6 Nov. 1800, Public Record Office.
5   MS 3782/13/53/114, Amelia Alston-MB, 30 May 1803.
6   MS 3782/13/53/112, Amelia Alston-MB, 13 Jan. 1802.
7   MS 3782/MB/General Corresp.1802/194, Mrs Nicholson-MB, 30 Jun. 1802.
8   MS 3782/MB/General Corresp.1802/114, Charles Dumergue-MB, 7 Apr. 1802.
9   MS 3782/MB/General Corresp.1802/86, Charles Dumergue-MB, 10 Mar. 1802.
10 MS 3782/MB General Corresp. 1802/275, Mrs Keen-MB, 1 Sep. 1802.
11 MS 3782/12/07/30, MB Diary 1802, 21 Sep. 1802.
12 MS 3782/MB/General Corresp.1803/1, Mrs Nicholson-MB, 1 Jan. 1803.
13 MS 3782/MB/General Corresp.1803/83, Mrs Nicholson-MB 29 Mar. 1803.
14 MS 3782/MB/General Corresp.1803/132, Sir Walter Scott-MB 13 May 1803.
15 MS 3782/13/53/ 116, Amelia Alston-MB, 22 Jul. 1803.
16 MS 3782/13/53/117, Amelia Alston-MB, 31 Oct. 1803.
17 MS 3782/MB/General Corresp.1803/336, Mrs Nicholson-MB 31 Oct. 1803.
18 MS 3782/MB/General Corresp.1803/409, Mrs Nicholson-MB, n.d. 1803.
19 MS 3782/13/48/4, Ambrose Weston-MB, 23 Feb. 1802.
20 MS 3782/12/72/104, MB-G.Scale, 26 Jul. 1799.
21 MS 3782/13/39/125, MB-Mrs Annie Watt, 1 Aug. 1803.
22 MS 3782/MB/General Corresp.1803/328, Mrs Nicholson-MB, 17 Oct. 1803.
23 MS 3782/MB/General Corresp.1803/378, Mrs Nicholson-MB, 5 Dec. 1803.
24 MS 3782/MB/General Corresp. 1803, Sarah Siddons-MB, 17 Dec. 1803.
25 MS 3782/MB/General Corresp.1803/378, Mrs Nicholson-MB, 5 Dec. 1803. Whoever Mrs Slade was, she was frightened of Napoleon.
26 MS 3782/MB/General Corresp.1803/387, Mrs Nicholson-MB, 15 Dec. 1803.
27 MS 3782/13/36/165, MB-MRB, 30 Oct. 1804. Docketed by MRB 'Interview with Dr Carmichael and dissatisfaction at his reserve'.
28 MS 3782/12/60/283, 'M.Boultons suggestions on the contemplated marriage of Miss M.F. to J.W.' This appears to be a draft letter, and there is no date. Whether it was ever sent there is no indication, but the fact that on one of the sheets Boulton refers to Patty as 'Mrs Brown' suggests that it must have been written after her marriage to William Brown in 1802.
29 MS 3219/7/51/B/28, Gregory Watt-JW, 27 May 1802.
30 MS 3219/6/61/68, JWj-Gilbert Hamilton, 26 Nov. 1804.
31 MS 3219/6/61/33, JWj-John Furnell Tuffen, n.d.
32 MS 3782/MB/General Correspondence 1805/62, Fanny de Luc-MB, 13 Jun. 1805.
33 MS 3782/MB/General Correspondence 1805/64, Fanny de Luc-MB, 23 Jun. 1805.
34 *See* Hibbert, Christopher, *George III* (1998), p.347.
35 MS 3782/MB/General Correspondence 1805/104, Fanny de Luc-MB, 5 Jul. 1805.
36 MS 3782/MB/General Correspondence 1806/5, Charles Dumergue-MB, 4 Jan. 1806.
37 MS 3782/MB/General Correspondence 1806/1, Fanny de Luc-MB, 1 Jan. 1806.
38 MS 3782/MB/General Correspondence 1806/85, Fanny de Luc-MB, 19 May 1806.
39 MS 3782/13/48/155, MB-Ambrose Weston, 10 Apr. 1806.
40 MS 3782/13/48/157, MB-Ambrose Weston, 9 May 1806.
41 Will of MB, Public Record Office ref. Prob.11/1502, 3 Jun. 1806, with codicils dated 7 Oct. 1807, 31 Oct. 1807 and 18 Mar. 1808 and schedule of legacies dated 9 Mar. 1808; MS 3782/14/83/4, notes on Deed of Settlement for Miss Boulton, in MB's hand, dated 3 Jun. 1806.
42 'The Maid of Buttermere': Mary Robinson, of the *Ship Inn*, made famous when Joseph Budmere stayed there in 1792 and praised her beauty to the skies in his popular *Fortnight's Rambles to the Lakes*. She became a 'tourist attraction'. In 1802 she married Augustus Hope, who turned out to be a bigamist and a forger. He was sentenced to death for forgery in Carlisle, where Wordsworth visited him before he was hung in 1803. (Thanks to Jenny Uglow for this information.)
43 MS 3782/13/53/123, Amelia [Emily] Alston-MB, 25 Jul. 1806.
44 *Ibid.*
45 MS 3782/MB/General Correspondence 1806/156, MB-Fanny de Luc, 20 Oct. 1806.
46 MS 3782/MB/General Correspondence 1806/158, F. and J.A. de Luc-MB, 24 Oct. 1806.
47 MS 3782/MB/General Correspondence 1806/178, Fanny de Luc-MB, 3 Nov. 1806. The Sucklings and the Nelsons were related.
48 MS 3782/House/ Corresp.1807/, William Cheshire-Charles Dumergue, 6 Jan. 1807.
49 *Ibid.*

50 MS 3782/MB/General Corresp.1807/8, Sophia Dumergue-MB, 24 Jan.1807.
51 MS 3782/MB/General Corresp.1807/28, Dr Carmichael-Henry Cline, 17 Mar. 1807.
52 MS 3782/MB/General Corresp.1807/29, Henry Cline-Dr Carmichael, 23 Mar. 1807.
53 MS 3782/House/General Corresp.1807/, William Cheshire-Charles Dumergue, 8 Apr. 1807.
54 MS 3782/House/General Corresp.1807/, William Cheshire-Charles Dumergue, 19 Apr.1807.
55 MS 3782/MB/General Corresp.1807/67, Charles Dumergue-MB, 22 Aug. 1807.
56 MS 3782/MB/General Corresp.1807/77, Charles Dumergue-MB, 8 Oct.1807.
57 MS 3782/MRB Special Subjects/Thornhill, Cornelius Dixon-Miss AB, 7 Aug. 1805, endorsed 'Drawing of Pump. Thornhill'.
58 MS 3782/14/83/2 & 3, Memorandum of agreement between MB and JWj, 12 Mar. 1808.
59 MS 3219/6/1/306, Annie Watt-JWj, 29 Feb. 1808.
60 MS 3782/Chubb, box of keys of Thornhill, containing list in Miss Boulton's hand, 25 Mar. 1808.
61 MS 3782/13/48/79, Ambrose Weston-MB, 18 Apr. 1808.
62 MS 3782/House/General Corresp.1808/, William Cheshire-Charles Dumergue, 13 Jul.1808.

Chapter 12 – The *subject*

1   MS 3782/MRB/Corresp.B 1787-1818/57, Bath accounts 1 February-15 March, 1809, Bill for accommodation at Bath for Mr and Miss Boulton.
2   MS 3782/14/76/53, MB-Miss AB, 11 Mar. 1809. The letter is endorsed 'Supposed to be the last letter written by him'.
3   MS 3219/4/33/32, JWj-JW, 14 Aug. 1809.
4   MS 3219/4/33/33, JWj-JW, 17 Aug. 1809. In adult life Matt is referred to by many correspondents as 'Mr R. Boulton', using his middle name Robinson in place of the old family childhood name of Matt.
5   MS 3219/6/9/32, JWj-Ambrose Weston, 17 Aug. 1809.
6   MS 3219/4/33/34, JWj-JW, 18 Aug. 1809.
7   MS 3219/4/33/35, JWj-JW, 22 Aug. 1809.
8   MS 3219/4/33/36, JWj-JW, 25 Aug. 1809.
9   MS 3219/4/49/88, J.F.Tuffen-JW, 29 Aug. 1809.
10 MS 3219/6/1/339, JW-JWj, 30 Aug. 1809.
11 See Dickinson, H., *Matthew Boulton* (1936), p.201.
12 Will of Helena Mynd of Ross on Wye, 1808. PRO Ref. Prob.11/1481, proved 9 June 1808.
13 Will of Matthew Boulton, 1806, PRO Ref. Prob.11/1502, proved 18 Sep. 1809.
14 MS 3782/13/48, Ambrose Weston-MRB, 5 Sep. 1809.
15 MS 3219/6/2/52. Sir Isaac Coffin-JWj, 29 Jan. 1811.
16 MS 3219/6/1/355, Ann Watt-JWj. 13 Jun. 1810.
17 MS 3219/4/34/5, JWj-JW, 17 Jun. 1810.
18 MS 3219/6/1/356, JW-JWj, 23 Jun. 1810.
19 MS 3219/6/1/357, JW-JWj. 25 Jun. 1810.
20 MS 3219/4/34/9, JWj-JW. 28 Jun. 1810.
21 George Freer, surgeon, of Birmingham.
22 MS 3782/13/40/24. JWj-MRB. 1 Jul. 1810.
23 MS 3219/6/1/363 Ann Watt-JWj, 23 Jul. 1810.
24 MS 3219/4/34/13, JWj-JW. 4 Aug. 1810.
25 MS 3219/4/34/16, JWj-JW. 27 Aug. 1810.
26 MS 3782/13/40/25, JWj-MRB. 28 Aug. 1810.
27 MS 3219/4/34/18, JWj-JW. 10 Sep. 1810.
28 MS 3782/general corresp. 1810/8, William Cheshire-Miss Alston, 20 Sep. 1810.
29 MS 3782/13/53/127, Amelia Alston-MRB. 22 Nov. 1810.
30 MS 3219/6/1/378, Ann Watt-JWj. 14 Feb. 1811.

Chapter 13 – *Leaving Soho*

1   MS 3219/4/120, Letterbook 1810-18, JW-J.F. Tuffen, 13 Jul. 1811.
2   MS 3219/6/2/W/255, J.Weston-JWj, 25 Jul. 1811.
3   MS 3782/14/83/6-7, Elliott & Holbrook-Miss AB, Dec. 1811.
4   MS 3782/14/65, Miss AB's 'Own Account' book for 1815-1821.
5   MS 3782/14/66, Miss AB's 'Own Account' book for 1825.
6   MS 3219/6/13/48, JWj-G.A. Lee, 29 Nov. 1815.
7   MS 3782/13/53/134, Amelia Alston-MRB, 22 Feb. 1815.
8   MS 3782/Bills of Mary Anne Boulton.
9   MS 3782/13/9/131, Charles Dumergue-MRB. 11 Apr. 1814. 'Someone has told the ladies in Salisbury

Square that you are coming to town before long; it may be that you have the inclination to take the opportunity to show this Babylon [London] to your disagreeable pupil and as, if you do not give her your name, she may not stay under the same roof, my ladies charge me to insist, although it is against my own inclination, that you bring Miss Wilkinson here to take possession of the room destined for the Misses Brandt, and we shall permit you to come and see her occasionally.' Whether Dumergue really disliked Miss Wilkinson or was being ironic is not clear – probably the latter.

10 MS 3219/4/120/Letterbook 1810-18, JW-J.F. Tuffen, 17 Dec. 1816.
11 MS 3782/14/65, Miss AB's 'Own Account' book for 1815-1821.
12 MS 3219/4/53/94 J.F. Tuffen-JW, 17 Dec. 1816.
13 MS 3219/4/120/Letterbook 1810-18, JW-J.F. Tuffen, 19 May 1817.
14 MS 3219/4/53/95, J.F.Tuffen-JW, 22 Jun. 1817.
15 MS 3219/6/1/513, JW-JWj, 21 Jun. 1817.
16 MS 3219/4/53/95, J.F.Tuffen-JW, 22 Jun. 1817.
17 See note 11.
18 MS 3219/6/13/36, JWj-Margaret Miller 8 Oct. 1815.
19 MS 3219/6/1/520, Ann Watt-JWj, 31 Jul. 1817.
20 Ibid.
21 MS 3219/6/1/521, JWj-Ann Watt, 2 Aug. 1817.
22 MS 3219/4/120/Letterbook 1810-18, JW-JWj, 9 Aug. 1817.
23 MS 3219/6/2/118, Miss AB-JWj, 8 Aug. 1817.
24 MS 3219/6/1/559, Annie Watt-JWj, 5 Apr. 1818.
25 MS 3219/4/121/27 (Letterbook Feb.1818-Aug.1819), JW-JWj, 6 Apr. 1818.
26 MS 3219/4/121/29 (Letterbook Feb. 1818-Aug.1819), JW-JWj, 9 Apr. 1818.
27 MS 3219/6/1/561a, Miss AB-JW, 9 Apr. 1818.
28 MS 3219/4/121/30 (Letterbook Feb.1818-Aug.1819), JW-JWj, 13 Apr. 1818.
29 MS 3219/6/2/B/121b, JWj-Miss AB. 24 May 1818.
30 MS 3219/6/2/B/121a, Miss AB-JWj. 25 May 1818.
31 Anne Robinson (5 Jun. 1818), Katherine Elizabeth (5 Aug. 1819), Mathew Piers Watt (22 Sept. 1820), Hugh William (30 Nov. 1821), Montagu (4 Apr. 1823), Lionel (5 Nov. 1826), and Mary Ann (23 May 1829).
32 MS 3782/MRB/General Correspondence 1818/131. MRB-JWj. 5 Jul. 1818. Endorsed 'Request for him to be godfather to my child.' Reply: MS 3219/13/40/69, JWj-MRB, 9 Jul. 1818.
33 MS 3782/14/32/13, Mrs Bell-Miss AB, 22 Aug. 1818.
34 MS 3219/4/37/39, JWj-JW, 2 Oct. 1818.
35 Ibid.
36 MS 3219/6/2/123, Miss AB-JWj, 3 Oct. 1818.
37 MS 3219/6/2/124, JWj-Miss AB, 3 Oct. 1818.
38 MS 3219/6/1/582, JW-JWj, 8 Oct. 1818.
39 MS 3219/6/2/R/44, John Rennie-JWj, 16 Dec. 1818.
40 Ibid.
41 MS 3219/6/2/125, Miss AB-JWj, 30 Nov. 1818.
42 MS 3219/6/2/127 JWj-Miss AB, 9 Dec. 1818.
43 The 500-acre Doldowlod Estate in Radnorshire was bought by James Watt senior in 1803, following earlier purchases of farms in mid-Wales. James Watt junior had alterations carried out to the house and took a keen interest in the planting of nurseries and orchards. After his father's death he had the original farmhouse extended to form the present Doldowlod Hall.
44 MS 3782/14/20/1819/1a/1-7.

Chapter 14 – Mistress of Thornhill

Note: so many household bills have been referred to in this chapter that individual references have not been given for every one. All are to be found in Miss Boulton's papers under the general number MS 3782/14/20-54 and MS 3782/14/67-70. Some of particular interest have been individually referenced.

1 Housekeeping bills.
2 Pye, Charles, A description of modern Birmingham (1818), p.106.
3 e.g. MS 3782/14/22/4/7, tax assessment 1821.
4 MS 3782/11/ [MBP 454] list of keys for Thornhill, 25 Mar. 1808.
5 MS 3782/13/39/125, MB-Mrs Annie Watt, 1 Aug. 1803.
6 MS 3782/13/142/(24), exercise book recording sale of Thornhill contents, 26-27 Mar. 1832.
7 See note 3.
8 MS 3782/14/27/10, Mary Rollston-Miss AB, Apr. 1826.

9   MS 3782/14/27/98, Thomas Davenport-Miss AB, Mar. 1826.
10 MS 3782/14/25/26-27, Mrs Brown-Miss AB, Aug. 1824.
11 MS 3782/14/Miss B. Miscellaneous loose papers/22, n.d.
12 MS 3782/14/60, Servants' Wages Book 1819-22.
13 MS 3782/14/83/22, 'Memoranda relating to servants' wages etc.' 1821-26.
14 MS 3782/14/83/20, list of duties of the footman and the butler, n.d.
15 *Ibid.*
16 MS 3782/14/83/22.
17 *Ibid.*
18 MS 3782/14/83/21, Description of the duties of the upper servant, cook, housemaid, footman and coachman, n.d.
19 *Ibid.*
20 *Ibid.*
21 *Ibid.*
22 *Ibid.*
23 *Ibid.*
24 MS 3782/14/20/22/6, Edward Townsend-Miss AB, 2 Feb. 1819.
25 MS 3219/6/79/42, Miss AB-JWj, 21 Jun. 1824.
26 MS 3782/14/83/19, 'Memorandum of Persons & Places for Furniture', J.F.T.-AB. n.d.
27 MS 3782/13/142/(7), J.F. Tuffen-Miss AB, 1 Mar. 1820.
28 MS 3782/14/83/3, undated list of rooms and their contents.
29 MS 3782/14/20/1/99, William Ryley-Miss Boulton, 18 Dec. 1819.
30 MS 3782/14/21/1/27, Thomas Hensman-Miss Boulton, Feb. 1820.
31 MS 3782/14/83/11, J.Wellsted-Miss AB, 13 Nov. 1819.
32 MS 3782/14/22/15, Gillow & Co.-Miss AB, Oct. 1820.
33 MS 3782/13/142/(24), exercise book recording sale of Thornhill contents, 26-27 Mar. 1832, lot no. 105.
34 MS 3782/14/22/1/15, Gillow & Co.-Miss AB, Oct. 1820.
35 MS 3782/14/25/5, John Whitehouse & Sons-Miss AB, 3 Aug. 1824.
36 MS 3219/6/37, James Watt Junior's notebook, May 1799.
37 MS 3782/14/21/3/1, S. Brereton-Miss AB, 7 Aug. 1819.
38 MS 3782/14/22/5/11, Cornelius Dixon-Miss AB, Aug. 1820.
39 MS 3782/13/142/(13), R. Bridgens-Miss AB, 6 Apr. 1820.
40 MS 3782/13/142/(24), exercise book recording sale of Thornhill contents, 26-27 Mar. 1832, lot no. 120; the tables sold for £17 0s. 0d. at auction.
41 MS 3782/13/142/(20), plan & drawing of sideboard, auction lot 125, sold for £13 0s. 0d.
42 MS 3782/14/21/1/57c, James Wellsted-Miss AB, 9 Nov. 1820.
43 MS 3782/13/142/(24), exercise book recording sale of Thornhill contents, 26-27 Mar. 1832, lot no.126, sold for £9 0s. 0d.
44 MS 3782/13/142/(14), 'Mr Gillow's estimate of curtains', n.d.
45 MS 3782/14/22/1/39, James & Robert Rickards-Miss AB, 30 Nov. 1821.
46 MS 3782/14/21/19, M.Boulton & Plate Co.-Miss AB, 3 May 1819.
47 MS 3782/14/24/3, M.Boulton & Plate Co.-Miss AB, 1 Mar. 1823.
48 MS 3782/14/21/4, Richard Chippindall-Miss AB, 22 Dec. 1819.
49 MS 3782/14/21/55, Rotton & Son-Miss AB, 8 Dec. 1819.
50 MS 3782/14/21/2, Christopher James-Miss AB, 26 Jan. 1820.
51 MS 3782/14/21/33, Mary Rollason-Miss AB, 15 Jul. 1820.
52 MS 3782/14/25/11, Mary Rollason-Miss AB, 26 Jun. 1824.
53 MS 3782/14/22/1, Mary Rollason-Miss AB, 11 May 1821.
54 MS 3782/14/21/17, J.Bedford-Miss AB, 20 Apr. 1820.
55 MS 3782/14/21/44, Sarah Bedford-Miss AB, 15 Sep.1820.
56 MS 3782/14/25/7, J.Bedford-Miss AB, 21 May 1824.
57 MS 3782/14/21/63, H.&R. Chamberlain-Miss AB, 13 Dec. 1820.
58 MS 3782/13/142/(9), H.&R. Chamberlain-Miss AB, 13 Dec. 1820.
59 MS 3782/14/24/28, H.&R. Chamberlain-Miss AB, 30 Jan. 1823.
60 MS 3782/14/83/3, memorandum of work to be carried out at an unidentified house, n.d. List of rooms and furniture, said to be in Matthew Boulton's hand, n.d. A comparison of the rooms on the list with the rooms on Miss Boulton's list of Thornhill keys, and with the floor plans, seems to confirm that the house is Thornhill. The furniture listed matches almost exactly the furniture which Miss Boulton bought from 1819, and which was sold at the auction after her death, suggesting that this list may in fact have been written by Miss Boulton herself, although the writing does resemble her father's.

61   MS 3782/13/142/(19), design by Baber & Co., Sep. 1805.
62   MS 3782/13/142/(6), Smith & Baber instructions on measurement, 29 Nov. 1819.
63   MS 3782/14/21/54, Richard Bridgens-MissAB, Sep. 1820.
64   MS 3782/13/142/(13), R. Bridgens-Miss AB, 6 Apr. 1820.
65   *Ibid.*
66   MS 37821/4/21/1/66, G. Morant-Miss AB, 19 Sep. 1820.
67   MS 3782/13/142/(16), memorandum 'Mr Gillows French curtains', n.d.
68   MS 3782/14/24/2/8, Rickman & Hutchinson-Miss AB, Jan. 1823.
69   MS 3782/14/24/2/1-9 (item 6 is Miss Boulton's own list of the other bills), 1823.
70   MS 3782/14/24/1/27, Thomas Dowbiggin-Miss AB, Nov. 1823.
71   MS 3782/14/24/11, Thomas Dowbiggin-Miss AB, 23 Jul. 1823.
72   MS 3782/13/142/(21), John Newbould-Miss AB, 4 Jul 1825.
73   *See* note 60.
74   MS 3782/13/142/(24), exercise book recording sale of Thornhill contents, 26-27 Mar. 1832, lots 50-56.
75   MS 3782/14/22/34, Mary Rollason-Miss AB, Christmas 1821.
76   MS 3219/6/5/186, sketch of 'oak dresser in the kitchen'.
77   MS 3782/13/142/(20), drawings of Miss Dumergue's kitchen range and another kitchen range, n.d.
78   MS 3782/14/21/36, John Slater-Miss AB, 4 Jul. 1820.
79   MS 3782/14/71-75, Miscellaneous Account Books.
80   MS 3782/14/48/33, Housekeeping accounts.
81   MS 3782/14/20-30, Housekeeping accounts.
82   MS 3782/14/75, Inventories book 1823-25.
83   MS 3782/14/21/53, John Crowder-Miss AB, 30 May 1820.

Chapter 15 – An Enduring Taste for Bonnets

1   MS 3782/14/27/2/10, Mme. Maradan Carson-Miss AB, 30 Dec. 1826.
2   MS 3782/14/29/1/2, M. Triaud-Miss AB, 4 Mar. 1828.
3   Hutton-Beale, Catherine, *Reminiscences of a Gentlewoman of the Last Century* (1891), p.29.
4   MS 3782/14/29/1/1, Mme. de Thier-Miss AB, 4 Mar. 1828.
5   MS 3782/14/35/34, Vickery's bill, 22 Jun. 1821.
6   MS 3782/14/37/14, Vickery's bill, 19 Jul. 1823.
7   MS 3782/14/26/5/13, E. Millin-Miss AB, 18 Aug. 1825.
8   MS 3782/14/27/37, E. Millin-Miss AB, 23 Sep.1823.
9   MS 3782/14/27/2/1, E. Millin-Miss AB, 23 Dec. 1826.
10   MS 3782/14/65, 'Own account' book 1815-21 (1817 and 1818).
11   Hutton-Beale, Catherine, *Reminiscences of a Gentlewoman of the Last Century* (1891), pp.213-5.
12   eg MS 3782/14/23/7/3, tax assessment for the year ending 5 April 1823.
13   MS 3782/14/25/6/17, James Clarke-Miss AB, 2 Apr. 1824.
14   MS 3782/14/58-62, small account books, Stable account, 1813.
15   MS 3782/MRB/Corresp.1819/74, Zacheus Walker jun.-Miss AB, 2 Dec. 1819.
16   *Ibid.*
17   MS 3782/13/17/8, Amelia Alston-MRB, 18 Sep. 1820.
18   MS 3782/13/17/10, Amelia Alston-MRB, 22 Feb. 1821.
19   MS 3782/14/35/36, Mrs Hall-Miss AB, 2 Jul. 1821.
20   MS 3782/14/36/12, 28 Oct. 1822.
21   MS 3219/6/75/23, Agnes Miller-JWj, 15 Aug. 1821.
22   MS 3782/14/27/3/23, Mrs Keen-Miss AB, Oct. 1826.
23   MS 3782/13/142/(24), exercise book recording auction of Thornhill contents, 26-27 Mar.1832, Lot 131.
24   PRO Prob.11/1763, Will of Miss Ann(e) Boulton, 1829.
25   MS 3782/14/29/3/55,56,58, bills.
26   MS 3782/13/23/58, Miss Ann Keen-MRB 4 Oct. 1828.
27   MS 3782/13/23/69, Miss Ann Keen-MRB, 14 Oct. 1828.
28   MS 3782/14/31/13, Obadiah Elliott-Miss AB, 26 May 1829.
29   MS 3782/13/54/1, MPW Boulton-MRB, 11 Aug. 1829.
30   MS 3782/13/55/1, Annie Watt-Mrs M.A. Boulton, 31 Jan. 1822.
31   MS 3782/13/23/71, Miss Ann Keen-MRB, 10 Oct. 1829.
32   Dr Johnstone-MRB, enclosed with letter above.
33   *Ibid.*
34   MS 3782/13/23/72, Miss Ann Keen-MRB, 16 Oct. 1819.

35 MS 3782/13/71/98, G. Barker-MRB, 18 Oct. 1829.
36 MS 3782/13/71/99, Dr Johnstone-MRB, 26 Oct. 1829 (enclosed with letter below).
37 MS 3782/13/71/99, G. Barker-MRB, 26 Oct. 1829.
38 MS 3782/27/13/124, J.Robinson-J.Mosley, 13 Nov. 1829.
39 Parish Register, St Mary's Church, Handsworth.
40 PRO Prob.11/1763, Will of Miss Anne Boulton, 1829.

Epilogue

1 MS ZA4946, W.C. Cartwright-W.C. Cartwright jun. (Paris), 20 Jun. 1845, Northampton County Record Office.

Appendix

1 Family trees: 1) various versions compiled by Boulton family members and others (on file at Soho House); 2) Dickinson, H.W., *Matthew Boulton*, p.24 (Cambridge, 1936); 3) in Delieb E., *The Great Silver Manufactory* (1971); 4) Dyott pedigree in Stebbing Shaw.
2 The Hall has gone but Curborough Hall Farm is still there, now a craft centre; the present farmhouse was built in 1871.
3 *Victoria County History* (VCH), Vol. XIV, Lichfield, p.233.
4 Shaw, Stebbing, *History of the Antiquities of the County of Staffordshire* (1798), p.376.
5 Will of Zachary Babington, 1687, Lichfield Record Office.
6 Parish Register, St Mary's, Lichfield; Stafford County Record Office, microfiche F20/1/2.
7 Dyott papers D661/1/97, 16 June 1655, Stafford Record Office.
8 Parish Register, St Chad's, Lichfield; Stafford Record Office, microfiche F29/1/1.
9 Parish Register, St Chad's, Lichfield; Stafford Record Office, microfiche F29/1/1.
10 Burial 29 Dec. 1698: Parish Register, St Chad's, Lichfield; Stafford Record Office, microfiche F29/1/1.
11 Will of Matthew Dyott of Stichbrooke, Lichfield Record Office.
12 *The Citizens of Lichfield in 1695: Census of Lichfield carried out for Gregory King and used in his 'Natural and Political Observations and Conclusions upon the State and Condition of England, 1696'*, Harl. MSS 7022.
13 Parish Register, St Mary Savoy, London, 11 Feb. 1699.
14 MS 3782/14/76/8, MB-Miss AB, 17 Aug. 1785.
15 Smiles, Samuel, *Lives of Boulton and Watt* (London, 1865), pp.163-5.
16 Longden, Rev. Henry Isham, *Northamptonshire and Rutland Clergy*, Vol.II (1938).
17 Parish Register, St Mary's Church, Stafford; Lichfield Record Office, microfiche F1399/2.
18 Freemen's Roll for the City of Lichfield (1652 onwards); Lichfield Record Office, D77 3/1.
19 Poll Books for 1710, 1714, 1718, 1721, Lichfield Record Office.
20 Birmingham City Archives, Bickley Collection MS373614, will of John Dyott, 1741.
21 Parish Register, St Michael's, Lichfield; Stafford Record Office, microfiche F27/1/3.
22 Correspondence between Simon Dyott and Stephen Simpson (solicitor), 1768-70, MS 381706 ZZ62A, Birmingham City Archives.
23 Parish Register, St Mary's, Lichfield; Stafford Record Office, microfiche F20/1/1.
24 Correspondence between Simon Dyott and Stephen Simpson (solicitor), 1768-70, MS 381706 ZZ62A, Birmingham City Archives.
25 Dickinson, H.W., *Matthew Boulton*, p.24 (Cambridge, 1936).
26 Smiles, Samuel, *Lives of Boulton and Watt* (London, 1865), p. 163.
27 Delieb, E.: *The Great Silver Manufactory*, p.17 (London, 1971).
28 Parish Register, St Martin's Church, Birmingham; Birmingham Reference Library.
29 *Aris's Gazette*, 23 May 1785; St Philip's Cathedral Register; Birmingham Reference Library.
30 IGI; and Delieb, Eric, *The Great Silver Manufactory*, op.cit.
31 Robinson, Eric, 'Matthew Boulton's Birthplace and his Home at Snow Hill: A Problem in Detection', in *Transactions of Birmingham Archaeological Society*, Vol. 75, 1957.
32 Smiles, Samuel, *op.cit.*, p.164.
33 The first St John's Chapel in Deritend was built in the late 14th century. The last chapel on the site was demolished in 1947. Hausted was its Chaplain from 1717-55.
34 *Aris's Birmingham Gazette*, 25 Aug. 1755.
35 Dickinson, *op.cit.*, pp.26-8.
36 *Birmingham Gazette and Express*, 16 September, 1909.
37 MS 3782/13/8/66, John Bentley-Matthew Robinson Boulton, 1 Feb. 1811. Bentley wrote to MRB announcing his intention to write a memoir of MRB's father Matthew Boulton, who had died in 1809, claiming he was particularly well-placed to undertake the task as he was distantly related to Mary and Ann Robinson, Matthew Boulton's wives, and had worked for the firm since the time of Matthew Boulton senior in 1737. MRB dismissed his claims as 'unimportant'.

38   Smiles, Samuel, *op.cit.*, p 165.
39   MS 3782/1/37 Boulton & Fothergill letterbook 1760-66, B&F-Abraham Dubois, 9 Mar. 1765.
40   Parish Register, St Chad's, Lichfield; Stafford County Record Office, microfiche F29/1/1.
41   Freemen's Roll (1652 onwards); Lichfield Record Office.
42   *The Citizens of Lichfield in 1695: Census of Lichfield carried out for Gregory King and used in his 'Natural and Political Observations and Conclusions upon the State and Condition of England, 1696'*, Harl. MSS 7022.
43   Will of William Robinson sen., Public Record Office Prob. 11/505.
44   *Johnsonian Gleanings*, IX, pp.101-2.
45   MS 3558/150/72, Marriage settlement of Luke Robinson and Dorothy Babington, 15 May 1724, Birmingham City Archives.
46   Parish Register, St Mary's, Lichfield; Stafford Record Office, microfiche F20/1/1.
47   MS 3782/12/103/6, Dorothy Robinson's memorandum of her children. n.d.
48   Parish Register, St Mary's, Lichfield; *op.cit.*, microfiche F20/1/1.
49   Parish Register, St Mary's, Lichfield; *op.cit.*, microfiche F20/1/1.
50   Will of Mrs Sarah Robinson, 1727; Public Record Office Prob. 11/618.
51   *Ibid.*
52   Freemen's Roll, *op.cit.*; Lichfield Record Office.
53   Will of Mrs Jane Robinson, 1760; Public Record Office Prob. 11/858.
54   St John's Hospital Records, Lichfield Record Office D88/6/1, D88/7/8 & D88/7/9.
55   Parish Register, St Mary's, Lichfield; *op.cit.*, microfiche F20/1/2.
56   Will of Elizabeth Bailey, proved 26 May 1737; Lichfield Record Office. Elizabeth (d.1735) was the wife of Francis Bailey, and the daughter of Dorothy Robinson's sister Katherine Babington and her husband Ralph Hawkes; she was therefore the cousin as well as the Godmother of Mary Robinson. She left land at Draycott, Staffordshire, to Mary, which was to pass to her cousin Anne Levett if Mary died without issue.
57   Parish Register, St Mary's, Lichfield; *op.cit.*, microfiche F20/1/2.
58   Will of Luke Robinson sen., Public Record Office Prob. 11/776.
59   Parish Register, St Mary's, Lichfield; Stafford Record Office, microfiche F20/1/2.
60   Parish Register, St Giles, Whittington; Stafford Record Office, microfiche F4834/1/3.
61   Parish Register, St Mary's, Lichfield; *op.cit.*, microfiche F20/1/2.
62   Parish Register, St Chad's, Lichfield; Stafford Record Office, microfiche F29/1/1. *See also* Molyneux, N., 'Matthew Boulton and his wives' in *The Birmingham Historian*, No.13, 1996. It has been suggested that Anna and Maria are one and the same person because the baptism of one and the burial of the other are only a day apart; without more evidence it is not so far possible to establish either their joint or single identity.
63   MS 3782/Miscellaneous bills/1752-1759. Edmund Hector's bill of 5 Apr. 1749 for £6 8s. 6d. for sundry medicines was receipted as paid by Matthew Boulton on 2 Feb. 1753.
64   MS 3782/13/37/(6).
65   MS 3782/12/108/2, Matthew Boulton's notebook for 1757.
66   MS 3782/Miscellaneous Bills 1752-58, Mary Froggatt to Mrs Mary Boulton, Jan. and Apr. 1758.
67   MS 3782/Miscellaneous Bills.
68   MS 3782/12/112/(72).
69   Parish Register, St Giles, Whittington; Stafford Record Office, microfiche F4834/1/3.
70   MS 3782/Miscellaneous Bills 1752-59, John Barker-MB, 26 Jan. 1758-14 Oct.1759.
71   Parish Register, St Chad's, Lichfield; *op.cit.*, microfiche F29/1/1.
72   MS 3782 Miscellaneous bills 1752-59.

Bibliography

Archive material
Matthew Boulton Papers (MBP), Boulton & Watt Papers (B&W), James Watt Papers (JWP), Birmingham City Archives, Birmingham Reference Library

Articles and papers
Robinson, Eric, 'Matthew Boulton's Birthplace and his Home at Snow Hill: A Problem in Detection', in *Transactions of Birmingham & Warwickshire Archaeological Society*, Vol. 75 (1957), pp.85-9.
Robinson, Eric, 'Boulton and Fothergill 1762-82 and the Birmingham Export of Hardware', *University of Birmingham Historical Journal*, Vol. VII, No. 1 (1959).
Quickenden, Kenneth, 'Boulton & Fothergill Silver: Business Plans and Miscalculations', in *Art History*, vol.3, no.3 (Sept. 1980)
Quickenden, Kenneth, 'The Planning of Boulton & Fothergill's Silver Business', in *Silver & Jewellery Production & Consumption since 1750* (UCE, Birmingham, 1995)

Books
Delieb, Eric, *The Great Silver Manufactory*, Studio Vista (London, 1971)
Dickinson, H., *Matthew Boulton* (Cambridge, 1936, republished in paperback, Leamington Spa, 1999)
Doty, R., *The Soho Mint and the Industrialization of Money* (Smithsonian, 1998)
Gale, W.K.V.: *Boulton, Watt and the Soho Undertakings*, Birmingham Museums and Art Gallery (Birmingham, 1970)
Goodison, Nicholas: *Matthew Boulton: Ormolu*, Christies (London, 2003)
Hutton-Beale, Catherine: *Reminiscences of a Gentlewoman of the Last Century* (1891)
Mason, Shena, *Jewellery Making in Birmingham, 1750-1995* (Chichester, 1998)
Moilliet, Andrew (ed.), *Elizabeth Anne Galton (1808-1906), A Well-connected Gentlewoman* (Northwich, 2003)
Porter, Roy, *English Society in the 18th Century* (Penguin, 1991)
Ransome-Wallis, Rosemary, *Matthew Boulton and the Toymakers, Silver from the Birmingham Assay Office*, exhibition catalogue, The Worshipful Company of Goldsmiths (London, 1982)
Schofield, R., *The Lunar Society of Birmingham* (1966)
Tann, Jennifer, *Birmingham Assay Office 1733-1993* (Birmingham, 1993)
Timmins, S. (ed.), 'The Plated Wares and Electro-plating Trades' in *Birmingham and the Midland Hardware District* (1866)
Uglow, Jenny, *The Lunar Men* (London, 2002)

Index

Numbers in **bold** refer to illustrations